W9-AHD-010

Bob Hope

THE ROAD

WELL-TRAVELED

LAWRENCE J. QUIRK

APPLAUSE

NEW YORK • LONDON

An Applause Original

Bob Hope: The Road Well-Traveled
By Lawrence J. Quirk

Copyright © 2000 by Lawrence J. Quirk

All rights reserved

No part of this publication may be reproduced or transmitted in any form or by any means, electronic or mechanical, including photocopy, recording or any other information storage or retrieval system now known or to be invented, without permission in writing from the publishers, except by a reviewer who wishes to quote brief passages in connection with a review written for inclusion in a magazine, newspaper, or broadcast.

Library of Congress Cataloguing-in-Publication Data

LC Catalog 00-108805

British Library Cataloguing-in-Publication Data

A catalogue record for this book is available from the British Library

ISBN: 1-55783-450-4

APPLAUSE BOOKS
151 West 46th Street
New York, NY 10036
Phone: 212-575-9265
Fax: 646-562-5852
email: info@applausepub.com

COMBINED BOOK SERVICES LTD.
Units I/K, Paddock Wood Distribution Centre
Paddock Wood, Tonbridge, Kent TN12 6UU
Phone: (44) 01892 827171
Fax: (44) 01892 837272
United Kingdom

SALES & DISTRIBUTION
HAL LEONARD CORP.
7777 West Bluemound Road
P. O. Box 13819
Milwaukee, WI 53213
Phone: 1-414-774-3630
Fax: 1-414-774-3259
email: halinfo@halleonard.com
internet: www.halleonard.com

CONTENTS

ACKNOWLEDGMENTS vii

PREFACE: AT FLOODTIDE — 1943 1

CHAPTER 1: The Rabbit Trap 3

CHAPTER 2: The Somnambulist of Euclid Avenue 11

CHAPTER 3: The Death of "Lefty" 19

CHAPTER 4: The Siamese Circuit 28

CHAPTER 5: Doctor Hope and Mr. Hyde 34

CHAPTER 6: The Phoenix 42

CHAPTER 7: Perlberg's Folly .50

CHAPTER 8: The Worldling of the Great White Way 61

CHAPTER 9: The Girl He Left Behind 80

CHAPTER 10: Radio Days 92

CHAPTER 11: The Cat Who Swallowed the Canary 104

CHAPTER 12: Ski Snoot and Mattress Hip 127

CHAPTER 13: Specimen Days .140

CHAPTER 14: The Champion of Champions 155

CHAPTER 15: The Great Lover 173

CHAPTER 16: Bob and the Peacock 191

CHAPTER 17: Global Affairs .203

CHAPTER 18: Off Limits 215

CHAPTER 19: The Facts of Life 234

CHAPTER 20: The "Sponsor" of Vietnam 250

CHAPTER 21: The Pits 263

CHAPTER 22: Staving Off the Reaper 287

BIBLIOGRAPHY 316

FILMOGRAPHY 318

INDEX 321

FOR JOHN COCCHI

A Proven Friend for Many Years

ACKNOWLEDGMENTS

With special thanks to my colleague and associate, William Schoell, who served as research assistant on this book, exploring all avenues, tracking down leads, and providing invaluable suggestions and advice.

And with continuing warm thanks to my publisher, Glenn Young; my associate publisher and publicist, Kay Radtke; my editor, Greg Collins; and Paul Sugarman.

Also my deepest appreciation to the many who, over the years of work on this book, provided information, reminiscences, and insights on Bob Hope, including those living and deceased who are named and quoted throughout this book, as well as those who spoke to me "off the record" and did not wish to be named or credited, but whose kind cooperation is deeply appreciated nonetheless.

Among those who were most helpful were Miss Phyllis Diller, who shared her memories of Bob Hope most generously with me; Pamela Lincoln, the well-known acting coach, who knew Linda Hope well in youth, was a frequent visitor to the Hope home, and who shared with me her memories and insights into Bob and Dolores Hope in the years she knew them well; also her mother, the actress Verna Hillie, who knew the Hopes, and whose husband, the late Frank Gill, was one of Hope's comedy writers; the late Louise Campbell, the talented film actress of the Thirties and Forties, whose husband, the late actor Horace McMahon, appeared with Hope in films; Jacque Lynn Colton, the actress-director, a neighbor of the Hopes for years; producer Curtis Roberts; actress-designer Barbara Barondess MacLean, and writer Gregory Speck, who provided memories and/or observations on Bob Hope; Miss Katharine Hepburn and her assistant, Sharon Powers; the late Charlie Earle, who was a publicity man for Paramount when Hope filmed at that studio. And with deep thanks to others among those listed and quoted in the text, including my old friend, the late casting director Billy Grady, who first introduced me to Bob Hope in 1950, thus initially facilitating interviews and informal socializing that I did with Bob Hope over the years; the late Hedda Hopper; the late Helen Ferguson; the late Ruth Waterbury; the late Louella and Harriet Parsons; the late Paulette Goddard and Lucille Ball among many others. And with special appreciation to my distant relative, the late actor Walter Brennan, who shared his memories of Bob Hope with me and facilitated introductions.

Also sincere thanks to Robert Dahdah, Don Koll, Doug McClelland, Doug Whitney, Robert Burns Gable. And the Cleveland Public Library (Ohio); the James R. Quirk Memorial Film Symposium and Research Center, New York; the Museum of Modern Art, New York, and its film library staff, including archivist Mary Corliss; the Staff of the Billy Rose Theatre and Film Collection, Lincoln Center, New York, and Dr. Rod Bladel; Ernest D. Burns, the late Mark Ricci; the British Film Institute, London; the staff of the Margaret Herrick Library of the Academy of Motion Picture Arts and Sciences, Hollywood; Jerry Ohlinger's Movie Material Store, New York; Photofest, New York, and Howard and Ron Mandelbaum; Mary Atwood and Ed Maguire, Joe Bly, John A. Guzman, Mike Snell, John Rothermel, Frank Rowley, the late Howard Otway, the late James E. Runyan, the late Mike Ritzer, Arthur Tower, Stephen Jerome, and others too numerous to mention, many of them quoted in the text. And with fond memories of two Hope sources, the late John Beal (1909-1997) who appeared with Bob in *The Cat and the Canary* and the late Joan Bennett (1910-1990) who helped Bob entertain servicemen during wartime.

AT FLOODTIDE — 1943

By his 40th birthday — May 29, 1943 — Bob Hope had gotten it all. He was beloved by the servicemen he entertained so faithfully at posts all around the world, that third year of World War II. His radio programs were "must listening." His movies were top box office attractions. He'd made good and solid friends among the top people in the worlds of entertainment, politics, and business. He'd co-starred with luminaries like Bing Crosby. He'd "romanced" onscreen some of Hollywood's more famous beauties. He was, ostensibly, happily married to the well-liked Dolores Hope for nine years. They'd adopted several children. He had money, beautiful homes, and his pick of women on the side.

He had all the travel and freedom he wanted, called the shots at the studio, presided over a coterie of gagwriters, yes-men, assorted admirers, and a houseful of servants. He was healthy, happy, vigorous, enjoyed his golf games, the camaraderie available to any highly successful man, and the respect that went with it. If there were things in his past he wanted to forget, relationships and feelings he sought to hide from the world — if there were hidden angers and tensions and even despairs — well, that went with the territory, didn't it?

It had been a long way up from the impoverished beginnings in Cleveland, Ohio, the early frustrations and disappointments in vaudeville, the down-and-out periods in Chicago and points North, South, East, and West. Yes, he told himself over and over, he'd pulled himself up by his bootstraps, and if he'd cut some corners along the way, if he'd hurt people without really wanting to, if he'd developed an iron-clad self-involvement that by his code was the only key to survival and the sole ticket to ultimate Big Time success, well, that went with the territory too, didn't it? To Survive, to Prevail — that was the philosophy he lived by from the time, in early youth, he realized that What Doesn't Kill You, Strengthens You.

Yes, some people had been sacrificed to his ambition, to his self-protectiveness along the way. Life was hard, life was cruel, and nice guys finished last, as he well knew. No great intellect, not all that well-educated, he battened off smarter people — the crackerjack gagwriters, the variety of associates whose brains he picked, whose philosophies he incorporated into his program. It was like what that guy Machiavelli said centuries ago, that it was a mistake to be too good when surrounded by others who were not good.

Yeah, that big four-oh birthday saw Bob Hope on top of the world, man. Nothing was denied him — but nothing. A time of flood-tide for an American icon who — his mirror told him to his ultimate satisfaction — could pass for 32.

So much had happened. So much was yet to happen. He'd survived the past. He was taking on that inviting, ever-more-upwardly-mobile future with the gusto, aplomb, humor, and resiliency that were always his to command. The darker, secret, hurtful aspects — he'd handle them too, as always. He was Bob Hope, Survivor Par Excellence.

CHAPTER ONE

THE RABBIT TRAP

William Henry Hope, Bob Hope's father, had many excuses. He said that the dust from his stonemason's work got caught in his throat and needed to be washed down with ale. He said he had to get out of the house now and then, for he felt stifled and hemmed-in by his wife and children. He told himself he drank because his way of life was changing, his livelihood eroding. For whatever reason, "Harry" Hope drank like a fish.

Once upon a time he and his wife Avis had had a pretty good life. They had an attractive stone house in Middlesex, England, where they raised chickens and planted flowers. The boys (this was before Bob's birth) had their own pony upon which they'd ride for hours. And there was plenty of work for a stonemason who had secret dreams of becoming an architect.

But then Harry began to drink and carouse, spending too much time and too much money on other women. He was a likable, charming man who appealed to both sexes, possessed of the knack for camaraderie that made him a good buddy to men, and that certain "X" factor that made women all too willing to share a drink — and more — with "Handsome Harry." Harry didn't want to hurt his wife — he'd often come staggering home from bars with gifts of candy and flowers for Avis — but he did hurt her, repeatedly. As the work dried up and the money ran out, as Harry spent what little was left on his precious booze, the Hopes found themselves moving into smaller and smaller quarters. It wasn't long before the pretty house and grounds — the beloved pony — were just a memory.

Harry's father had also been a stonemason and builder — he built several churches in America. Grandfather Hope wanted to bring his family to the United States but was vetoed by his wife, whose oft-repeated response to his suggestion was, "When they build a bridge across the Atlantic." Grandpa Hope made sure that Harry and his six brothers all had a trade —plumbing, bricklaying. Even the two sisters became corset-makers. Grandpa chose Harry to follow in his footsteps, but it wasn't long before stonemasonry was a dying art, a skill no longer required in the brave new concrete-and-steel machine age of the 20th century.

Avis Towns (Bob Hope's mother's maiden name was for years incorrectly spelled "Townes," but research has indicated that "Towns" was the proper original spelling) was to become Harry Hope's wife on April 25, 1891. She was the foster daughter of a retired sea captain, Abraham Lloyd, and his wife, May. Avis's real parents had died in a ship-wreck. Early memories of her life were always shadowy. When she and her new husband Harry left Wales to move to Middlesex, she never saw her foster parents again.

Avis was nothing if not fertile. And William Henry had no problems fulfilling his husbandly duties. The babies came in rapid succession: Ivor in 1892, James Francis in 1893, their only daughter Emily in 1895, and Frederick Charles in 1897. Possibly it was the death of the cherished Emily in early childhood that began the downward spiral for the Hope family. Avis was inconsolable. She loved her baby boys, but Emily —the sweetest and most vulnerable child, her own daughter — was the pride and joy of her life. Harry tried to help lift Avis out of her depression, but this essentially reserved and inarticulate man was unable to do much beyond supplying temporary psychological salve.

Although Emily died before Bob Hope was born, he'd tell an oddly tasteless joke years later regarding her: "She starved to death, poor thing. With seven brothers at the table, she never got anything to eat." (Emily had, of course, died before all the brothers were on hand, so Hope added inaccuracy to tastelessness.)

The birth of a fourth son — William John, called Jack — shortly afterward (there was apparently no slowdown of work in Harry Hope's bedroom) helped make up for the death of Emily and saved Avis's sani-ty. But now that Harry had performed his male function and given Avis a new child to replace the one lost, he seemed to lose all interest. Still bitter about the lack of work for a skilled tradesman such as himself, still overly fond of the ale — and of other women. Being with these women was one of his means for reasserting his masculine pride as the family coffers dwindled and the Hope family habitats became increasingly shabby and grim.

The Hopes had moved to Eltham by the time the fifth son, Leslie Towns — much later to become world famous as Bob Hope — was born on May 29, 1903. Years later, his oldest brother, Ivor, was to tell Leslie of the early years of Hope family prosperity — ponies, gardens — but Bob remembered only a drunken, rather bullying father, a warm, encouraging mother, and siblings who ran the gamut, in their attitude toward him, from warmth and friendship to utter indifference and even hostility.

When the Hopes were obliged to move again, to Weston-Super-Mare, where Harry had grown up, it was for Harry a final comedown, a return to his home town in defeat. Presently, there was yet another move, this time to Bristol, where he hoped he could find some work. His hopes didn't pan out, and Harry now spent almost all of his waking hours in barrooms. He'd come home later, sodden with drink, reeking of cheap perfume and of even cheaper women, this time without the reconciliatory gifts of flowers and candy. There was no money for appeasing Avis's hurt and jealousy and growing disillusion any longer; it had to be carefully saved for booze.

Avis, who'd indulged certain show business dreams before giving them up for marriage — she sang quite well and had done some concert work in Wales — gradually transferred her aspirations to her youngest son, Leslie. She grew to rely increasingly on her children for solace and emotional support. Little Leslie would entertain her and make her laugh. Ivor, the eldest, was the surrogate father, looking after the other children, pouring dad into bed, trying to earn money doing odd jobs here and there, as did Avis. Jim was the surrogate husband — her closest friend and confidante. (This relationship between mother and son — the feeling Jim had that he was the "favorite" and therefore entitled and destined for Great Things — would be the cause of much friction between Jim and Bob in later years.)

While Avis brooded and raged and allowed an understandable bitterness to overtake her, a drunken Harry would try to give her the only thing he had that had never failed her: his manhood. This finally resulted in the last thing the Hope family needed, another mouth to feed. Young Sidney was born in 1905.

Avis, maternal as ever, welcomed him; the Hope family finances did not. The bright-eyed comical little Leslie, too young to know better, was the family's sole eternal optimist (if unconsciously) and the literal "hope" of the desperate family. His good humor and high spirits were in sharp contrast to the despair and gloom of his parents and older brothers.

"He learned early in life that it pays to make people laugh," his brother Jack (William John) remembered. Circa 1907, when Hope was about four, they'd go to see his Great-Great-Aunt Polly, a 102-year-old widow. (She was not to be the only centenarian in his ancestry, which accounts for his hitting 95 in 1998 and still counting.) For this still live-ly and alert old lady, Leslie Hope would do his impersonations of the people he'd seen along the way. "He'd stick his little hands in his pock-ets and push his little tummy out to make Old Polly laugh, and she'd give him a cookie," Jack was to recall.

Leslie developed an aptitude for entertaining an audience — even if it were only made up of relatives — at an early age. He'd sing songs — garnering laughs when his voice cracked — recite poems, even dress up in his mother's clothes and flounce around like an Edwardian-era harlot, giving his "act" hilarious twists. His antics would particularly delight his mother, who saw some of her artistic leanings and talents reflected in the boy.

It was a good thing little Leslie could make Avis laugh, for by this time there was precious little else to laugh about. Harry, she feared, was in the process of leaving her. In fact, he was already gone, physically. He'd gone to America because his brother Fred told him that stonema-sons were still in demand there. Avis, though, was almost certain he had, in actuality, abandoned her and the children. True, he sent her long, glowing letters about how wonderful Cleveland, Ohio, was, but she could only imagine him in the arms of another woman, or falling off a bar stool. Harry had not been much of a husband — at least, when on his feet — but she was bound to him heart and soul, and she still har-bored the illusion he'd make something of himself once again.

Meanwhile, lovable Leslie was demonstrating he could be just as adept at getting into trouble as he could at making people laugh. Once he nearly died when he went out over his head in the water at Herne Bay near Canterbury. Like most children his age, he felt tireless and invincible and was a bit of a showoff. He didn't have the energy to make it back to shore and had to be rescued by Ivor. Leslie's inert, motionless body, white-faced, was laid out on a pier, and work began on him. After a few tense minutes, he started breathing. He was taken to a nearby hotel to fully recuperate. Ivor was embarrassed by the fuss made over this rescue and in later years wouldn't even admit he was the one who saved his younger brother.

Hope also acquired his legendary ski-nose through foolhardy childhood larking. One day, climbing up an apple tree, determined to reach the topmost and the juiciest, reddest apples, he lost his balance.

His nose was never the same.

Gradually, Avis, left behind in England and constantly worried, began to believe in Harry's epistolary depiction of life in faraway Cleveland. She allowed herself the luxury of imagining him steadily, gainfully employed, his drinking under control. He expressed so much love and affection — for her and the boys — in his letters, and seemed so much to want to effect yet again a renewed family togetherness in Ohio. He began begging her to take the kids and join him. Avis persuaded herself, against her better judgment, that with a radical, intercontinental change of milieu, everything would revert to what it had been in their pony-riding years. Didn't she owe it to the boys, she reasoned, to reunite them with their father, to see them brought up in the best possible circumstances?

And so, in the year 1908, when little Leslie was five years old, Avis Towns Hope packed up her family and left for Cleveland, three thousand miles and a world removed, environmentally and culturally, from the Victorian-Edwardian ambience she'd always known. Edward VII ruled over England that year, and Theodore Roosevelt was President of the United States.

During the long ocean voyage to America, in crowded, unpleasant conditions in steerage, Avis would many times ask herself if she'd made the right decision. Could she and the boys have managed on their own back in England? Was it perhaps not more prudent, indeed expedient, to have her alcoholic husband out of their lives? But she still loved Harry — charming, roguish Harry. He was the father of her children, after all. She missed him, wanted to feel his arms around her again, wanted to drift into sleep in his embrace. She really did love him for better or for worse. Or even for from bad to worse. Moreover, if his fortunes had risen dramatically in America, she was determined she and the boys would get their fair share after all their years of humiliation and privation.

Avis and her brood, after a dusty, uncomfortable train ride cross-country from New York through New Jersey and Pennsylvania to Ohio, finally touched down in bustling Cleveland. After the initial thrill of life in a new country wore off — and it wore off in short order — Avis discovered that her husband's upbeat letters were more than a little off the mark.

Harry had used his talent for overstatement to convince her that the Ohio metropolis was a city paved with gold. Perhaps on certain streets it was, but in the neighborhoods where the immigrants lived (and where the weekly pay after seventy backbreaking hours of work averaged ten dollars) the streets were coated with an entirely different, much more pungent substance. Harry, true, did better because he was a skilled tradesman, but not by much. He was excited to have his family reunited around him, and the boys thought of it all, at least in the beginning, as an exciting adventure. But Avis — weary, disillusioned, lonely Avis — revved herself up to pretend that all the tears she found herself shedding were, miraculously after all, only of joy at being reunited with her husband. She told herself, again and again: tomorrow will be better, can only be better. But her deeper instincts told her otherwise.

Her deeper instincts were right. Life in Ohio was largely a reprise of what they'd gone through those final years in England. They had only exchanged King Eddy for President Teddy. Worse, the people from all nations who now surrounded them were busy, pushy, ambitious, and sharp, as well as crass and competitive; older Clevelanders might look down on them somewhat but there was no "class" system here on the scale of the one back home. Money and Power and Winning were all among the more enterprising Clevelanders. There was none of the laissez-faire slower-paced element of even the lower-class English here. America had come into its own among the leading nations of the world, and wanted all comers to damn well know it.

As for the Hopes, they found themselves living in a dreary, one-family house that cost $11.50 per month. It rated no higher than any equivalent dwelling they had known in England, and had the added disadvantage of being in an unfamiliar ambience, a fresh new set of customs, manners, and mores to which they would have to adjust, pronto, do or die. Soon the children were busily exploring the ways of their peer group, and gradually over time would plane away the Britishisms in their accent and manners. It was that or risk extinction. American bullies, they found, had even sharper cutting edges than their English counterparts. The first "Americanism" in their speech canon, one of the Hope brothers later recalled, was "Keep your guard up!"

As for Harry, he was running true to form, having found American bars on a par with, and indeed exceeding, the raunchy free-for-all spirit in the English pubs — and every bit as entertaining, as were, of course, the "looser" American women. Avis, for her part, kept close to home, watching the smaller of her brood, and trying to keep herself from falling apart altogether.

Not only had Harry not changed his basic habits and mindsets, he still could not, would not, accept that it was no longer possible for a man to make a decent living as a stonemason. Continually self-deluding, he spent more and more time in sleazy bars and in the company of sleazy ladies of the evening in whose company he could "assert his manhood" and forget that in the outside workaday world he was a failure.

At home his boozy entreaties for lovemaking won his wife's acquiescence because she had succumbed to boredom and inertia as well as simple human need. She would put up with his beer-heavy body and fetid kisses and constantly remind herself that this bloated but still attractive man had once — oh, it seemed so long ago — been her Prince Charming, straight out of the more roseate English legends of yore. She'd try to recall that other man as they made love. It was a strange marital romance — if that's what it was — as replete with anger and resentment as it was with animal passion. Whatever it was, for present purposes, it worked.

It resulted in yet another son, who was to be the last, George, born in 1909.

Soon enough, Harry's Cleveland relatives grew tired of paying his rent. They knew, as did Avis, that there was no realistic chance of his making a living in his chosen profession. His brother Fred grew increasingly fed up. As embittered and disillusioned as she was by her husband, Avis still loved him and was not about to let her condescending relatives put him down. Neither did she want her boys to be out on the street because of the paterfamilias's chronic inability to make, let alone hang onto, a buck.

Avis went to see Fred and family and reminded them that it was at Fred's urging that Harry had elected to take his chances in America and that, accordingly, Fred owed them something in return. Outraged, almost at the limits of their patience, the "Fred Branch" of the Hopes declared that there was a limit to what they could do or, for that matter, what they should do. Out were trotted such long-hairy clichés as "God helps those who help themselves." Harry's penury had become a bore. Though essentially a proud woman who had always kept her own counsel, Avis found herself literally begging. She would always resent having had to do this. She did win a short reprieve, but Fred made it clear she could not count on his help for much longer.

It was crisis time, no ifs, ands, or buts about it. The boys determined, especially for their mother's sake, to go out and get breadwinning jobs. Soon the Hopes moved to a larger house where they could take in boarders for added revenue.

It was 1910 now, George was a year old, and Harry and family all became naturalized citizens of the United States of America. The "jickey" accents were rapidly fading, the family — certainly the boys and Avis — were toughening up, American-style, "speeding up the pace to keep abreast" as brother Ivor later recalled it. Americans they were, Americans in the Land of Opportunity.

As for Avis Hope, her attitude about their future still reflected the family name.

CHAPTER TWO

THE SOMNAMBULIST OF EUCLID AVENUE

In later years, Bob Hope became inordinately fond of relating an incident that allegedly happened to him as a boy selling papers in Cleveland. A man in the back of a big limousine drove up to young Leslie's corner and, handing him a dime, asked for a paper. Hope had to run off to get the man his change. By the time he returned he'd missed out on selling papers to numerous other customers. The man in the limo tendered the advice to always keep change handy so as not to miss out on sales, along with some other sage observations as to the ways of American commerce.

As per Hope's reminiscence, a streetcar inspector then ran up and told him the man he'd just spoken to was John D. Rockefeller, Sr., "The Richest Man in the Country."

This probably apocryphal story (perhaps the streetcar inspector honestly thought it was Rockefeller) nonetheless illustrates the way Hope in later life was to talk as if his success were preordained. Like many celebrities and wealthy people, he saw himself as possessing something special, some outstanding, latent quality that set him aside from the mob — something that would ensure he ran into the right people, in the right place, at the right time. Hence there was no such thing as Luck. Some people were destined for greatness.

As Leslie Hope grew into his teens in Cleveland, he knew he was different from other people in certain less glorious ways, at least. He had, unlike his dutifully hardworking neighbors, a horror of the workaday world, and a need, a compelling urgent need, to be the center of attention. As much as he loved and respected his mother, he saw only too clearly the essential hopelessness of her situation. He developed an iron determination to avoid repeating her pattern, let alone his father's. For his father he could generate only a great pity, which more often than not congealed into outright contempt. While, as is often the case in traditional families, his mother did most of the disciplining (Harry

Hope was too inebriated to care what his boys were up to), Avis would at times call upon Harry to do his part when all other control measures failed. Overzealous from alcohol and frustration and an ever-growing self-contempt, furious that the boys' bad behavior had necessitated his temporary emergence from his dreamy stewed stupor, Harry would beat the boys with a strap to within an inch of their lives. In years to come, Bob Hope would try to cover up for his father, according him more charity than the man deserved, but Harry Hope was more drunk than social drinker, and his corporal punishments bordered on outright child abuse.

Young Leslie also had problems in school and with the friends he chose. The kids, merciless in the usual tradition of peer cruelty, made fun of his nondescript clothing and the leavings of his English accent and (to them) vaguely sissy first name. Soon they were reversing his name from Les Hope to "Hopeless." But they'd picked a spirited, angry, fearless target. Leslie became a scrapper by necessity; he was easygoing enough to take some good-natured teasing, but when the name-calling got too nasty, when the jabs landed too close to home, he'd lash out with his fists (fists well trained and seasoned by practice sessions imposed in one-for-all-all-for-one style by his older brothers) and pummel viciously anyone who dared go too far.

Often he'd come home to his mother all bruised and bloody, having left his playground opponents in the same condition. It was all coming together to shape his permanent psychological stance: the abusive, alcoholic failure of a father, the decent and caring but somewhat pathetic and pixillated mother, the essentially self-absorbed older brothers (who once they had salvaged the remnants of family pride by teaching Leslie to fight had left him to his own devices), and the patronizing, scornful Cleveland relations. And then there were his enforced feisty rejoinders to the teasing he endured at school. All combined — throw in as well the everlasting-poverty and hard work and uncertainty about the future — to create a bitter, protective shell within which Leslie Towns Hope could hide and keep forever intact his essential nature. The sweet, playful child still lived inside this shell — a child that, in decades to come, would be coaxed out of hiding only by the prospect, and thrill, of keeping the whole world entertained — but outside that shell was a new, more ruthless, more self-propelled creature who established himself firmly in charge. Leslie Hope at 13 in 1916 hated the life his parents and those about him were forcing him to lead, and as his high school years wore on, he determined to escape it any way he could, by any means that came to hand.

Leslie began to hang out with a rough crowd. As one of his brothers later put it, "It was not so much a matter of: if you can't beat 'em, join 'em; for Leslie it was: beat 'em and *then* join 'em — have it both ways!" Though in today's world of teenagers with guns and "wilding" these boys were about on the danger level of "The Little Rascals," they were still by any standards a tough, mean crowd. Leslie and fellow members of his "gang" — the Fairmount Boys — would chase the members of the rival "Cornell" gang and beat them over the heads with sticks, often aiming for even more sensitive portions of the anatomy. In time, lashing out against all the hurt he'd endured, and in the only way he knew how, Leslie became something of a bully. Circa 1919, age 16, he had firmly incorporated as unspoken motto: "Get them before they get you."

Sometimes Les Hope and his companions would land in real trouble, such as the time they broke into a local sporting goods store out of sheer bordom and stole some tennis equipment. They proceeded to play with the balls and racquets in a parking lot located only a couple of blocks away from the store. In short order the Cleveland police put two and two together and Les Hope and cohorts were rounded up and put in jail. The boys were released a few hours later — the theory being that they'd learned their lesson — but the beating Harry gave Leslie afterward was far worse than his consternation at being incarcerated.

The assorted strains that besieged young Les Hope began to manifest themselves in outré ways; for instance, sleepwalking. Once he walked out of the family home early in the morning clad only in a long nightshirt that barely covered his "family jewels." He proceeded to saunter, still soundly asleep, for several blocks to a drugstore located at 105th Street and Euclid Avenue, where he knocked loudly on the door. Cops in the neighborhood had already familiarized themselves with young Hope's midnight jaunts, and one would approach him, put a raincoat over him, and lead him home. Hope always maintained that he was asleep the entire time.

Although the police were sympathetic to a point — they knew of the family environment — some maintained that young Les Hope's "sleepwalk-grandstanding" was actually a plea for attention, a way to get his parents to stop fighting (one of the more unpleasant family customs Harry and Avis had increasingly taken up) and concentrate their energies on his "problem." For a while it worked: the parents haggled over methods to keep Les from "sleepwalking-out" and Avis finally hit on the idea of tying one end of a rope around Leslie's leg, and the other one around his brother Jack's. For a time this worked too — until Jack expressed increased resentment at being woken up out of a sound sleep at all hours. Possibly hit by the realization that his somnambulizing was simply serving to irritate his brother instead of getting his parents' attention, Leslie's nocturnal excursions diminished and soon ceased altogether.

One of Leslie's closest friends during this period — and one who shared most of his adventures (and misadventures) — was Whitey Jennings, a cool, slick customer who taught him how to hustle semipro locals down at the poolhall, among other pursuits. The boys picked up quite a bit of change at the poolhall and before long Leslie was spending as much time there as Harry did in the barrooms. When one of Harry's relatives mentioned this to Leslie's mother, the ever-more-realistic Avis shrugged it off, sniffing wearily but pointedly that "Les is down there finding himself." Her instincts, by now finely honed, told her a boy could be doing worse things than hanging out in poolhalls.

As Leslie's brothers had their own pursuits (often of the amatory kind) and his parents were too bemused by the pathos of their own situation to keep much of an eye on him, Whitey Jennings quickly became Leslie's role model. The two were inseparable and often got involved in schemes that, however exciting, were borderline dishonest. One source of income was competing in Cleveland-area picnic races. Sometimes the races would be run at the same time in different parks, so the boys would call up one place and get the organizers to delay the race until later in the afternoon by pretending they were from a newspaper and wanted to send a photographer. Meanwhile they'd run in the race at, say, Euclid Beach, then head over to Luna Park and enter the race there. Of course, no photographer ever put in an appearance.

Les and Whitey made sure of winning by sprinting off in that half second between the starter's hollering "Get set!" and "Go!" — which of course a regular racing setup would never have countenanced. Another of their tricks, automatically outlawed in professional racing, was digging starting holes, which none of the other contestants ever did. The only real competition was a fast young lad named Henry whom they would literally bump off the track at intervals to slow down. The Hope-Jennings combine won a lot of money, courtesy of their assorted strategies. Leslie rationalized his actions by quoting a motto of Olympic coach Mike Murphy: "A man who *won't* be beat *can't* be beat!" Shunted aside in young Les Hope's strategic concerns were such terms as "Fair

Play." Here lay a questionable philosophy, which was to be firmly ingrained in young Les Hope by age 18 in 1921 — a philosophy which, in ever changing forms adapted to the particular circumstances, would serve the later Bob Hope throughout his life.

Meanwhile Les Hope's ingenious "petty larceny"-style gimmick ensured he had spending money whenever he wanted it. When he was a delivery boy for a local bakery, he'd bring cakes to upscale suburban neighborhoods and put on an act for each housewife, feigning exhaustion and worry. He'd declare he'd had a terrible time finding the house and had spent all the traveling money his bakery allotted him. Taking pity, the women would offer him more money so that he wouldn't have to walk all the way back to town. His scheme worked very well until he applied it to the same housewife twice in a row and the matron notified the bakery. Young Les was sacked.

Leslie in his later teens tried a variety of odd jobs but didn't last very long at any. None to him smacked of a future, and none, he knew instinctively, began to tap his greatest gifts and needs — to him they lacked that certain "glamour" or "excitement" or "kick" — nor did they give him a chance to indulge an ever-more-obsessive need — to show off. To young Les Hope they all had the stench of stonemasonry, of failure. Failure — his father's failure — that he wanted to avoid at all costs.

As early as Les's seventeenth year, pal Whitey Jennings was steering him into an occupation he felt, at that point, came nearer to "filling the bill." In his cocky, casual way, Whitey bragged one afternoon that he was going to be a boxer — moreover, had already signed up for the Ohio State Amateur bout schedules.

This did not sit well with Leslie. By now a highly competitive boy, he found it annoying that Whitey was going to take on, and possibly shine in, something he believed himself more suited for. He had certainly "boxed" enough ears in his day and felt he was real good with his fists. Even worse — Whitey had had the gall to call himself "Packy West" after the then-famous boxer, Packy McFarland. So Les decided to go Whitey one better and call himself "Packy East" — a name that not only competed with Whitey's but mocked his friend's choice. It was typical of the anything-for-attention-I-can-do-better-than-you-can attitude that Hope had already ingrained into himself at that age.

However, his "career" as a boxer was to knock him down a peg — or two — or three. At 128 pounds, he was just two pounds over the bottom-most limit for the featherweight division and had to register as a lightweight. He was to claim years later — and with considerable reminiscential chagrin — that he'd have done much better in the feather-weight class. As it turned out, he "creamed" his first opponent, who stupidly kept looking over his shoulder for instructions from his second. Whenever the opponent's back was turned, Les Hope would hit him hard, the lesson "a man who *won't* be beat *can't* be beat" being kept duly, and firmly, in mind.

Young Leslie Hope managed to go straight to the semifinals at Moose Hall. This time his opponent was one "Happy" Walsh, so christened because he had a habit of grinning like a jackass every time he was socked. Happy didn't do much grinning during his match with Packy East, however. This time, Les was outmatched, and in spades. Happy, who went on to become a local champion, made mincemeat of his opponent. Although Les tried his best to dodge Happy's blows with fancy footwork, and even got in a few licks of his own, the outcome was foreordained. By the time Hope was scooped up from the floor, he scarcely remembered what had hit him.

Leslie Towns Hope, Boxer, it was apparent, would have to find a new career.

Much of the young Bob Hope's contradictory, complex nature shows up in an incident when he and Whitey Jennings were riding freight trains one afternoon. They'd sit in the "blind baggage" car right behind the engine and ride fifty miles out to Ashtabula and back. On this occasion they decided to ride back to Cleveland from the Ashtabula train yard on the famous Twentieth Century. They climbed up into the "blind" and enjoyed the ride until the train began to slow down near Cleveland. The time to jump off had come.

The space between the engine and the blind begins to narrow as the train slows down. Les always liked to let Whitey get off the train first, but just as Whitey was about to jump, the space narrowed and closed on his knee. Whitey cried out in agony and fell back into Leslie's arms. He was sure thet his kneecap was crushed. When the train came to a complete stop, Leslie managed to get his pal off the train — then simply left him lying on the side of the tracks, moaning and whining in pain. Leslie ran off to a nearby candy store that Whitey's aunt owned, where he hollered out, rapid-fire, a nearly unintelligible story to the astonished woman. But instead of waiting to take her to where her nephew was lying, some instinct for self-preservation kicked in and made him run off to his own house instead. It never occurred to him that the woman might not have understood him or might need to be shown exactly where the badly injured Whitey was.

Luckily, the station master came upon Whitey's prostrate form lying at the side of the track and took matters into his own hands. As the boy slowly recuperated in the hospital, his pal Leslie slunk around in a panic that day and the next, convinced that his buddy was dead and that he, Leslie, was somehow responsible. He felt guilty that he had deserted him at the track and had failed to return to him; he simultaneously felt he'd done his basic duty and could not be held in any way responsible. Or could he? But when all was said and done, Leslie Hope had absorbed Whitey Jennings's lessons well. It was every man for himself. Les hadn't deserted his friend at the side of the tracks; he'd only been looking after himself. If he didn't — who else would?

When he wasn't in pool rooms or otherwise getting into trouble, young Hope haunted Cleveland's movie palaces, which by 1921 were taking on architecturally palatial ambiences. Of course there were the cheapies and grind shows and old theatre houses fallen to movie status; Hope neglected none of them. He'd take his ill-gotten gains from park races or gullible housewives with sweet tooths and kind hearts and hie himself to the Alhambra or the Park movie theatres. Charlie Chaplin especially appealed to, and inspired, him, but at the time it was intrepid, swashbuckling Douglas Fairbanks, Sr., that Les most wanted to emulate. He was enthralled by dashing Doug's exploits, and he and Whitey would spend afternoons swinging from trees and slashing each other with invisible swords or battling mythical dragons. Among his other favorites were Rudolph Valentino, Richard Barthelmess, and Wallace Reid.

But while Les Hope at 18 was fancying himself the suave, handsome hero, others saw him more as a kid comic. His brothers suggested that he enter a Charlie Chaplin lookalike contest in Luna Park. One of them gave him an old, bedraggled black suit to wear. He borrowed a derby hat and a pair of brogans from dad Harry and made a moustache by smearing ashes over his upper lip. Then he broke off a small tree branch to use as a cane. Thus equipped, he "Charlie-walked" off to Luna Park and gave it his all. Although much of the applause he won for his impersonation in Luna Park that day came from family members — who looked forward to splitting the money he'd win — the audience, as it turned out, genuinely concurred, and registered that opinion loudly.

Knowing that, of all his cheering family on hand that day, it was his mother who truly loved him the most, and feeling sorry for her, Leslie decided to use his Charlie Chaplin contest winnings to buy her a new stove. The brothers announced themselves mightily disappointed by this prosaic way of spending the winnings (Dad Hope, for one, to *his* extreme annoyance, was to find no way to cadge drinks out of it), but Leslie, in his view, had done the right thing. While Avis was deeply pleased by the boy's thoughtfulness, no doubt even she must have wished he'd chosen a less practical gift to enliven her rather drab existence.

This was Leslie Towns Hope's first real taste of showbusiness. The bug had bitten, he was infected, and he was already on a roll.

CHAPTER THREE

THE DEATH OF "LEFTY"

It was now, in the earliest years of The Roaring Twenties, that Leslie Towns Hope began to mull over, more and more, the possibilities inherent in a show business career. He'd held down a series of boring daytime jobs to earn basic money, once he'd left school. He said of his academic record in later years, "The less said of it, the better." To be sure, it was monumentally undistinguished; no scholar was Les. He'd always preferred action to analysis, working out angles for survival as opposed to abstract cogitating. Sitting in classrooms while insistent teachers tried to pound into him dates, figures, and subjects that bored him, smacked too much of the workaday world he abhorred. His keen natural intelligence, he felt, took in all of life and people and the ways of the world that enabled him to survive, flourish, push on. He learned all the basic — readin', writin', 'rithmetic — tools for getting on, then discarded anything that didn't further his immediate life purposes. "He was a bright, bright guy," one of his brothers later said, "and he read, and kept up with what he needed. What he didn't need, he threw out. He felt it slowed him down."

At 18, he found that nights and weekends contained the most excitement, promise, and mystery. Les Hope was never one to stint on fun, pleasure — and romance.

Les's first big crush was on one Mildred Rosequist, a vaguely pretty brunette who resembled (somewhat) the perky, blonde Una Merkel, later famed for playing onscreen roommate-sidekick to Jean Harlow and other luminaries of the screen. Saucy, lively, funny, Mildred was no slouch at dealing with the "public" where she worked at the cosmetics counter at a downtown Cleveland department store. She'd turn her bright smile and flashing eyes on all who promised, however tentatively, to be suckers for a compact or a lotion.

Smitten at first sight, Hope took to coming by during lunch hours, flirting with her and coming up with what he considered at the time funny jokes and gags to get her attention. His big aim: to enveigle her into a lunch date. As she was to recall years later, Mildred Rosequist was not overly impressed with the brash youngster with the funny nose who seemed to be "trying too hard." But eventually his persistence wore her down and she agreed to a date.

Their first outing was an unmitigated disaster, or so she remembered it. Dinner was okay enough, she recalled, though he made sure not to put too much of a dent in his meager salary by his choice of restaurant. He even told Mildred what she should order — "Mr. Take-Charge from the word go," as one later girlfriend would style it. He made sure what she ordered was relatively inexpensive. Most of the conversation was dominated by his accounts of his variegated exploits real and imaginary — she hardly got a word in edgewise. For Mildred, matters started down the chute when he insisted she accompany him to what he called a "super swell" party one of his friends was throwing.

At the party, Leslie made sure that everyone knew who Mildred had come with — her attractiveness built up his stock — then proceeded to largely ignore her while he "worked the joint." After an hour of neglected boredom, during which she failed to catch sight of him, she made some inquiries and found he'd lost himself in a world of his own — off playing craps with the boys in a back room.

Miss Rosequist, who had her own brand of ego, wasn't taking any of this. She stormed out of the party in a noisy snit that caught all eyes. "That was one time I upstaged him — and it wasn't the only time, either," she later said.

Unfazed, intrigued with her sauciness and snap, Leslie applied all his artful aggressiveness to make it up with her. He succeeded, "but only after she'd given me a tough time," as he reported later to a pal.

It was at this time that he sought out specific training as a song-and-dance man. He'd heard that a once-well-known black entertainer named King Rastus Brown was giving dancing lessons. Hope immediately signed up for them. Pool winnings and the like that had fomerly gone only for movies and other pleasures were now saved up to pay for lessons with Brown. Brown, with his born showman's instinct, immediately sensed young Les Hope's natural ability and encouraged him by every means he had on hand, giving him honest, piercing criticism when warranted, and getting Les to look at himself objectively and clearly, so that he could correct any flaws in what he was projecting.

Meanwhile, though he'd effected a thawing in Mildred's attitude toward him after the party debacle, he "scored" with her only to a point.

Even then, in the early stages of their on-again, off-again relationship, it was apparent he cared more for Millie than she for him.

Among the jobs he was taking on, and hating, at the time was one as a butcher's assistant. His Uncle Fred, the same man who'd patronized his family when they first hit America and Cleveland, was his ever-more-exasperated employer. "You don't have the interest!" he'd bellow. Later Les would mimic him, adding "Interest in what — dead things being cut up?" Uncle Fred finally gave up on him and fired him when he found Les and his then-pal and co-worker Johnny Gibbons applying his King Rastus Brown training by tap-dancing for the customers one time too many.

Les, ever more serious about the elusive Millie, then landed another "steady, solid" (translated: "deadly") job as a lineman for an outfit known as the Cleveland Illuminating Company. With the proceeds from this he hoped to buy Millie "a real nice, fancy, classy" engagement ring. He seemed oblivious at the time that Mildred's interest in him was at best casual. He amused her with his wisecracking and clowning, but as one of his brothers was later to recall, it was apparent she had no deeper interest in him.

When Les finally had enough money to pay for a ring, he demonstrated his youthful failure to equate expense with quality by rushing out and buying the cheapest one he could find — cheap but "flashy" — one that, in his own phrase, "just demanded attention!" When he showed it — eagerly, happily — to Millie, she at first took it as a joke. "But it's so small" was her initial putdown. To the tough little scrapper who'd conned housewives out of money and fought till he dropped in the boxing ring and made a policy of taking no guff from anybody, this was the lowest of low blows, one that left him flat on the mat.

Millie was not without sensitivity, and sensing that his feelings were badly hurt (and still having her uses for him, if only for companionship and laughs) apologized, with a hug for a bonus. So he took her dancing. Marriage was still miles from her thoughts — certainly with Les Hope — but Les Hope, or "Hopeless" so far as his courtship of Millie went at that point, failed to distinguish between his being "amusing" as against "attractive" — which to Millie he was not. But, as Victorian novelists used to put it, Millie continued to foster in him a feeling that "he might dare hope."

Soon Les found a way to combine the personal with the career aspects as concerned himself and Millie the Unattainable. Not far from Millie's downtown Cleveland department store was a dancing school named Sojack's. Dangling hopes of extra money and "certain" stardom, he sold Millie on signing up with him for dance lessons given by an ex-vaudevillian named Johnny Root. Millie didn't have Les's natural ability, as it turned out, but she was reasonably light on her feet and, on their own time after work, she and Les worked up some passable routines. When they felt themselves sufficiently rehearsed, they managed — thanks to Les's gall and persistence — to get a three-day engagement at a social club in the Brotherhood of Engineers Building — hardly, as Millie snickered, a romantic name for their first appearance together.

Everything went swimmingly for the first two days — the Les-Millie combine didn't exactly galvanize — much less mesmerize — the audience, but neither did they garner hisses. The third night, however, was a disaster.

Millie and Les, it seems, had themselves a real knockdown (figuratively) fight backstage, and just before they were to go into their number. All along, Millie, who'd not been bitten, let alone infected, by the showbiz bug, had been letting herself be carried along solely by Les's ambition — certainly he had enough for both of them — but she found herself increasingly riled by his impatience with her, his insistence on hogging the spotlight, and his habit of snapping at her when she made a mistake — and she made her share. Out she went on stage that night, still fuming. Right in the middle of their dance — catching an irritable glance from Hope when she took a wrong step or was too slow to swirl — Millie walked off the stage and left him standing there in mortification.

At a loss for once, a red-faced Hope was soon recovering his poise and sass, and although he'd never been so mad at another human being in his life as he was at Millie, he proceeded to work up a smile and give out in his best pizzazzy style as he told some snappy jokes he remembered. He managed to get through the next few minutes with his dignity intact — in fact it was to prove, though he didn't at the time realize it, to be a good object lesson in how to "cope" with the unexpected — and he wound up the proceedings decently enough, to judge from the audience response.

But he was livid, shaking all over with rage, and he caught up with Millie backstage and really let her have it. Whereupon she rocked him on his heels by her counterattack, giving as good as she got. Where was all this money he'd told her she'd make? she demanded. "But Millie — these are charity benefits," he rejoined. "This is the way every performer gets started." But what Millie didn't know was that Les pocketed ten dollars a performance for these "benefits" with Mildred's share exactly zilch. True to form, when Hope and Millie won a handsome silver cup in a dance contest, Hope kept the cup.

Les wasn't through with Millie yet. After he got her calmed down and purring-up in a few days with sweet talk, flattery, and more phony promises, he tried to sell her on the idea of touring with him. Millie got her back up at this, inisting that her mother absolutely forbade it; also, she had strong reservations of her own. Temporarily stymied in his ambitions, Hope then went after what he considered a hot opportunity when Johnny Root announced his retirement. Les asked if he could take over as the school's dance instructor. Many at the school labeled this a particularly brazen and thoughtless request — Root, after all, boasted a long and solid history as an entertainer and this Hope kid, in their eyes, was a callow neophyte — but on the other hand there was no arguing Les was a quick study, had natural ability and talent and more than his share of drive, and might be right after all, if not exactly what the doctor ordered. He landed the job.

There were immediate problems. For one thing, the job didn't pay enough. Hope also failed to summon the requisite patience with his pupils. and condescended rather offensively to those he recognized as talentless. Then he figured that if he wasn't actually performing he might as well be corraling more greenbacks, so he left Sojack's to take a job at the Chandler Motor Company. Once again, to his chagrin, he had "settled for the salt mines," and all for filthy lucre, such as it was. The tedious, deadly work drove him up the wall, but presently he was relieving his frustrations singing in a quartet comprised of himself and three other Chandler employees. Unfortunately, his boss at Chandler didn't appreciate his musical ability — particularly when he saw fit to display it during working hours — and Les was canned forthwith.

Hope then decided to take a chance on another dancing student he'd met at Sojack's, Lloyd Durbin, whose nickname was "Lefty." Lloyd was a shy, pale, inoffensively amiable young fellow who knew his way around a dance floor even if he lacked any professional experience. Les saw that the raw material was there to work with, and he took note of, and admired, the way Lefty could come up with fresh new routines of his own invention and execute them neatly and energetically. Remembering how he and Whitey Jennings always used to stack the deck in their favor in any and all pursuits, Les applied the same principle when it came to his and Lefty's performances in amateur contests at local vaudeville houses.

First he'd make sure all his relatives came. Then, using his by-then-well-honed charm on various pretty usherettes, he'd get the girls to leave a side door open so his pals could slip in free. Via this means he insured his own large cheering squadron, planted in strategic spots around the theatre. Soon he and Lefty Durbin were winning more than their share of contests. Although he often baited friends who cheered for him with promises of free meals afterward if he won, often these dinners would never materialize.

It was now 1923, and Hope had celebrated his twentieth birthday. Lefty and Les paid a call on an agent named Norman Kendall, who was responsible for booking acts into a small Cleveland showcase called The Bandbox. Kendall looked around for something right for the lads and later managed to book them on the same bill as the silent comedian Fatty Arbuckle, whose stardom in films had evaporated a year or so earlier after a scandal that erupted during a wild party.

Rotund Fatty had been accused of manslaughter when a young pretty girl died of internal injuries after a Coca-Cola bottle was allegedly thrust into her vagina. Although Arbuckle was acquitted after two sensational trials, the publicity was too much for a film public that in the early 1920's did not like to think of their eunuch-like comedians as entertaining carnal desires. Fatty was also peculaiarly asexual in appearance, obese, with a doughy, childlike demeanor. With his picture career in ashes, Fatty was making personal appearances in small skits in one-horse towns circa 1923. Later, under the name of William Goodrich, he'd direct some films; he died a disappointed, broken man at 46 in 1933. At the point when the boys encountered Fatty he was undergoing the most pathetic of his comedowns.

To Les and Lefty the Bandbox was nirvana. They put together a clever parody of an Egyptian dance complete with a painted desert backdrop with pyramids and the like. At the end of the dance they'd pantomime dipping their derbies into the Nile, then — to the audience's delighted surprise — actually pour water out of their hats. (While the patrons' attention was cleverly diverted by the other partner, Les or Lefty would fill the derbies from a pouch concealed beneath their garments.)

Despite his greatly reduced circumstances, Arbuckle was not embittered, and to his co-performers proved cheerful, generous, and encouraging. He took note of the boys' act, called them into his dressing room, told them they were talented, and offered to introduce them to Fred Hurley, a producer who put together "tabloid shows." These were mini-musical comedies that toured small midwestern towns and which paid each act $40 per week. Les and Lefty were quite excited but their hopes were almost dashed when they met Hurley, who looked them over and said outright he wished they could do more than "just dance," adding, "Maybe you'll learn new tricks on the road." Relieved to be hired after the initial uncertainties, the boys shook hands with the producer and were soon on their way.

East Palestine, Ohio, was the first stop for their show, *Jollie Follies*. Although the revue was strictly smalltime, Les's "success" on the circuit went to his head. He began to strut and saunter about as if he were a big-time vaudevillian, alienating many of the other performers and new people he met. Everyone he encountered sensed the steely ruthlessness that was so much a part of his character, and at 20 it was already fully honed and sharpened.

Lefty, on the other hand, was well-liked by the people they worked with, and had the more pleasing, unassertive personality. Les patronized his partner; he was certain — probably correctly — that Lefty would have gone nowhere without Les to push him. It was with some surprise, however, that his less-than-friendly fellow performers viewed Les's first attempt at comedy one evening. An actor playing an emcee in a sketch couldn't go on and Les was hastily drafted to take his place. Hope not only easily adapted to the routine, but improved upon it with his asides and bumbling mannerisms. Truly funny, he knocked the audience out. Everyone in the company would have expected the more amiable Lefty to be the natural comedian; but Hope — stinker or not, personally — had to be given his due.

Hope's ego was almost out of control by the time he next landed in Cleveland. His family — especially his brothers — was not impressed, nor were they particularly supportive. To them, Les's pride seemed totally out of proportion when by most people's standards the tour was strictly small potatoes. Inwardly, Les bristled — why weren't they happy for him? — and the seeds for many future disagreements and ultimate bitterness in regards to his family were firmly planted. He was convinced they were jealous of him. Even his mother wasn't as sup-portive as he expected. The only one who *did* seem impressed was Millie Rosequist's mother. But it was too late for Millie to join him now; she had her chance and muffed it.

Traveling around in a tabloid show was not the most blissful expe-rience, no matter how Les chose to slice it. The company — thirteen people — would be doubled up in drafty, odious rooms in dilapidated theatrical boardinghouses. The beds they shared had lumpy, uncomfortable mattresses and were often infested with bugs. The bathrooms — which they also shared — usually consisted of a toilet, pitcher, and basin, with no sinks or bathtubs. Towels were scarce, and had to be reused each day, until finally theyd acquired so much grime they were nearly black. The theatres were always small and crumby, with moth-eaten wardrobes — when there were any — and backdrops and sets that were ancient and falling apart.

Offstage, when he wasn't rehearsing, the 21-year-old Les Hope of 1924 would fill his time with amorous pursuits. Millie was out of sight and out of mind. One wench that he found particularly attractive was named Kathleen O'Shea, who did a piano specialty. One night he complained of a chest cold and went up to her room hoping she'd rub some salve on his afflicted area and that this might lead to more adventurous endeavors. Unbeknownst to Les, the manager of the small hotel they were in saw him sneaking up the stairs, and went to get a shotgun. He distrusted theatrical people to begin with, and wouldn't have any of that kind of stuff going on in his hotel — especially when he wasn't part of the fun. The old man kicked in the door to Kathleen's room to find Les with his shirt off and Kathleen with sticky fingers. Pointing the gun at Hope, the manager ordered the frightened fellow back down to his own room or else.

Meanwhile, Lefty Durbin was undergoing a frightening experience that he had to face on his own. There was no one to turn to — certainly not the self-absorbed Les Hope, who spent all his free time chasing down the ladies and thinking up new angles. Lefty didn't want to tell anyone, but he was feeling more and more tired and on some nights barely had the energy to get through the act. And he was steadily losing weight, more than he should have, even considering that while on tour they didn't always eat properly. Soon Lefty had developed an almost constant fever, along with a bothersome cough. Les — always eager and concentrating on the spotlight, the audience, the applause, his great plans for the future — didn't even notice. It was a terrifying situation for the young man to be in. What was wrong with him? He was also afraid that if he told old reliable Les, Les would replace him pronto. And Lefty needed the money. He just *couldn't* be sick.

Finally one night, Lefty Durbin, only 22 years old, collapsed on stage. He doubled over in pain, blood dribbling out of his mouth. The crew rushed out, carried the boy back into the wings, and set him down on an old couch once used in a set but now discarded — exactly as Lefty must have felt.

Having completely failed to notice any of his partner's symptoms, Hope insisted that Lloyd must have eaten a bad piece of cream pie at a greasy spoon and that all he probably had was a case of food poisoning. The act was not in danger! he assured himself and others. There was no need for anyone to panic. Lefty would be feeling better in no time.

But Lefty didn't get better. Hope was told to take him back to Cleveland by train. A cot was set up for the ailing youth in the baggage car. Annoyed by the whole business, Hope would periodically go back and sit with his partner, hoping to see signs that Durbin would eventually — and rapidly — recover. They were missing shows, losing money — it was all a bother! All this trouble over a lousy cream pie! Both men were preoccupied with their own grim thoughts during the long, lonely ride to Cleveland.

Although years later Hope would continually insist that Durbin died of food poisoning, grudgingly admitting the kid must have had a weak constitution to begin with, Lefty actually died three days later in Cleveland of consumption. Many at the time theorized that Hope had noticed Lefty's symptoms but refused to acknowledge them and what they might signify, that the last thing Les wanted was for Lefty to take time out and break up the act.

True, Hope was probably human enough to feel sorry for his late partner, but, as always, his thoughts were chiefly reserved for himself. How would Durbin's death affect *his* career? What was to happen now? Could he continue in *Jolly Follies* without a partner? He'd never before done a solo full time, and he didn't as yet consider himself sufficiently prepared for the challenge.

Although in later years Hope would briefly allude to his partnership with Lloyd Durbin, as the decades went by the man receded deeper and deeper into oblivion until Hope usually told people that his next partner, George Byrne, was his first.

George Byrne fared better teaming with Les Hope than Lefty Durbin, but not by much.

CHAPTER FOUR

THE SIAMESE CIRCUIT

Hope's fears about his career coming to an end after the death of Lloyd Durbin proved groundless. Producer Fred Hurley still saw potential in Hope, and quickly hired another entertainer, the above mentioned Mr. Byrne, from Columbus, Ohio, as a replacement side-kick.

Compared to himself, Hope always characterized Byrne as "like a choirboy." Byrne, like Durbin, was much more quiet and unassertive than his hustling, ambitious partner. Still, they liked each other and performed well together, some said more smoothly than Hope and Durbin ever did.

Les had an itch to do more comedy bits, but to his chagrin was always cast as straight man. This, he felt, wasn't taking full advantage of his talents — or, more to the point, putting him at the center of attention. His greatest dream was to have a solo comedy spot, even though he still had trepidations about it. At least when you had a partner, you didn't have to sink or swim on your own.

In an effort to expand the appeal of the act, Hope and Byrne practiced singing together after hours. They figured a few songs added to the dancing would show everyone how versatile they were. They made the mistake, however, of never telling Hurley what they were up to. One night they simply came out, did their usual steps, then opened wide and started warbling. They failed to make much of an impression.

Hurley was furious. Not only had the boys reworked their act without showing it to him, but the bad notices they started to get threatened to put a dent in business. Nonetheless, Hurley recognized that the boys were getting tired of the same old routine and realized they both needed — and were ready for — a change. Singing, though, was out. But maybe comedy was the answer. Hope hadn't done badly in some of the sketches, and he was sure Byrne could carry his end.

The solution emerged: Hope and Byrne and two other guys in the company were formed into a comic quartet. But even the solution came with its own share of problems. For one thing Hope was stepping on lines, mugging, trying to hog the act. Even worse, he kept laughing on stage at the antics of the troupe. "It's the *audience* that's supposed to laugh," Hurley told him. "Not you." Hope duly attempted to rein himself in, but at each performance it was the same: he'd crack up. Finally Hurley told him sharply that if he didn't cut it out, *he'd* be cut out. Hope managed to restrain himself after that.

Oddly enough, those early days in the comic quartet created a habit that Hope never did successfully break in later years — smiling at his own jokes. Even in his film appearances he developed a way of winking at the audience, as if to tell them he was enjoying it as much as they.

Les still had a penchant for finding trouble. One evening he wanted to take George to see his brother Jim, who was living in Pittsburgh, some miles away from their current hitch. One of the locals who hung around backstage to chat with the showgirls overheard him and offered to drive the two of them the whole way. Byrne was resistant. He didn't know the guy very well, but as usual Les took the expedient route and decided to take the man up on his offer.

They were unaware that the fellow worked as a chauffeur for a local doctor and had borrowed his employer's fancy car — while the doctor was out of town — without telling the doctor's wife. She called the police when she noticed it missing, and in short order Hope and Byrne were to hear the din of sirens and to see the flashing of red lights pulling up behind them. Panicking, the chauffeur-on-leave embroiled all parties in a speed chase that finally wound up in a back alley, where the driver quickly disembarked and ran off into some bushes. Left holding the bag, Hope and Byrne had to spend the night in jail with assorted lowlifes — including a man who kept bragging about how he beat his wife (he was the mildest of the cases) — until the whole thing was settled in the morning.

There was no indication at this time of his life, late 1925, age 22, that Leslie Towns Hope would really amount to much of anything. None of the people who worked with him saw anything particularly special. They saw the raw ambition and pride and ruthlessness, but that alone, in their view, wouldn't put someone on top. As a performer in those days he was promising, pleasing, but essentially mediocre. When he finally did make good in major terms, it seems to have really surprised those who knew him at this time.

Meanwhile Les continued to see Mildred Rosequist whenever he was in Cleveland. They danced about the subject of marriage, discussing it, never confirming it. Mildred, on her end, wanted to hear all about this Kathleen O'Shea whom Les's youngest brother George had read about in Hope's letters and had blabbed about to Millie. Hope would assure her that Kathleen was just a friend, someone he worked with. Hope and Millie would neck, nothing more. Kathleen, it seemed, was providing Les Hope with more of what a young man really required. Typical of young males of that, or any, period, Hope found Mildred appealing and thought of her as wife material precisely because she denied him. Kathleen, who "put out," was never seriously thought of as a possible bride. In any case, Kathleen soon left the show to open a dress shop in Morgantown.

It was about this time that Leslie Hope changed his first name to what he conceived to be the more masculine "Lester." Being on the road in close quarters with so many actors had opened his eyes to facts of life he'd never encountered, such as men who liked other men sexually. He was afraid the ambiguous "Leslie" would cause people to get the wrong idea about him. He pursued a series of women with a passionate abandon as if to prove that he — Lester Hope — was as "manly" as anyone could get. Throughout his long life — because of his weakling father, his English origins, and early associations with makeup, costumes, and other aspects of theatre life — he'd undergo a foolish homosexual panic at the slightest provocation. The thought of anyone thinking him "queer" was enough to drive him crazy. He would never piss at a urinal next to anyone, always in a booth. And he hated guys who playfully "groped" each other.

His difficult adolescence, with its variegated privations and distortions and parental and fraternal imbalances, had created deep-rooted insecurities and confusions within him. Throughout his lifetime, his ambivalent feelings about homosexuality as well as his own sexuality were never to sort themselves out. Womanizing to him was always an affirmation of his masculinity, his "straightness."

In Detroit, Hope and Byrne managed to hook up with an agent named Ted Snow. Snow booked them into Detroit's State Theater for $175 a week. At the State, Hope was deeply influenced by the snappy patter and delivery of the M.C., Fred Stitt. Hope also liked the way Stitt took current events and turned them into jokes. Stitt's approach to comedy was one to "stay" with Hope for many decades.

Snow also got the boys a nightclub job at the Oriole Terrace for another $75 a week. Hope and Byrne felt themselves rolling in dough.

They decided to go on a shopping spree and came back with brand new clothes, trunks, and a whole set of flattering publicity photos. Their newfound wealth would have lasted longer if they hadn't gone in for poker and crap games late at night after the club was closed. Each week they'd lose much of their earnings.

It was in 1926 that 23-year-old Lester Hope and George Byrne decided to go for broke and make their way to New York City. Surprisingly, considering his restless, peregrinative wonts, it was the first time Hope had seen Manhattan. Both halves of the act were thrilled (it was new to George too) by the city's energy, glitter, variegated human scenes, tall buildings, and colorful vastness. Les's blood was really racing now. Here was where it was all happening! Here was the Big Time! He determined to make good in this town do or die.

Fortified by initial cockiness — even the more timid Byrne perked up, after his own fashion — the boys reassured themselves that in no time at all they'd be turning New York City on its ear. The going, alas, proved more rocky than either anticipated.

With partner Byrne in tow, Lester Hope marched into the B. F. Keith New York office and managed through sheer gall and push to get not only an interview but some bookings. But the theatres were strictly minor and, worse yet, paid poorly. They were used as showcases for performers hoping to attract the attention of decent agents, who in turn would slug it out for their new clients in quarters where it counted. Soon the Ohio duo was scuttling from one fourth-rate vaudeville house to another, all over the New York area, with Les-the-Intrepid shoring up George-the-Wavering's morale at every point.

Many of these barns were firetraps and rat havens in depressed, rundown areas — and the clientele was even more depressing. The Hope-Byrne combine would peer out through the curtain hole and see mostly empty houses featuring people sleeping off drunks. Some were even quarreling and, in the more remote shadows, making love. These dilapidated vaudeville houses — ubiquitous in 1926 New York — also attracted many people who literally wanted to get out of the rain or needed a place to sleep. On more than one occasion, Hope and Byrne would go into their act only to be greeted by a large chorus of snores. Loud, vicious marital spats would break out in the middle of a number. The floors were sticky with spilled booze; the Prohibition bathtub gins and scotches and beer leaked from inside jacket pockets where they were concealed. The hole-in-the-wall dressing rooms stank of piss and vomit. Soused customers often urinated in their seats or in the aisles, or threw up during a performance. In some of these theatres, while the acts were dying onstage, tubercular patrons would literally die in their seats; the lights would go up, the crowd would exit, and the drably clad "ushers" — often in torn shirts and soiled pants — would find the corpse of someone who'd passed away during a comedy skit, still sitting and staring dead-eyed at the stage. They had not, in most cases, died laughing.

By leaving a set of their spanking new photographs at the William Morris office, the Hope-Byrne duo managed to land one of the most bizarre bookings ever. Agent Abe Lastfogel liked what he saw in the photographs, got in touch with them, and booked them into the RKO-Keith circuit, on a double bill with Daisy and Violet Hilton. Thrilled as they were by the opportunity, the boys still greeted this particular gift horse with mixed emotions. For the Hilton Sisters were, by 1926 standards, a "famous" set of Siamese twins.

Joined together at the spine, Daisy and Violet were likable, almost pretty young women born in Britain and raised in Texas. Exploited by their foster mother's (and midwife's) daughter Edith and her opportunistic husband after the foster mother's death, the twins sued to get out from under their financial control. Past masters (or, again in 1926 terms, mistresses) of self- promotion, the Hiltons were always making headlines. They were never camera-shy. When Violet was denied a marriage license (Daisy had already married) because authorities in twenty states had already "ruled they were one," they insisted that the American Guild of Variety Actors charge them only one initiation fee. (The Guild eventually agreed.) At one point Violet did manage to marry; then reneged, admitting it was a publicity stunt, and got an annulment.

In their act on the Keith circuit, the twins would come out on stage and talk about their lives, then sing and dance and play musical instruments. Hope and Byrne would then join them on the stage and dance with them back-to-back. The boys would get to do their own act immediately following.

Les gritted his teeth and determined to go through with it — it was a terrific opportunity, no doubt about that — but privately he was utterly repulsed. The twins were obvious grotesqueries and in more ways than one (or two). Although his attitude toward them warmed as the months went by, while they traveled from Philly to Washington and from Baltimore to Youngstown, Ohio, he felt like a freak himself as he and George terpsichored around the stage with two women who for all intents and purposes amounted to a two-headed monster.

Rehearsing provided its own macabre comedy. When first Hope and Byrne took the hands of their respective twins for the dance number, they each tended to move in the wrong direction, causing the girls to cry out their pain in unison. Les was always fearful they might whirl too fast, literally tearing the girls in two. Behind their backs he made lewd jokes that had the crew guffawing. "Two girls, one twat," for instance. For the record, the Hilton Twins actually had two of everything, but Hope found it hilarious to foster speculation as to what unique phyical properties they might boast and how they went about making love. What would one twin do, for instance, while the other was copulating with her husband? It gave new meaning to the term "extramarital" affair. Sexually precocious as ever at 23, Hope admitted to some sexual curiosity about the duo but usually concluded with his standard quip, "They're too much women for me."

The act lasted six months, into 1927 — audiences loved, and were intrigued by, the Hiltons. It would have lasted longer, at least with Hope and Byrne, had the boys not demanded more money when they got to Providence. This was a misstep. Everyone knew that the twins were the real draw. The producers refused to pay the two hoofers another cent and they found themselves headed back to New York on the next train. Although they probably could have swallowed their pride and stayed on for the same amount of money, they'd already had their fill of the peculiar ways of the Hiltons. Or, as Hope pronunciamented to the somewhat depressed and indecisive Byrne, "We've *got* to do better than this!"

They moved into the Somerset Hotel, the management of which was understanding about late payment of bills by unemployed show people. Luckily they'd held on to some of the money they made with the Hiltons. Bloody but unbowed, they put on their shoes and hit the sidewalks of New York.

It wasn't long before "The Sidewalks of New York" hit back.

CHAPTER FIVE

DOCTOR HOPE AND MR. HYDE

Earl Linds, a choreographer who knew the boys and had seen their act, got in touch with them about auditioning for a new Broadway show entitled *The Sidewalks of New York*. It was to be produced by Charles Dillingham with words and music by Eddie Dowling and Jimmy Hanley, respectively, and would star Dowling's wife Ray [sic] Dooley, at the time a big Ziegfeld Follies headliner. In the musical, Dooley plays a young woman who's been raised in a convent. Now she's on her own in the big city, searching for romance and excitement.

The producers had already signed up Ruby Keeler as a tap dancer, largely because of her current tempestuous and notorious romance with Al Jolson, whom she would later marry. The show needed a few guys to do specialty dancing and act small speaking parts. Les and George were confident they could fill the bill. They did. They met with the approval of the powers-that-were and were hired.

Although Hope was overjoyed at finally being cast for his first Broadway show — and a big, snappy, and glittering one at that — he was disappointed that his and George's parts were so small. They were only one of two pairs of hired dancers. (Incidentally, Hope became good friends with Alan Calm, one half of the second team. It was one of the few genuinely warm relationships Hope established at that time. Years later he hired Calm for TV and movie stints as a stand-in and dialogue coach.)

The Sidewalks of New York first opened in Philadelphia at the Garrick Theatre on September 5, 1927. For Hope, at 24, there were two bits of additional good news. First, it was decided yet another number would be added to the show featuring Ruby Keeler and the four male dancers. Second, Barbara Sykes had wired him she was coming to Philly.

Characteristically, Hope had continued his frenetic pursuit of all the females available. The ones who rejected him left him angry and bitter. The ones who accepted him won, in short order, his patronizing scorn. Mildred back in Ohio — she who had kept her erotic self safely secure on a pedestal — remained in his respectful regard. He stayed in steady touch with her, sending her long letters detailing (and inflating) his part in the show and assuring her she was often in his thoughts. At the same time, Kathleen O'Shea was still busy in her dress shop and Les wanted to stay in her good graces, too. So when he saw a pretty item in a Seventh Avenue shop that he felt she'd like, he'd mail it to her.

But now Barbara would have the great advantage of being in the same city as Les. Barbara was a perky, aspiring actress who peregrinated around town in the company of a number of men. Her romance with Bob began when a mutual friend introduced them, and was soon going full steam. She undoubtedly saw in Hope — who was, after all, in a Broadway show whatever his place in the pecking order — someone who could be a useful contact.

For a time, however, it seemed Barbara was fated never to arrive. She was seeing a piano player — her true passion as opposed to the useful contact she saw in Hope — and her midnight rendezvous with *him* kept delaying her and screwing-up her schedule. She proceeded to keep Hopeful Lester on a string, sending telegram after telegram detailing her arrivals — then never showing. Finally, unwound temporarily from the piano strings of her lover, she arrived in Philly all breathless and eager. Anxious to show her off to his confreres, Hope arranged a party in her honor at the Maidstone Apartments where the cast was staying.

The party — bolstered by over fifty guests and several bottles of bootleg booze — became a frenetic, noisy affair in no time. Music played loudly, drinks were passed around, as well as bodies, and before long the word had gone out and others involved in the show were knocking on the door requesting entry. Among these was Billy O'Rourke, a chorus boy and drag queen who marched in with his friends, all of whom were totally clad in lace and lipstick and other feminine accouterments. As the theatrical community, in 1927 as in any other time, tended to tolerate and accommodate the "different," this caused only a minimum of stir. Hope, however, as Barbara was later to recall, felt more than a little uncomfortable and clung to her even more tightly. However, everyone was so soused at this point it hardly mattered.

Except to the house manager, who angrily climbed to the floor of his apartment house from which issued the pounding noise and raucous chatter and demanded to be let in. The first people who met his disbelieving eyes were flamboyant Billy O'Rourke and his "gal-pals." The house manager nearly had a fit. Horrified at the thought of "perverts" carousing in his apartment building, the manager hauled in the Philadelphia police. The drag queens fled into the night and most of the other guests quickly vamoosed.

Those who remained continued to party in relative quietude or began passing out. Les and Barbara found an empty bed and flopped into it drunkenly, arms and legs entangled. There they spent several hours until it was morning — or, rather, afternoon, whereupon hangovers had to be nursed so that the performance could go on as usual.

Sidewalks finally opened in New York on October 3, 1927, at the Knickerbocker Theatre and was immediately certified a hit. Which made the blow that Hope and Byrne sustained shortly thereafter all the more painful. The producers called them in and explained that, since there was more than enough dancing in the show, there was no way to justify to the backers the added expense of keeping them on. Hope and Byrne were, in short, cutting into the profits. The other team of dancers, having been hired first, would handle all the required hoofing. Les and George got two weeks notice and the boot.

Once more they were unemployed. And only a few days before they'd been on top of the world and the toast (at least in their own minds and letters home) of Broadway!

It was strategy-session time again. The first thing they did was get themselves a new agent, a fellow by the name of Milt Lewis. The best he could do for them initially, however, was the second billing out of eight at a big showcase theatre. Hope had summoned from his temporary depression a reinforced cockiness. After all, he'd made it to a Broadway hit show, however briefly. So what if he got fired from it? Some people *never* made it to one, *ever*. As for those headliners, he'd show *them* who was boss!

As usual, George Byrne had to go along with whatever Hope suggested — or, rather, insisted upon. George was wise enough to know it was Les Hope's drive and persistence that had gotten them as far as they had. He was also no match for Les's sheer force of personality.

George Cukor, who'd known George Byrne in the early days, once told me that Byrne had been secretly in love with Hope. It seems Byrne never confessed his love to Hope, sensing Hope's fear of anything homosexual, and was fearful of a brutal rebuff and inevitable exile. Whether Hope knew of his partner's feelings remains an as-yet unanswered question to this day. Although he may have sensed them but blocked it from his mind.

Cukor, later a famed Hollywood director, was very active in the theatre of the 1920s, and ran a stock company for a while in Rochester, New York. Gay himself, he was attracted to George Byrne and tried to persuade him he had a future as an actor. "But George wouldn't leave Lester — he adored him, depended on him, was essentially feminine to Lester's masculine — I always thought it would have been better for George if he'd broken loose sooner than he did. I know he got badly hurt."

The headliners to be overtaken at this particular theatre were an old, highly experienced comedy team, but Hope felt sure they were no competition for the younger, more energetic — fresh from Broadway! — Hope and Byrne. Although the greatest asset of the team had been their dancing (the very reason they'd made it to Broadway) Hope decided it was time to play that down and play up the comedy routines.

Unfortunately, Hope failed to come up with fresh jokes — it was before the days of the ready-to-wear gagmen he'd later keep in servile stock — and the old routines he sported were already familiar to everyone in the audience. The new act bombed. After that, even Milt Lewis went cold on them.

Tails between their legs, they were soon back at the William Morris office, prepared to throw themselves on anyone's mercy. An agent, Al Lloyd, a man with a kindly nature, took pity on them and went so far as to suggest ways they could improve their act. He also set out to win for them more appropriate bookings. But there was a senior agent on hand, a less patient, ruthless little fellow named Johnny Hyde (the same Johnny Hyde who'd later Svengali Marilyn Monroe to success) who was completely unimpressed by Hope-Byrne and wanted nothing to do with them. He'd heard their act was bad — not actually having seen it himself. He vetoed Lloyd's decision to take them on, declared there was no place for them with William Morris. He refused even to talk to them, relaying his advice that they should "Go home and start over." The ultimate expression of patronizing contempt.

This was, by all reports, the nadir in the careers of Hope and Byrne. The most prestigious talent agency in town had told them they were losers — or at least Hyde had, and his word was what counted. They'd blown it, lost everything they'd worked for. Frustrated and furious, cursing at Johnny Hyde, Hope began to take out his anger on the only target available: George Byrne, the man who'd followed him with doglike faithfulness through all their ups and downs. George was to blame. George had ruined everything. George was too passive, too life-less, too indecisive. George the drag, nerd, burden, loser, who, in Hope parlance, failed to hold up his end.

George took it hard. "Without him I'm nothing. Less than noth-ing," he told George Cukor (weeping, as Cukor later remembered) on the phone. Hope, of course, endlessly rationalizing, endlessly self-absorbed and self-motivated and self-protective, simply couldn't admit his own failure or the fact that it'd been *his* approach to the act that had made them bomb at the showcase. And, as matters stood, they didn't even have enough ready cash on hand to tiptoe their butts back to Ohio — not that Hope, at any rate, wanted to.

Still indecisive, still toying with a possible need for ticket-money back to Cleveland, the boys accepted with considerable bitterness some inferior bookings. One week they wound up at a small theatre in New Castle, Pennsylvania. It seemed the manager needed someone to announce the coming attractions. After a doubtful look at Les Hope, he elected the newcomer "for lack of anyone better suited."

Having developed a deeply resentful and defensive "don't-give-a-shit" attitude after the New York debacles, Hope decided to "play around" with his assignment. He proceeded to poke witty but risky fun at the upcoming acts. The next week's comic was a Scottish entertainer, so Hope dredged up a few impromptu jokes about Scotsmen. Ditto with each of the other acts. Every night the Intrepid Les added more and more jokes, encouraged by the audiences' — and the manager's — response. It was his first real taste of stand-up comedy. And his first real taste of going solo. Soon Les Hope was wandering around talking to himself — and over and over a not particularly original refrain resound-ed: "He travels *fastest* who travels *alone!*"

George, of course, saw it coming. He knew that, however unjust-ly, Les blamed him for their negative notices, knew Les felt he himself and he alone was the comedian of the two, and that doing a dance act with Byrne — an act that seemed to have long since reached the limits of its potential — was a ticket to nowhere. Over and over Les recited the mantra from long ago: "A man who *won't* be beat, *can't* be beat!" In this steely determination, this manic urge to make it and make it big — wanting major success, wanting it with all one's mind and heart, soul, and being, *would* make it happen — there was simply no place for sen-sitive, introverted, secretly lovelorn George Byrne.

Many years later the future Bob Hope would insist, on more than a few occasions, that it had been *George's* decision to break up the act, sensing (in the Hope version) that Hope had a much better chance of making it without him. Even if this version were true, it would only be because Hope's ever more contemptuous, dismissive, and aloof attitude toward George had triggered his partner's natural self-sacrifice. But it's more likely, and this is backed up by informed sources, that Hope simply took Byrne aside and unceremoniously told him they were through.

William Haines, another well-known Hollywood gay who'd crossed paths with Byrne, felt George had been utterly broken-hearted by the parting. Hope suspected Byrne's love for him, according to Haines, and wanted to get in the clear. In 1928, George's "Love That Dared Not Speak Its Name" was on the verge of turning openly, embarrassingly loquacious. Or, at least, so Hope feared. In any case, Les had no intention of waiting around to find out. No, sir! Byrne had already told friends he felt Hope was rigidly repressing his gay instincts. Les opted to repress George instead.

The irony of all this was that George Byrne, who'd struggled and suffered through thick and thin, in good times and in bad, for four long years as a sidekick, was the sole human being (with the exception of Hope's mother) who was genuinely loyal to Les Hope.

The brothers had given him no real love; from them there was only jealousy. Agents had dropped him when he didn't serve their purposes. Professional associates had been fair-weatherites through and through. Even old buddies had seen Les only as a fun-and-games comrade. And the women: Mildred had never really responded to him. Barbara Sykes had tried to use him for her purposes. Chorus girls and ladies of the evening had pocketed his dough and eaten his meals and accepted his flowers and trinkets — but to them he'd been just another horny guy. George Byrne, alone, had loved Les Hope for himself, unconditionally. And when George went, Les was to find himself truly, frighteningly alone. That aloneness was not to be dispelled for five long years.

Pitiful, broken Byrne went on as best he could. For a while he was in a four-member comedy dance act. In the mid-Thirties he decided to quit show business altogether. George Cukor again had urged he try acting, but Byrne, humble and self-effacing as always, felt he lacked the requisite ability. Never bitter or envious of Hope's later success, he was always to speak of him in glowing, complimentary terms. Byrne drifted back to Columbus, Ohio, and took up a job with the Defense Construction Supply Center, where he worked for twenty-five years (1941 – 1966). He'd intended to retire in 1967, but on December 15,

1966, age 62, he died. George Cukor and others opined that Byrne had loved Hope to the end of his life. (Oddly, the Byrne and Hope families *were* united, when George Byrne's sister Mary married Bob Hope's brother George. Mary and George were to have three children to perpetuate the blending of the Hope and Byrne blood.)

Oblivious to the rare treasure he'd lost, and wishing to make a fresh start amidst friendly surroundings, Hope returned alone to Cleveland. To family, friends, and neighbors, he put up a fairly jaunty and positive front. He gave no hint he'd been booted out of Broadway and turned down by major agencies who felt he had no future. Cocksure and boastful as ever was he — at least on the surface. He smiled patiently, even ruefully, as he listened to his baby brother George, a year or so out of high school, tell him proudly that he was taking dancing lessons in the hope of joining Les's act later. This was the last thing Les needed to hear. There was no place in his scheme of things for a clinging greenhorn brother. Hadn't he just gotten rid of a clinger? "We'll see, kid," he laughed dismissively.

Lester Towns Hope, a man who'd always preferred action to analysis, was forced to face the possibility that his "meteoric rise to the top" might have come to a complete and deadly halt. He also was facing these gloomy thoughts by his lonesome now. Part of him liked that he'd share the spotlight with no one. And deep, deep down, a part of him was scared. It was a feeling he recoiled from.

Somehow, some way, he insinuated himself by early 1929 into bookings as a solo act in different theatres in Cleveland and environs. He told jokes in blackface, the blackface serving two functions. First, it "looked" comical. Second, given the current state of his insecurity, it was a mask he could hide behind. The last thing the 25-year-old needed was for his fears to be seen, or even sensed, by others.

One night, however, he was running late and didn't bother with the blackface. The act was well-received but he was still nervous about how it would go over if he weren't "funny looking." The audience laughed just as hard as they ever did, and it was suggested to him that he go out with a clean face from that night forward. It was all right with Hope — putting on all that greasepaint had always been a bother. And he was pleased that his jokes and delivery were funny. But underneath there was a certain nagging doubt about this happy turn of events.

Hope had always felt and maintained that the best comics were funny-looking physically. He had, in fact, affected the blackface in part to disguise what he feared were his too *good* looks. Always he'd been a vain fellow, studying himself in the mirror, admiring his sleek hair and smooth skin. Now he studied his reflection in a different way. Was there really, after all, something *funny* about him, something that audiences were laughing *at*? Sure, he'd never had trouble with women, but the real beauties, the gals every guy wanted, always seemed a trifle distant with him. At least until they knew he was in show biz, or saw him as useful in some other way. He was getting the first inkling that perhaps he wasn't as handsome as he thought. He was to find out, for sure, some years later — and in the most dramatic, larger-than-life way possible.

Still, he reassured himself, his present act, such as it was, was doing okay, and once more there was reason to be positive about his eventual prospects. Ignoring the ominous feelings in the back of his mind about his looks, he basked in the audience's applause.

Lester Towns Hope was a solo. He'd proved he could do it. The best was surely yet to come.

CHAPTER SIX

THE PHOENIX

After his success in his home town, Lester Hope wanted to try the big time again, but he wasn't quite ready for New York. He decided it was better to hone his act in Chicago and then make his way to Manhattan armed with solid, big-city notices and letters of introduction. He was to learn to his dismay that Chicago in 1929 was not the best place for a vaudevillian.

Vaudeville was dying out in the late Twenties. The big thing in the country was the motion picture, and old vaudeville halls were being converted to movie theatres in record numbers. Although most theatres still booked a few vaudeville acts to entertain patrons after the double-bill or single movie program, the competition for these limited spots was keener than ever. The booking business for the vaudeville circuit was lorded over by the Radio-Keith-Orpheum organization and if you weren't one of the favored few it was hard to get jobs. Hope had sadly overestimated the opportunities awaiting him in Chicago.

Years later Hope would tend to put a sunny complexion on the whole Chicago business. "I was out of work for a few months in 1929 when I was getting started," he said in the early Sixties. "That's the only time I've been out of work in thirty-two years. Was it real tough? Naw — nothing like that. It was nothing, absolutely nothing!"

It seemed like nothing to Hope decades later because it was one of the only times he had to scramble for bookings and was constantly turned down. A few months out of a career spanning three quarters of a century does in retrospect seem inconsequential. Only it was not so inconsequential during these months he was actually living it.

Hope had absolutely no contacts in Chicago. No one had seen him perform, and his Broadway-New York credits left agents and the-atre managers singularly unimpressed. If he was so good, why wasn't he still in New York? they wondered. Every day he would think of going back to Cleveland where it was more likely that he could get jobs, but he couldn't stand the idea of returning a failure yet another time. He was always good at putting up a brave front, true — he had done just that after returning to Ohio from New York — but there were limits to what people would believe. Besides, he'd stepped on a few toes in Cleveland, alienated people with his brash, cocky manner — they'd never let him forget it if he returned without an armful of clippings and lots of moola.

Hope was able to survive by virtue of some money he'd saved up from bookings in Cleveland. He took a room in a cheap boardinghouse, and ate most meals in a cafeteria where he struck up an acquaintance with a pretty waitress, who fell eager victim to glib tongue and charming manner. She gave him free donuts and coffee, sneaking him an occasional sandwich. He also said he'd pay her back and maybe she believed it. He'd play craps and poker, win some money, hang out with other hopefuls just as down on their luck as he was. They'd have some drinks, console each other on how tough it was, and trade ideas on how to survive.

Young men in the theatre in those days, as now, had several options when jobs were scarce and money running low. They could take other kinds of work on a temporary, part-time basis. They could chicken out and go home. They could even turn to prostitution.

Hope knew about this last possibility, of course, even listened to other young actors tell of their erotic exploits, conquests, whatever. (In later years, Jimmy Dean and Rock Hudson, among others, would recall in detail the "help" smitten older men had given them.) Hope had no objection to a john buying him a beer, telling him the sad story of his life — Hope could incorporate some of this as fodder for his act. But when push came to shove — or hand-clasp or groin-squeeze — he would become extremely nervous and shy off. Or so he liked to say. Whenever the subject came up retrospectively, he would say he ran for his life, that there were certain levels he could not bring himself to stoop to.

Whatever the problems, pursuits, people, and ambiance which he found himself subjected to in that grim 1929 Chicago period, he did, by his own admission, almost accept failure and board the next bus for Ohio. Until he ran into an old friend he'd met while touring some years before: Charlie Cooley. Cooley was a successful vaudevillian and he bought Hope coffee so they could talk about how things were going. At first Hope gave out with the usual malarkey — things were going great, couldn't be better, buddy — too proud to admit he was on his last legs.

After a while, however, when Cooley caught him in several lies regarding theatres and bookings, Hope had to confess that things were frankly lousy. He hadn't had a job in months. It was an extremely humiliating and trying moment for him. To his relief, Cooley didn't rub it in.

Instead, Cooley promised to see what he could do, and in only a few days' time, to Hope's surprise, Cooley came through. He got a friend and agent named Charles Hogan to hire Hope as master of ceremonies at a West Englewood theatre for three shows over Decoration Day. The fee: a heaven-sent $25. Over-anxious, still a bit cocky — he had done Broadway, after all — Hope took the job determined to make the best of it. At first he came on a little strong, then found his stride and got a good reaction from an audience that appreciated his sense of humor. He worked out so well that he was transferred to the Stratford Theatre (which ironically had been a movie house converted to a vaudeville theatre, bucking the trend) when the original M.C. demanded too much money and became difficult to deal with. Audiences responded so well to Hope in this engagement that his stay was extended for a lengthy run.

Back on his feet again — although far, far from where he wanted to be — Lester decided it was time for yet another name change. Since no one in any city, certainly not the William Morris agency — had been impressed with his New York credits, he deemed it high time to wash away his whole back history and start all over again. Start all over again — boy, did that have a familiar ring! Once it had been Leslie Hope. Lester Hope. Hope and Byrne. Now it was to be just "Bob Hope." In his younger days he'd always been a fan of automobile racing, one of his idols being the race-car driver Bob Burman. It was from Burman that he took his new first name. Now he was really on his way as a solo act: new name, new image, new everything. And, most of all, new Hope.

He liked "Bob" for other reasons. Leslie had been too feminine; Lester too outrè. These names had seemed to create a distance between him and the people he wanted — and needed — to please. Bob — it seemed more down-to-earth — just like his audience. Bob Hope it would be.

During that 1929 run at the Stratford there emerged, starting at age 26, the Bob Hope that audiences nationwide and abroad would one day come to know and love. It was at the Stratford, encouraged by such people as fellow performer and comic Barney Dean, that he came to refine his snappy patter and rapid delivery. Here he developed the precise, expert timing that was to become his trademark. He began thinking up clever bits of business to put across while performing, and added sound effects to the act. If one joke bombed, he'd rapidly follow up with another that would, hopefully, click. His humor, to say the least, was broad — but it was also nothing that patronized the audience or went over their heads. They came to love him for it.

In those days people would often return to the Stratford to see the whole show again — a second, a third, even a fourth time. In the case of a song or a dance act, this wasn't a problem, but for the comics it was a headache. Jokes being heard for the second or third time rarely went over big. Hope determined to keep his act as fresh as possible, no matter how many repeaters were in the audience. He took to cannibalizing old joke books for "new" gags, and flung out one-liners he'd heard on the circuit from other performers. Anywhere and anyhow he could dredge up what he felt was the "right" material, he would use — the words *"won't* be beat — *can't* be beat" reverberating in his consciousness. He was out for the jackpot — to get everyone in the audience, right up to the third and fourth-time repeaters, to find him absolutely, irresistibly hilarious each time out. New material — no matter where it came from — that was the ticket; that was a must. Now that he had a firm grip on this latest chance, Bob Hope wasn't going to relax it.

One night, in a theatrical hangout near the Stratford, Hope made the acquaintance of a young lady named Louise Troxell, an aspiring actress. He worked up a prime infatuation for her right from the start, and made up his mind he'd incorporate her into his act. She wouldn't be his partner, as such, but come out to serve as his foil in a certain segment — à la George Burns with Gracie Allen. Louise, anxious for her first real taste of show business, did not require much coaxing.

It seems odd at this point in his life that, after eschewing co-performers and developing what had become a successful solo act, Hope would want to share the stage with anyone else, even if it were clear she was only a complement to him (certainly not an equal in time-span or billing). There were, however, several reasons for Hope's decision. First, he was really stuck on Louise, whom he conceived of as that kind of "classy" dame always "above" — and therefore always elusive to — him. She was, for one thing, extremely good-looking, and moreover she lacked the vulgar, common demeanor of so many "actresses" of the day. He was, in short, falling in love with Louise and wanted her near him as much as possible. He'd also developed a fear of those constant rumors about young, unmarried men in show business and had grown weary of fending off advances from gay fellow players and "tired-businessmen" types. Rumors were still in the air concerning Leslie Hope's alleged relationships with such men as Lloyd Durbin and George Byrne. Show business stories traveled quickly from city to city along the lines of "oh, yeah, he and Byrne," and "weren't he and Lloyd . . . ." Everyone in 1929 Chicago was, for instance, enjoying crude jokes about "the Oliver Twists" — the young starving men and how they survived. Even if unfounded in Hope's case — or so he always stridently insisted over the decades — such musings could be embarrassing. So, it seemed to the newly christened Bob Hope that having a beautiful young woman traveling with him would polish up his "look" ("image" was not the popular term in 1929) and solve all his public — or rather private — relations problems in one fell swoop.

At this time he was also straining to whip up fresh material performance after performance. It got so bad he resorted to "borrowing" bits of business done by well-known comics — a not uncommon practice, to be fair to him — such as Jay C. Flippen's way of cocking a brown derby on his head while twirling his cigar around in a funny, highly distinctive little mannerism. "I twirl *my* cigar in the *opposite* direction!" was Hope's standard reply when he was accused of filching from Flippen. Bob also figured that having Louise in the act would generate fresh new gags by hook or by crook, thereby taking some of the burden off his shoulders.

Last but not least, Hope was still not as confident a solo as he projected himself as being. Telling non-stop jokes in front of an audience — many of them repeaters — was a lot harder than doing dance routines with a partner.

The Bob-Louise Act went over all right, and before long the duo was touring Kansas City, Wichita, and points South and West. Hope much preferred touring to one long theatre stay because he could repeat the same carefully tilled gags. Their reviews, to his delight, and relief, were overwhelmingly positive. By this time, Hope was collecting some $300 per week — a far cry from the measly $25 he'd hungrily snapped up in Chicago.

He and Louise then put together a new act, which they christened "Keep Smilin'" and took it out on the road as the featured comedy spot on a four-act vaudeville bill, one put together by an organization known as Interstate Time. All went well on the tour until the group reached Fort Worth, Texas. Hope strutted out and laid his usual jokes and impeccable delivery on the audience — but there was virtually no response. And no laughs.

Bob did everything he could to recover, to get the audience in his corner, but it was no go. He applied every savvy trick in the book; nothing seemed to work. Humiliated, he left the stage in a huff to curse Texas audiences in salty language in his dressing room.

Suddenly the door opened and in walked a somewhat unprepossessing fellow whom Bob did not realize was the manager of the Interstate Vaudeville Circuit, Bob O'Donnell. "You're good, son," O'Donnell told him, "but you have to learn how to relax." Over the next half-hour O'Donnell detailed how Bob should always adapt his own tempo to the tempo of his audience; that there was such a thing as delivering at too rapid a pace. The machine-gun approach, he emphasized, didn't work for everybody. These were, after all, laconic, laid-back Texans.

Hope was never anxious to get gratuitous advice, no matter who gave it. Overly sure of himself and his own approach, he nodded smugly until the man finished and finally left. Hope felt like he'd just been patronized. Who *was* that guy to tell *him* how to do comedy after all his years in the business? Even when he learned who the man was, Hope remained in a snit. Still, much of what O'Donnell said began to sink in. Perhaps he *was* trying too hard. Perhaps he *did* come off — at least to these Texans — as rather desperate. He determined to try to get a feel for the audience, adjusting his tempo subtly as he went along. But he'd never learn to relish taking advice.

Bolstered by good notices and plenty of clippings, Bob and Louise decided to leave the company and brave Big, Bad New York yet again. Hope felt much more confident that he'd make it this time. "He" meaning he, not he and Louise. Louise was an asset to the act, but, with no billing, he was the only star. Hope now had all the advantages of being a solo *and* having a partner.

Through correspondence, the B.F. Keith office in Manhattan had expressed an interest in the New Bob Hope, and when he arrived in New York he hastened to their headquarters. But when he was ushered into the office of his new agents, two gentlemen named Morris and Fell, they didn't seem to know who he was. Unfazed, Bob launched into an all-out recital of his credits and background. He was haunted within by the specters of the treatment Johnny Hyde of the Morris Agency had foisted on him and was out to nip that in the bud. (He had "gone back and started over," hadn't he, as per Hyde's contemptuous advice?) Overwhelmed and somewhat intrigued by their new client's intensity, Morris and Fell finally eased the brash 26-year-old into a seat and talked to him about possible bookings.

As he listened to their plans for him, however, Hope began to experience the sinking sensation of theatrical déjà vu — he'd been this-away before. To his dismay, they were discussing low-class showcases on 14th Street like the Jefferson — now *that* had a too-familiar ring! Showcases? Wasn't he past that by now? For a while he forgot that he was now *Bob* Hope, someone new who rang no Big Apple bells. But he'd be damned if he wound up yet again in those flea-bitten fourth-rate vaudeville shacks when he and Louise had become a top act in several other major cities. As soon as he got to a phone he made calls to the William Morris office and the Publix Circuit.

Like many entertainers before and since, Hope was a victim of politics and the pecking order, at the mercy of agents and theatrical managers who mercilessly controlled the lives, careers, and general welfare of the artistic people among whom they doled out the breaks. He somehow had to convince "them" that he, Bob Hope, feisty, fresh and new, wasn't a loser any longer — if for that matter (his ego talking now) he'd ever been! The trouble was: if Publix took him on, they weren't the Power Players the Keith people were, and while the William Morris Agency could offer him representation, they couldn't actually book him into theatres the way Keith could. If only the Keith office would come through for him!

Finally they did. Hope was booked into Proctor's, an uptown theatre on 86th Street. The headliner was silent movie actress Leatrice Joy, whose career was on the wane. Audiences were more attracted to the show because of Joy's notoriety — she was the former wife of film star John Gilbert and the mother of his child, Leatrice Joy Gilbert. Still, this drew the unsuspecting audience on which her fellow performers, like Hope, could capitalize.

Hope was soon excitedly reviewing the material he planned for Proctor's. But there was one hitch. Before his debut at that spot, the Keith office wanted him to warm up his act at a theatre out in Brooklyn for the week preceding.

Hope willingly went out to Brooklyn, but in the back of his over-confident mind he began to wonder if he was being tested. If he failed to pass muster here, would he be booted from the Proctor's slot before he had a chance to register? Too nervous at the time to think straight, he went into the same kind of act he planned to perform at Proctor's. That was his big mistake.

The Brooklyn audiences of 1929 were not those of the more

upscale and more expensive places like the upper-Manhattan Proctor's. The Brooklynites tended to favor more physicalized comedy, replete with pratfalls and falling-down pants and shirts that broke outward — tired but still (to them) amusing comedy routines of a more time-tested and vulgarized nature. Bob's patter went over like a lead balloon. Talk. Talk. Talk. All he did was *talk*. This crowd wanted action, slapstick, pizzazz! He was soundly booed, his brightest sallies lost in the resounding raucous din of the cavernous house.

After bombing in Brooklyn, Hope's nerves were really frazzled by the time he opened at Proctor's — though it was a relief to learn he was, at least, still on the bill. He walked out on stage in front of a much more high-toned crowd, remembering they were fascinated by the Leatrice Joy-John Gilbert connection. The first line out of his mouth, addressed to a whispering dowager in the first few rows, was "No, lady, I am *not* John Gilbert." To his vast relief, the audience howled.

From that moment on he had the Proctor's crowd in the palm of his hand. Louise joined him on stage later, and their well-timed, well-posed bantering also went over big. His Proctor's run, it seemed, was going to be a smash.

Soon Johnny Hyde, no less, was out in the audience, later sending word he wanted to talk to Hope. Like the proverbial shark sniffing blood, Hyde smelled success in the air and wanted his percentage of it. He had, he later admitted, never imagined that "Hopeless" would make good. While Bob knew, in spite of himself, that Hyde's advice of yore (granted that it had been offered with disdain and contempt rather than with compassion and concern) had actually turned out to be good advice, in after years he could never forget how it had made him feel like a loser. At that point, he indulged the sweet luxury of telling Hyde, by Proctor messenger, that he couldn't possibly see him until after the last show, setting the appointment for midnight.

However, after the second show of the night, Lee Stewart of the Keith office came into Bob's dressing room and offered him a $400 per week contract with the prestigious Orpheum circuit, three years guaranteed. "$450 and I'll do it!" Hope snapped. Stewart agreed on the spot. In 1929, $400 a week was an absolute fortune in show business terms. If he needed any proof that he had made The Big Time, Hope had it now.

As for Johnny Hyde of William Morris? Hope didn't keep the appointment but he did leave a message — and not the kind they permitted over Western-Union.

CHAPTER SEVEN

PERLBERG'S FOLLY

Now that his career was really cooking with gas, Hope decided it was time to do something about the one major problem with his act: coming up with fresh material. He knew he couldn't continue indefinitely with rehashed gags from yesteryear, or tired new slants on ancient routines. Left to his own devices he had a reasonably quick wit and was slickly and smoothly adaptable, but he needed, as of 1929, an *inexhaustible* supply of new jokes. The solution became obvious: hire a professional gag writer.

The man elected was Al Boasberg, who had written for many top vaudeville acts including George Burns and Gracie Allen; he had, in fact, come up with the routine that set a whole new, and profitable, direction for their act. Boasberg also wrote jokes for Jack Benny, among others. Hope would take Al out for some Chinese food, sit him down at a table, and make conversation with him until the wee hours of the morning. Every time a funny line or quip came out of Al's mouth, Hope would scribble it down on a menu or napkin. Al could take any situation and make a joke out of it; if a gag wasn't quite working, Al knew how to fix it and make it funnier.

But now that he had fixed one problem, Bob found himself with another headache: Louise. At first she'd been satisfied with coming out on stage for a few minutes of his act and serving as foil-straight-gal for his jokes, but now that they'd become so successful she wanted more — more stage business, more money, and — (worst of all to Hope's thinking) — she wanted her name to be billed alongside his!

By this time Hope was firmly and permanently sold on himself as basically a solo act. Louise to him was just window dressing, a little bit of gravy on the side. As he saw it, any halfway pretty girl could do what she did. Hope was furious at her demands. It was *his* talent and persistence that had driven them to the top; Louise was just along for the ride. He called her an ingrate. She called him a bastard. He would have replaced her in a minute but he didn't want to go through the bother of training someone else to do their routines. Besides, they worked well together and audiences liked Louise.

Even though Hope's fee had steadily risen since Louise first joined his act, Hope hadn't given her a single penny more than they'd first agreed upon. It seemed never to occur to him that he was being greedy; he just saw this as good business sense. Louise was no more important to the act than she'd ever been, in his view — so what was all this about her getting more money? But to keep her quiet he raised her fee — but only slightly — and told her to be grateful.

The raise worked for awhile, but before too long shouts and screams and the sound of thrown and shattered cold cream jars could be heard coming from the dressing rooms. Hope and Louise argued bitterly over her time on stage. She saw Hope getting the lion's share of attention and applause and she wanted her piece of the pie. She knew better than to expect him ever to give her billing — Bob and Louise: A Comedy Team, for instance — but, she reasoned and insisted, the *least* he could do was give her a few more minutes on stage, while expanding their sequence together so that she needn't feel like a glorified chorus girl. Hope implied that there were ways pretty girls could get ahead in this business — if they were smart — but Louise was bright enough to know that the womanizing Hope would only have felt, and registered, contempt for her if she'd given in to his suggestions.

While Hope might have been initially infatuated with Louise when they originally got together, his interest had dwindled gradually to mere sexual curiosity — which she had no intention of gratifying. She made it clear to him that theirs was strictly a business relationship. He, for his part, realized that in no way had she ever returned his feeling — it had been the classic case of The One Who Loves and the One Who Permits Herself to Be Loved — but only to a point.

Bob had always wanted to physically possess this attractive, teasy woman. He'd originally figured their weeks together would give him time and opportunity to win her over, that she'd come to see him as more than an "opportunity," but it was not to be. She had, in Hope's view, committed The Cardinal Sin: she hadn't stuck to his prearranged schedule and fallen in love with him. She wasn't as malleable as he'd figured her to be. She turned out, in his view, to be just another grasping, cold-hearted show-biz bitch who thought only of herself and her own ambitions. Hope's hackles were raised when he met other men as ambitious as he; in a woman, he found it intolerable.

Bob refused to knuckle under. He decided it was time to throw Louise out on her ass. His romantic plans for her hadn't panned out as expected, and as far as the act was concerned, she was becoming a liability. He was essentially a solo and that was that! He decided to write to Millie Rosequist and ask her if she'd be willing to replace Louise. Spurred on by his anger at Louise's romantic rejection of him, and wanting to hedge his bets for Millie's cooperation by sweetening the pot, he threw in a marriage proposal along with the business offer. With his new success, he figured, he would make far more palatable husband material than he ever had before.

There were countless girls — a number of whom Bob was dating — who would have loved to step into Louise's place, but the last thing Bob now wanted was a grasping showbiz type of the usual stripe whose ambitions would eventually come into conflict with his own. Chorus girls were okay to sleep with but not to work with. Millie, however, who'd stayed back home in Cleveland and whose protective mother had forbidden her to go on the road, was still — or so Bob imagined by that relatively late date 1929 — innocent and lacking in show biz aspirations. What he didn't take into account was that just because Mildred didn't want to be an actress didn't mean she was just sitting home twiddling her thumbs, waiting for his calls and letters.

Having been ignored by Bob for months on end, Mildred must have registered a certain satisfaction when she told Bob she couldn't possibly join his act and certainly couldn't accept his offer of marriage. "I'm engaged," she wrote him, "to somebody else."

Bob was more exasperated than devastated. While he'd never stopped caring for Millie — his first true sweetheart — he was more interested in his career than in marriage at this point. Millie, true, might have made the perfect, pliable partner for his act. Unambitious, naive, innocent of sharkish show-biz ways, she'd have been much easier to manage than Louise. But it was not to be. He wished Millie the best of luck and sat down to figure out which concessions he could make to Louise to keep her in line — without inadvertently giving her more power than she deserved.

Years later, Millie, who'd married a policeman, visited Hope backstage at the NBC studios. She reminded him that it had (supposedly) been her mother who had forbidden her to go on the road with him when they'd first put their act together. "If my mother were around today," she told him, "I'd slap her in the mouth." Hope took real satisfaction in hearing her say it; even decades later he could still bear certain grudges. But he reminded Mildred that it was, after all, she herself who had turned down his marriage proposal, not her mother.

When Bob's act on the Orpheum Circuit opened in Cleveland later in 1929, he looked forward to having his mother come for the opening night. He was disappointed when she told him she couldn't attend. "I'm too nervous," she said, "and I'll only make you nervous, too." He failed to notice his mother's wan complexion, her lack of energy. Because he sent her money all the time, he couldn't help but figure that for once in her life she was free of financial woes; so to his way of thinking she should, of course, be happy. True, his father was still the same as ever — but his mother must be used to his wayward ways by now. And so, just as Bob had ignored the signs of illness in Lefty Durbin, he was too preoccupied with his self-concerns to see that his mother was in the first stages of a fatal illness. When she surprised him, however, by showing up for his matinee performance the following day, he couldn't help but feel deep gratification.

Not much later, the tour worked its way to Chicago, where, predictably, Hope told jokes about the reigning king of Cicero, Al Capone. Over the years, Hope has been fond of telling how Capone and/or one of his henchmen (there have always been minor, sometimes major, alterations in this story) had phoned and politely but firmly told him to take out the jokes about Capone and his mob from the act. It was typical of Hope's always over-inflated ego that he would a) think Capone would take the time to come see the show he was in, and b) take the time to call him on the phone to lodge a protest about the jokes, which actually tended to colorfully reaffirm Capone's tough image and probably would have pleased the gangster. It's more likely, in retrospect, that a practical joker made the call, knowing Bob, in his self-importance, would take it seriously. Anyway it worked. For days Bob would stare nervously at any suspicious-looking strangers who came backstage, and when it came time to traverse the lonely stretch of dim alley from the stage door to the street he'd wait until he could go with a group. Meanwhile, everyone giggled at his childish behavior.

Shortly afterward, Bob received a communication from his mother. Avis was worried about her baby, George, now 20 years old, who ever since graduating from high school had been floundering about looking for a job. Earlier, he'd had great hopes of joining his brother's act and was now so "depressed" about being continuously left behind in Cleveland that Avis worried he would "do something desperate." "Is there anything you can do for him, son?" mother pleaded.

Bob was not especially crazy about the idea of another Hope in the act. He was amused by George's hero-worship but also resentful that the kid should get an easy break into showbiz when he himself had found it so hard; he also recognized that there were fewer opportunities in vaudeville than when he was starting out. Whatever his feelings about his father and siblings, he truly cared for Avis. "Send the kid and I'll see what I can do," he told her.

Telling himself he was crazy, kicking himself at times for the decision, he decided to work in George as a "stooge" in his act. To keep George from getting too big for his britches, he'd hire an additional stooge so his brother would be only one of a pair. Further, the salaries dispensed would be so low that it wouldn't put much of a dent in Bob's income. The stooges' stint was to sit in the audience and start heckling Bob in the middle of his act. Hope saw rightly that this idea might open whole new possibilities for fresh material. In the back of his mind was the thought that if the stooges worked out, he could eventually expand their roles. And kick Louise out on her butt.

The other boy Bob chose for stooge duty was one Toots Murdock, who came from a well-known family of vaudevillians and was said to have a lot of energy and talent of his own. He also had a drinking problem, which in time was to prove a major headache for Bob. Bob tried to be tolerant — as he had been tolerant, and endlessly, of his father — but when he looked at Toots he couldn't help remembering the awful things that drunks could do to other people, their wives and children included. He figured that what Toots did on his own time was his business, but when Toots started showing up drunk for work, the boss found it necessary to act.

The thing that most infuriated Bob was that the inebriated lad was somehow getting *more* laughs than his boss, which was not the way it was supposed to work. The stooges were only to yell out mildly funny insults to which Bob would respond with hilarious sallies that brought down the house. Instead, Toots, nearly falling out of the balcony he was so drunk, would come up with his own lines and have the audience in stitches. At first everyone thought he was a brilliant actor playing the part of a drunk; to Hope's chagrin, when the audience realized Toots was really three sheets to the wind, they laughed even harder.

The kid was upstaging Bob Hope — and that was the most Mortal of Mortal Sins in the Hope scheme of things. Hope insisted the kid stick to the script. He also told him to get sober for the long haul — or else! Toots was cramping Bob's style and Bob laid it on thick, giving him such a tongue-lashing that the lad flew straight after that — for a while, anyway.

Hope also had trouble with his younger brother. Bob discovered that George had showbiz aspirations but not the dedication and ambition that should have gone with them. Older brother tried to make George understand that younger brother would have to expand his repertoire and hone his skills if he were to graduate beyond stooge-status, in the act or anywhere else. Also, Bob had no intention of letting George batten off him forever.

The two were soon having bitter arguments. "Why should I practice my dancing," George would yell at Bob, "when you're not going to let me dance in your act?" George continued to be resentful that Bob didn't give him more to do, and stubbornly resisted the idea of breaking out on his own. More than once over the next couple of years George would go home to Cleveland in a fury, only to have Avis intercede with Bob to take him back yet again. Working on George to *get* him to go back, she always gave the same advice: "Les needs you."

George didn't care for Louise Troxell, and was jealous that she appeared on stage with Bob while he did not. "She thinks she's Mrs. Bob Hope!" George would tell fellow performers. Whenever George was in Cleveland during breaks, he would run into Mildred Rosequist and would implore her to drop her fiancée and go back to Bob. Mildred wanted no part of it.

It was now 1930, and Bob, at 27, was back in Manhattan after a tour. Hope and Company found themselves booked into a theatre that was showing *All Quiet on the Western Front,* Lewis Milestone's classic film about the vicissitudes of young German soldiers in World War I. *All Quiet* was an incredibly moving and powerful film which ends with the death of the boyish hero, Lew Ayres, as he reaches for a butterfly on a battlefield and is shot by a sniper. There wasn't a dry eye in the house. Bob was forced to go into his act directly after the movie ended, the timing being highly unfortunate, for his snappy patter seemed not only lame and lightweight but totally out of sync with what had preceded it. When he finally realized at one of the performances that the audience was too saddened and choked up to laugh at his nonsense, Hope flew into one of his worst tantrums.

"Get me into another theatre fast!" he told Lee Stewart of the Keith office. As soon as feasible, Hope was booked into Proctor's on 58th Street. Champing at the bit to get his audience howling again, he arrived at the new theatre all bright-eyed and bushy-tailed only to see

on the marquee yet again: Now playing: *All Quiet on the Western Front!*
Hope made yet another frantic call to Stewart, who tried to be understanding yet proved adamant on one point: Hope would have to fulfill
this engagement, like it or not. "If you don't, you'll never play the
Palace," Stewart warned.

The Palace in New York was the theatre every performer aspired
to. This was the worst of times for Hope to get a reputation as being
"difficult" with a reluctant cancellation of his bookings "when conditions were not favorable," or via any other front-office excuse that came
to mind. Hope was no fool. He knew when to anticipate trouble. He'd
come too far now to muff the ball. He went on after *All Quiet* and with
high energy and clever ruses soon had the audience drying its tears over
Lew Ayres' onscreen death.

That same year, 1930, Hope and Al Boasberg, who was still
churning out gags and comic ideas that Hope sopped up voraciously,
came up with a new act, or revue, titled *Antics of 1930*, which was very
similar to the screwball comedy of Olsen and Johnson's *Hellzapoppin*.
Louise was included in the act as well as the stooges George and Toots.
Bob and Louise had learned to get along by hardly talking to each other
when they weren't working or "on," and Toots wasn't getting quite as
polluted during showtimes. George, Toots, and Louise still provided
pretty good support for Bob at a fraction of what other aides might have
cost him. There was also no denying that whatever the feuds and has-
sles backstage, they made theatrical magic once they got in front of an
audience. They proceeded to take *Antics* on tour all across a country
already in the first mean throes of the Great Depression. Bob, realizing
that economic conditions could reach into sbow business costs, hiring
and firing, etc, kept his ski nose to the grindstone more than usual and
avoided ruffling any front-office feathers.

It was in *Antics* during 1931 that Bob, who was spurring on
Boasberg to deliver really snappy material, began to break a few showbiz taboos. His jokes became laced with sharp topical references and
subtle but gamy double-entendres. He'd gingerly test the audience with
a racier gag to see how far he could go; if it worked he'd test out an even
gamier one the following night. Although at that point he was still not
all that much on target as a political humorist, heads of state and political honchos and other movers and shakers presiding in the *Times* and
the magazines were no longer sacrosanct to Hope — or absent from his
material. He got a lot of mileage, for instance, from then-President
Herbert Hoover's "Prosperity is just around the corner" statement, ren-

dering it — in a variety of forms — the punchline for numerous gags, all touched up by Boasberg in different speeds and styles.

It was about this time, while *Antics* was running in Los Angeles, that a screen test was arranged for Hope. Although Louise would appear with him, he went along with it. He'd have preferred to test alone — it would only make her more difficult, he worried.

The test was the brainchild of a Hollywood agent named William Perlberg, who'd been told of Hope's act by his old freind Boasberg. As soon as the L.A. run of *Antics* came to an end, Bob and Louise rode out ot the Pathé Studios in Culver City to perform the act before the cameras. Hope thought it went over well. Certainly the crew members seemed to enjoy it.

Bob went on to San Diego with the rest of the Antics company and anxiously awaited a call from Perlberg. Although he feigned nonchalance, and claimed years later he'd been indifferent, he was actually on pins and needles waiting for the result. The screen was now the American medium, and the Talkies era that began in 1929 was in full flower by 1931. Stage and vaudeville figures by the carload were "going Hollywood" that year, and stage star Helen Hayes would win an Oscar for her *Sin of Madelon Claudet*. Compelling voices and sharp personalities were on demand in Movieland that year, and the theatre mediums were being thoroughly raided. Bob felt that perhaps his time had come in films. He was 28, and rarin' to go, recognizing that exposure on thousands of movie screens all over the country would vastly expand his recognition factor and earning capacity. Films, he sensed, would be the culmination of all he'd striven for over the last decade. Via that medium he might know Fame and Fortune beyond even his wildest dreams. That was to be his cue now: Think Big!

Meanwhile, Bob's performance in *Antics* wobbled as he contemplated Those New Hopes. He was coming in late on cues —something he'd never allowed himself in the past — and was unduly rough and temperaemtal with his co-performers backstage. The results of that test had become so important to him he could hardly eat. Films — if he failed that test, what? Vaudeville was a dying art form. Should he jump back to the stage, expand his persona and his name recognition there? His rapidly accelerating thoughts rendered him tense by day and sleepless by night.

Finally, summoning all resources of confidence, he made a call to Perlberg when the act returned to Los Angeles. When he asked how the test had gone, he heard only silence at the other end of the line. For lack of anything else to say at that point, Perlberg asked Hope if he wanted to see the test for himself. Then Perlberg tried to dissuade him, saying Bob should look at it when he was less keyed up. This should have given Bob fair warning, but he insisted on seeing the footage. Perlberg quietly made the arrangements. When Bob asked what he thought of the test, Perlberg's only reply was "Judge for yourself, Bob."

The next day in that small screening room was one of the darkest Bob Hope was ever to know in his entire life up to that time — and he'd known the pits of setbacks and defeats. He had by that time seen a thousand pictures of himself in various poses, and (as had always been his constant practice) studied himself a million times in any mirror that came to hand, but he'd never seen himself larger than life on a movie screen. "It was a new and shattering experience," he recalled years later, "to see myself as others saw me."

As he sat there alone in the darkened projection room, he began to sink lower and lower in his chair. He didn't like anything at all about the man he saw up there — neither his mannerisms nor his voice nor his style of delivery — but what especially appalled him was his face. For up until that afternoon, Bob Hope had honestly believed himself to be genuinely handsome.

The man he saw up on the screen was not handsome. There was something funny — almost goofy — about his face, and his nose was much too big and oddly shaped. His voice was too high-pitched, his mannerisms almost effeminate. Had Hope enjoyed a more realistic and balanced idea of his essential appearance before he went into the screening room he might have taken note of his considerable assets: at 28 he was actually an attractive (almost handsome from some angles) young man with a pleasing manner, but he'd always pictured himself a sort of Valentino type with a dash of Doug Fairbanks Sr. thrown in. The screen test was to him — to his sensitive, unduly self-critical appraisal — a crushing blow. He was nothing at all like the person he'd always pictured.

Yes, the test was indeed a dismal failure as Perlberg had tried to tell him. Whatever qualities Bob Hope had simply did not translate to the screen — at least not on this occasion. Perhaps he'd been too nervous to truly get himself across. Possibly he'd overplayed too blatantly. So many reasons, or excuses, for this fiasco crossed his harried mind.

Walking numbly out of the screening room, Hope slunk off the Pathé lot as quickly as he could. He spoke of the test to no one, and no one asked. They could see something was wrong just by looking at him.

Stripped of self-confidence, he barely got through the next performance of *Antics*. At night he'd forsake parties and other social activities and lie in bed trying to convince himself that the moving picture could lie. He didn't want to see anyone or go anywhere.

But the human mind and spirit — especially for an energetic, ambitous 28-year-old — has an infinite propensity for bouncing back. Hope in short order accepted that, whatever he looked like, he had sufficient attractiveness and talent to have made it this far — and much farther yet even if no movie career was in the offing. In spite of his lack of matinee-idol handsomeness, he reasoned, he still had plenty of women ready to roll in the hay with him, and the ability, on stage, to roll 'em in in the aisles.

Besides, there was literally no choice *but* to go on. What else could he do? Surely he wasn't *that* bad-looking. Gradually he began to accept his new "image," even to admire it as he had the old one. Weathering this major disappointment as best he could, he forced all negative thoughts into the background of his mind and spirit and concentrated on the work at hand.

Eventually *Antics* made its way to Cleveland. There George continued his campaign to get Millie to drop her cop (whom she was taking forever to marry, it seemed) in favor of Bob, while Bob himself strutted about popinjay-style, flushed with the pride of stellar (at least in vaudeville) success. Old acquaintances who were initially happy for him would eventually tire of the unrelenting bragging Bob went in for. Hope may have treated his old friends as if they were peons, but he was to be humbled even here in his unassuming hometown in an unexpected way.

One day his oldest brother Ivor came to ask him a favor. Ivor was sales manager for the Cleveland Metal Works. His boss had heard about his kid brother's success in show business and figured Bob would be the perfect person to preside over the dedication of a new plant in the capacity of Master of Ceremonies. Hope knew it couldn't have been Ivor's idea — all his brothers felt overshadowed by his success and were vaguely, if not overtly, resentful — but he knew Ivor was on a spot. It wouldn't look good for his brother if he didn't agree to do the stint.

Nevertheless, Hope let his brother sweat it out for a few days before consenting.

He was to regret he ever did. The plant workers — forced to attend — were not exactly an appreciative audience. Jokes that would have gone over well with more sophisticated audiences sank without a trace at the plant.

When the first few jokes failed to elicit a positive response, Hope knew he had a rough few minutes ahead. Nothing he did got so much as a chuckle out of these men. When it was all over and Hope beat a hasty retreat, he blamed Ivor for setting him up. "Why the hell did you ever ask me to do that?" Hope yelled at him.

"It was my boss' idea," Ivor reminded him.

Once outside the Cleveland environs, however, Hope quickly forgot about this untimely and unfair fiasco. For he had gotten a wire from New York. *Antics* had been booked at the Palace. He'd made it!

CHAPTER EIGHT

The Worldling of the Great White Way

Hope was determined that not a single person in New York would fail to know he was about to open at the Palace. On the train from Cleveland he began cooking up schemes (which he later attributed to Palace publicity people) that would get him as much attention as possible, including items in the all-important newspaper columns. His first step was to hire — for a pittance — a few starving actors, hardly in short supply in New York in that Bottom-of-the-Depression year 1932, to act as fake pickets outside the Palace. These grungy characters were deputized to march around in front of the box office holding up signs that read "Bob Hope Is Unfair to Stooges, Local 711!"

This tactic did not sit well with the manager of the theatre, who was afraid passersby might take the pickets seriously and boycott the performance. Hope denied responsibility, putting the blame on the publicity man, Arnold Van Leer — who'd gone along with the scheme, thinking it sassy and witty. Van Leer talked turkey with the manager, explaining that like it or not the pickets were attracting the requisite attention. The press agent placated the manager even further by calling columnists to ask them to "set the record straight" about how the whole thing was a gag. This, of course, generated further publicity. Van Leer, in an interview many years later, said of Hope "That man was an indefatigable fiend when it came to putting A-Number-One ahead! He'd have made a great press agent for others, except the only guy who ever won his enthusiasm was himself!"

Beatrice Lillie, the fey, eccentric British comedienne, was the headliner. Hope and his crew (Hope, as usual, got sole billing) were in the second spot. Although his act was a credible one, well-received by the tough, highly discriminating and not easily pleased Palace regulars, his debut could not be said to have been auspicious. He failed to get the notices he felt he deserved. His ego highly affronted by what he felt were deaf and blind critics, he momentarily toyed with the idea of cancelling the rest of his engagement. It was to turn out to be only one of his frequent fits of pique over one thing or another, and he was easily persuaded to reconsider.

However, the night after the opening — stung by the bad or dismissive notices — Hope was more edgy than usual. It was a Sunday night — the night when, traditionally, any celebrities in the audience would find themselves rousingly introduced and invited to come on stage. Two comedians, Ted Healy and Ken Murray, who were introduced by Hope (part of his job was to M.C.) felt a little sorry for him; they could see he was floundering. Murray was an experienced vaudevillian and Healy was the man who a while later would form The Three Stooges (they later dropped him as, in their view, superfluous).

Murray and Healy, former Palace M.C.'s themselves, took pity on the relatively less-experienced Hope, whose basic talent, however, was quite evident to them. Flanking Hope, they got the audience laughing and relaxed in short order; result: Hope licked his nervousness and before long was firing and slinging his lines in well-served volleys. Hope always maintained, as did others, that part of Murray and Healy's zest on stage with him came from the knowledge that they were showing him up, even if the audience didn't catch on.

Ken Murray's later observations on Hope always smacked of noblesse-oblige graciousness. "His talent was obvious as all hell," Murray said. "He'd hit the big time with the Palace and he knew it, and, well, the guy was pushing it a little too anxiously. I was happy to help him hit his bull's-eyes. He'd have no doubt done it without me on hand, given enough time, but in that spot the sooner the better! Palace audiences were impatient and their attention spans were short. You had to keep on top of it or you were ground under it."

It was true that a Palace performer had to watch his performance carefully and keep on top of his material at all times. Although much of the attendance had dwindled with the onset of talkies, with a consequent eradication of censorship restoring the box office take, the live acts still had to compete with such stellar 1932 film personalities as Clark Gable, Joan Crawford, and Norma Shearer, as well as with the pre-1934 Production Code steaminess of film plots. There were, however, on the Keith circuit some forbidden areas and subjects — and jokes — Keith's still targeted "family audiences." Some elements that had once been banned, such as slang words, expressions like "God damn" and skimpy, tight costumes, were now permitted, but political and sexual humor — which Hope had started purveying with natty éclat

— was still very risky.

All "partners" on the Keith circuit were handed a list of verboten routines and lines. (Hope was the first to snicker ironically when the performers had been styled by the front office "our partners in serving the entertainment needs of a wonderful and responsive public that is entitled to the classiest and finest entertainment we can offer.") Hope and Boasberg used all their ingenuity to circumvent rules that Boasberg, in particular, considered outrageously rigid and confining. "To listen to these guys reining us in," Jack Benny later quoted Boasberg as saying, "you'd think guys had no dicks and gals had no twats and the stork brought the brats and you conceived the stork — or storkesses — by sneezing! It was a howling joke — on the public!"

It was also about this time that Hope commenced a series of feuds with other comedians that would drag on for decades — though the rivals might put up a friendly front in public or while performing. One of Hope's major antagonists was Milton ("Uncle Miltie") Berle, who had the misfortune to play the Strand across the street from the Palace while Hope was "in residence." Hell broke loose one night when a fiddler in the orchestra tipped off Hope that Berle was using one of Hope's best gags up at the Strand across Broadway.

Hope, livid and stuttering with rage, didn't even bother to take off his makeup, he was in such haste to find out if the report were true. Since Berle came on after he did, Hope cabbed up to the Strand (though it was a seven-minute walk), got a ticket and watched Berle's routine. Sure enough — out popped the identical joke, winning for its perpetrator a response as rousing as any Hope was getting down the street. Hope wasn't taking it. He confronted the hapless Uncle Miltie outside his dressing room and the air was suddenly full of obscene invective, accompanied by Hope's threats to yell to the audience "He copped it from me! Come see the Real McCoy down at the Palace! This dickhead is just a second-rate gag-stealer and imitator!"

Berle, a scrapper himself with an ego equal to Hope's, thereupon accused Hope of stealing the gag from him! Recriminations, accusations, threats of physical harm filled the air. "He was a mean one," another comic said years later of Hope. "I thought I had Napoleon's ego but this guy thought he was Jesus Christ! I never liked him and hated the idea of ever having to work with him."

Although over the years both would kid each other about gag-stealing in their acts and feign friendliness superficially when forced to rub shoulders in public, their relationship in private was always icy and wary. One of Hope's milder observations on Berle over the years was that he was "delightfully unabashed" about stealing good — and bad — gags.

The Berle-Hope feuding — which audiences thought hilarious fun, along Bob-and-Bing lines later in the 1930's — was in reality deadly in its earnestness. It reached a point where Berle's mother confronted Hope at a social occasion when he was yet again accusing Berle of "pirating my stuff" and shouted, "My Milton wouldn't stoop so low! My son stoops high!"

Hope tried a variety of tactics to get even with Uncle Miltie. On one occasion he was aided by his comedian buddy Richy Craig, Jr. (who like Lefty Durbin was to die an early death of tuberculosis). Bob and Richy found out that Berle was going to do four benefits in one night and since most comedians followed the practice of saving the same special ("boffo" was the word for it) routine for a benefit, the Hope-Craig combine were already familiar with the jokes Berle would use (and vice-versa, for that matter). Hope and Craig were also doing the same benefits as it happened, but preceded Berle in the program, before Berle had even arrived.

At the first two benefits they did all of Berle's material, then swore the audience to secrecy. When Berle finally came out and did the same material he'd bomb without knowing why.

Finally, a Berle ally tipped him off. The last two benefits started somewhat later in the evening and Berle managed to get there earlier than Hope and Craig. This time Uncle Miltie pulled a reverse switch and beat the other two to *their* gags. When Hope and Craig did their routines later to loud silence they knew they'd been hornswoggled. "I think he came to respect me in time," Milton Berle said years later. "He found I gave as good as I got. And in an odd sort of way we found it amusing wondering what either of us was going to pull next!"

Years later, Hope was furious when Sid Caesar borrowed one of his old routines for Caesar's TV show. In the late 1920's Hope favored a bit in which he'd swallow some medicine and say "I forgot to shake the bottle," whereupon he'd jump up and down vigorously on stage. Caesar did the same gag on his TV show, prompting Hope to send him a mock-friendly message that he, Bob, had originated that gag and if Caesar saw him do it he'd know he wasn't the thief. "Bob could be very cutting and sharp whenever one of his major or minor 'vital interests' was threatened. And when he was mad, he wasn't the least bit funny," an associate later said, adding, "but don't quote me until he's pushing up dandelions!" (The latter observation meant facetiously, maybe.)

Right into Old Age Bob Hope would loudly complain about "infringements" on his material from oldsters and "those new young whippersnappers," though his rivals would snap back that he himself showed, allegedly, no scruples about "borrowing" jokes from others. One of Hope's standard responses would be that there were just so many jokes to go around, for Chrissake, and some sounded remotely or closely alike often coincidentallly or serendipitously. "That's the smartest dodge double-talk I ever heard," Walter Winchell said of this.

Walter Winchell, whom I knew well, always held Bob Hope's comic abilities in high esteem and gave him many plugs in his column. In 1966 Walter told me, "Hope was probably the most naturally gifted comedian of his time and I've known the best!" Asked how he felt about Hope's often-reported "egomania and ruthlessness," Walter snapped "Shrinking violets belong in monasteries, not in dog-eat-dog showbiz."

Hope's Palace engagement went over so well that, before 1932 was well advanced, he began getting tapped for parts in musical plays. He'd come a long way since 1928; among his more minor assignments (one he didn't even include in his credits for 1928) in that earlier year had been a thirteenth-billing stint as Screeves the Butler in *Ups-a-Daisy* at the Shubert Theatre in Newark — some trifling nonsense about a man who pretends the adventures of a famed mountain climber are his own. Now it was 1932, age 29, not 1928 age 25, and Hope jumped into a new production called *Ballyhoo of 1932*.

Ballyhoo was a collection of frankly risqué sketches based on a new and popular periodical of the same name that was vulgar, albeit entertaining, and was enjoying a good run on the newsstands. Billy Grady, who managed Al Jolson, had taken an interest in Hope after seeing him at the Palace. He persuaded the *Ballyhoo* writer-producers to take an interest in the comedian with the object of casting him. Grady had no interest in Louise, however, and, as it turned out, neither did the *Ballyhoo* producers.

Billy Grady, an old friend of mine, discovered many luminaries, including Jimmy Stewart, and later wound up as casting manager at MGM. Of Hope Grady said to me, "When I first saw him he was the pushiest, meanest son-of-a-bitch you would want to know. What an ego! I was always surprised his head didn't burst out from it and that it didn't liquefy and coast down that ski nose of his. He held the gospel that nice guys finished last and he was no nice guy. I always felt he thought of his fellow human beings as being meant to be maneuvered as per the dictates of his own self-interest. Later, when he hit top Hollywood success he mellowed somewhat — most of 'em do — but he never let his guard down. He followed, all his life, the theory that it's harder to stay up there than get up there. I'm not sure I agreed with that — all those who *didn't* make it, there wouldn't be cemeteries enough to hold 'em. He was also one of the most insecure guys I ever met — never seemed to relax and enjoy life and give the competition thing a rest. But I suppose, negative as it all sounds, it worked for him. You can't quarrel with success!"

Louise Troxell, though she always prided herself on keeping her eye on all that went on around her, didn't realize she was off the team until it was almost too late. The *Ballyhoo* project gave Hope his cue to make his long-delayed move on her. Their relationship, ironically, had improved of late. Louise was shrewd enough to know that even if Bob was tight, unpleasant, and on occasion outright mean and rude to her, he was also a Guy Going Places and she'd gotten pretty far riding his coattails already, hadn't she? She was "purrier," sweeter to him than usual these days, hoping it'd soften him up and expand her role in the act or give her more money, along catch-the-fly-with-honey-not-vinegar lines. Soon they were billing and cooing — Hope's libidinous ego, at long last, was getting the salving from Louise it craved, and rumors flew among their associates that she was pregnant and they were getting married.

But when Louise found out that Bob was going on to *Ballyhoo* without her, "Boy, did that broad pull a stinking fit!" as Billy Grady remembered. She hadn't really wanted to marry Bob because she wasn't in love with him. The Hope pizzazz and toughness that had made unrequited-lover George Byrne's legs go weak left Louise standing tall and erect — and unimpressed. But, as of late 1932, she reasoned that if marriage was the price of going onward and upward with Hope, she'd pay it. According to one source, Hope married a "Grace Louise Troxell" (Grace was her professionally unused first name) in Erie, Pennsylvania, on January 29, 1933. When and where the marriage, obviously short-lived, was annulled, remains unknown. Certainly Hope was always to treat this short-lived union as if it never existed. Troxell later remarried and settled in the Chicago area, her involvement with Hope, be it professional or personal, by then conclusively over.

Billy Grady felt that Louise liked Bob reasonably well, even cared for him a little, but especially when she found she was being left out of *Ballyhoo* "She really frosted on him." Bob as a gateway to success was one matter; Bob by his lonesome quite something else in the Troxell scheme of things.

Bob, according to Grady, couldn't have cared much — he was no more in love with Louise than she with him. Rumor had it that he'd gotten into her panties, yes, and it was said that he'd even financed an abortion. How this jells with later statements about Bob's alleged sterility is up for speculation — unless he contracted, as was rumored, a venereal disease later.

The exact circumstances of their final parting were, of course, known only to Hope and Louise Troxell, but part they did. Around this time, Bob also got rid of his youngr brother George and fellow-stooge Toots, and he did little to help George with his career thereafter. ("God, he didn't have the talent!" Bing Crosby once reported Bob confiding to him.)

With Louise, Toots, and Baby Brother out of the picture, Bob at 29 in early 1933 was able to fully apply, and with a vengeance, his well-known "Travel Alone, Travel Faster" theory. He turned away from them without one look back.

The Keith office, with which Bob was still connected, had no problem letting Bob do the *Ballyhoo* show because they knew it would only enhance his value on the vaudeville circuit when he returned. *Ballyhoo* had been put together by composer Lewis Gensler, choreographer Bobby Connelly, and the editors of the magazine, a sort of *Spy* of its day, albeit with more spice and humor.

Ballyhoo played Atlantic City and Newark before opening in Manhattan. In the out-of-town tryouts, things were as hectic and discombobulated backstage as they were upfront and onstage, where the doings were *supposed* to be frantic. Right in the middle of the show in both towns blown fuses knocked out the lights. As if this weren't enough, audience panic and confusion were accelerated by malfunctioning generators that caused smoke to waft over the stage and into the first few theatre rows.

On both occasions, Hope was the man drafted to go out front and keep the crowds, which were on the verge of rioting, as calm as possible until the malfunctions could be corrected. He succeeded admirably, proving to one and all that he was often at his best while under pressure. His heroic efforts, unfortunately, did little to help *Ballyhoo* survive the bad critical notices when it arrived on Broadway. Thanks to frantic advertising and hyping, however, the show managed to slink along for almost four months before closing. Hope meanwhile did not miss opportunities to console himself with the gorgeous babes the producer hired for the chorus — showgirls "of Ziegfeld caliber" (according to Billy Grady) many of whom were ready, willing, and able to show Bigshot Bob a good time in the sack if he in turn made a promise (often unkept) to boost their individual fortunes. Grady and others later theorized that Hope's later rumored impotence began in this period via one venereally infected showgirl too many.

Bob's next Broadway show, *Roberta* (1933) was his biggest jump forward yet. This one featured music by the legendary Jerome Kern of *Showboat* fame, including the memorable "Smoke Gets in Your Eyes." (It would later make a hit 1935 movie with Irene Dunne, Fred Astaire, and Ginger Rogers.) The zany plot dealt with a football player (Ray Middleton) who inherits a Parisian dress shop after his aunt dies. Bob got to work with Fred MacMurray, then a handsome and promising 25; Sydney Greenstreet (still eight years away from his impressive 1941 *Maltese Falcon* movie advent); and George Murphy, later the popular movie song-and-dance man and future U.S. Senator from California. The women in the cast included Tamara and Lyda Roberti, a sassy Polish comedienne with a spicy, teasy accent whom Hope found particularly delectable. Bob quickly mounted a campaign to win her over. But "My own special blonde bombshell," as he referred to her, had plenty of other suitors. Bob resorted to bringing his Scottie dog — which he hamed "Huck" after his comedy character in the show — backstage to attract the women, along "love my dog, love me" lines. Once they'd been lured over to pet and rhapsodize over the little darling, Bob would swoop in for the kill — sometimes it worked, more often it died like a dog. This didn't improve Bob's overall mood. Wasn't he in the Broadway Big Time now, for Chrissake? What broad dared resist him?

Forgetting he was now part of an ensemble cast and not the head of his own *Antics* crew of galley slaves, Hope began stepping on toes right from the first. Jealous of Fred MacMurray's good looks (and Fred was a looker, as all the showgirls noted, as would millions of filmgoers two years hence), Hope patronized him as a green kid and former saxophone tootler who couldn't put over comedy (Fred proved him wrong there later in films) and who needed coaching (Bob's?) in putting over his scenes. Decades later, Fred MacMurray was still feeling resentful toward Hope. Questioned once about working with him, the usually amiable and mellow Fred hesitated, then said, "He was tough — very tough. He thought he was right on everything and everyone else was wrong. No middle ground for him. He was a pain in the ass."

Next, Bob went in for fat jokes, the avoirdupois-afflicted Sydney Greenstreet being target number one. But as Sydney reported it ten or so years later, "I could out-act him and he knew it, so I started patronizing that Big Mouth Hope by giving him acting tips. He really shrank down to size when I told him mugging in vaudeville was one thing, polished acting another." Reportedly, in the late 1940's when it was suggested Sydney Greenstreet would add heft (histrionically that is) to a projected Hope vehicle, Hope, with his elephantine memory, vetoed him.

But the brash Bob didn't stop there. He made passes at every woman in the show, according to MacMurray (a man who, despite his come-on sexiness looks-wise was actually a chivalrous Puritan with women who had two solid lasting marriages [he was once widowed] and a reputation totally free of scandal, as his Hollywood chroniclers loved to unite in relating). Reportedly, comedian Jack Benny once made a crude crack about MacMurray to the effect that he must have masturbated a lot to relieve sexual tension, so his virtue was overrated. This crack sounds like something Hope, who never liked MacMurray, might have dreamed up.

The problem with *Roberta*, as Hope saw it, was that it didn't make him the center of attention the way other, admittedly lesser, shows had. He threw his weight around in other ways. He actually had the temerity to give suggestions to Jerome Kern and his lyricist, Otto Harbach. But according to George Murphy, who became good friends with Hope, Hope's suggestions for playing up the comedy routines actually saved the show from the scrapheap. Meanwhile, a change of directors couldn't seem to improve the pacing or the strangely ossified quality which handicapped even the best scenes. True, Hope's constant input — some of it rejected, some of it reluctantly incorporated — was designed primarily to expand his part and put him more in the spotlight, but the suggestions often had oddly positive and constructive side effects, opening up the show and turning what, despite the fine music, was for some weeks a sow's ear into a sparkling soufflé. Otto Harbach, however, resented Hope's blithe interferences, however helpful, and conducted loud arguments with him. "An impossible, impossible amn," Harbach would say of Hope years later. "It's his way or no way — a monstrous, inflated ego of the worst kind."

But Hope's instincts, especially when it came to building up his own originally comic but lightweight role, proved to be the correct ones. The *New York Mirror* critic, for one, didn't think there was *enough* of him, stating, "Hope makes the most of his role of Huck Haines the crooner. But [he] is capable of somewhat more robust fun. His smoothness, slick dancing and imitation piano playing are only slight indications of his real comedic powers. Would it be sacrilege to ask Mr. [Max] Gordon [the producer] to cut out some of the vapid love talk and interpolate one of the boy's monologues?"

With notices like this to stick up on his dressing room mirror, Hope was to prove particularly embittered when, two years later, he failed to get the role in the film version. Still, his success in *Roberta* gave him a second shot at Hollywood. Paramount in 1933 asked him to play a role in a Ginger Rogers-Jack Oakie feature, *Sitting Pretty*. Although the deal would have been a lucrative one, Bob told his agent, Louie ("Doc') Shurr to turn it down. The reason he gave the newspapers was that he was doing so well on Broadway he didn't need Hollywood; privately he was still hyper-sensitive about his onscreen appearance and afraid a move to pictures might spell finis. He admitted later to tormenting himself with nightmares about shooting the first scenes in *Sitting Pretty* only to have the powers-that-be tell him he was horrible. He could picture them sending him back on the first train to New York. Now that was one mortification he didn't need. Broadway was his metiér, he was at long last convinced. All the evidence to date shored up his decision.

There's a story that years later he was talking with the eminent Laurence Olivier, who that same year, 1933, at age 26, had been rejected for the lead opposite Garbo in *Queen Christina*, after tests that didn't work out. (John Gilbert got the role, at Garbo's request, to shore up his sinking cinematic fortunes.) Hearing Olivier tell of this disaster, Bob joked to friends, "Think of what *I* escaped in 1933!"

Hope's agent "Doc" Shurr, incidentally, was a tiny man with a big ego who fancied himself God's Gift to Women. Billy Grady and others who knew "Doc" were full of stories about his bedroom prowess, many of them along the lines of "little-guy-but-big-dick." Hope was to use Doc as a model years later when he began playing "the great lover," or rather campy overblown variations thereof, in many of his films. These usually highlighted a man who couldn't understand why so many of the women he met found him completely and utterly unattractive.

Milton Berle was to recall when Hope "aided and abetted" a practical joke involving a variety of hookers sent to Shurr's office when the agent was interviewing possible female leads for Hope's next picture. (This was when Hope had finally made it big in films years later.) Hope and several cronies rounded up every sleazy prostitute they knew — some of course more "classy" and come-hitherish than others — and directed them to the proper address. These ladies were supposed to drive the Priapic Mr. Shurr crazy with their deficiencies in the acting art. The joke, however, backfired. Shurr knew they were hookers — once upon a time he'd hired several of them himself. He proceeded to make love to every one of them on his wellworn and more than slightly sagging-springed "casting couch." The bill Bob and his pals paid for Shurr's multiple pleasure must have been astronomical.

Two pivotal events occurred during the run of *Roberta* that provided beginning-and-ending phases in the life of Bob Hope, who on May 29, 1933, reached his 30th birthday. He was to meet his future and permanent wife, Dolores, and his mother passed away.

By 1933 Hope had known for some time that Avis was terminally ill from cancer; indeed that sad knowledge, which he for months tried to avoid completely absorbing psychically and emotionally, had first come to him during a Capitol Theatre engagement between his run at the Palace and the opening of *Ballyhoo*. His ill-advised attempt to get Louise Troxell to marry him during that period, despite the lack of genuine love on either side, had been partly predicated on the belief that his mother would be pleased to see him take a wife before she died.

By 1933 Avis was confined to her bed while Harry Hope, completely unable to deal with the imminent family tragedy, withdrew even further into his alcoholic escapisms. Hope had always reacted oddly, indeed singularly, to the inevitabilities of his mother's serious illness, employing what today would be called the psychic principle of denial. In 1933 terms, however, he "just didn't want to think about it. If he didn't think about it," he reasoned, "it would just go away." Those people — and they were few — who did receive his confidences about his mother's condition were more than a little startled when he suddenly added a new bit to his act in which he'd sing a terribly sentimental love song to his mother. It wasn't the song itself that was so startling, but what followed: an old woman would walk out of the wings and beg Bob for money. "Get lost, mom!" he'd snap. Even those who knew nothing of Avis's illness thought the gag strikingly disrespectful. Negative reactions from all quarters later forced Hope to take it out of his act. A psychological explanation for this odd happenstance might be that Bob, essentially a cold person, at least up to that time in his life, was using crude comedy to ward off deep feeling of a kind he couldn't deal with. Like his father, though in a different way and context, he was running away from a reality more shattering than he'd ever known.

A while before, in the early 1930's, Hope had bought Avis and Harry a big house in the more upscale Cleveland Heights section so they could be near his brother Fred and family. After Avis's death the house was to function primarily as a living tomb for Bob's father, who'd spend his time aimlessly wandering about the house, drinking and mourning obsessively, and steadily deteriorating physically, until he finally passed away three years after his wife, being then in his mid-60's.

Harry's death was to prove only mildly upsetting to Bob. There were things that had passed between them over the many years that the son just couldn't forgive; Harry's weak character and directionless life had affected all their lives too adversely, and in Bob's view too unnecessarily. To him the life of Harry Hope had been one long waste. But Avis's passing was for him monumental. It was his mother more than anyone who'd encouraged him when he was a child, who'd brought out his nascent abilities and who had energetically applauded his early efforts at entertaining. He recognized now the supportiveness, the nurturing sustenance of her love, carried on unstintingly through decades. He realized that what he'd once interpreted as a lack of encouragement early in his career had only been a symptom of her worry that he might find himself utterly lost in the threatening quagmire of lost hopes that so many other showbiz aspirants perish in. For several years now he'd proved to her he would survive, even prosper, in his chosen field, and she was still his Biggest Fan and Rooter. Thinking of her, of the gap her death would leave, aware instinctively that the one person who'd given him Total, Unconditional Love in all his tumultuous, combative, egocentric, defensive thirty ears on earth, would no longer be there for him, he surrendered, for once, to the human condition he shared with billions of others — and wept.

Determined to lose himself in his career — trying with all his might to drown out thoughts of death and sorrow and finality, he took on a new show, *Say When*, a musical-comedy by writer-producers Jack McGowan and Ray Henderson about two vulgar vaudevillians who campaign for the affections of a pair of debutantes on Long Island. The show opened in 1934.

Lucky Luciano, the famed mobster who ate at the same Italian restaurant on 46th Street that Bob frequented and who'd nod hello to him before Hope even knew who he was, turned out to be one of the investors. Remembering his "brush" with Al Capone in Chicago, Hope confided to fellow cast members that Luciano's participation made him nervous.

The actual star of *Say When* was Harry Richman, a famed theatrical performer of his day. The show had been constructed as a vehicle to showcase the Richman talents, but Hope, as was his usual wont, worked behind the scenes to make his own part more substantial and get the audience sharply aware of him. He was to wind up with the lion's share of the good reviews.

Years later, in one of his "rewriting history" excursions, Bob Hope claimed that Harry Richman had been at a disadvantage because he had the weak part of an "unsympathetic lover" and no decent songs with which to put himself over in a stellar way, hence came off second best to Hope. The truth is that Hope did everything he could to make the producer-writer team play up the comedy elements — and his part — and there was little Richman could do when it came to taking center stage.

According to the Hope version, Richman called him into his drawing room on the train from the Boston tryout to New York, toasted his success in the show with a glass of champagne, and even apologized for being so "weak." The truth is that Harry Richman had a very strong ego of his own, and if he'd given Hope a glass of champagne there most likely would have been poison in it. Richman did everything he could, subsequently, to take back the show from Hope, but the creators sensed that playing up the comedy *would* ensure the show's success, so it was a losing battle. As it turned out, Depression audiences were ridden with other distractions and said "When!" to *Say When* after only a fair run. But it was yet another Broadway credit for Bob.

One of the more interesting characters in the cast of *Say When* was one George Gurgeson, a native of Brooklyn who insisted he was in actuality Prince Michael of Russia's Romanoff dynasty, defunct since 1917. No one could figure out if Prince Mike Romanoff, as he called himself later, actually believed this, or was putting on one of his many super-con acts, characteristic of the era. Anyway he played it up for all it was worth, winning for himself a brief but striking Broadway career and an extensive set of press clippings. A notorious tightwad, Gurgeson would borrow money from everyone in the cast, even Hope — not exactly prodigal with his change. Then he'd go out on the town as Prince Michael, replete with top hat and tails and an assumed demeanor to the imperial manner born. Later Mike Romanoff would open a highly successful Hollywood restaurant frequented by the top stars of the era, but by that time he'd been exposed as a phony, being no more of a

Romanoff than the man in the moon. While appearing together in *Say When*, Mike and Bob often rubbed each other wrong, Harry Richman's explanation for their lack of simpatico being that "two big showoffs like that should never be at closer quarters than a mile!"

After *Say When* closed there was a dry spell for Hope while his agent dickered with producers over suitable assignments; meanwhile he did "guest spots" here and there and waited for the next big opportunity. It came in late 1935 with a new show, *Ziegfeld Follies of 1936*. Ziegfeld, though dead since 1932, was on everybody's mind that year, since William Powell was starring in films in *The Great Ziegfeld* with Myrna Loy and Luise Rainer to smash business. The headliner this time was Fanny Brice, a famed Ziegfeld entertainer who was privately a lonely woman who'd turned to booze and pills to make life bearable. She'd taken to marrying men (like Billy Rose) who were notorious philanderers and there was even a criminal in her romantic background. "Funny Girl" she had been called by her admirers, but her life offstage had been more sad than happy. She was to appear in the 1936 Ziegfeld film, and her "My Man," a song she delivered in a heartrending, simple, sincere style, had become her trademark, signature piece.

During the stage version of Ziegfeld Follies there were numerous attempts on the part of the producers and their aides to hide the truth of Fanny's instability and deteriorating condition, but the signs were there for all to see. The first major warning came when *Follies* was running in Philadelphia prior to the New York opening.

Fanny needed uppers and downers to get her through the days and nights. If she got the right pills in the right quantities, she was fine. If she got the wrong ones, matters turned baleful. One night she mixed up her pills and took sleeping tablets at intermission. By the time she went out to do her last number, the combination of pep pills and sleeping pills had wreaked havoc and she had no idea, literally, of where she was. She kept starting the number over, stopping — then starting again — trying pathetically to get her bearings. This went on for several agonizing minutes while the orchestra conductor did his best to cover for her, guiding her as best he could to the right passage. It was no use. The stage manager had to ring down the curtain. Watching from the wings with an appalled fascination, Hope found himself horrified at the prospect of ever going dead like that before an audience. The love and approval of audiences was the most important thing in his 32-year-old life. He felt that, had audiences known the truth about Brice, they would have scorned her. Years later, when Hope related the anecdote, he officially "cleaned it up" so that the drugs Fanny was taking became simple cold pills.

Eve Arden was also in the cast of *Follies*, appearing in sketches such as the one where Hope played an exasperated director working with the child star, Baby Snooks, portrayed by Fanny (and one of Brice's more famous and beloved characterizations). Arden confided to Bob she was afraid she'd forget her lines. He counselled her to do what Fanny did when the same thing happened to her: grab him around the waist and wrestle him toward the wings until the lines came back to her. Audiences were certainly perplexed on those occasions when Brice or Arden would suddenly start tusseling with Hope in the middle of a sketch. "But they laughed," Arden recalled, "and that's what mattered!"

Eve Arden was always to speak well of Bob Hope. "I keep hearing what an egomaniac he was," she said decades later, "but I and others I know found him damned helpful and supportive toward fellow players. Maybe he just liked me — I don't know — but he was, well, brotherly to me during that show. But then I suppose he could afford to be. He was getting the best lines and situations."

Although the star, Fanny Brice, got the lioness's share of the notices for *Ziegfeld Follies of 1936*, Hope got his share of favorable attention. "Bob Hope renders suave first-aid treatment to many ailing comic skits," the New York *Post* critic said. Another critic who must have warmed the very cockles of Bob's vain heart wrote, "He is one of those rarely seen comedians who doesn't have to look funny in order to get a laugh." During the show's run, and due to Brice's deteriorating condition, Hope found himself waging a constant battle to keep the sketches moving and sounding right, and hence was applying more "first aid" than even the critics perceived.

Later in 1936 Hope appeared in *Red, Hot and Blue*. This show was a product of the *Anything Goes* team: Russell Crouse, Howard Lindsay, and Cole Porter. William Gaxton, the star of *Anything Goes*, was supposed to head the cast of *Red, Hot and Blue* until Ethel Merman, the temperamental high-voltage star who could give Hope or anyone a run for his money in the Ego sweepstakes, and who was also set for the show, complained to the creators that she wanted more to do — much more.

Gaxton had had his share of problems with Merman backstage, and certainly didn't want her crowding his act on stage to boot, so he beat a hasty retreat with a "Thanks but no thanks." So Crouse and his associates decided that Bob Hope might make the perfect replacement

— and cost less, besides.

With Gaxton gone, Merman and her co-star, Jimmy Durante, began a bitter Battle of the Billing. Since Hope was not as well known as Gaxton at the time, and had, moreover, never actually starred in a show of this nature, he was never really in the running for the lead. Durante and Merman between them kicked up such a fuss that Crouse finally threw up his hands and came up with the notion of crisscrossing their names in the same-size type above the title. He even went so far — hoping to embarrass them into realizing their pettiness — as to switch their names on a bi-weekly basis. Neither Durante nor Merman ever saw anything in the least peculiar about it.

Hope was cast as a lawyer and Merman's love interest. She played a rich widow who pined for Hope while being courted by Durante, a polo player of questionable character. Although the show was by no means a failure, it was not as successful as its predecessor, *Anything Goes*, and the backstage goings-on between the co-stars were in fact more interesting than anything going on out on the stage.

Hope admired the talents of Durante and Merman but often found them a trial to work with. No matter how often Hope would rehearse a scene with Durante, Jimmy would blow his lines or go completely blank during performances. He did know how to cover himself — or would manage to get the audience on his side by making a joke out of his alleged faulty memory. But to Hope the direct result was Durante corralling more laughs and more attention. Something about Durante's convenient amnesia just didn't ring true. Hope to his anger was later to discover that Durante's "memory lapses" were totally bogus, with Durante planning precisely every line and movement in advance, and with the help of an associate. Hope saw the purpose too: more time and more gags for Durante onstage.

On other occasions Durante would deliberately have "accidents" that would get the audience — and nearly himself — in stitches. For instance, Hope and Durante would do a bit where a special appliance on the floor of the stage, attached to their shoes, would permit them to lean precariously over the orchestra pit at any angle. Desperate for even more attention, Durante would sometimes recklessly forego the appliance, winding up tumbling into the orchestra pit while Hope stood by helplessly — and foolishly — watching. Ever more irritated and nonplussed, Bob was finding this kind of upstaging impossible to counter. Hope knew that all eyes in the house would be on Durante as he floundered and slipped among the violins and tubas, and he was at a loss to bring attention back to himself or trump Jimmy's ace in some other way.

Durante also shrewdly took advantage of Bob's ego — it took one to know one — by delegating Hope to do benefits for him when he was otherwise engaged — or indisposed — or off indulging his gambling and racing pursuits. Durante would ask Hope to accompany him to a function and maybe Hope would do a little bit in the middle of the show. Jimmy's trick was to perform for a few minutes at the beginning, introduce Bob, and then exit out the back door while Hope was left to entertain the crowd, often sans material and all by himself, for the rest of the show. Later, Hope would get angry at Durante, and ask where the hell he'd gone, making him promise to stick around if by any chance they did another benefit. While Hope loved the opportunity to show off in front of any and all audiences, he could only do just so many gags, despite his formidable repertoire, and knew full well that people — most people — in fact had come to see Durante, not him. Soon, Durante would ask Hope to go to another benefit — again the Hope Ego demanded he comply — and pull the exact same trick on him.

Finally Hope accepted that Durante was going to pull this business every time, and took steps one night to forestall it. As soon as Hope was introduced he looked around to see if he could spot Durante, who'd made the mistake of going out through the audience of the Athletic Club they were appearing in instead of using the back door. Before Durante could leave, he was accosted by fans wanting autographs. Hope told a few jokes — one eye on Durante — then pointed at Jimmy and yelled into the microphone, "Let's bring Durante back for your favorite number!"

Durante couldn't escape. There was too much applause. And the spotlight was on him. When Durante returned to the stage, Hope walked off and quickly left the stage for good to do some barhopping. The next day he walked into his dressing room to find that in a fit (Durante had obviously had big plans for the previous evening) Jimmy had thrown powder and smeared makeup all over the walls and mirrors. Hope then and there made up his mind: no more benefits with Durante.

As naughty and contrary as Jimmy Durante could be, at least he never complained behind his back about Hope's performance. The totally self-involved and insecure Ethel Merman — who could carry on like the toughest male of the species when affronted — was shrewd and savvy enough to recognize in Hope a gifted comic of the first water, and moreover someone who could take some of the spotlight off her performance. She thought Hope was mugging too much and getting too many laughs for her comfort. She told Crouse and his associates that Hope was "ruining" the show with his clowning. They were shrewd enough to know the real reason for her concern, but they also knew she was a bigger star, hence more important to the show than Hope. Still, onstage at least, the chemistry was right. But how to keep Merman happy without offending Hope or getting him fired?

They decided to tell Hope — as in tactful a manner as possible — to tone himself down. They never hinted that Merman had complained, but Hope was probably smart enough to know better. He also knew Merman could get him sacked if she really put up a fight about it. Hope let her get more than her share of laughs but he was never to forgive her for her pettiness.

Merman had other reasons for disliking Hope. She liked some of the same chorus girls he did. Although by that time married, Hope still had a wandering eye. Merman — hypocritically — was angry enough that a married man would make time with the showgirls, but when they were showgirls she herself was attracted to, that was too much.

Merman's lesbianism was well known in show business circles. She had a belting drive, a kinetic force in her acting, clowning, and song-delivery that one Mermanophile characterized as 75 percent masculine, 25 percent feminine. In fiercely homophobic and benighted 1936, it was true that lesbians could get away with more than gay men — even so-called "straight" women were huggy-kissy with each other and given to emotional displays for people of their own sex — but nonetheless her sexual ambivalence (she could be fiercely man-mad at times, too) troubled Merman. Hence her overreaction to Hope — he was in her way romantically, and it humiliated her into the bargain to know that he was on to her girlie pursuits and in his mind downgraded her for it. His experience with Merman, others later felt, accounted in some measure for his ever more homophobic stance in future years.

The Hope-Merman relationship was never better than icily polite and cooperative. They were too much alike, both temperamental, both insecure, both lusting after every comely woman who presented herself to view. Hope never got over the humiliation of having to give in to her on all matters, personal and professional, because she was the bigger box-office draw, and he found her backstage tantrums and blowouts repulsive and madly infuriating.

Durante and Merman were both to be quoted on Hope in future years. When I interviewed Jimmy Durante in the 1950's, he said grumpily that he never understood "how Bob got so big in movies. I always thought him second-rate and phony as they come. And he didn't know his place in a show's pecking order. He didn't know how to blend into the whole." Merman's observation: "What a goddamned ego that bastard had! No respect for fellow performers. Everything was for himself. The goddamned show had been created for him alone — he thought! I'd rather bed with a porcupine than ever share a stage with him again!"

But La Merman and Jimmy the Great were to prove angels compared to some of the people Bob Hope would work with in the very near future, on screen, on TV, and — of course — on radio.

CHAPTER NINE

THE GIRL HE LEFT BEHIND

Dolores Reade was an attractive, talented nightclub singer in New York in 1933 when she first met Bob Hope. Sixty-five years later she is a pretty, petite, elderly woman who — all of Hollywood seems to agree — deserves an Academy Award all her own for sticking by a man who to all intents and purposes spent the larger part of his six-decade marriage ignoring her. Still, Dolores hasn't exactly lived the life of a welfare recipient, and to a man of Bob Hope's mindset that alone should preclude any complaints on her part. For though Hope may not have been generous with his time when it came to his wife and children, he was certainly generous with his money. He has seen to it that Dolores lives like a queen. And as late as Christmas 1991 he was even "co-starring" her with him in a charming sequence where they sang to each other, while riding in a sleigh, for his Bob Hope special. It was touching to see these two people, both in their late 80s, who'd weathered all those years together and had emerged, obviously, fond friends. Indeed, more than that: whatever his preoccupations over those sixty-five years, whatever his strayings, Dolores had represented the harbor, the place to return to, home. And luckily for Bob, she had come along just in time to replace the only other woman who ever was to give him the unconditional love he needed deep down — his mother Avis. Certainly, all agree, this loyal, loving, eminently decent lady Dolores Hope has given him just that: unconditional love. And he met her the year Avis died, luckily for him. Later, disillusionment and bitterness, and increasing remoteness, was to characterize their relationship, especially in old age, and in their private life. (Publicly, all seemed fine straight through.)

They met when he was doing his *Roberta* run on Broadway. Co-star George Murphy, the Howdy Doody lookalike who later entered politics and served as inspiration for a similarly aimed and oriented Ronald Reagan, took Bob to the Lamba Club for some drinks. After a while, Murphy suggested they move on to a place called the Vogue Club on 57th Street. At this time Murphy had taken it upon himself to turn Hope into a sort of Man-about-Town (not that Hope needed much urging), telling him how to dress, where to buy clothes, which clubs to frequent. Hope on his end put up with Murphy's somewat patronizing manner because he sensed the sharply dressed and smoother Murphy might be helpful in unforseen ways.

Murphy liked the singer at the Vogue Club — Dolores Reade — but Hope was even more smitten, not just with her smoky, soft voice, but with her looks, her manner, her entire persona. When introduced to Hope by Murphy, Dolores saw a young, well-tailored and charmingly mannered, boyish fellow, then 30 years old, who, in the subdued light of the club and dressed to the nines, was "almost handsome," as she later tactfully put it. Hope walked Dolores home when the club closed and found out all he could about her via discreet but pointed questioning. She'd had the usual upward struggle, similar in some respects to his own, had honed her fine singing talent with assiduous study and a host of seasoning performances, and already had a coterie of admirers who went back to the Vogue Club just to hear her put over a song in her own inimitable style.

Bob was particularly gratified to learn that Dolores had no current boyfriend, and wasn't especially attracted to George Murphy. He gave her two tickets to the matinee of *Roberta* the following day and made her promise to visit him in his dressing room afterwards.

Dolores made the performance of *Roberta*, but to Bob's surprise, she failed to show up backstage. Hope's ego was painfully affronted, and he went about all evening muttering about ungrateful bitches who thought you were good enough to accept free tickets from but not good enough to get to know better. He had worked himself into a lather by the time he got to the Vogue Club later that night. He accosted Dolores and demanded to know why she hadn't shown up.

Bob certainly felt mixed emotions when the object of his affections confessed that she didn't go backstage because she'd thought he was only a chorus boy in the show and was embarrassed and slightly overwhelmed to see he was actually one of *Roberta*'s major players. Hope's keen annoyance at her ignorance of his stardom waged silent battle with his profound relief at knowing she hadn't simply "dumped" him. He began his courtship in earnest.

Hope didn't win over Dolores Reade right away. For her, it was certainly not love at first sight. Hope became a bit of a nuisance, hanging around the club once the performance of *Roberta* was over, chasing away all other suitors, picking minor fights with the more persistent among them as if regressing to his Packy East days. Yes, Dolores found herself flattered — but not thrilled — by the attention. He'd walk her home every night, impressing her with his basic charm and thoughtfulness, and slowly, slowly, he began to win her over. Dolores recognized a soft, caring side to him when he spoke to her of his mother and her sufferings. And Hope was grateful for, and deeply touched, by the compassion Dolores showed him.

They may have been in love by then, but there was Dolores' widowed mother, Theresa De Fina, to win over first. Hope's first contact with this Italian woman was over the phone, via which she would implore him to bring her daughter home "at a reasonable hour." Mrs. De Fina knew that a nightclub singer couldn't get in by midnight, of course, but those long walks home — or the hours they spent in Bob's Pierce-Arrow car parked outside the Delmonico Hotel where she and her mother lived — delayed Dolores's bedtime to well past dawn.

Finally one night Dolores brought her mother backstage at *Roberta* to meet her boyfriend. Mrs. De Fina didn't quite meet the Bob Hope she'd later come to know, however. Hope was in full "corrective" makeup for his role as Huck Haines, with a more attractive skin tone and special cosmetics that made his nose seem less peculiar. When she met him a second time without the makeup, Mrs. De Fina wondered why he didn't look as good as before. In any case, she was impressed with his charm and gentlemanly manner. But that didn't mean she wanted him for a son-in-law.

For one thing, Hope — spurred on by Murphy — was becoming quite the Broadway ladies' man. His personality and pleasant looks — plus the fact he was the co-star of a hit Broadway show and had a fancy car and lots of cash to spend — made him an extremely eligible bachelor among the chorus girls and other ladies on-the-alert. And even meeting his future mother-in-law didn't alert him to disguising the off-putting braggadocio that went with his success. Mrs. De Fina, in the final analysis, couldn't take "lover boy" seriously and used her influence to get Dolores to accept an engagement with a Miami nightclub instead of with Mr. Hope.

Although Bob was later to claim he "pined away" for Dolores while she was in Florida, it's probably more accurate to say that while his heart may have languished for her his other body parts were still active elsewhere. There's little doubt that he truly cared for Dolores and wanted to marry her, but separation would hardly have prevented such a randy chap from continuous easy scoring with nubile delectables. Hope kept calling Dolores begging her to come back, but his little black book became very dog-eared.

Though at this time Hope had plenty of women to take care of his sexual appetites, he did need someone to handle his emotional needs. In the past that had been Avis, but now his mother was dying; she needed him more than the other way around. She was too preoccupied with her worsening health back in Cleveland to dote on Bob as she had before. There was, as he increasingly admitted to himself, an inner core of loneliness within himself that wouldn't let him face the future on his own. He desperately needed a supportive presence. And while the chorus cuties were fun to sleep and hang around with — and while they kept his mind off his fears and insecurities — he knew none of them really cared for him deep down as much as Dolores did. Dolores also seemed mercifully free of that hardboiled, opportunistic edge the "chippies" had. So Hope kept putting in long-distance calls to Miami.

Whatever he said to her had its effect; she cancelled her engagement halfway through and came back to New York. But she didn't alert Bob in advance, planning to surprise him. *She* was the one who got the surprises — two of them. First, Bob wasn't in New York; he'd gone to Cleveland when his mother took a turn for the worse. Second, the gossip columns were afire with a chorus girl's statements that she and Bob were engaged.

When Bob got back to New York, Dolores wasn't talking to him. Her mother felt vindicated; everything she'd warned her girl about "that Lothario" was true. Through a subterfuge, Bob finally got Dolores on the phone when her mother was out, and told her he hadn't even seen that particular chorus girl in months. (Hope's acquaintances wondered if Louise Troxell had had something to do with planting the story; she was reportedly still bitter about not being cast in *Ballyhoo* with Bob.)

The only way Hope could convince Dolores it was her he loved and not some chorus girl, was to marry her. Plans were quickly made for the knot-tying, which took place on February 19, 1934, in the bucolic town of Erie, Pennsylvania. Dolores Reade Hope was 29 at the time of the wedding; her new husband was 30. The cast of Roberta threw them a nice celebratory party to make up for the fact that Hope's commitments to the show prevented him and his bride from having a decent honeymoon.

When *Roberta* closed, Hope decided to incorporate Dolores into his act. After his usual comedy shtick, he'd bring her out from the wings for a song. During her number, Bob would gush and flirt and try to crack her up, nibble on her arm, and finally lie down behind the footlights and stare up at her in genuine rapture. The audience laughed appreciatively because they knew the couple was in love.

As far as the act was concerned, however, all was not wedded bliss. Hope demanded the same strict attention to detail from Dolores he expected of any other performer. And when he didn't get them, he got furious. As Dolores put it, "What he expects is perfection. He never lets down for a moment on stage and heaven help you if *you* do! Sometimes I'd not pay too much attention and that was fatal. Bob would get very angry and right on stage in the middle of the act he'd crack, 'What's the matter with you? Tired?' I soon learned not to anger him; if I did, there was nothing to do but take the consequences."

To say that Dolores was unsettled by her new husband's snapping at her right on stage in front of hundreds of people — although he'd try to make it seem funny, like part of the act — would be an understatement. "Having the tenor in a band rib you and taking it on the chin, on the stage, from your new husband, are not the same thing," she said. "But I lived. And through the years I've learned to respect his merciless code that the show must go on." Publicly over the years, Dolores has always had a tendency to cover for, or gloss over, her husband's less admirable traits, although privately it's a different story. Some friends feel, however, that even in her private life Dolores has tended to let Bob get away with too much for the sake of a marriage that increasingly became more of a business arrangement.

Dolores was, in fact, relieved when Hope signed for *Say When* and she went back to being a solo. For one thing, she didn't need Hope to perform; his buzzing around her while she sang was, frankly, an annoyance. And she wasn't taken with the temperament he displayed if he felt she let him down. This figured to a great extent when she decided to retire from showbiz shortly thereafter.

But first she did a single act at Loew's State in Boston while *Say When* was previewing in that city. The morning Dolores opened, an exhausted Hope overslept in his room at the Ritz-Carlton and never got to see her. Piqued, Dolores called him afterward and said she was going to quit. She claimed the problem was with the lights and the band, and that nobody liked her, but it was more likely she was furious that her husband had never shown up to support her. Finally Hope came over and threw his weight around, ordering the manager to dim the lights more and getting the orchestra to play softer. His "suggestions" were adhered to and Dolores had no more complaints, but then her only true complaint was that Hope had been ignoring her. It was something that time would teach her to get used to.

When they were first married Bob and his bride lived frugally, even though he was making a lot of money. They lived in a modest furnished apartment with a bedroom, kitchen, and living room. Then they moved to California in 1937 when Hope started doing motion pictures. Because he never truly believed his film career would amount to much, he kept lugging Dolores from one furnished home to another, staying at each rental for just as long as it would take to shoot a new picture. Finally Dolores pleaded with him to buy them a home and he went out and purchased a house in the San Fernando Valley. Dolores didn't participate in the selection process; Hope just came home, put her in his car, and drove her over to the house he'd chosen.

Hope had been hit very hard when his mother Avis passed away, but Dolores was there for him, as he'd always known she would be. Years later he'd complain that his brothers, on the other hand, were not there for him at all. When asked if they'd given him any moral support, he said bitterly, "Supportive? They were thrilled because I was supportive of them!" He was always to feel that his siblings, even though most of them had careers of their own, were parasitical and exploitive of his fame.

Not that his relationship with Dolores was without its strains.

In the tradition of the unenlightened decade they lived in, Dolores always deferred to Bob — but that didn't mean she liked it. At the first sign of unhappiness, Hope would remind her that he was supporting her in grand style, bought her whatever she wanted, and gave her a generous allowance as well. The more money he made, the more elegant their lifestyle became. Dolores went where he went, did as he told her, eventually stayed home in their San Fernando Valley dwelling while he made pictures, caroused with his writer friends, and indulged in matters extramarital. Hollywood insiders debated whether the woman was superhumanly forbearing or merely masochistic.

The biggest contention in their marriage was the lack of children. Hope didn't want children all that much — his relationship with his siblings had proved to him that large families weren't always the happiest and he barely had time for Dolores as it was — but he was bothered by the rumors that Dolores's barrenness engendered. Jokes were being told about their love life, and worse, about his virility. Hope has claimed for years that it was because Dolores was unable to bear children that they were forced to adopt, but stories had always circulated that the real reason was Hope's low sperm count, to say nothing of those rumors that an old venereal infection had left him sterile.

Still, as Hope put it, "I was content with a wife and show business and golf." He also knew that his buddies were aware of his extramarital adventures and knew he could "cut the mustard." The public might wonder why he had no children but as long as his box office wasn't affected he didn't care.

Dolores, however, wanted children. Not only did she have the parental instinct that was totally missing in her husband, but she was lonely, she needed something to do. So she began a campaign to get him to adopt a child that lasted well over half a decade.

Hope was eventually worn down, figuring that a baby in the house would keep Dolores occupied and less concerned about his whereabouts. Marriage was not about to keep him from indulging the same "Devil May Care" attitudes as always. He developed a new tack for public consumption. As he was to tell columnist Hy Gardner: "A house isn't a house without a child in it, and since we've been married for five years we think we'd be very selfish going along this way without giving some orphan a chance to have the things we would have liked to have had when we were young." That was in 1939, by which time Hope's Hollywood career was thoroughly launched.

The lucky baby came from an adoption agency known as The Cradle in Evanston, Illinois, run by a stern managing director named Florence Walrath. Mrs. Walrath looked the Hopes up and down, her sharp, knowing eyes missing nothing, and made it clear it was *they* who must prove suitable for the child, not the other way around. She then took them to see an adorable baby girl. Dolores was delighted with her, as expected, but when Mrs. Walrath asked Hope for his opinion, all he could muster was a "She's all right, I guess."

Time stood still for Dolores. They'd gone through a great deal of trouble just to get this appointment, and now that they were on the verge of getting a child, Bob's disinterest was blowing it all. Gathering her wits, she informed Mrs. Walrath that her husband was simply afraid to appear "soft" and "sentimental" and had difficulty showing his feelings. Whether Mrs. Walrath believed Dolores, or was simply touched by her obvious and rather desperate need for a child, she decided, in September of 1939, to let them adopt the 8-week-old baby. The Hopes called the girl Linda.

More children were to follow. They were like expensive Christmas presents meant to appease a lonely and embittered woman who needed someone to love and need her as much as she herself needed someone to love. The second child was a boy, Tony; the Hopes had asked Mrs. Walrath to keep an eye out for a suitable brother for Linda when they first went to The Cradle.

Tony became a member of the family in 1940, not long after Linda's first birthday. When World War II resulted in U.S. involvement, Dolores pestered Bob for yet another child, but he begged off, citing the possibility he might die on one of his overseas tours. (As his children were to see very little of him, it would hardly have made a difference.) When the war ended and he returned home safely, he had no choice but to keep his promise and make yet another visit to The Cradle.

This time Mrs. Walrath had on hand both a boy and a girl, either one of whom, she felt, would be perfect for the Hopes. Dolores went off by herself for a little while, trying to decide which of the two babies to choose. When she got back she discovered that her husband had made this most momentous of decisions for her by deciding to adopt both children. Eight-week-old Honora (nicknamed Nora) and three-month-old Kelly joined the family in 1946.

The Hopes wouldn't allow pictures of their new children to be published. When they had adopted Linda a news story read, "They intend to keep this private joy of their lives truly private, [as they] fear publicity might be harmful to the baby girl."

Dolores quickly set about putting all of her energies into raising the children. Even had she wanted to continue with her career, her husband would have vetoed it. She, too, developed an "official line" that was part reality, part myth: "If it weren't for the children, I'd go with him; I'd probably be part of the act as I was in the old days when he did benefits for every charity on the East Coast. But he's very firm about this; he wants me at home with the children, all of us here to come back to. This is his security and the essence of it stems from his own childhood. TheHopes may not have been affluent but they were warm and hearty and happy together." Thus ran that set of fictions.

Although not afflicted with the curse of demon rum, Bob Hope was essentially as much of an absentee father as Harry Hope ever was. He did his best to act like a parent whenever he was around, but the children, to him anyway, often proved distracting, annoying, even nerve-racking. Once, when hewas playfully roughhousing with Linda and Tony in the early 1940's, they accidentally poked him in the ribs. He called Dolores up angrily from his office later on and complained that the brats had hurt him.

Then there was the time Hope had a run-in just with Tony. Several guests — friends and associates of Bob's — were having breakfast in the Hope home when Bob came down to join them. The other children said "Hello, Dad!" but five-year-old Tony piped up, "Hello, Bob Hope!" Although in recent years Hope has strangely amended the story to illustrate how often he was away from home, when he first told it he used it as an example of how the boy "could be fresh" and labeled the remark a wisecrack. He went over to the kid and told him he could say things like that in private but not when people were around. At 12, Tony was shipped off to St. John's Military Academy. According to friends, he grew up with a chip on his shoulder and became too difficult for even Dolores to handle. Reportedly, however, she was heartbroken at Bob's insistence on sending the lad away.

Linda, perhaps, had a better relationship with her father. "I think we missed him a lot when we were growing up," she says. "The thing about him was that when he was there, the quality of time was so terrific that it did make you miss him when he wasn't there." Dolores would also stress in interviews that it was the quality, not the quantity, of her husband's infrequent appearances that mattered.

The children saw more of their father when he was working at Paramount Studios, which was located not far from their house. Linda recalls, "We had a breakfast room on the ground floor that looked out on a little patio. Every morning he'd go out the glass door, do a 'Shuffle Off to Buffalo,' then be gone."

Dolores says that as a child Nora was the one who really beguiled her husband, and predicted she'd wind up in show business. Kelly she characterized as the most "sensitive." According to Dolores, Bob had to discipline Kelly as much as, if not more than, Tony. "He doesn't want him to grow up fresh. He doesn't want Kelly to be spoiled by everyone who succumbs to his charm — and then grow up to 'kick people around.'" (As usual, Hope reveals more of himself than he realizes.) Hope told Kelly's teacher he'd give her twenty dollars to donate to her favorite charity for each time she "bopped" Kelly. The Catholic sister told Hope even he didn't have that much money.

Dolores also occupied herself with volunteer pursuits when she wasn't busy with the children. According to her brother-in-law, Jack Hope, some years after her marriage "she was one of the originators of the AWVS. She has been pretty active in the agricultural work the organization is doing, recruiting men and women to help relieve the farm help shortage. Not long ago [this was in 1942] she got a whole town in the San Fernando Valley to close down and go out and pick the tomatoes that were rotting in the fields."

In 1949, the six Hopes were joined by Dolores's mother, whom Dolores had persuaded to leave her apartment in New York and come out to sunny California. Dolores was feeling the need for adult companionship as well as the children's, and she knew her mother was also lonely. In 1955, Hope wrote a piece for *McCall's* (or had it ghosted for him) entitled, "My Favorite Mother-in-Law," in which he told in allegedly comical terms how his mother-in-law dropped unsubtle hints about the things she "needed," and managed to get a new car, a private box at the Santa Anita racetrack, and many other expensive gifts out of him once she'd arrived in California. Intended as a tribute to Dolores's mother, it was instead an embarrassing tribute to his own generosity, a slap in the face to Mrs. De Fina, and a trenchant reminder that when Bob Hope did nice things for people, he never let them forget it.

With the household now swollen to seven people (or more accurately six, as Hope was rarely there, particularly when his mother-in-law was around), Dolores by 1951 was campaigning to get new, larger quarters. She'd set her heart set on Beverly Hills. Real estate agents were contacted and Bob drove around by himself looking for the house *he* wanted (after all, as he let everyone know, it was his money). In the end, he decided to buy the lots on either side of the house he had and simply expand it. He also built, for his convenience and privacy, a brick business quarters adjacent to the house.

Nowadays Dolores Hope is held in higher regard in a number of circles than her husband is. Her friends have drawn a protective shell around her, as if she is a proud, fragile soul who cannot stand the least suggestion of reality entering through the shell surrounding her — as if she has made a choice to put up with certain facts of her life and marriage but wants these facts to be utterly private and sacrosanct, even when in her heart of hearts she knows they're not. Time and again this author was told by interviewees, "I don't want to talk about Dolores, I don't want to hurt her. I'll talk about Bob but not about Dolores." Or, "I simply can't discuss Dolores." But those who did talk, even off the record, have made it clear Dolores has had to put up with plenty in over sixty-five years.

Sometimes Dolores, surprisingly, came out in the open — somewhat. "There were times I wanted to pack it in," she once confessed to columnist Cindy Adams. "But that's perfectly normal. And Bob felt the same way because he's perfectly normal. But responsbility and commitment get you through. Thank God, because it's like getting through a course in school you know you're better off for having finished."

However, Hope's hectic Hollywood lifestyle, weeks and months away from home, and many casual infidelities did hurt, and occasionally humiliate, Dolores over the years.

Even *The New York Times* once reported of the Hopes that "It is no secret in Hollywood that there is little intimacy left in the marriage," quoting a press agent who described Bob as "a little Rabelaisian. With all the beautiful women he's acted with, it would be pretty hard to resist temptation." Dolores's life was also described as "a vale of tears." One writer characterized Hope as "one of the cleverest Casanovas of Hollywood," a reputation that Hope has done little to deny, given his ego. Although he claims that "in pictures you don't have a hell of a lot of time" for infidelities (the opposite, given the slow pace of filmmaking, is usually true). Dolores herself has said, "No person living has the kind of unspotted life that is the perfect example of clean living."

Despite Bob's infidelities, over the years Dolores has become convinced she's his Main Woman. A few acquaintances don't feel sorry for her at all. "She's got it made," says one. "All people talked about for years was Bob's randy appetite but Dolores has also gotten to go to glamorous social events, wear beautiful clothing and expensive jewelry, and meet interesting celebrities. Bob certainly gives her a lot of money. Besides, she always has been an attractive person in her own right. Maybe she was getting some of her own all those nights that Bob was bedded with some starlet. I hope so, for her sake. Yes, Dolores Hope has it made and she knows it — and that's why you'll never hear her kicking."

Whatever Hope has paid for his wife's loyalty, she *is* very loyal, and supportive. "My husband puts limitations on himself that should never be there." she once said. "His capabilities are unlimited and he could be — yes, I mean it — he could be President."

One of those who observed the Hopes' home life first-hand was Pamela Lincoln, now a well-known acting coach who runs an acting school and coaches TV reporters and anchors. She and Linda Hope were close friends when they were in their teens and early twenties, and she has recalled the young Linda as "extremely bright, with a wonderful sense of humor — a genuinely kind person." She recalls that Linda gave Pamela's son Damier "a wonderful baby shower." The daughter of actress Verna Hillie and the late Frank Gill, who was a comedy writer for Hope, Pamela Lincoln is a great admirer of Dolores Hope. "She was a wonderful family woamn," Pamela says, "and she got Linda and me involved in her volunteer work at Our Lady Queen of Angels Hospital, where Dolores was also a champ fundraiser. Dolores was very generous, always looking for ways to help others."

Pamela recalled also that "Dolores was very hospitable, ran a beautiful home, was well-organized. I think she gave Bob Hope a wonderful atmosphere, domestically. He always looked happy and contented when I saw him; he'd wander in, ask how we were doing. I thought him and Dolores very down-to-earth, very accessible; I always felt very welcome there."

Pamela's mother, the actress Verna Hillie, recalled that her husband, Frank Gill, always enjoyed working with Hope. "Frank said he was galvanic, kept the guys on their toes, got their best inspirations out of them by keeping the atmosphere electric, keeping the ball in the air. Frank always admired Dolores also."

Actress Louise Campbell, whose late husband, Horace McMahon, appeared with Hope in such films as *Beau James*, also thought Dolores a wonderful wife and mother. Her husband would tell her that Hope was "a lot of fun to work with, " that he got the impression Bob and Dolores "had a wonderful marriage, that Dolores was well-organized and solicitous of Bob's every need."

Jacque Lynn Colton, the actor-director, is a neighbor of the Hopes. A member of the National Board of AFTRA, she recalls Hope being honored with an award from that organization a few years ago. "I felt he was in his glory surrounded by so many admiring colleagues there to honor him," she says. According to Colton, the Hopes are the most admired and respected couple in their area, and Dolores, at 88, was "the most popular woman in the neighborhood." Colton feels that Bob and Dolores Hope are "deeply devoted to one another — it shows in their faces, the way they act together." (Again, the Hopes put a good face on things in public at least.)

Pamela Lincoln gets the last word on the woman who has been Mrs. Bob Hope for over sixty years: "Everybody — and I mean everybody — likes Dolores."

CHAPTER TEN

RADIO DAYS

It was Bob Hope's appearance in a vaudeville show at the Capitol Theatre in 1932 that led to his performing on the radio. The Loew's corporation, which owned the Capitol, developed a radio show entitled "The Capitol Family Hour" for which they'd book entertainers appearing in their vaudeville theatres, thereby to publicize their shows. The program, which aired Sunday mornings, was hosted by the Capitol Theatre's manager, Major Edward J. Bowes. For years Bowes had run radio talent contests which broadcast from the Capitol's stage.

Hope was happy to do a radio show — it certainly gave him less anxiety than appearing in a motion picture, ski nose and all — but he wasn't at all happy with the host. Bowes had let success go to his head and was determined not only to run the show but be the funniest man on it. Playing innocent, Bowes asked Hope to send him a copy of the jokes he planned to use on the show. "I just have to give it a once-over," Bowes told him, intimating that it was merely a formality and the material was only to be checked for broadcast standards. Hope complied.

On the morning of the broadcast, however, Hope learned of the major's duplicity. As soon as their banter began, Bowes began to appropriate Hope's jokes, coming out with the punchlines before Hope could get a word in edgewise. As this sorry situation continued, Hope was forced to take the major's intended role and play the straight man. Hope did his best to protest against this rude injustice, but Bowes sloughed it off; he had a right to get some laughs, too, didn't he? he said. Hope was furious at the new arrangement but as Bowes was the boss there was little he could do about it. At least it would help publicize his appearance at the Capitol he reasoned, and once he had the crowd in front of him, it would be his turn to show what he could do.

Hope had better luck working with Rudy Vallee on "The Fleischman Hour." Hope let Vallee do the singing and Vallee didn't steal any of his jokes. But there were other problems. It took Hope quite a while to get used to the microphone; radio was a whole new discipline. Even though there was a studio audience he could perform to, Hope's disembodied voice would be the only thing most listeners heard and he knew he had to put himself over or else. First he talked too loud and emphatically; then not loud enough. He was so nervous that the engineers could pick up a thumping sound that turned out not to be his heartbeat but the bump of his foot kicking the mike stand after each joke.

He did not, initially, make a very good impression on the air waves. One critic wrote:

> For the life of me I can't understand how Bob [Hope] dares to endanger his reputation by appearing before the mike with such dull, stale, and unfunny material as he used last night. As an example: his burlesque dentist's skit was about as forced and boresome [sic] an attempt at humor as I've ever heard on the radio. If this sort of stuff were being spouted by some poorly paid comedian on a minor station, one might make allowances. But after all, Bob Hope has a name in the entertainment world. And he should do something to safeguard it.

In 1935, Hope went on "The Bromo Seltzer Intimate Hour." It was here that he zeroed in on a new foil in much the way he'd bantered with Louise Troxell. Her name was Honey Chile (Patricia) Wilder, and Bob met her in the office of his lascivious agent, Doc Shurr. Wilder was a Georgia Peach with a thick Southern accent and wonderful looks. Hope found her a refreshing change from the Ethel Mermans of the world; it was relatively rare for a funny lady to look good, too. He worked with Honey Chile in a few theatre engagements and found her completely at ease in front of an audience. Then he took her onto the Bromo Show with him for a fifteen-week engagement. Hope had been married over a year by this time, and he spent much time reassuring Dolores that his relationship with Honey Chile was strictly professional.

Hope later was to arrange for Wilder to make a screen test and she had a brief career in pictures, but made more of a mark on Broadway. Unfortunately, the ratings for the Bromo Seltzer broadcasts were not very good and Hope was soon back on the vaudeville circuit.

As Hope remembered it: "I used to check in with an agency

because that agency represented the [stomach] powder I was pitching for, and when I got there I had to read my radio script out loud to this outfit . . . six or seven Yale or Princeton advertising types, all wearing tab collars, would form themselves into a jury, listen to my material, and decide whether to go 'Tsk-tsk' or say, 'This week we're going to have a smasher.' That account meant millions to them and, boy, they wanted to pull it off. But apparently that wasn't the way to do it."

Hope's first lengthy radio contract was with the Woodbury Soap Show (26 weeks) in mid 1937. This coincided with his trip out to Hollywood to appear in his first feature film, *The Big Broadcast of 1938*, released some months later. Although the Woodbury Show was normally broadcast from New York, it was decided to keep Hope on the program and have him do his segment direct from Hollywood on a coast-to-coast hookup. Hope was thrilled with the new arrangement — which allowed him to "conquer" two mediums at once — but his joy turned to horror when he realized he'd forgotten to make sure the NBC Hollywood people had arranged for a studio audience. If he didn't have an audience to bounce his jokes off, he was sunk. His pacing and delivery — should he quickly follow up a joke that didn't work with a new one, etc. — were dependent on the reaction of his audience. But it was two days before his transcontinental debut and there was no time to arrange for tickets to be printed and distributed.

Hope went to ventriloquist Edgar Bergen, whose show broadcast from the studio next door, and asked if he could borrow his audience. Once Bergen's show was over, the perplexed crowd was guided by ropes and ushers not up to the exits but into Hope's studio. It was an extremely close call. Bergen's show ended right when the Woodbury Show began and Hope's spot commenced only five minutes into the hour. While a few folks with prior engagements somehow made their way out of the building, the rest, half-restless, half-intrigued, stayed and listened to — and laughed at — Hope's show.

While still in California, Hope signed for "Your Hollywood Parade," which was emceed by actor Dick Powell. Hope did a ten-minute monologue which, the critics later opined, was the only thing about the program that was worth listening to. Hope made jokes about movie stars and their private lives, and also worked in some other kinds of topical humor. Virtually all of his material was written by Wilkie Mahoney, who'd meet with Hope several times a week for marathon gag sessions. Hope insisted on more and more material from Wilkie, but usually threw out 90 percent of it, retaining only what he considered

Knocking his radio audience dead, 1935

were the top-drawer gags. Even that 10 percent amounted to a stagger-ing pile of jokes considering how fast Hope used them up via his rapid delivery.

"Even when I use my writers," Hope later insisted, "there are things we hammer out, then polish together. Wilkie and I had fun. We sat in a room together, with a typewriter between us, shagging ideas back and forth. If you have a gag-type mind, gags pop out of it at a time like that. Not only that, but you get several slants on each gag, so you play around with them and select the one you want. Wilkie and I used to sit up and work until four or five in the morning [often six or seven, by his own admission]. We'd walk up and down and laugh and kid, and it opened up our brains the way freshly ground horse-radish opens up your sinuses."

In 1938, age 35, Hope finally got his own radio show, sponsored by Pepsodent toothpaste. The Pepsodent account was handled by the Lord and Thomas agency, which hired Hope to replace Amos and Andy. The amount of new material he'd need was so tremendous that Hope went all-out and hired a battery of professional writers to help him and Mahoney. These seven men, known for a time in the trade as "The Dauntless Seven" were Milt Josefsberg, Norman Panama, Al Schwartz, Mel Frank, Jack Douglas, Norman Sullivan, and Mel Shavelson. Fifty years later, Shavelson, Panama, and Sullivan were still writing the occasional gag for Hope. Shavelson was to collaborate with Hope on his autobiography. Within months after the hiring of the Original Seven, some were fired and replaced by others. Until the two weeks' notice of the fired men was up, the ranks of writers would occa-sionally swell to eleven. At one time Hope fired Frank and Panama for having the temerity to ask for a $25-a-week raise (Frank and Panama worked as a team). Years later he hired them back.

Hope worked up the logistics implicit in many men writing a show together by giving them as much work to do as possible. Each man was assigned to write one complete script a week on the same subject. Then the writers would get together with Hope for a script conference. There each man would read his script aloud while Hope recorded the others' responses. Each joke that got the loudest laugh would go into the master script. Somehow it never occurred to Hope on these occa-sions that personalities might enter into it. If, for instance, several of the writers were mad at, or jealous of, the guy reading his script, they wouldn't react favorably to his sallies. Newcomers had a particularly tough time. If the fellows didn't like somebody, his jokes would receive only polite titters and within a short while he'd be jobless.

Hope also got his money's worth by making the writers combine the best jokes into a 90-minute script for a 30-minute show. The cast would perform the entire ninety minutes for a live audience a couple of days before the actual broadcast. The segments that went over best — adding up to thirty minutes — would go out on the air each Tuesday.

The writers always had to adjust their routines to suit Hope's convenience — and working schedule. Hope had movies to shoot by 1938, and benefits galore to attend, not to mention a more private social life and fun schedule that didn't include wife and family. It wasn't uncommon for his writers to work fifteen hours straight to come up with gags and then meet with him at three in the morning and spend more hours reciting joke after joke for The Master's approval. A certain bond grew between those writers who liked each other; they'd arrange to laugh extra hard at each other's gags so the jokes would be included and Bob would be pleased.

Writing jokes for Bob Hope was to become these men's whole existence, crowding out everything else. "That was our whole life," said Mel Frank. "Bob is probably responsible for more interrupted orgasms, either with their wives or — well, whomever — when his rush phone call sent a hapless writer out of bed and into his pants," Jack Benny once joked. This sally was reported to Hope who cracked (or maybe one of his writers cracked for him) that had Jack Benny been on his writing team he'd have arrived first because in bed he hadn't even gotten it up, let alone worked up an on-the-way orgasm. When Mel Shavelson wanted to take time off for his honeymoon some years later, Hope allowed him exactly one afternoon, kidding that the new Mrs. Shavelson was "the bride left high and dry."

Some of his writers, off the record, reported the demanding Hope as not an easy man to like. He was determined to become a major radio success and if treating his writers like galley slaves made for a better show, so be it. It's unlikely he felt any qualms, for, to be fair to Hope, his writers were among the best paid in the business. The trouble was: paying large salaries got Hope to feeling he could take over their lives at any and all times, and according to his varying whims. In his code, these guys were there to give service, and that was it. Hope paid each of his writers $100 a week (good money sixty years ago) but he balked at it and mightily resented it and made sure he got his pound of flesh from each in return. He got a power-kick out of the way they figuratively — sometimes literally — snapped to attention when he barked an order, noting how they worked up sweats trying to outdo each other by turning in more copy, figuring the more they wrote the more chance their pet gags would make "the finals." Hope also took perverse pleasure in watching the galley slaves' faces as their jokes were read aloud one by one and they had to decide whether to laugh at a rival's gag or "poker-face" it. As he put it: "If they could get laughs from the other worried gentlemen whose jobs depended on keeping a straight face, the joke went into the show." (Freud and other analysts would have doubtless had a field day of their own dissecting the psycho-sexual dynamics or whatever of Hope's lip-smacking enjoyment of his power over other men.)

Hope's legendary cheapness with regard to his writers — inviting them to his home to work, then sending them out to restaurants, at their expense, at mealtimes — reflected his anger at paying what he considered exorbitant salaries, yet he was shrewdly objective enough to know that if he wanted the best gagmen in the business, he'd have to pay decently for it. That didn't mean he had to like it. "He hated it!" one "slave" later chortled.

The men who worked for Hope got used to his ways, but not one became close friends with him. They were employees and he was the employer, and Hope rammed the caste-system inequities of this right down their throats every chance he got. His egoism, condescension, and resentment forced his writers to view him as a rapacious monster "with a bottomless need for jokes and blood and sweat and even tears in no particular order."

The Pepsodent show was typical of the radio program of its day — music, comedy, lots of guest starts, a singer or two. Two of the female vocalists who lasted the longest were Judy Garland and Doris Day, both of whom, by the 1940's, were difficult, although in individual ways. Judy got off to an early start in her life and career exhibiting neurotic tendencies and popping pills. Hope liked her and enjoyed and respected her talents, but had little patience for her "crises" and depressions and manic highs and lows on days when she didn't feel like working. Day, too, had her problems, and didn't always come on like a seasoned, hardened trouper of the kind Bob felt most comfortable with. Every little thing seemed to upset her and before "going on" she was usually a bundle of nerves. Day had to have things just so, her way, or she'd stew and become uncommunicable and unpleasant. "These egotistical broads" was usually a variation on Bob's reactions to their temperaments, but he, of course, was no slouch in the egotism-temperament sweepstakes himself.

One "colleague" (though to Bob probably an underling) that he did seem to enjoy working with was Jerry Colonna, a pop-eyed, jittery, rather flibbertigibbet comedian who got much exposure thanks to Hope on radio shows and U.S.O. tours, but somehow never became a truly major figure on his own in the entertainment world. For one thing, Jerry was just too weird — and weird looking. His comedy tended to be extremely broad, his looks were downright ugly, and when it came to spotlight-grabbing, he was no threat whatsoever to Hope — one of the reasons, doubtless, that Hope hired him and kept him on.

In the early 1940's, Bob hired two ladies, Blanche Steward and Elvia Allman, to do parodies of two well-known debutantes of the period, Brenda Frazier and Cobina Wright, Jr. The gag was that these two ladies were supposed to be the ugliest dogs that ever lived, with Elvia and Blanche providing the horrendous voices while the audiences' imagination would do the rest. Unfortunately, the names of the characters were left simply as Brenda and Cobina, the same as those of the real-life duo, and this was adding insult to injury so far as Cobina Wright, Jr. was concerned. She initiated a tough lawsuit. The characters were dropped.

The irony in this was that Hope had only chosen the names of Frazier and Wright because in reality they were cultured beauties — the exact opposites of the Brenda and Cobina on the show. In a way, it was a reverse compliment, had they seen it that way, especially the litigious Cobina. There was never any real offense intended, nor even social satire. No negative cracks or points were made on the air about upper-class people or the social register. Hope's radio show was strictly a collection of shallow wisecracks with no underlying significance or satirical edge. Even the topical jokes were more silly than scathing. Hope told jokes in his usual scattershot style, but — probably this was his intent — there was no Hope "personality" as such. He just proceeded from gag to gag, pausing only for an advertisement or musical number.

This approach to his radio program changed as time went on, and the writers were responsible for it. For one thing, the work would go easier on them if Bob developed certain "public" characteristics — along the lines of Jack Benny's famous prissiness and stinginess — that would lend themselves naturally to easy gags, give them something ongoing to bounce off of. So they adapted some of Hope's actual characteristics — his preoccupation with the female sex, his rampant egomania — and exaggerated them; then they added some fictitious traits somehow associated with his public pose — such as a cowardly nature. This eventually became the accepted Bob Hope persona and carried over to his films. The new "Hope Mystique" that the whole country came to recognize opened up new avenues for comedy and was in no small measure responsible for Hope's unprecedented popularity in several mediums over the next few decades.

Hope's show for Pepsodent over the years was not only popular but influential. When the wife of the show's announcer, Bill Goodwin, gave birth, a contest was held to name the baby. At that time Yehudi Menuhin, the classical violin prodigy, was attracting wide attention (among a completely different class of people from those who listened to Hope, of course) and Colonna suggested "Yehudi!" Before long, the name caught on and came up again and again in sketches and gags until Yehudi became a character — a mythical person the cast kept searching for — in its own right. "Who's Yehudi?" became a national catch phrase to millions of people who had no idea there was a famous classical violinist of that name. Reportedly, when the "Yehudi" gag finally seeped into higher-brow circles and The Great Menuhin himself was apprised of its use as a gimmick on the Hope show, he thought it "vulgar but harmless." Considering the notorious touchiness of classical artists whose egos put Hope's in the shade, Menuhin showed considerable flexible tolerance. "He probably figured the Hope radio audience was so déclassé anyway that they'd never associate their Yehudi with him, so why bother protesting?" Gracie Allen once observed.

The show was, to be sure, almost canceled on one occasion when fans felt Hope and Colonna had gone too far. A sketch in which Colonna played Santa Claus ended with Hope murdering Kris Kringle. The switchboard immediately lit up with calls from outraged parents determined to guard the "pleasant innocence" of their small-fry, and in the days that followed, letters and telegrams of protest poured in by the cartload. A stern warning soon came in short order from the Lord and Thomas agency, which insisted on scrutinizing Hope's scripts much more closely thereafter. Pepsodent, after all, could not be put in the position (they huffed) of sponsoring a program which offended family audiences. Luckily the brouhaha died down as quickly as it began and Hope and Company were saved from certain disaster. One writer almost got fired from the Hope contingent for sassily suggesting that a sexed-up Santa seducing one of the more nubile family daughters might be just the ticket. Hope, prurient as always in private life, huffily insisted on the maintenance of his prissy on-radio manners, and told the writer "not to get wise" at his expense!

Hope's writers were also the original creators of the "feud" between Bing Crosby and Bob Hope; they modeled it after the feud Jack Benny and Fred Allen had worked up, to their public advantage, feeling that it, too, would be an unending source of fresh material. Hope also got a lot of mileage out of Desi Arnaz, who in the mid 1940's became his show's musical director. This was due entirely to the pleading of Desi's wife, Lucille Ball, a guest star on the Hope show, when she learned there was a vacancy. Lucy pulled out all the stops in her campaign to get Hope to hire her husband (in Lucy Bob always admitted he'd met his match in egomaniacal ruthlessness and persistence, calling her "a dame with balls"). Lucy never let up, raining on Hope Desi's press clippings and rave notices, determined as she was to have hot-blooded, Latin Desi, who had an ever-active crotch area and a fanatically roving eye for feminine allure, by her side in Hollywood where she could keep an eye on him instead of bouncing around the country in his tight pants and colorful open shirts, bedding all willing women. Hope (it took one to know one) was always intrigued by the well-named Ball's pizzazz and persistence and her career self-interest and self-perpetuation, and took priapic Desi on. Secretly, he identified, in another way, with the woman-mad, philandering Arnaz, who, knowing where his bread was buttered, nodded eagerly and repeatedly when Lucy told him over and over that it was just the ticket to keep their marriage (at least at that time) from eventually going on the rocks.

Unfortunately, Hope's obliging of Ball was not to produce the desired effect in the long run. It seemed that one of Desi's duties was to audition female vocalists for the show, since they had decided that a different young lady each week would lend some variety and spice and contrast to the departed Frances Langford. A lot of comely feminine flesh passed through Arnaz's office, and he took full advantage of the assorted juxtapositions, as, reportedly, did Hope, with Arnaz passing on the more choice specimens to him. More upset than ever, Lucy decided some tit-for-tat was in order and that Desi was taking her too much for granted, so she began a fake-but-convincing romance with her screen co-star of the moment, Franchot Tone, an ex-Mr. Joan Crawford famous for his racy amours (he later had to undergo facial plastic surgery after one of his love-rivals, Tom Neal, punched him out).

Although Hope and writers, with their comic and brash inventiveness, always squeezed laughs out of Desi and his comical hispanic accent, Desi, left strictly on his own, couldn't even elicit mild titters from an audience as sorry for him as they were baffled by him. An excellent musician, with natural rhythm and a fine musical sense, Desi was devoid of any real humor. Desi may never have picked up Bob's facility with stand-up comedy, but he did absorb the ways and means employed by Hope to run his show in flawless professional fashion. A great aper, of the more constructive and self-seeking kind, Desi's inner shrewdness and canniness belied his somewhat wide-eyed and buffoonish exterior and wild accent, and he adapted many of Hope's production methods and overall principles when he parlayed to success his and his wife's *I Love Lucy* and other shows produced by the Desilu Empire in the 1950's. It was during this later period that those who had sneered at Lucy's choice of Hot Tamale Desi as a husband came to realize that he was bright, clever, and ruthless. Hope later tried to take credit for Desi's improved acting and clowning on the Lucy show — "he stood around and watched me, so how could he go wrong?" being one of his more salient observations on Desi.

Hope's radio popularity had soared during the War years, but by the late 1940's there was persistent nagging and fault-finding from the critics, who commented that some of the material was veering on stale and repetitious; worse, the ratings declined rather precipitously. Hope, who never took challenges lying down, thereupon mustered considerable reshuffling of backstage and on-mike talent to get himself on top of the ratings yet again. By this time he was plugging soap for Lever Brothers instead of toothpaste for Pepsodent.

He'd signed a ten-year contract with Lever Brothers in 1945, but demanded to be released from it five years later, charging the sponsor with being "a big obstacle" to his creativity and production methods, and of offering him "no cooperation." Lever Brothers announced themselves as only too happy to switch to Arthur Godfrey, then in his ascendancy, while Hope, having made the kind of deal that satisfied his plans and projections, signed, after much pro-and-con discussion, with the Liggett and Myers Tobacco Company.

Of course, by the early 1950's, Television had become the bright, exciting, novel recreational factor in American homes, with radio gradually taking a back seat and giving itself over mostly to musical programs and topical items. But the transition was gradual, and Hope hung on with radio for a while longer, signing a 1952 contract with General Foods to do six daytime shows a week. The fee that went into the Hope coffers: a cool two million smackers. Each show would be broadcast at 9:30 in the morning for fifteen minutes. The show moved later to 11:45

a.m., and Hope went on to add twenty-six weekly nighttime shows in January 1953.

The background routine for the new daytime show differed radically from those of the old nighttime broadcasts. Gone were the story conferences, and the writers no longer had to write five times as many jokes as were used. Head-scripter Howard Blake has recalled that he'd write up outlines of the guests and subjects for each day, then each member of his staff would be assigned a particular segment. Blake would then collect all the scripts, edit or reject them, and combine them into a finished script to be sent to Bob — who got them only hours before taping and never met with the writers at all. This was Bob's chosen method in the early Fifties — he was Big Time in Spades and could delegate some of the work — and he trusted Blake to follow his standards.

Blake, who knew his business, remembers encouraging ad-libbing; he'd mark places in the script where he thought it advisable for spontaneity. He encouraged Hope to slow down somewhat (Hope had just turned 50) but recalled that it was "hard to do it too much because at a certain point he ceases to be Bob Hope." Blake (this was in the early Fifties) also thought it had become repetitious, stale, and no-longer-timely to overdo, or even run at all, Bing Crosby gags. He also felt Hope should do less gag-stuff involving the likes of Phil Harris, the young Marilyn Monroe, and, of course, that perennial favorite, Bob's ski nose. He recalled not being terribly successful at getting Bob to de-emphasize these subjects and approaches. Bob at the time seemed to feel that the tried-and-true could be freshened up, recycled, whatever — later he began to get Blake's point, though; being the egoist he was, he adjusted slowly and reluctantly.

Hope's radio agent, James Saphier, felt the switch to daytime radio would provide longevity for Bob's broadcast career. As Saphier saw it at the time, "Bob felt daytime audiences were going to be larger than nighttime. Daytime television [on the other hand] hasn't been successful — a woman can't do housework at the same time." As Saphier put it, "Bob can be on [daytime] radio ten years or more, while nighttime radio can't possibly afford him much longer."

But by the late Fifties, Bob had finally and conclusively veered from radio. But he was never to miss it — movie and television work was there for the asking, and he concentrated on those.

CHAPTER ELEVEN

THE CAT WHO SWALLOWED THE CANARY

Bob Hope's first real taste of the movies — aside from the debacle of his 1931 screen test — occurred during the time he was appearing on stage in *Roberta*. His agent, Doc Shurr, was contacted by an East Coast outfit, Educational Films, that specialized in two-reel shorts. They offered to pay Bob $2500 a picture for six pictures. This was in 1934. Bob, then 31, was told he could film the shorts out at the studios in Astoria, Queens, in the daytime, then get back to Broadway each night for his role as Huck Haines. Each short would take only three days to shoot. Despite his misgivings, even after three years, as to his on-camera appearance, Hope liked the fees offered, and moreover felt he'd appear to better advantage in films now that he was more established as a showbiz personality — he was also more confident than he'd been at the time of that disastrous first screen test. A lot of water had, after all, gone under the bridge since 1931.

The first short was entitled *Going Spanish*. The zany premise had Hope driving through South America with his fiancée and her mother when they arrive at the town of "Los Ham and Eggos," which is celebrating "Don't Do It" Day, this being, according to the film, "the one day a year when it's impossible to insult or be insulted." The rule was to immediately start singing to the person you've insulted, and they must smile and forgive all.

In spite of some genuinely amusing sequences arising from the complications of the premise, *Going Spanish* isn't very good except for Hope. Right from the start he registers, and gets tellingly across, that trademark cocky assurance and Hope-style suavity. He's appealing, confident, expressing star quality and swagger in equal measure, and it's easy to see from this first filmic outing how a big film career eventually materialized for him.

He looks almost handsome in the footage, ski nose notwithstanding, and a head somewhat too large and a brow too high. Leah Ray is also delightful as the storekeeper's daughter, who wins Hope's heart after his fiancée runs off with the handsome "King of the Pampas" (but who actually works in the livery stable).

Hope didn't think much of himself, however, in this first on-camera outing in a plotted story; he still hadn't gotten as used to, and accepting of, his appearance as he'd thought. Considering how well he comes off in the movie, it's difficult to imagine just what he expected: a variation on Doug Fairbanks or Rudy Valentino, his early screen idols, to say nothing of the top current 1934 heartthrobs, Clark Gable and Warner Baxter? True, his reasons for not liking the script were valid enough. He ran into columnist Walter Winchell at the Rialto Theatre on Broadway where the short was showing, and the brash columnist asked the comic his opinion of the picture. Hope quipped, "When they capture John Dillinger, they're going to make him sit through it twice." (Hope later claimed he did express dismay over the picture, but that the Dillinger joke might have been Winchell's idea.) Dillinger, the most notorious criminal of the 1934 era, *was* later to be killed in Chicago after seeing William Powell, Myrna Loy, and Clark Gable in *Manhattan Melodrama*. One of Hope's writers later was to joke that had Dillinger seen the Hope short, he might have saved the cops outside the theatre the bother and shot himself.

Jack Skirball of Educational Pictures (later a top Hollywood producer of features) wasn't pleased with the negative publicity stirred up by Walter Winchell's Dillinger joke about Bob and the picture in his column. He called Doc Shurr, and in the screaming match that followed dropped Hope's option. (Skirball, in 1934 anyway, was obviously not an adherent to the school of thought that publicity, any publicity, was a plus as long as the name was spelled right.)

When Shurr told Bob what had happened, Hope accepted the news with mixed emotions. He didn't have long to entertain ambivalent feelings, if that was what they were, for Shurr then got him a deal with Warner Bros. to make six shorts for a tightwad but shrewd producer named Sam Sax who, unlike Skirball, obviously felt publicity was, well, publicity. The mostly forgettable Hope two-reelers that ensued in 1935-36 included *The Old Grey Mayor*, in which Hope co-starred with irascible, gravel-voiced, scene-stealer Lionel Stander, a character actor who was to make his mark in Hollywood.

On the set Hope had the same problem he'd weathered while performing years before in vaudeville — the antics of fellow players, this time Stander, broke him up. A simple scene of Hope running out of a

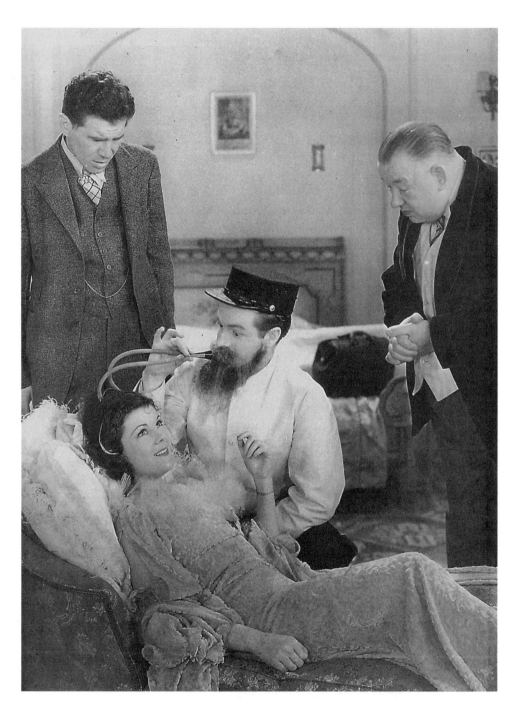

An early short: *The Old Grey Mayor,* 1935. With Ruth Blasco,
Lionel Stander and Sam Wren.

telephone booth and bumping into Stander couldn't be shot because Hope was doubled up with laughter. Finally the director took him aside and reminded him — it was like a replay of earlier vaudeville incidents — that the audience, not the actor, was supposed to laugh. The admonition didn't work. Hope ultimately "sobered up" only when feisty Sam Sax showed up on the set to see what was going on and told him bluntly he'd be fired if he didn't stop cutting up.

Whatever else the Warner shorts did for Hope, they did season him up, make him more camera-wise, enabled him to watch himself in various situations before the camera. Quickly made, sloppily done, they showcased him to some advantage, and he became more self-accepting of himself onscreen. He made them in New York during the day, doing various Broadway shows of the 1935-36 period in the evenings. The shorts, trivial and forgettable as they were to prove, served one crucially important function. They helped, along with his stage appearances, in bringing him to the notice of Paramount executives in Hollywood.

After completing his last Broadway stint in 1937 — Hope was 34 that year, a relative latecomer to Big Time Hollywood Movie features — he was signed to a major contract by Paramount. The deal was for three pictures a year for seven years, at $20,000 a film to start. Every other term of the contract was extremely favorable — for the studio. Paramount, as per contract, could drop Hope any time they felt like it without so much as a farewell penny.

Hope was cast in his first Hollywood feature, *The Big Broadcast of 1938*, when Jack Benny, who'd starred in *The Big Broadcast of 1936* two years earlier, turned it down.

Hope arrived in Hollywood in September 1937 with, as he put it, "A log-size chip on my shoulder." He'd heard a lot back in the East about the dire experiences of other Broadway people who went West to brave the camera and then found themselves treated more cuttingly and dismissively than the lowliest chorus boy. Hope had been a star in New York, and he had no intention of putting up with any abuse Hollywood-style. By his own admission, it was to be a few years before he fully took in the fact that even a Broadway star was a newcomer so far as Hollywood was concerned, and couldn't expect the same publicity or build-up as was accorded an established movie figure. Not that he could really complain. He got good parts and starring roles almost from the beginning. Those Warner shorts had gotten a wider exposure than he at first realized, and had put him through the door. But it took time for him to become a major Hollywood player; in the early period he was

With Shirley Ross in his first feature, *The Big Broadcast of 1938*, 1938

often impatient and jittery, off and on the set. When he first arrived in California he told his agent that if his parts weren't big enough and he felt he wasn't being treated right and properly appreciated, he'd be on the first train back East — back where they did appreciate the talents of Bob Hope.

Even though two years had passed, Hope, of course, was still nursing his hurt feelings over having been left out of the 1935 RKO film version of *Roberta*; this slight had left him particularly bitter. Virtually everyone who'd been with him in the Broadway show had been left out of the movie, too; to him, the difference was that cast members like Fred MacMurray had been welcomed to pictures (by 1937 MacMurray was solidly established as a Paramount leading man after 1935 hits early in his screen career opposite Claudette Colbert [*The Gilded Lily*] and Katharine Hepburn [*Alice Adams*, on loan to RKO]). Always envious, in spite of himself, of Fred MacMurray's extreme handsomeness and virile presence, Hope was determined to make up for lost time, any way possible, now that he too was ensconced in the City of Angels.

Doc Shurr, always a watchful friend and agent, had confided to Dolores that selling Bob to the movies wouldn't be easy, and keeping him ensconced once he'd had his baptism by camera, even less easy. "He's unique," Shurr said, indicating by his expression that "unique" had a negative coloration in Bob's case. But Dolores had firm faith in her husband as a movie figure from the very start. "If you can't sell him for movies, radio, everything," she shot back, "you might as well close up shop."

What Bob saw around him in the Hollywood of 1937 would have given pause to far more confident stage performers. The Movies were in their Thirties heyday. Bob had been taken on by one of the major studios, Paramount, to be sure, but there were others just as major, just as competitive, also with exhibition outlets cross-country. There were RKO, and MGM, and Warner Bros., and Columbia, and Universal, as well as a host of independents like United Artists and Samuel Goldwyn, going on down to the smaller outfits like Monogram and Reliance. Glamour was being busily purveyed that fall of 1937, with Garbo shining in *Conquest* for MGM, and Katharine Hepburn and Ginger Rogers in RKO's *Stage Door*. Bette Davis was making her major starring breakthrough picture at Warners, *Jezebel* (released in 1938). There was plenty of comic competition, too, led by the Marx Brothers, who'd made big hits at MGM in *A Night at the Opera* and *A Day at the Races*. Deanna Durbin, the lovely young singing star, was Universal's bright new personality, and at Columbia there were screwball comedies with the likes of Irene Dunne (who'd starred in the screen version of *Roberta*) and Cary Grant. Clark Gable was the top male romantic star at MGM, and Fred Astaire and Ginger Rogers the top dancing team at RKO. The studios and their stars were fed by mammoth publicity machines, with columnists and feature writers and fan magazines like *Photoplay* cueing in the country on even the most minor gossip tidbits about the private and on-set partying life of the Hollywood Elect.

At Paramount, Bing Crosby was riding high as a singing and romantic lead, with the aforementioned Fred MacMurray at his heels. Hope knew he would have to summon, full-force, no-holds-barred, all the egoistic, self-confident, go-for-it hardness he could if he were to survive this world of glittering stellar competition, ruthless studio overlords, and publicity saturation nationally.

Hope's arrival that September of 1937 in Hollywood certainly did not bode well for the future. He had expected a contingent from the studio to greet him and the ever-faithful, ever-encouraging Dolores when they stepped off the train in Pasadena (it was customary for stars to avoid fans at the L.A. station by leaving at Pasadena). But there wasn't a soul from Paramount on hand. No stretch limo (or the 1937 equivalent thereof), no bowing boys with flowers, no publicity chief or studio exec with outstretched hand.

When they repaired to their first quarters in film town, Dolores kept up Bob's spirits along the lines of "you gotta start somewhere to get somewhere." She remembered later that when she went to get her hair done no one had heard of her husband; all the facial reactions registered blank. In Hollywood that fall of 1937 Bob Hope was a nobody. As so often in his career incarnations, he'd have to start all over again, in a sense. The prospect energized him while it wearied him. But with Dolores pumping aggressive adrenaline into him, he went to the studio for his first meetings with an "I'll show 'em" attitude and stance, betraying no insecurity or uncertainty.

The myth Hope upholds some sixty-one years later is that the makeup people and studio executives and publicity people at Paramount all ganged up on him to insist that he get plastic surgery for the ski nose. As he was essentially a comedian, was associated with comic roles, and had been seen already in those comedy shorts, and since comedians in Hollywood weren't supposed to be good looking, it's more likely that the studio people, who knew exactly what they were getting, considered his looks just right for their purposes; in fact, several executives thought him rather handsome for a comic, which would have both nonplused and pleased him had he known. Ronald Colman they already had; this Hope was signed to make 'em laugh. They were actually more optimistic about Hope than Hope was about Hope.

Billy Grady, by then casting director at MGM, who'd known Hope well in New York, was one of those who held a favorable view as to his film prospects. "I always felt he'd make it," Grady told me in 1964. "He was different, unique, very much his own man, didn't look or act like anyone else. And he was confident, alert. He'd won his spurs in the toughest arenas, Vaudeville and Broadway. I just felt he'd do fine in Hollywood. It was a matter of the right parts in the right pictures. And as I remember, he got them, too, almost from the start!" Grady on another occasion expressed regret that Hope hadn't come out in 1929 or 1930 or so, at the start of the sound period. But he added, "He wasn't as confident then — for Bob it was slow but sure — all in its own time. And then the Big Payoff!"

There's a story, sometimes denied by Bob Hope, sometimes confirmed, that he proposed that the studio pay for plastic surgery on his nose, though his wife was firmly against it. Finally the head makeup man told him that fixing the nose would take away what individuality he had. "You don't see Durante doing anything about his proboscis, do you?" was the selling point there. (Durante had already made his mark in films several years before.)

The makeup men, of course, were expert in maximizing assets and minimizing defects of any performer's features, as were, for that matter, the makeup people who'd advised Bob for his *Roberta* role on Broadway. For several years, Bob was to prove indecisive about his screen makeup, trying this, then that. In 1939 he hired his own makeup man, Charlie Berner, whose task was to concentrate on That Nose. Charlie applied shadow to each side of the nose and ran a white line down the bridge to make it look straighter. The more costly, and risky and time-consuming, elective plastic surgery, which would have meant costly weeks or months of healing while he missed picture assignments, was by that year 1939 conclusively dismissed as a choice. "And thank God it was," Paramount director Mitchell Leisen once said, discussing Hope and his cinematic mystique. "It was one of the cardinal points of Bob's individuality."

Leisen directed Hope in that first feature, *The Big Broadcast of 1938*. Hope played a radio announcer named Buzz Fielding. Leisen noticed on the first day of shooting that Bob needed toning down for

his cinema advent — at least in a major feature. The two-reeler directors had tended to let Bob have his way, more or less, but the more
demanding and experienced Leisen knew Hope needed direction and
focusing. Indeed Bob tore into his role on all cylinders, projecting the-
atre-style, overdoing every gesture and shouting all his lines, totally
heedless of the camera's intimacy and tendency to exaggerate the performer's speech and movements. Leisen guided him into underplaying,
told him to rely more on his eyes, that in a motion picture — with one's
image so much larger than life — the eyes mattered much more than
they did on stage; the eyes, Mitch emphasized, had to mirror for the
camera the emotions the actor was supposed to be feeling. Trouble was:
at first Hope took Leisen's advice much too literally, rolling his eyeballs
around and from side to side in a way that, Leisen recalled years later,
made his director wince.

Leisen might well have found it necessary to tone Bob down in
The Big Broadcast of 1938, which began shooting that fall of 1937, but it's
difficult to imagine he was ever that bad in the first place. A look at his
first two-reeler of 1934, *Going Spanish*, shows a man quite confident in
front of a camera and not at all overly theatrical. What is more likely is
that Hope was nervous and anxious to make just the right impression in
his first big Hollywood feature and tended to overdo.

Mitch Leisen was always to speak rather fondly of Hope, and
there were rumors that Leisen, a promiscuous homosexual whose
adventurings were always on the thin-ice side, had developed the same
intensely romantic crush on Hope that the former vaudeville partner,
hapless George Byrne, had. Leisen had heard from George Cukor, Billy
Haines, and others on the Gay Circuit of Byrne's unrequited love for
Hope — though in fairness to Byrne, it had been Love, while Leisen
was probably more motivated by sensual curiosity — a curiosity that, in
Hope's case was to go ungratified and certainly unreciprocated. Hope,
after all his years in show business, doubtless sensed Leisen's interest,
knew of his orientation, but kept him at bay, tactfully but firmly. Since
Leisen, it seems, never made any overt passes, all went smoothly
between them on that first film, and in fact, as Hope later admitted, he
learned a lot about cinema technique from Mitch Leisen.

Also in the cast of *The Big Broadcast of 1938* was a woman Hope
had already encountered professionally in New York, and who was to
work with him quite often in the Hollywood years to come. This was
Dorothy Lamour. Hope had met her originally when she was singing in
hotel cocktail lounges and uppercrust dining rooms in Manhattan; for a

while he'd, reportedly, nursed the same kind of crush on her that he had on his by-then wife Dolores, who had, of course, proven in the long run more receptive.

According to Dottie Lamour, it was she who was responsible for Hope's success at Paramount. She wanted to sing the big number "Thanks for the Memory," but let them give it to Hope because she knew he needed to make an impression in his first feature. She's also claimed that when the studio wanted to drop Hope's option — they had somehow, and rather inexplicably, lumped him in with Jack Benny as a type — she pleaded with them to keep him and even offered to let them cut her salary in half and give the other half to Hope.

With all due respect to Dorothy Lamour — a fine entertainer in her own right — her claims should be taken with a grain of salt. First of all, "Thanks for the Memory" is a number meant to be sung by a man and his ex-wife to one another. Lamour might have taken the song away from the actress who sang the ex-wife part, Shirley Ross, but obviously she couldn't have taken the place of Hope as the husband. And while the studio might have entertained some doubts about Hope at the beginning, after the success of *Broadcast*, which all agreed was in large part due to the Hope-Ross rendition of "Thanks for the Memory," the studio had no intention of dropping the promising Bob Hope's option. It's much more likely that Lamour's ongoing bitterness over Hope's subsequent treatment of her and his often dismissive attitude colored her perceptions and gave her a peculiarly creative memory; it would, of course, have been in her mind a fitting revenge on Hope after all those years to suggest she'd been responsible for his movie success in the first place.

Possibly Lamour might have done Hope other favors or services in his first picture and after shooting had ended — there being the usual gap between the conclusion of filming and release — and she might, after many years, have had a blurred memory as to the exact nature of those favors — but her remarks as outlined above, do have a self-serving sound nonetheless.

Hope worked with Martha Raye for the first time in *Broadcast*. Raye was not much different offscreen than on, and covered up her dismay at being unattractive — and constantly weathering that unattractiveness being referred to and exploited in films — with a brash, often abrasive manner that could set many of her fellow players on edge. One gag in the film involving Raye almost slashed the careers of Hope, Raye, and others in untimely fashion. She was to stare into a six-foot-high and 75-foot-wide mirror behind a bar, only to have it crack into a dozen

Paramount publicity photos, 1937 – 38

pieces when confronted with her ugliness. Normally such an effect would be created by planting a few prop men behind the mirror with mallets, poised to hit it at the proper moment. However, a new, ambitious effects man decided to try a special compressed air chamber behind the mirror. Instead of cracking, the mirror splintered outward in thousands of deadly quarter-inch jagged shards. Everyone, luckily, escaped injury — except for W.C. Fields, whose head was grazed and who ran off the set screaming for his lawyer.

Fields was certainly the Holy Terror of the picture. Mitchell Leisen characterized him as "the most obstinate, ornery son-of-a-bitch I ever tried to work with. Really." Fields would go wandering off for several hours, then come back soused and difficult, ignoring the script and inserting ancient routines he'd performed a hundred times before (and then charging the studio thousands of dollars for "script revisions"). Fields tended to stick to himself and his drinking, but Hope would sneak into the great comedian's dressing room from time to time for a chat. One day a man from the Community Fund charity came by to ask Fields for a donation. Fields insisted that he only gave money to the "F.E.B.F." Foundation — Fuck Everybody But Fields. Hope and Fields gradually warmed to one another, enjoying each other's ribald, often vulgar humor and trading one-liners that would never have made it onto the screen or to the stage at the Palace.

The Big Broadcast of 1938 is basically a variety show with the thinnest of plots tagged on — a race across the ocean on a new boat with a bunch of oddball characters interacting and generating mischief. While never outright hilarious, the film is consistently amusing, and boasts such highlights as W.C. Fields' retread (but still funny) routines, Martha Raye's clowning, and even Kirsten Flagstad, incongruous but majestic, singing Wagnerian opera. But the best moment is the Hope-Ross duet of "Thanks for the Memory," which is actually a very clever, rather pretty number with the couple recalling the bittersweet times before their divorce. As director Leisen put it: "The only part that was any good was 'Thanks for the Memory'" —a slightly unfair put-down of other good performances and sequences, granted Leisen's right to his opinion.

Leisen was partial to the number. He insisted to the composers that the tempo should be slowed down, and he went against custom and recorded the number while it was being performed before the camera, instead of having the actors mouth the words to pre-recorded voices and music. It made all the difference. Critics praised the number, as well as Hope and Ross, and a major film career was launched. Ross herself always praised Hope as a "consummate professional," laughing off (she liked Dolores Hope) sly columnar references to her and Hope "heating up" during production.

When Paramount picked up his option after *Broadcast*, Hope decided to hire a business manager. He was making much more money than he had on Broadway, and he found Hollywood contracts long, confusing — and boringly tedious when it came to his efforts to dissect and elucidate them. Perhaps he didn't quite trust Doc Shurr. Who better to trust, he reasoned, than a member of his own family? (Although he made no bones about not feeling that way about all of his siblings.) Bob gave his brother Jack a call in Akron where Jack was working in the retail meat business. Jack, a restless guy with creative yens, was also an aspiring songwriter and had a casual interest in show business — or perhaps secretly it wasn't all that casual. When Bob suggested he come out to Hollywood to work for him, it didn't take long for Jack to make up his mind.

Although the two would have their clashes on this and that over the years, Jack in time turned out to be the only Hope brother to successfully capitalize on Bob's showbiz career, though the others would give it, on occasion, a college try. "I think it was a matter of meshing temperaments," Billy Grady later said. "Of all his siblings, Bob got along best with Jack, perhaps because he trusted him."

Hope's next picture was *College Swing* (1938) in which he again appeared with Martha Raye. But this time it was his song duet with Raye ("Howdja Like to Love Me?") that became the show's big hit. Originally Hope's part in the film was so small it was practically a bit, but he appealed to (some said "put pressure on") the producer, Lewis Gensler, who had co-created *Ballyhoo*, Hope's earlier Broadway show, and Gensler (who later said Hope was a "Prime Persuader") agreed to expand Bob's role. It still didn't amount to that much: he had to share screen time not only with Raye, but with Betty Grable, George Burns, and Gracie Allen, the latter two champion scene-stealers. As a well-seasoned vaudevillian himself, Hope could relate well enough to the Burns & Allen duo, but as he later kidded to friends, "I spent most of the time staring at Betty Grable's legs." At that time Grable was 22, and a lusty bachelorette who liked her men and her pleasure wherever they presented themselves. Her starring career at 20th Century-Fox was a couple of years ahead of her. Her marriages, to such as child-star-grown-up Jackie Coogan and band leader Harry James, never were to compete in

With Martha Raye in *College Swing*, 1938

the publicity sweepstakes with her amours and mischief-making pro-
clivities in all areas. Grable never thought much of Hope as a sex symbol though she thought him witty. "But he always left me cold," she said
when a *Photoplay* writer asked her circa 1939 if she and Hope had
romanced. "Besides, the guy was married," she added. "Even I have my
principles, believe it or not!"

Another obstacle to Hope's "making out" among the distaff cast
and bit-players on the *College Swing* set was the ace competition presented by handsome John Payne, who was to number actress Anne
Shirley among his wives. The sight of Payne always sent Hope's morale
plummeting. A prime hunk of Thirties and Forties Hollywood, Payne
had the broad-shouldered, well-muscled, slim-hipped body and chiseled
features that Hope always envied deep down, and to Hope's chagrin it
was Payne who caught the eye of all the pretties on set.

College Swing presented Hope with a situation different from what
it had been on Broadway and even in *Broadcast*. Here, to his extreme
annoyance, he was just one of a crowd. *Broadcast* had not been released
when *College Swing* was in production, and Hope couldn't throw around
any star-weight as in the past. Hope tried to befriend Payne — that was
one way to get the girls, even if they were Payne's cast-offs, he figured
— but Payne found this odd-looking makeout artist forgettable if occasionally funny. Once during a lull in shooting, Hope knocked on
Payne's door with a card game in mind but after some rustling and
swearing behind the door Payne emerged with his shirt off and lipstick
all over his ribs and nipples and hollered at Hope to go hang out with
Edward Everett Horton.

Unconsciously Hope might have borrowed a lot — tailored to his
own style, of course — from the older comedian and one-time
Broadway character actor Horton, who had built up a big sidekick-to-
handsome-male-stars character reputation in Hollywood by 1938.
Horton's persona was that of the mischievous, fey, but totally unlikely
lover-boy. He was homely, cadaverous, rather effeminate and fussy —
and like Franklin (Fussbudget) Pangborn and Eric (Slow Burn) Blore,
was one of the homosexual stereotypes Hollywood enjoyed using for
comedy relief, leaving their basic sexual orientation strictly to the imagination of the audience, most of whom, in the Thirties, caught on soon
enough.

In 1933, in a scene in *Flying Down to Rio* in which handsome blond
Gene Raymond (later the husband of Jeanette MacDonald) stripped to
the buff in front of Horton, there was unkind laughter at every showing

because Horton mischievously let his eyes go wandering below Raymond's waistline. Pangborn was usually to figure as a department store manager or hotel clerk, fussy, fidgety, Nervous Nellie-ish. He was to provide in 1942 one of the few humorous scenes in Bette Davis's *Now, Voyager* (a heavy dramatic love story) what with his fussing and matchmaking as a den mother type tour director. Eric Blore, too, drew his share of laughs, half-appreciative, half-disdainful from audiences who found that his constant casting as valet to handsome actors and his leers and grimaces made them uneasy yet titteringly amused.

Hope was to get to know all these actors, whose private lives were objects of constant speculation (according to George Cukor they were all "gay as bitchwolves in private life") and as their counterparts had in New York, they made him nervous and jittery; at the same time he was trying with all his might to copy elements of their clever styles that would fit in with his own fey stances but not go "too far" in threatening his sexual image. Jack Benny, with whom Hope liked to compare notes, also borrowed some effeminate "fussbudgety" mannerisms from "The Big Three of Fey Funmaking" as Hedda Hopper rather pointedly termed the Horton-Blore-Pangborn combine. Hope's plan with The Three, as he told Benny, was to incorporate what he needed from them professionally without getting too close to them personally — how that worked out only Hope and The Three would know.

Hope and Horton came to know each other rather well during *College Swing* and their styles, as evidenced onscreen, did sort of rub off on each other. The main difference between their personas before the camera was that Hope's loverboy would more actively pursue the gals (even if he was always a bit surprised when they responded) while Horton's shtick was to play the essentially prissy, self-contained woman-hater who would react with sputtering shock — but (at least on screen) grudging enjoyment when the girls pursued him.

Hope adapted some of Horton's shtick in onscreen romantic matters, but never came on as woman-hater. Inwardly Hope wanted to think of himself as John Payne but was afraid he came off more as Edward Everett Horton. (Horton's reactions to handsome, muscular young Payne have never been recorded.) Hope could essay the Nervous Nellie persona as well as Horton but always added a touch of comic virility and adolescent horniness that was beyond Horton's range.

It was during the *College Swing* shooting that Hope first started the friendship with Jerry Colonna that would bring Colonna a "side-kick" spot with him at a later date, and worked for the first and only time with director Raoul Walsh, a no-nonsense meat and potatoes director who favored more masculine-oriented fare (as he did later at Warners to great effect) and who reported later that *College Swing* was one of his "more silly, insubstantial vehicles that I rushed through shooting in record time just to get the damned thing off my back." Nor was the plot any great shakes — Gracie Allen inherits a college and hires vaudevillians as teachers. Walsh, asked years later what it was like to work with Hope in what was only his second film, dismissed Hope with the curt observation, "I was hardly aware he was in the movie."

Gracie Allen was later to note that Bob felt a little down during the shooting, feeling the Burns-Allen duo was heavily overshadowing him, but the kindly Gracie said she kept reminding him, "Your time will come."

It was back to a reprise with both Martha Raye and Betty Grable in Hope's third 1938 film, *Give Me a Sailor* (which Billy Haines was to joke should have starred Franklin Pangborn, given his penchant for "sea food," as cute young sailors were termed at that, and later, times). The plot dealt with Raye and Hope deciding to honor a childhood pact to keep her sister (Grable) and his brother (Jack Whiting) apart when the last two decide to marry. Although Hope got some good reviews for *Sailor* — The New York *Daily News* critic wrote that the picture "opens new vistas for Bob Hope, who comes to the fore for well-deserved honors" — he was not too thrilled with yet another smallish role and asked Doc Shurr to feel out other studios where he might find roles more tailored to his talents. He got a good slice of humble pie rammed down his throat when Shurr was obliged to report that the competing studios were not exactly falling all over themselves to obtain his services. The best offer he got — and at only half of his $20,000 per picture fee — was a part in a Universal comedy. The producer, however, found Hope just a little too goofy and cast a more urbane and — a fighting word for Hope — virile actor in the part.

Luckily, the success of *Big Broadcast of 1938*, which had finally been released, improved Hope's fortunes — somewhat. Paramount decided it would be good business to cash in on the hit song delivered by Hope and Shirley Ross. One of their properties was a stage play by Albert Hackett and Frances Goodrich entitled *Up Pops the Devil*. They decided to name the picture for the song and entitled it (naturally) *Thanks for the Memory*. Also in the cast were such as Hedda Hopper, Laura Hope Crews, Eddie "Rochester" Anderson, an engaging black comedian, and Patricia "Honey Chile" Wilder, from the Hope New

York past and for whom Hope had also obtained a small part in *Broadcast*.

The plot had to do with newlyweds Steven and Anne Merrick (Hope and Ross); he is an aspiring novelist, she is a former model who decides to go back to work to support them while he writes. The title tune was reprised nicely, and Hoagy Carmichael and Frank "Most Happy Fella" Loesser provided a new hit tune, "Two Sleepy People." The film, for all its romantic charm and the well-paced direction by George Archainbaud, came and went rather perfunctorily, though critics praised Hope's "offhand charm" and "featherweight insouciance." (He later said the latter phrase gave him pause — had they confused him with Horton and Pangborn?)

Nor did his next two films represent much more of an advancement. Both released in 1939 (Hope turned 36 that May 29, as he noted with some semi-hysterical alarm), *Never Say Die* and *Some Like It Hot* (the first *Some Like It Hot* — nothing to do with Monroe-Lemmon-Curtis) were relatively trivial offerings. *Some Like It Hot* was to win further obscurity decades later when it was retitled *Rhythm Romance* for TV re-runs after the Monroe 1959 film stole all the thunder. *Never Say Die*, directed by Elliott Nugent, a stage veteran, employed the "comic" (so the screenwriters thought) device of someone, in this case John Kidley (Hope) mistakenly believing he has only a short time to live, with a resultant loosening of inhibitions. (Guess in what direction.) As an odd-ball millionaire, Hope runs from husband-hungry Gale Sondergaard (miscast) straight to Martha Raye, an oilman's daughter fated to marry a prince (Alan Mowbray at his most pompous and affected) but who really loves her dopey sweetheart Andy Devine. Monty Woolley (two years before his hit in *The Man Who Came to Dinner* at Warners) was also in the cast.

Andy Devine was the bizarre comic actor with the most unique voice in Hollywood — it rasped and razored and groaned away like sandpaper on glass. Andy had been used, amazingly, for a sort of comic relief in the Norma Shearer-Leslie Howard MGM production of *Romeo and Juliet* in 1936 and surprisingly took his Shakespeare in stride. His having a small part in *Never Say Die* was to prove useful to Hope. When Hope and Andy wanted to take off from shooting to play golf on sunny days, Andy would go to work on Martha Raye, telling her she was being shamefully overworked and exploited by the producers and ought to slow down for her health's sake. After this brainwashing from Devine, Raye would pull a faint or claim a major indisposition, shooting would shut down temporarily, and off golfing the boys would go.

Hope found it interesting — and profitable — to compare the respective thespian styles of Mowbray, Devine, and Woolley while shooting *Never Say Die*. Andy was an original, a law unto himself, but Mowbray's high-falutin' affectations (Mowbray was not gay but many thought he was), Woolley's grumpy harrumphing, and for that matter the slithering silkiness of Gale Sondergaard, all got incorporated into Hope's comic style later, though in subtle, highly overlayered forms.

As for his other film, *Some Like It Hot*, based on a play co-authored by Ben Hecht (who would have a bitter run-in with Hope a decade and a half later) and Gene Fowler, Hope took the opportunity to draft his chief radio gag writer Wilkie Mahoney to punch up Lewis Foster's screenplay (reportedly much to Foster's resentment). Hope also added many lines for himself, courtesy of Mahoney, which didn't sit well with the other cast members. This time around, however, Hope was the undoubted star of the shenanigans. No Martha Raye or Burns and Allen to steal the spotlight, only obliging and friendly Shirley Ross and witty Una Merkel, both of whose styles meshed with his own while allowing him the edge. Hope, already bossing his sets, and with director George Archainbaud sympathetic to his aims, maintained later that it was time to protect his interests and stake out his gains.

In this film Hope is Nicky Nelson, who runs an amusement parlor on a boardwalk and hires Gene Krupa and his band to publicize his show. Shirley Ross, an easygoing gal who never quite emerged from Hope's aggressive shadow to make it on her own, gave pleasing romantic foil thesping, and Una Merkel, always amusing over at MGM as sidekick for such as Joan Crawford and Jean Harlow, was given to understand that all the mugging and clowning was to be left to Hope. Handsome Richard Denning, in his way, posed as much a threat as Bodyboy John Payne had, but Hope saw to it that Denning's opportunities to show him up in romantic posturing were kept strictly limited and muted. Denning was later to say of Hope, in a masterpiece of euphemistic understatement, that "One always knew who was running the show in a Bob Hope picture." (Hope was always to opine that *Some Like It Hot* was his all-time worst picture, but he was to sink lower than that when the Sixties came along.)

Hope took a step upward with his next picture, *The Cat and the Canary*, released in November 1939. This was an updated spoof of the "old dark house"-style film of the silent era. *The Cat and the Canary* actually began life as a suspense play by John Willard; in the 1939 Hope version, directed by Elliot Nugent, most of the scares were replaced by giggles, as Hope wanders around a spooky old mansion where dead bodies keep dropping around him and a beautiful heiress, played by Paulette Goddard, shows up to provide a form of "love interest." The murders are precipitated by the reading of a will leaving a fortune to Goddard.

The film was well received and extremely successful. It has been said that *The Cat and the Canary* represented the first time Hope synthesized all he'd learned from vaudeville, Broadway, and his early Hollywood experiences, and creating — with the help of Walter De Leon's and Lynn Starling's screenplay — the essential characterization he was to display in most of the Hope movies that followed: the cowardly "hero" who meets his fears head on with a bold, silly quip. This of course was the same direction his radio writers were pushing him in. Hope by this time had recognized that this persona would really work for him and his style of comedy. Some who knew him, like director Elliott Nugent, were later to opine that it was ironic in the extreme that such a ruthless, egotistical, aggressive person as Hope would choose as a permanent, definitive screen characterization something essentially so dorky and self-effacing. The fact that it worked as well as it did suggests that Hope was not only a better actor potentially than he ever allowed himself to be, but by 36 had arrived at a realistic assessment of the extent, and limits, of the characterization he'd have to essay to win maximum screen success.

John Beal, then 30, acted with Bob in *The Cat and the Canary*, and has provided a good assessment of Hope as he knew him then: "Nobody gives Bob credit for the extraordinary discipline and precision of his style. It was a pleasure to play with Bob because he was always on top of things, and moreover, always there for his fellow actors. I kept hearing stories of his upstaging people and always trying to hog the action but I never found him that way. He knew ensemble playing backwards and forwards and actually inspired the people acting with him in his scenes to give their best — and when they did, he saw to it that they got their minute or more in the sun." Asked about Hope's alleged romancings with pretty co-stars and bit players, Beal replied, "I knew nothing of that side of him. I knew him as a consummate professional."

Paulette Goddard, one of the many lovely ladies who costarred with Hope, was a feisty beauty with a fascinating romantic history and a series of marriages to such as Charlie Chaplin, actor Burgess Meredith, and the novelist Erich Maria Remarque. She was high-spirited, a "fun" gal, and a match for Hope when it came to ego. Nor did she mince words in speaking of him. "God, he thought he was The Deity's gift to women, but he amused them more than he excited them. I for one never thought he had much sex appeal or whatever it was he thought he had. He did try to upstage me; he never got away with it. My scenes with him were fifty-fifty exposure. I saw to that. Sure he'd have liked to get me in bed, but he left me cold, never had a chance in hell."

The New York Times ran an excellent analysis of Hope's comic style in Frank Nugent's 1939 review of *The Cat and the Canary*:

> " . . . the lights dim and an eerie wail rises when the hopeful legatees assemble in the manse in the bayous for the reading of Uncle Cyrus's will. Over them all broods Bob Hope, with a chin like a forehead and a gag line for every occasion. Some of his lines are good ("I'm so scared even my goose pimples have goose pimples") and some are bad ("Let's drink Scotch and make wry faces") but good and bad profit alike from the drollery of Mr. Hope's comic style. It is a style so perfidious we think it should be exposed for the fraud it is. Mr. Hope's little trick is to deliver his jests timidly, forlornly, with the air of a man who sees no good in them. When they are terrible, as frequently they are, he can retreat in good order, with an 'I told you so!' expression. When they click, he can cut a little caper and pretend he is surprised and delighted, too. It's not cricket, but it is fun."

Hope would always credit *The Cat and the Canary* as being the film that really metamorphosed him into a bona fide movie star. Paramount quickly readied a follow-up (Hope was to make his first "Road" movie with Bing Crosby in between) entitled *The Ghost Breakers* (1940). This was another comedy version of an old thriller filmed at least twice in the silent era.

In *Ghost Breakers* Hope had yet another filmic run in with Paulette Goddard, who still maintained to friends that he was tops in comedy but zilch as romantic fodder (not that she ever cared to find out) and the supporting cast included handsome Richard Carlson (who in this new era of Hope Self-Satisfaction and Self-Confidence posed no threat to

Ghost Breakers, 1940

Bob's romantic self image or so Hope maintained), Anthony Quinn (who later said that Bob was "a hoot and a howl" — whatever that meant), and Paul Fix, the saturnine character actor whose views on Hope are not on record. The director was George Marshall, who was working with Hope for the first time on this film but would be reteamed with him often over the decades.

Marshall was always lavish in his praise of Hope's "professionalism, impeccable timing, wonderful story sense, adaptability, superior sense of humor. Maybe other directors had problems with him — a lot of that is chemistry and mutual interests, having enough in common creatively, not as personal as people make it out to be — but I always found him wonderful to work with." He added, "We had our run-ins at times — what two people all tensed up over getting a picture out don't — but my memories of him are happy, and I still laugh remembering the goofy times we had and Bob's ability to make light even of heavy situations — off screen as well as on."

Paulette Goddard gave Hope a dressing-down one time when he pulled a stunt she thought way out of line. Without leave, he borrowed her little motor scooter — Paulette loved to use it to show off her wonderful legs in tight-fitting shorts — and wound up falling down hard on the pavement at 35 miles an hour, skinning his knees and twisting both his ankles. The next scene required him to walk down a flight of stairs, but he couldn't make it. When Bob tripped and fell, still shaky from the scooter accident, Marshall had to cancel shooting for the rest of the day. An annoyed and exasperated Paulette exited the set shouting over her shoulder at Hope, "See what your damned show-off stunts cost the studio!"

Ghost Breakers does not hold up especially well all these years later. The plot has to do with Hope and Goddard traveling to Cuba to investigate her so-called "haunted" castle. Although the movie promises to be fun at first, it starts to die a slow painful death after about 45 minutes, with even the "eerie" castle scenes failing to perk up the proceedings. George Marshall's direction is largely on furlough here — the material must have defeated him — and Walter De Leon's dated script doesn't contain enough chills or laughter for a half-hour sitcom, let alone an 82-minute feature. The one who comes off to best advantage is the amusing Willie Best as Hope's black pal and employee.

But parodies of old silent thrillers were not all that Hope was pulling out of his hat by 1940. It was time for him to hit the road with Bing.

CHAPTER TWELVE

SKI SNOOT AND MATTRESS HIP

B ob Hope was 29 and Bing Crosby a year younger when they first met in 1932. They bumped into each other on the street near the actor's hangout called The New York Friars Club and spent some time trading stories and comparing notes on their careers. Eight weeks later they were on the same bill at the Capitol Theatre.

Bing was better known than Bob at the time. He had a hit record, "I Surrender Dear," which he had recorded after leaving the Paul Whiteman band, and then his own group, The Rhythm Boys, to go solo. He had a national radio show in 1932 and had become a film star at 28 with his major role in *The Big Broadcast of 1932*. (Hope's *Broadcast* film was six years in the future.) Hope later described Crosby on the occasion of that first meeting as being "extremely cordial" to him.

It was a year before Prohibition ended and during their run at the Capitol Bing and Bob would repair to a speakeasy called O'Reilly's Bar and hoist a few while they traded jokes and stories, and eventually came up with the idea of teaming up on stage. It seemed like a natural.

They'd do variations on old vaudeville routines such as one bit where they'd play two people — different kinds of people — meeting each other on the street. First they were farmers. Hope would point his thumbs down while Crosby "milked" them. Then they were politicians. As soon as they finished shaking hands they'd pick each other's pockets. And so on.

Their "friendly enemy" mutual putdown shtick basically began at the Capitol. But they were only amiable co-workers at this time; they saw little of each other socially in the years between the end of their Capitol run in 1932 and Hope's 1937 relocation to Hollywood. Indeed, they never really socialized much together — aside from playing golf — through all their long association.

Their acquaintance was renewed circa 1939 when Bing invited Bob to join him in doing some of their old Capitol routines at the opening night of the Del Mar racetrack, which Bing operated with Pat O'Brien. Entertainment would be put on for all the Hollywood guests. Bob and Bing were a hit with the audience, among whom was Paramount's production chief, Bill LeBaron. It was he who got the idea of putting the two in a movie together.

The property which eventually became *The Road to Singapore* began life as a serious drama entitled *The Road to Mandalay*. Two writers under contract to Paramount did a complete rewrite, changing it into a comedy and tailoring it for the talents of George Burns and Gracie Allen. When that didn't work out, more changes were made and the studio tried to get Jack Oakie and Fred MacMurray to team up. Both were unavailable at the time, so the project was dusted off once more and handed to Hope and Crosby. The title was changed because "Singapore" sounded more dangerous and exotic than "Mandalay."

By this time Hope and Crosby had both guest-starred on each other's radio shows and the phony comical "feud" that had started at the Capitol continued on the radio and made its way full-grown onto the movie screen. "It was a thing we fell into," Crosby said. "It grew out of the fact that when we appeared on each other's radio programs and in the Road pictures, it seemed easier for our writers to write abusive dialogue than any other kind."

To round out the cast and provide the curves, Dorothy Lamour was also enlisted. She found working on *Singapore* a sometimes frustrating experience. She'd dutifully study all her lines the night before, only to arrive on the set and find the boys mouthing completely different dialogue. Helplessly but valiantly, she'd try to work in a gag edgewise, to no avail. Minutes would go by while the only words tossed about were those of Hope and Crosby insulting each other, maneuvering back and forth in their cool, bantering manner. While Dorothy and the scriptwriters fumed, director Victor Schertzinger would simply stand there and keep the camera rolling.

Schertzinger's assistants would get ready to shoot the whole scene over in medium shots or closeups, but Schertzinger would tell them not to bother, that the master shot was okay. The director, who could be painstaking when he cared to be with other pictures and other stars, was so impressed with the way the boys worked together that he never wanted to change a thing and normally used the first take.

This did not sit well with screenwriters Don Hartman and Frank Butler. For years both Hope and Crosby were to perpetuate the canard that they ad-libbed on the set, throwing in gag after gag, insult after insult, straight off the cuff. Actually they brought in their own radio gag writers, as well as ex-vaudevillian Barney Dean, to "spice up" the lines and give them more interplay. Hope would even try to undercut Bing by telling his writers to go to Crosby and offer him a comeback for one of Hope's insults. Hope would, of course, already know what Bing was going to say in response to his jab and would say it before Bing could, or come up with something to top it.

In any case, Hope and Crosby never ad-libbed; every line they uttered was the product of some writer, be it the Paramount contract men or one of Hope's or Crosby's gagsters. Schertzinger didn't concern himself with what particular gags the boys worked up or who wrote them; he just knew that whatever they were doing it worked, so he gave them a free hand.

Lamour found herself the victim of cheap practical jokes as well as script manipulations. In one scene she was swathed in special imitation suds cooked up by the prop department (real suds would have melted under the hot lights) for a washtub sequence. First Hope grabbed some of the "suds" and threw them at Bing and Dorothy during their lunchbreak. Bing grabbed some himself and both men teamed up against Lamour. Finally, Lamour just grabbed the biggest can of suds she could find, chased the two men into the commissary, and dumped all its wet messy contents over their heads. Schertzinger was not pleased because after lunch shooting had to be delayed because the three stars' hair and clothing needed time to dry.

Hope had himself a sadistic field day making fun of all the preparations Crosby put himself through before facing the camera. First he'd put on pancake makeup to keep his skin appearing smooth and dry, but it itched terribly and began to flake after a while, causing Bing to screw up his face in comical grimaces whenever the camera was turned elsewhere. Crosby was also afflicted with protruding ears and these had to be glued back against his head with spirit gum or adhesive. By far the worst mortification was the hairpiece or "scalp dolly" Crosby had to wear to cover up a noticeable bald spot and a receding hairline. Hope was most merciless in his teasing of Crosby when it came to his toupee, and on and off screen he took to referring to Bing as "Skinhead." Bing also had a rear section that tended to be flabby; for this Bob dreamed up "Mattress Hip."

Hope was jealous of the fact that Crosby was a legitimate romantic idol while he was not. Although the scene in Crosby's 1932 *Broadcast* film when the women drop what they're doing to run after Bing for kisses and autographs and literally sweep him into a building and up several stories was played for laughs, Bing was considered genuinely attractive to women and had them swooning in the aisles. When women, however, ran after Hope in his movies, it was never more than a farcical situation. Crosby was better looking and slimmer and at least appeared to be taller than Hope, and Hope could never quite forgive him for it. There was always an edge to his wisecracks, and though Bing usually took it graciously, or appeared to, and gave as good as he got, there were times when he almost lost his temper.

Eventually he'd think of a way to get vicious revenge on Hope for the latter's cutting remarks. Bob accordingly learned a reluctant, wary respect for Bing. The two never really developed a close, warm friendship offscreen, chiefly because of Hope's envy and the nastiness it engendered, nastiness he would cover up with a smile and a quip — as if to say, "I'm only kidding so don't be offended." Nonetheless this aspect of the Hope-Crosby interplay was very real and sharp.

Crosby hated wearing his "skull dolly" so much that he always preferred to wear a hat on screen whenever he could get away with it. This phobia reached ridiculous lengths in *Road to Singapore* during a sequence when the two men hit the sack for some shut-eye. Hope fully expected them to remove their hats once they were in bed, but Bing wouldn't allow it. Schertzinger insisted they take off the hats, but again Bing flatly refused. The director had to bring in producer Harlan Thompson to talk sense to Bing, but when the confab was over it only proved who was boss: Bing. The hats stayed on.

There was more in contention between the boys than Bing's hairpiece and their share of the lines. They even fought over camera angles and closeups, and between the two of them directed the picture more than Schertzinger did. Dorothy Lamour wasn't the only one to find shooting on *Singapore* a trial. The great character actor Charles Coburn lost patience with the antics of the twosome and almost walked off the picture. "They're rampant egomaniacs!" Coburn shouted at anyone within hearing distance, and it took the combined efforts of producer Thompson and director Schertzinger to keep him calmed down. Anthony Quinn was again on hand for a Hope picture, and according to character actor Pierre Watkin (a staple of many a film with his solid playing) both Hope and Crosby started envying Quinn's handsome looks and lithe body (he was then 33) and subtly put him down at every turn. "Quinn almost punched them out, and well he should have," Watkin reported.

The "plot" of *Singapore*, such as it is, has Hope and Crosby on a woman-hating kick — tired as they are of what they allege are marriage maneuverings and power connivings — and they decide to live together without distaff company in a tropical bachelor hut — until Lamour comes along and sets them off against each other.

The film was released in March 1940, and one critic thought Lamour appealing as the native girl but felt Charles Coburn's talents were criminally wasted — as well they were. Seen today, *Road to Singapore* is a featherweight exercise with few real laughs, albeit an amiable atmosphere. Surprisingly, it did quite well at the box office. Plans for a sequel were quickly formulated.

That was *The Road to Zanzibar*, released in the spring of 1941. Again the basis for the second Road film was a serious script originally called "Find Colonel Fawcett." It was gagged up and tailored for Hope and Crosby. The original screenplay dealt with two adventurers traveling through the jungles of Madagascar. Unfortunately Paramount executives felt it bore too many similarities to an earlier film with Spencer Tracy that 20th Century-Fox had released under the title *Stanley and Livingstone*, and it had to be scrapped — at least in its original form. The new version had Hope and Crosby playing sideshow nitwits who travel around Africa, encounter con gals Dorothy Lamour and Una Merkel, and wind up paying for the girls' safari ostensibly aimed at finding a "missing father." The Merkel-Lamour combo have quite a racket going: Lamour joins a slave auction block while partner Merkel finds a sucker who'll bid for her to keep her out of the hands of the heartless slave traders. Merkel and Lamour had juicy roles here and made the most of them, and the boys found themselves with more competition on their hands than usual.

Paramount's publicity flacks went into overdrive on *Zanzibar*. Press releases had Leroy Prinz, the studio dance director, scouring Africa for months for authentic tribal costumes and boasting that "the original conga as danced in the heart of Darkest Africa is shown in one sequence."

Some comedy that never made the screen had to do with the slave auction scene which employed over three hundred black extras, not all of whom were dark enough and hence had to be made up as "blacker" men. Fifteen extra makeup men had to put on the dark makeup themselves to prove to the extras that it was a simple greasepaint that wouldn't provide a permanent stain or make their faces break out. Paramount prop men needed so many plants for the jungle scenes that they ran

Una Merkel, Dorothy Lamour, Bing Crosby, and Hope in
The Road to Zanzibar, 1941

through their stock in the backlot greenhouses and had to import
greenery from as far away as Arizona.

Among the *Zanzibar* supporting cast were Iris Adrian, as blowsy
and sensual as ever; Eric Blore, doing his usual sly homosexual shtick;
and sexy Joan Marsh. Iris Adrian, who appeared in several Hope films,
was widely reported at the time to be having "a thing going" with Hope,
denied by Ski-nose along, as Hedda Hopper wrote "he doth protest too
much" lines. Certainly there was genuine fondness between the two,
and years later when she was older and work was scarce, Hope got her
a part in *The Paleface*. Adrian's type was of a kind that had appealed to
Hope in his 1920's barnstorming period: frankly sensual, direct, open.

Eric Blore found Hope's egomania and often cruel offscreen wisecracks (obviously the hapless Blore was the latest threat to Hope's "all-man" self-concept) distinctly unamusing. Hope enjoyed making fun of Blore's upper-crust, too-too British mincing mannerisms, but he was to get a dose of his own medicine before long.

Producer Paul Jones noted that Hope received most of his fan mail from women — which Hope made sure Bing and everyone else knew about — and decided that director Victor Schertzinger (on his second Road film with the boys) should film two endings: in one Bing gets Lamour at the end, and in the other Bob makes off with the girl. Reportedly, the sneak preview audience made the final decision on which would claim the lady's hand. The verdict was foreordained, and Paramount Publicity made the most of it: the fans dictated that Hope was never to get the girl. But never.

Like *Singapore*, the *Zanzibar* road movie is a perfectly amiable concoction, with some very funny sequences (the best has natives mistaking Bob and Bing for gods) but frequently lapses into the rudimentarily silly and is a distinctly minor item in their pantheon. Although the boys play together with polished professionalism, Crosby comes off as so relaxed and laid back that he hardly seems to be giving a performance. Offscreen, in spite of his often tyrannical and indeed downright brutal nature in his domestic life (as son Gary was later to describe in an autobiography) Bing was indeed more relaxed than the perpetually live-wired and high-strung and impatiently and nakedly ambitious Hope. This essential difference in their natures also translated into different reactions to jealousy, insecurities of various kinds, and attacks of a personal nature. Hope's approach was to jab away with wisecracks until one hit home. Bing would assess the situation, ponder it a while, then strike home straight and true with what he knew to be the cruelest jibe he could come up with. With Hope, in one area there was no contest, as Bing well knew — what Hope was most insecure about was his manhood.

Certainly this essential difference in their respective natures transferred with amazing veracity to the motion picture screen.

This combative interplay went on and on, in film after film, to the boys' relish, and audience delight. Whenever Hope's remarks about Crosby's gradually thickening waistline and thinning air cut too deep (which was more often than not: Crosby was fully aware that a singing idol and romantic lead could reach what he called "flaw-ceiling" and phfft went his career) Crosby, and this was offscreen, would make a quiet, almost deceptively polite, rejoinder about Hope's lack of natural children. The implication — put across ever so softly and obliquely — was that if Hope were a real man he would never have had to adopt kids. He'd make sure that his sons made their often noisy and rowdy presences known to Bob. During even rowdier offscreen battles, Crosby, pushed too far and for too long, would come right out with it and throw any gay rumors he'd ever heard about Bob right in his face. Bing would affect a limp-wristed posture and accuse Hope of exaggerating — if not all-out fabricating — his distaff conquests. He also never let Hope forget that Der Bingle was the one women — many, many women — found attractive.

They reportedly almost came to blows one day when Bing said he felt he should give the Road pictures a rest and suggested that Bob "carry on" with a *Road to Greenwich Village* film in which he'd have sole star billing as a rooming house owner in the (even in 1941) rumored homosexual ghetto of New York City, with his colorful tenants, all running in and out to get "things" fixed and be comforted with coffee and consolation. (Obviously a 1941 variation on the *Tea and Sympathy* play title of 1953 — or possibly Robert Anderson heard of the "C & C" and switched it to "T & S" twelve years later.) Anyway, the Greenwich Village plot for Bob, as Bing concocted it, would have Edward Everett Horton begging to have his faucet fixed, Eric Blore needing attention for a burst pipe, Franklin Pangborn asking Bob to help him hang up frilly curtains, and Grady Sutton (another "gay" stereotype actor) threatening suicide in the basement after being deserted by his boyfriend. And instead of Lamour or Adrian, Bob would wind up with Alan Mowbray, who'd pay his rent, and cook and knit for him.

Jerry Asher, a regular fan-magazine contributor during the Fifties, used to tell the story of the day Bob and Bing began fighting while traveling in a golf cart from the course to the clubhouse after a close game. The two began shouting at each other, then Bob began flailing out violently with his hands until Bing had no recourse but to jump out of the cart and make his way to the clubhouse on foot. An angry Hope avoided Crosby for the rest of the afternoon. When Bing was asked by fellow golf enthusiasts over drinks what in hell he'd done to get Hope so mad at him, Bing laughed and chortled, "I called him a fag." He later added nonchalantly that he'd only been kidding and that Hope had "as always, overreacted." Himself a dyed-in-the-wool Homophobe of the first order, Crosby had a habit of calling anyone he didn't like or who irritated him a "faggot" or a "queer." Lindsay Crouse, Bing's youngest son by his first wife, Dixie, once related that when Bing caught him masturbating one time, he yelled, "That's bad enough, but if I ever find out you're a fag I'll goddamn *kill* you!"

On another occasion, in the Fifties, Crosby had the audacity to wax judgmental about the way Hope treated and/or ignored his adoptive children. Crosby was himself hardly an exemplary father — his son Gary was to give horrendous details of what amounted to rampant child abuse on Crosby's part in his book *Going My Own Way*. Gary was steadily and relentlessly beaten with great severity until at one point in his late teens he told his dad to stop — or else! Always something of a physical coward (the very trait he always tried to lay on Hope) Bing stopped. When Bing proffered his unwanted child-rearing advice to Bob, Hope reacted less to Bing's hypocrisy than to the fact that anyone — anyone at all — should have the temerity to tell him how to deal with his own children. When Crosby would taunt "How can you do that to your kids?" Hope's standard rejoinder would be, "But they're not my kids, remember?"

Actually Crosby was on thin ice tormenting Hope about homosexuality when he himself had been the subject of many rumors that he'd been the "kept boy" of prominent homosexuals in the music field during his leaner days in the Twenties. Writer-publicist Jim Reid told me back in the Sixties that he felt Bing's tendency to beat his sons gave reason to believe he was exorcising some latent homosexual sado-masochism in his nature.

Gary Crosby and others maintained that Hope and Crosby rarely saw each other socially more than two or three times a year. As the two didn't really like each other all that much — certainly not deep down where it counted — any more than that would probably have resulted in homicidal assault. Occasionally others got Bing's goat — where it hurt most. Gay director Mitchell Leisen once circulated, after Bing's first wife Dixie's death, the story that Dixie had left her sons independent trust funds "to keep them out of their father's power and free from his encroachments" — "encroachments" being one of the code words in the story. When Bing heard this, he broke down Leisen's door and beat him up within an inch of his life, shouting every homosexual epithet he could think of.

Sometimes the Hope-Crosby twosome got into arguments over more trivial matters — although anything to do with one of Bing's movies might not be considered "trivial" by Hope. In 1944, when Bing played a priest in *Going My Way*, for which he won an Oscar ("one of my dad's more hypocritical impersonations," Lindsay Crosby later called it), Hope wanted Crosby to appear as a priest for a cameo in Hope's latest movie. Crosby rejected the situation as being in extremely poor taste. ("It was in the Crosby period when he was more Catholic than the Pope," as Helen Ferguson the publicist put it.) In his autobiography, Crosby blamed the idea for the bit on "some joker at Paramount" but he'd been perfectly aware that it had been Hope's idea. Since Hope had always had a more irreverent sense of humor (more of any kind of sense of humor than Bing, in fact) he felt Crosby's attitude was ridiculous. Hope and others took honest glee in hearing the story from impish, mischievous Barry Fitzgerald (Bing's co-star in *Going My Way*) that Bing would come to the set sporting a hard-on in what Barry termed "his priest pants." "They're too tight, Bing — get a bigger size," Barry told him, but Bing primly retorted, "Priests' pants are never too tight!"

On one occasion Bing was the guest star on a Hope radio show, performed before a live Hollywood audience. They were supposed to do a skit together, after which Bob would bid him a verbal adieu, thanking him for appearing, and Bing would walk off the stage while Bob carried on. Instead Bob launched right into his monologue once the skit was over. There was no graceful way Bing could leave the stage while Bob was performing, so he just stood there in the spotlight with his arms folded, waiting for Bob to finish. Crosby, of course, had heard Hope's routines over and over, and didn't crack a single smile — even a pale one — during the entire performance.

Backstage Hope screamed at Crosby in manic rage. Hope's usual method of showing irritation at somebody was to put him down via nasty wisecracks; Crosby had never seen Hope lose control in public. Right in front of the other actors, the technicians, the sponsors' representatives, anybody and everybody, Hope whipped Crosby's ass bloody for just standing there and not laughing at his jokes while he did his act. "Why did you just stand there like a fuckin' corpse?" Hope hollered. Privately incensed at Hope's public raging, Crosby professed later to be amused by it. "Hope is so intense," he'd say later. "Everything has to be perfect when he's on. He's all wrapped up in what he's doing," adding, "I can't be like that. Life is too short."

Bing loved to tell of the time he and Bob were playing in a golf tournament in Cleveland before approximately 100,000 people. Also playing were the governor, Frank Lausche, and golf pro Harry Picard. Both Bob and Bing were wearing long silk Hawaiian shirts that were not supposed to be tucked into trousers, and subsequently were flapping about in the breeze.

A man hidden in the crowd kept yelling out wisecracks, mostly about the pretty Hawaiian shirts. Bob drew the brunt of the sallies. Finally on the sixteenth tee Hope was just about to swing when this heckler yelled out, "Hey, Bob, your slip is showing!"

Even the gag writers occasionally risked rubbing Hope's ego raw by picking up on the "gay" stuff (in those days "queer" was a more popular term) Crosby taunted Hope with. In one radio interchange, Hope says to Crosby, "Why do we fight? You know I really like you." Crosby's reply: "Only when you've been on Army bases too long."

Crosby also got annoyed by what he referred to as Hope's "heavy-handed jesting about my being a human Fort Knox." Crosby knew that in actuality Hope was wealthier than he was (for which Hope partly had Crosby to thank). Yet when a profile in *Time* magazine suggested strongly that Hope was a tightwad, Crosby wrote an angry letter to the magazine declaring that anyone (like Hope) who forfeited large personal appearance fees by doing at least two benefits a week could hardly be called cheap. The editors conceded the point but couldn't help adding mischievously that "Bob Hope from time to time has been known to put undue pressure on a nickel."

Crosby on occasion would do generous things for Hope. He once flew from Chicago to South Bend, Illinois, to give him a birthday cake on stage at a naval installation. But he seems to have had ulterior motives in his public defenses of Hope. In the case of *Time*, Crosby undoubtedly saw any attack on Hope's wealth as an attack on his own. If, after all, a magazine could claim that Hope was a wealthy tightwad, what would stop them from coming after Crosby next? Crosby's philanthropy (such as it was) was not anywhere near as well-documented as Bob's was. "I don't use my good works to get publicity like he does — he'll do anything for attention," Bing once cracked.

Bing had contributed to Bob's wealth (Bob's camp claimed it was the other way around) via their many business ventures in common. Along with a Texas golf buddy, Monty Moncrief, the two were partners in certain oil land leases, which in time were to greatly increase their personal fortunes; in fact, they provided Hope with the initial capital he needed for other monetary adventurings. To rescue some of their considerable incomes from the jaws of the IRS, both formed their own corporations early in the game: Hope Enterprises and The Crosby Company.

Hope also aroused Crosby's ire over a venture that Hope was, at first, not a part of: The Bing-Lin race horse stable. Hope's gag writers, knowing where and by whom their bread was buttered, came up with a whole line of gags about the "nags" Hope was breeding and running. Bing's partner, Lin Howard, who took great pride in their stable, deeply resented the ridicule. He reasoned that he and Bing would never sell the colts they were raising if Hope's radio gags turned their horses into national jokes. Crosby also took note of the fact that Hope used no material on the subject when Bing-Lin won a race. But gradually the racehorse venture flourished, despite Hope's jealous efforts to sabotage it via the radio waves. To Bob's chagrin, Bing's horses were winning a good part of the time. Soon Bing-Lin was operating a new race track at Del Mar.

"Ski Snoot" and "Mattress Hip," as Bob and Bing dubbed each other, was always to contain a strange and inherent love-hate relationship. Their work together — vaudeville, radio, movies — and their financial alliances formed in time an unbreakable bond that substituted for any genuine affection feeling or loyalty but was, in its way, intense and pervasive.

Sometimes Demon Sentiment — more theatrical than deeply felt, in the opinion of Jim Reid and other onlookers — would out, as when Bing, according to Bob, at the funeral of Bing's first wife Dixie, who'd died a lingering cancer death, "threw himself into my arms and sobbed," adding, "We were two guys hugging each other and for that minute [Bing] couldn't go on." Obviously the strain of this highly emotional moment had created an artificial closeness in the two men: both had known one another for decades by that time, had been through a lot together — but it was not true closeness. A cold man with few real friends, a man who alienated his children, it was not as unnatural as it may at the time have seemed for Crosby to turn to Hope — his Road buddy — for a few moments of comfort.

But the distance between them was in a genuine sense quite vast, and beyond bridging — if for that matter it had ever been. There might have been a certain grudging affection and fondness — tender words rendered harsh in their inner and outer parlance — and shared memories, but never a true, loving friendship. There was, always, too much bitterness, resentment, mutual dislike — even if buried beneath the surface, spurting out at odd moments — for that.

Crosby was never to accompany Hope on any of his jaunts overseas. When Hope was given a tribute by the Friars Club, Crosby didn't even bother to appear. When Bing was asked why he had missed the dinner honoring his sometime co-star and alleged "best buddy," he merely snapped, "I wasn't hungry."

In truth, at moments like that, Crosby was articulating what he really felt about Bob Hope, what Hope had made him feel about Hope, in all those forty-five years from 1932 to 1977, the year Crosby died.

The jokes, the taunts, the chewing-outs, the desperate, sheer intensity of Hope's jealousy and ambition, the blood-drawing sallies about homosexuality, a subject both men felt nervous about for different reasons, took their toll in the final analysis. Bob and Bing were co-workers, comrades of a sort, associates in business, golf partners, many things. But never really friends. It was not surprising for larger reasons.

For Bob Hope let few people get too close.

CHAPTER THIRTEEN

SPECIMEN DAYS

When Bob and Dolores went over to England on the Normandie in 1939, the Captain asked Bob if he'd entertain at a ship's concert for the Seaman's Fund, but Hope was only interested in resting and relaxing; performing for free (otherwise than at benefits) was the last thing on his mind now that he was a star. Edward G. Robinson was another passenger, and looked up Hope to have a talk with him once he found out from the captain that Hope had refused. "I think it would be a nice thing to do," Robinson said pointedly. Later Robinson, who had the gift of kidding himself and enjoying it, remarked that the passengers would much rather hear Hope's jokes than listen to Robinson making with the rat-a-tat-tat gangster talk and cracking wise a la *Little Caesar*, which he'd been prepared to do if Hope held out.

While they were traveling through Europe, World War II grew more menacingly imminent, and American tourists reversed course for America. Bob and Dolores hastily crossed the Channel from Paris to London and boarded the *Queen Mary* at Southampton, along with many others anxious to get back to America before real hell broke loose. The boat was so overcrowded that some passengers had to sleep in the hallways. It was to be the famous ship's last civilian voyage until after the war; meanwhile it was to be converted to military transport and other war use.

"Balloon barges were up, England was on the alert," Dolores recalled. "'They'll work it out,' Bob kept saying. 'There won't be a war, there can't be.' He'd grown up in a world that had seen the folly of war and he never thought men would fight on such a scale ever again. Then in mid-ocean we were blacked out and loudspeakers blared forth the news."

The scenes in the ship's salon were sobering. Men and women, many of them British, openly wept or sat glumly in total silence, absorbed with baleful thoughts and fatal prophesies. Hope had been scheduled to do another act for the passengers, but didn't think anyone that night would be in the mood for laughter. This time, Harry Warner of Warner Bros., who'd just had lunch with the captain, sought out Hope to tell him that the captain felt it would be a good idea to go ahead with the entertainment anyway. A lot of these people, he stressed, could use some cheering up. Hope at first talked seriously about the terrible new war looming, but then went into light gear, replete with gags about the overcrowding on ship, and whipping up new lyrics to "Thanks for the Memory," which in one short year had become his immediately recognizable trademark. The best gag had to do, to wild audience amusement, with the exclusive cabin Hope had been assigned — it had "Gentlemen" on the door.

But it was to be in early 1941 — a year and a half later — that Albert "Cappy" Capstaff, the producer of Hope's radio show, came up with the idea of broadcasting live from army bases. At first Hope couldn't understand why they just didn't bring servicemen to the regular studios, but Capstaff emphasized that the sheer numbers involved — at least a thousand at each base, often much more — made this prohibitive. Hope's first show that year — the year the United States actually entered the War — was for the Army Air Force at March Field in Riverside, California — many similar shows followed at various service locations.

When Hope's sponsor at that time, Pepsodent, saw how high the ratings were soaring due to the broadcasts from service bases, they agreed to pick up the costs no matter where Hope and company decided to go. Certainly the higher ratings also played a very important part in Hope's decision to continue entertaining servicemen over the next few years, though to his eventual surprise it was to bring rewarding spiritual and emotional dividends for him personally.

But that was in the future, and at first he began adjusting his usual material to suit his new audiences. He and his writers set about to thoroughly familiarize themselves with G.I. terminology. One gag, for instance, never got past the word "head" because the soldiers used that word for "bathroom." Hope also memorized precisely the names of top brass at each base; the servicemen got a kick out of it when he mentioned the names during his act and proved what a "regular fella" he was by poking fun at the officers, who, in turn, tolerated the jibes with good humor, and even joined in the laughter because they knew it eased officer-enlisted man tensions harmlessly.

Hope was rehearsing one of his monologues on December 7,

1941, with his writers, as usual, in mandatory attendance when Dolores rushed into the room and announced that the Japanese had attacked Pearl Harbor. Hope incongruously burst into laughter; he recalled later that it had sounded too incredible, like something out of one of his sketches. Dolores got them all "making long-faced" soon enough when she rushed to the radio and snapped it on. A New York Philharmonic broadcast ended with the playing of "The Star Spangled Banner" while the Carnegie Hall audience rose to its feet and sang fervently. As Hope noted, "Patriotism Is Back in Style"; he determined to capitalize on it, but there was still a small voice of nascent personal feeling, even fervor, already stirring beneath what appeared his surface opportunism.

In Beverly Hills well-known actors, and directors like Otto Preminger, went on duty as air raid wardens. During the blackouts barrage balloons were often misidentified as Japanese planes, with a resultant mass pandemonium erupting with Preminger and other wardens running around like latter-day Paul Reveres, movie stars having hysterical fits. One feminine star won rueful laughs in the "trade" papers by screaming that the chlorinated water in her swimming pool had turned blood red — that was feisty, highly strung Lupe Velez, the Mexican Spitfire (some of her movies carried that name in fact). It turned out that a studio gagster had put red dye in the water. Soon there were reports of L.A. area anti-aircraft guns firing at non-existent aircraft and army generals making exasperated broadcasts to calm down a populace already overstimulated by the movies they not only made but looked at in the film palaces from Pasadena to Santa Monica. (Steven Spielberg was later to make a movie, *1941*, which described the West Coast scene at that time, and those who remembered didn't think it was exaggerated — at least not much.)

The Treasury Department in Washington later organized what they called a "Victory Caravan" in which Hope and other movie personalities would ride across the U.S. selling war bonds. An eventual billion dollars' worth of bonds would get raised thanks to the efforts of such as Joan Bennett, Charles Boyer, Cary Grant, and Merle Oberon, but, as Joan Bennett later recalled, it took its toll on actors accustomed to plush dressing rooms and luxurious surroundings who found themselves sharing close quarters on an uncomfortable train instead. Joan Bennett, however, in a 1977 interview, singled out Hope for praise above all others: "He would go anywhere, any time, give it all he had. And I think in time he came to love it, and to love the guys he was brightening up."

Joan Bennett and Merle Oberon, among others, described scenes that belonged in movie farce: feminine stars abandoning "daintiness" and "poise" in fights over who got to use the bathroom first. (Cary Grant cracked that "Burst bladders were the rule rather than the exception.") Desi Arnaz, with his wild accent and frenetic hip-and-shoulder renditions of Latin-style songs, drove everyone crazy playing "Babalu" over and over again; Pat O'Brien later recalled that he threatened to bash Senor Arnaz' brains in if he heard one more note.

Oberon and Bennett both recalled, perhaps facetiously, that they could never figure out whether Hope's frequent passes at them were camp silliness or the real thing, adding that even had he been serious there would have been no private space available for monkey business.

Except for two instances when illness prevented him from traveling, Hope broadcast all of his radio shows from service bases during the 1941-45 period, with the sponsor paying for all traveling costs. Hope and his groups reportedly did many extra shows at additional bases when time permitted.

In 1942 Hope did his first extensive tour in a non-combat area — Alaska — visiting bases in Anchorage, Nome, Cold Bay, and other locations. Here he established additional momentum for the later worldwide trips designed to bring servicemen laughs and escape, and for which Hope would become renowned.

His U.S.O. and other activities kept him out of the service, true, but as a man of 40 with a wife and children, he would not have been taken anyway. In all likelihood, with his sure, strong grasp on current realities, he recognized that Patriotism was "In," Patriotism was "Fashionable," Patriotism was "The Thing"; hence it was important careerwise to identify himself with it in the public mind. And it gave him widespread exposure and brought tremendous good will on himself. And being what he was, coming as he did from a background of ruthless, disciplined efforts at self-promotion and self-perpetuation, Hope could not have helped relishing the waves of love and respect he was arousing in Americans because of his broadcasts from bases around the world.

He could not, true, have avoided second thoughts at times; what if he were to be killed if he were in the wrong area at the wrong time; what about Dolores, and the kids, and the money and the fame and the other ambitions he still had on the back burner — one bullet, one burst of machine-gun fire, one plane plummeting to earth on which he was a hapless passenger, would finish off Bob Hope. This prospect chilled him; whatever else he might be, he was a fierce lover of life, its myriad pleasures and excitements and novelties, its variety and challenges.

Three other entertainers also deserved much of the credit that Hope tried to retain for himself: Frances Langford, Tony Romano, and Jerry Colonna. They were in there pitching constantly, always "there" for Hope on all occasions, in all situations. Langford's womanly poise and down-to-earth approach and heartfelt singing style perked the boys up; Colonna made the perfect second-fiddle foil for Hope; Romano, well-liked by the men, lent his professionalism one hundred percent to their many stops during the tours.

On his tours, Hope discovered things the average American was never to know, such as how Russian troops in the Northern Pacific were being trained to fly aircraft and handle landing craft-tanks in preparation for the assault on Japan that U.S. atom bombs were to beat them to by the end of the war.

To be sure, there would be some close calls on assorted flights — such as engine failure and windstorms and climactic conditions — that Hope and Troupe undertook, and all of which they were to walk away from.

In mid-1943, around the time that the famed U.S.O. was formed, Hope, who had just turned 40, decided to do some extensive touring of combat areas, citing publicly his guilt at being "safe at home" while the boys were jeopardizing their young lives on the front lines. Hope, with his usual canny eye on the public relations aspect, and what in later decades would be called his "image," had taken note of the public criticism that he and his people had tended to frequent "safer," non-combat areas while other performers were literally risking life and limb in worldwide danger spots. Hope's old *Roberta* co-star, Tamara, for instance, was to be killed when the plane carrying her U.S.O. contingent was shot down. Hope was not letting a woman outshine him in areas he recognized were crucial in retaining public esteem, which doesn't mean he didn't sincerely mourn his old stage colleague Tamara's death.

Hope wasn't all that anxious to go into the crucial areas, and for a while shrewdly manipulated his "pussycat" screen persona to forestall the move. But he came to realize that his non-combat-area tours wouldn't shape up as much — nor his radio ratings go higher — if he kept out of the "hot spots" while such film stars as Clark Gable and Jimmy Stewart were in the service and hot to trot in the risk-action for which they were to win commendations.

Giving the troops plenty of Hope in 1943. With, left to right, Tony Romano, Jerry Colonna, Frances Langford, Patty Thomas, and comedy writer Barney Dean

Abe Lastfogel, then head of the William Morris Agency, was president of the U.S.O. camp shows and the members of his agency, both those who enlisted and those who helped on the home front, were highly esteemed in show business circles for their contribution. It was Abe Lastfogel who personally arranged the Hope itinerary, once Hope determined he'd go where the hot-action was, and let chips fall where they might. Lastfogel later paid tribute to Hope's services. Hope let it be known that Pepsodent picked up the tab for the tours.

There were to be many rumors about Bob Hope's homoerotic affinity for the servicemen, along the lines of the sentiments Walt Whitman expressed in his famed tome, *Specimen Days*, in which he unabashedly wrote of his love for the wounded soldiers of the Civil War, whom he nursed in Washington, D.C. hospitals. Even during the Korean War, in which I served as an Army sergeant, the rumors persisted — indeed, flourished. I personally always found Bob Hope a warm and kind person in that period, as did many other soldiers; though there were criticisms of him as an opportunist using his service entertainments to enhance his career, I, and others, sensed an underlying sincerity, and indeed a fervor.

Stories proliferated about his secret kindnesses to servicemen after their tours were up and they were again civilians, how he set some of them up in businesses, made loans to them. And there were the stories that he'd fallen in love with a few, including one boy who'd lost an arm in combat and whom Bob had comforted in a hospital. Here, in what he conceived of as "legitimate" and "paternal" solicitude, Bob could relax the self-imposed cautionary tensions that had existed since the George Byrne days.

Of course there was always the threat of extortion or blackmail. Reportedly, according to such as George Cukor and Billy Grady, attempts along these lines had been made by the more callous and opportunistic recipients of his kindness, but Bob had seen to it that these soldiers (and later veterans) were either "leaned on" or repulsed by police friends, with no money or other extortionate forms of largesse paid out then or ever.

A number of men I served with in the Korean War, however, joined along with me in their admiration for Hope's efforts to entertain them, and sensed, as I did, his sincerity and warmth. If others felt he was opportunistic, possibly that was part and parcel of his approach (he was, after all, only human, and had learned the uses of self-interest early on, the hard way) but the sincerity was there too.

Others who have observed Bob Hope through the years feel that he could be kind, sensitive and giving if he felt the recipient of what he used to call, self-derisively, his "sucker self and sucker acts" were worthy.

Longtime show business observer Gregory Speck, author of the well-received book, *Hollywood Royalty*, has felt that Hope's personal kindnesses kept pace with his professional celebrity. "If you study his performances carefully, that kindliness comes through. I know he is supposed to be a cold man — cold and calculating and self-involved — but that other Bob Hope is there, inside, and he has emerged at times, personally and in his work — perhaps more often than is perceived."

Barbara Baroness MacLean, an active participant in the Hollywood scene of the Thirties and Forties, both as actress and as designer, felt that Hope was a more creditable actor than he was given credit for, and that he could be a nice guy indeed "if he knew you and trusted you and felt you were on the up and up," as Barbara put it. Barbara was among those who noted that Hope did a lot of nice things for people nobody ever knew about, especially if they were people who didn't approach or pressure him. Then he liked to surprise these people with a kind act out of the blue.

"But certainly he was no patsy," Barbara insisted. "And why should he have been? Life was hard for him at the beginning; he pulled himself up by his bootstraps and felt other people developed character along God-helps-those-who-help-themselves lines."

As for his marriage problems and his many infidelities, Barbara MacLean adopts a charitable view, dismissing these stories with "Everyone has their problems and pressures — who knows the deep-down heart of another human being?"

Certainly (and as a Korean War soldier in service for three years, I believe this) the plight of the servicemen and the suffering and quiet heroism Bob Hope observed did move him — and if in some cases it became all-out love, who is to judge his heart?

Hope got together for a talk with Major Clark Gable when he encountered him at the Flying Fortress Base in Poolebrook, England. Gable had enlisted in 1942, though already 41 years old, after his wife, Carole Lombard, the first American entertainer to die "in action" (in a plane crash after a bond-selling tour) was lost to him. Gable had just returned from an Air Force mission and admitted he was still shaky. He told Hope that nothing he'd seen or done in the movies had prepared him for what he had to see and do amid the actualities of combat. This was no "movie-style" heroism, he told Hope. Some of the pilots would return in one piece only to jump out of their planes and refuse ever to board them again. (Some of course did, conquering their fears.)

The servicemen couldn't always escape the realities of their lives via Hope's acts. The dichotomy between what was really going on and the escapism Hope and Troupe offered, didn't give comfort to every soldier, especially those who had their "baptism of fire," those who had seen their buddies blown to bits, dying in agony and fear.

Some servicemen even gave strong indications that they felt they were being patronized. Others did little to disguise their resentment that Hope could pick up his marbles and go home whenever he felt like it, while they had to await the end of the game and whatever it brought. There was a feeling among some servicemen that Hope was getting privileges, mobility, freedom denied to them; that he fancied himself some variety of Lord Bountiful dispensing largesse in the best noblesse oblige tradition — an attitude admittedly more prevalent among the more intelligent, perceptive servicemen. At home Hope would tell various groups around the U.S. about the rough conditions and cramped

Keeping those servicemen happy, 1943

quarters and tense situations, but he and his home audiences knew — and so did the servicemen — that at worst he'd be enduring them for a few weeks, not for months and even years on end, as did those boys out there.

Aside from what was happening on stage, bizarre bits of real-life comedy would intrude into the battle theatre at unexpected moments. At Ferryville in North Africa, Hope had just stepped up to the microphone when a light tank appeared suddenly behind the crowd of servicemen before him and began pushing its way ruthlessly through, forcing men to run out of its path in every direction. To Hope, the tank seemed relentlessly out of control and headed right for him — a ski-nose-flattener *par excellence* if ever there was one. He was about to fling himself off the platform when the tank came to a sudden stop directly in front of the stage. The top of the tank opened and out popped a young G.I. carrying a folding chair. He set the chair up on top of the tank, sat down, and ordered Bob, "Okay, fella, start the show!" The laughter that ensued was nervous, tense, but explosive nonetheless.

Hope was to remember conditions in North Africa as more unpleasant than anything he'd experienced yet. Since the water in their dilapidated hotel was shut off at 5 p.m., the tour members would have to fill the bathtub before they left in the morning so they'd have water to wash up with when they returned. Masses of hungry mosquitoes and other horrifying insects would descend on Bob as he lay in bed. And just as sleep came he'd be woken up by convoys that would pass by and make the whole building tremble ominously.

Hope would tell about swatting at the insects frantically with a copy of *Reader's Digest*. He'd wake in the morning with huge lumps all over his body and worry that he'd contracted malaria. During a bombing raid Hope and party had to crawl into a sewer until the "all clear" sounded.

In 1944 Hope took his merry little band to the South Pacific — the usual gang plus Barney Dean and the tap-dancing Patty Thomas. Their first show was well-received in spite of the fact that the P.A. system was malfunctioning and the soldiers could hardly hear anything. Hope used his clout on the general in charge, arguing that there was no point in his troupe coming some 20,000 miles if no one could hear the act; from then on the Powers That Be in the Military Command saw to it, somehow, some way, that the microphones were tested ahead of time throughout the South Pacific.

It was in the jungles of Dutch New Guinea that Hope, along with everyone else in his troupe, contracted the dreaded "jungle rot," a pernicious skin disease that can affect virtually any part of the body and can lie dormant for years after its initial onslaught, resurfacing during especially humid periods. Hope would visit the wounded in the wards after doing his shows and would take agonizing step after step because of the blisters on his feet. Still he was luckier than some of the soldiers, who got jungle rot over their entire bodies.

On a flight from the South Pacific to Sydney, Australia, the pilot, who back in the civilian life of peacetime had been a neighbor of Hope's, allowed him, as a special favor, to fly the Navy Catalina plane. Hope was piloting the craft when the engines gave out. The neighbor, a Lieutenant Ferguson, ordered him out of the cockpit and suggested that everything on the plane that could be jettisoned be thrown off immediately. Hope, Barney Dean — who was slow to catch on that they were in deep trouble — and Jerry Colonna got to work. Eventually, with altitude still failing, they made an emergency landing in a lake. Their flight was over an hour late.

Hope managed to meet most of the big-time generals during his travels.

In Palermo, after the fall of Sicily, Hope was invited by an aide to have dinner with General George S. Patton at his headquarters. Tony Romano had already planned a big spaghetti dinner for everyone and Hope was forced to send his regrets. The aide insisted: Patton wouldn't take no for an answer. He went further — he made it clear that both men would be in serious trouble if Hope refused. Hope and company arrived later at the Palace in Palermo where Patton was quartered and ate dinner while Patton chatted. They put on an impromptu mini-performance for him. As they were leaving, Patton took Hope aside and explained the real reason for his summons. Although Hope wasn't to learn the details until later, Patton had slapped an injured G.I. in the hospital and subsequently found himself suffering from what a later decade would term "a severe image problem." He told Hope, "I want you to tell the people that I love my men."

While in Algiers Hope also met General Dwight D. Eisenhower. Ike assured Bob and the other troupe members that conditions were safe there, as there had not been a bombing in months. Confident they could get much-needed and extensive rest in Algiers, they retired happily — but in the early morning hours of the following day Hope was awakened by the sound of bombs dropping and an associate pounding on his door yelling "Air Raid!" Still in their night clothes, Hope,

Langford, and the others raced for the nearest air raid shelter vowing never again to believe a general.

Bob Hope was never to forget the white crosses over the graves of Marines he saw in the South Pacific. But his deepest, strongest, most racking and pervasive memories were of conditions he saw in the hospitals. He and his crew would wander from ward to ward, dispensing what cheer they could, making jokes like "Don't get up!" to someone with a broken leg, but on occasion Hope's upbeat spirits would be tested in the extreme. "I saw a boy lying there with both of his feet just ragged chunks of meat," Hope was later to recall. "They were shaving around the bone in preparation for an imminent and crucially necessary amputation. This was too much for me."

Working with a ghost writer, Carroll Carroll, who adapted Hope's copious notes into book form, Hope described a typical army hospital scene in his book *I Never Left Home*:

> Then a guy pulled aside a curtain and there were seven teams of doctors and nurses, two of each, all operating at once. What a picture! Sometimes even now, for no reason that I know of, I shut my eyes and see that scene: the glaring lights, those surgeons working so surely, the nurses helping them and other nurses running back and forth with the speed of an operating assembly line. It sounds terrible. It looked pretty grim. But lives were being saved by those men. Every one of those surgeons looked at least twelve feet tall to me.

It was in the hospitals visiting and comforting severely wounded soldiers that Hope found himself most touched by the plight of the men and most proud of his U.S.O. involvement. Hope had come to these scenes — and those he'd in fact witnessed since the beginning of the war — as a man not particularly giving and caring by nature. He was selfish and single-minded and by long habit concerned primarily with his needs, his purposes. But it would have taken a heart of stone not to be moved by what he saw in the operating rooms and wards during World War II.

Many in the various Hope troupes were deeply affected by their hospital visits and were to tell of them for years afterward. Frances

Langford, a compassionate woman, collected letters wounded boys had written and saw to it they were forwarded to the proper locations. "It was wonderful to entertain the boys and make them forget their tensions and worries and boredom," Frances told me years later. "But I felt I really justified my existence — and presence there — when I did my best to comfort those boys in the hospitals. They were so patient and wonderful. They made me feel so humble to be in good health and sound of body. I only wish I could have helped more than I did."

By 1945, the final year of the war, the mood had changed overseas as on the home front. The soldiers were dog-tired of combat and the stresses and tensions; tired of being away from loved ones; tired of the repetitions, the grime, the dirt, the discomfort; tired of watching buddies die or get sent off to medical units. The charged energy of anticipation and terror, loneliness, and alienation from the civilian ambiances they'd come from, gave way in time to weariness, disillusion, a pernicious and pervasive anomie of spirit. Now in 1945, when Hope and his little band came to offer comfort, the troops tended to shout, in increasing numbers, variations not of "Come back soon!" or "We love ya!" but, rather, an urgent "Take us home with you!"

That last year, Hope took a larger group than usual and toured England, France, and Germany. Despite the problems in these countries — the bombings, the demoralized civilian population, the desolation and hunger they often encountered, conditions were not as bad as in the 1941-44 combat zones. For these reasons, more entertainers volunteered to accompany Hope. Bob had been to London before, during, and after the Blitz and still couldn't get over it and when room service at Claridge's Hotel informed him there was no soap. Hope eventually learned to hoard one small cake of soap while watching it slowly dwindle. At a show in Nice, France (this was after the 1944 liberation of France) Hope was peremptorily told by an American major that it would be politically inadvisable to introduce on his show the famed entertainer and sometime Hollywood star Maurice Chevalier, who was suspected of having been a Nazi collaborator during the War. To his great credit, Hope stuck doggedly to the rule that a man was innocent until proven guilty and he wasn't going to have this greatest of French entertainers sitting in the audience unrecognized and unappreciated. He overruled the major's injunction and brought Chevalier to the stage. Chevalier got a standing ovation after his number. He was never to forget Hope's kindness and generosity.

Hope was in Nuremberg in 1945 for the G.I. Olympics when it was announced at the stadium that Japan had offered to surrender. This was in August; Germany had given up in May. "The whole stadium of guys," Hope was to remember, "seemed to rise twenty-five feet in the air!"

Time magazine was to honor Bob Hope, for his efforts throughout World War II, with a cover story and photo, and the legend, "First in the hearts of servicemen." Ratings for his radio show went through the roof. As of 1946 he became one of the country's most popular and beloved entertainers. Asked now to give serious speeches around the U.S. about the War and "his boys," Hope couldn't rely any longer on his gagwriters, so he hired a new "straight writer," Glenn Whedon, to help him "sound like Henry Kissinger without an accent" as he was to put it in reminiscing many years later. In his own, hardly self-deprecating though humorous words, Bob Hope had become "Mount Rushmore."

In later years, working with Carroll Carroll and other ghostwriters, Bob Hope churned out several volumes devoted to his war as well as his civilian appearances. In these books — a typical one was *Don't Shoot, It's Only Me*, published in 1990 — Hope tends to repeat the same stories over and over again (often with different details) and manages to relate everything that happened in the war to some aspect of his career. The same near-death experiences are recounted in dramatic detail; the same false-humility stances are set forth; one carries away a sense of distortion and occasional exaggeration and even of untruth due to his self-serving, subjective approach to the material.

Hope himself mentions in these books that he wasn't the only entertainer who went overseas during the war (though whether the idea of mentioning others was his own or his ghostwriter's remains in the realm of speculation). Jack Benny, for one, did many overseas shows during the same period, as did Fred Astaire, Gary Cooper, Jimmy Cagney, Al Jolson, Ann Sheridan, Edgar Bergen, Andy Devine, Joe E. Brown, and many others. Hope, however, got his *Time* cover story, among other reasons, because his radio shows kept the American public regularly informed of his exploits, which he capitalized on, and in overkill style, as other performers did not. Once, in a moment of levity (presumably at least) he characterized some of these entertainers as "publicity shy" — something that could never be said of him.

Hope could never psychologically throw off the dross of his longstanding self-advancement and self-perpetuation; his insights acquired during the war were always to be leavened by ulterior motives. In the Forties he did a magazine ad for a group called Appreciate America, which denounced racism in the United States and compared it to the "Master Race Superiority" philosophy of the Nazis. Admittedly ahead of its time, and admirable in its intent, it might have come across as even more admirable had Hope in his private life broken free of some of his own long-held prejudices and fears. And had it not been a clever way to remind readers yet again that this "Paramount Star" always had a new picture ready for audience viewing at the local Rialto?

CHAPTER FOURTEEN

THE CHAMPION OF CHAMPIONS

Although Hope kept busy on his U.S.O. tours during the Forties, he was by no means idle in films and at the box office. In 1941 he was named "Champion of Champions" by *Motion Picture Daily*, and the *Motion Picture Herald* was to list him in the years coming up one of the ten best money-making stars from 1941 to 1951 (with the exception of 1948). All the publicity he garnered from his wartime tours of Europe helped to advertise his motion pictures. His press representatives and marketing men always made sure his latest feature film was mentioned in any newspaper reports of his overseas exploits. On the way to the top in those years, Hope didn't miss a trick, which explains the cynical attitude of many Hollywood insiders, especially executives at rival studios, toward him.

Never satisfied, always restless to break new ground, Hope came out in 1941 with his first book, *They've Got Me Covered*, which was actually written by one of his gagwriters, Carroll Carroll. His radio sponsor, Pepsodent, paid for the printing of the book, while his movie studio, Paramount, helped generously with the promotion. Although according to his promoters several million copies of the book were sold, Hope was always to claim he received nothing in profits because too many copies were offered via a box-top promotional gimmick.

Later, when Carroll co-wrote *I Never Left Home*, proceeds went to the National War Fund. Hope finally admitted to getting some royalties from his third Carroll-ghosted tome, *So This Is Peace*. Hope, his sponsors, studio and press flacks did everything possible to turn these books into bestsellers; the actual author, Carroll, was to win only a pittance, comparatively, for his hard and extensive work. Paramount executive Bill LeBaron, who was always to wax hot and cold about Hope, later remarked that Carroll should have gotten 25 percent of the sales profits "not only for the writing, laborious as that was, but for putting up for weeks and months with such an egomaniac as Bob Hope."

After finishing up *Road to Zanzibar*, his second film with Bing, Hope worked on the service comedy, *Caught in the Draft*, which was released on the Fourth of July, 1941. The plot has to do with a movie star, Hope, who enlists primarily to win the hand of the colonel's lovely daughter (Dorothy Lamour). Lynne Overman and Eddie Bracken were also cast, as his agent and chauffeur respectively. They also enlist with Hope. The script was hastily written around the title, considered a natural with the draft boards working overtime that summer of 1941.

The director, David Butler, was an extremely portly fellow whose proportions provided great sport for Hope. One afternoon they were filming a scene in "No Man's Land," which was full of ditches, foxholes, and deep mud cavities. The 300-pound Butler proceeded to dash about shouting orders when he made a misstep and wound up submerged to his neck in a mud hole. Hope wouldn't let anyone rescue the director, insisting they leave him there for a good while with Hope bent over in laughter and Butler bellowing in humiliation and rage. A derrick had to be called into use to get Butler rescued. Butler, trying to get in the last word, later said he always felt there was a large dose of vicious sadism in Hope's general approach to humor.

On the last day of shooting, the cast and crew had to wait around until the sun went down so they could shoot a sequence that took place at dusk. Bored and impatient, Hope took off with his makeup man for a ride through the Malibu mountains, stopping to enjoy some of the breathtaking sites — and, incidentally, to check out real estate to buy. The two completely lost track of the time, and when they finally did get back — too late to shoot the scene, which had been done with a double — Butler was livid. But he knew that by that time Hope had far more clout with the studio, so he took out his anger on the makeup man. Lamour, stuck with Hope for yet another picture in which she essentially played stooge for him, later called it "the usual horrid mess." Actually it was one of Hope's best and funniest features.

Paulette Goddard was again drafted to co-star with Hope in *Nothing But the Truth*. By this time she'd developed a healthy contempt for his pushy, egoistic manner, though she was to speak politely of him for public consumption. In this, Hope played a stockbroker who makes a $10,000 bet with three associates — Edward Arnold, Leif Ericson, and Glenn Anders — that he can tell the truth and nothing but the truth for the next twenty-four hours. Goddard is on hand as Arnold's niece, who gives Hope his $10,000 to put in the pot. *The New York Times'* Bosley Crowther reported that the picture was "an ancient farce comedy already seen twice in films, which derives from an idea so obvious that it no longer supports a parlor game. Yet Paramount, plus director Elliott Nugent, plus the ever-entangled Mr. Hope kick it around so blithely and with such candid applications of hokum that you can't help but find it amusing, despite the fact that you — and they — know it's a 'sell.'"

One sequence in the film has Hope wrapping himself in a woman's negligee and hiding in an empty bait tank on a houseboat to escape pursuers. A moment later, the tank is lowered into the water. The gag has Hope later reappearing covered with anchovies. Royce Findley, the property man, had to sail into the choppy Catalina Channel at dawn and scoop up thousands of anchovies using chopped meat for bait. When most of these died upon being transferred to a studio tank, Findley had to set out all over again and capture some more. The decision was made to film the sequence earlier than intended before the second batch of anchovies perished.

First a test was made using Hope's stand-in, Len Hendry, who found the water hard to take as it had to be very frigid to keep the anchovies alive and kicking. Half the anchovies were already dead when he was pulled up out of the water. Then Hope, who wouldn't have minded if the sequence had been scrapped entirely, put on the wet negligee with the air of a man approaching the gas chamber, and dutifully entered the tank. Lousy actors, the anchovies immediately fled out of sight to the bottom. Hope was pulled from the water along with many more anchovy casualties with the joke going around that they'd been frightened to death by Ski-Nose's appearance.

The situation was now getting desperate. There were only enough live anchovies left to film the sequence once and only once. There was no time to send Findley out to the Catalina channel for more of the creatures. It was then that director Nugent came up with an inspired solution. The anchovies were removed from the tank, Hope was inserted, and then the fish were poured into the water over Hope; this spared their by now notoriously delicate physiques and got the required shot.

Many years later Elliott Nugent was to tell me that Hope was one of the most difficult performers to direct because he always had his own ideas about everything and anything: "Some of his ideas were good and others not so good," Nugent snapped, "but he was such a fathead that you couldn't tell him anything. Looking back, I could kick myself for deferring to his approach most of the time, just to have quiet and peace.

Victor Moore and Irene Bordoni, seated, with four standing chorines and Bob on the set of *Louisiana Purchase*, 1941

If you crossed him, he could be damned mean."

Hope's final 1941 picture, released at Christmas time, was *Louisiana Purchase*, from a Broadway musical that featured Irving Berlin songs. Irving Cummings directed. He, too, was no great fan of Hope's. Asked later what it was like to work with him, he clapped his hand to his head, rolled up his eyes and moaned, "Please, don't get my blood pressure up." In this, Hope plays Jim Taylor, who's framed for graft by some associates and becomes the target of a senatorial investigation. The odd plot hardly seemed like comedy potential, but the movie won some praise for certain sequences, especially one in which Hope filibusters Congress.

Irene Bordoni, a musical comedy star who'd known great success on the stage and wouldn't let anyone forget it, didn't get on well with Hope. "It was a case of her ego being bigger even than his, so Hope hated her guts," Frank Albertson, a cast member, was later to crack. Among the several attractive ladies in the cast, Dona Drake was the one to really capture Hope's eye. Dona in 1941 was a luscious blonde starlet with the most sensual of lips, seductive eyes, and a figure that curved lethally in the strategic spots. Hope was to get Dona into his supporting cast whenever he could, and indeed she turned up in several of his other early Forties films. Then he appears to have lost interest. Dona Drake, asked about Hope in later years, replied succinctly, "I recall him as funny, kind and sweet. For the rest, my lips are sealed."

Classy Madelaine Carroll, the English actress who'd figured in many historical dramas, found herself incongruously the co-star of Hope's next picture, *My Favorite Blonde*, his first for 1942. Gale Sondergaard and George Zucco, both distinguished character actors who had appeared with Hope in *The Cat and the Canary*, were also again on hand. While they acted well enough vis-a-vis Hope, director Sidney Lanfield described their private attitude toward Hope as "barely tolerant," with Zucco "upstaged" by Hope in one scene too many, calling the star "a clown but not an actor." In this, Sondergaard and Zucco were Nazi agents figuring in a plot that had Hope as a small-time entertainer with a trained penguin act getting involved with beautiful blonde spy Carroll.

Although Paramount contract writers were brought in to do the finished script, the original story, *Snowball in Hell*, had been written by two of Hope's former radio writers, the team of Norman Panama and Mel Frank (both of whom would be creatively involved with Hope many times over the years). With this film Hope also began an association with director Sidney Lanfield, who went on to direct several other Hope features. Lanfield didn't care for the egoistic, do-it-my-way -or-else Hope at first, but they eventually reached an accommodation. Despite the temperamental and working-method differences between them (and on some points during the shooting, Hope, to his surprise, found himself uncharacteristically giving in), the real reason Hope wanted to work with Lanfield again was because *My Favorite Blonde* proved so successful at the box office. Hope never argued with success.

Hope was especially pleased that the script gave him something to do aside from the extremely broad comic turns he'd seemed to be getting stuck with in picture after picture before *Blonde*. He complained at the time he was getting too much of the "slapstick and double-take" stuff, and *Blonde* represented a welcome departure. The role of Larry Haines, the hapless performer with a penguin as pal and co-worker, was always to be one of his all-time favorites because it provided more range than he'd been accustomed to.

At the time *My Favorite Blonde* was shooting, Madeleine Carroll was living on a high cliff across from Catalina Island, where she could watch Navy boats and searchlights scanning the water for Japanese submarines while reconnaissance planes flew overhead. There were pockets of soldiers in the countryside all around her house; she'd give them, in her words, "cakes and cookies in return for chevrons and fraternity pins." These she would pin on her dress in rows, "like an admiral," as she laughingly put it, adding, "I'm proud of my platoons of new friends."

To Hope's consternation, she also had a very special friend he didn't know about. Meanwhile he was broadcasting to one and all (all except homebody Dolores, of course) how smitten he was with the fair Madeleine, harping constantly on her beauty in his radio broadcasts and, as Sidney Lanfield somewhat disgustingly put it, "following her around like a puppy." He'd been her admirer for at least two years before *Blonde* went into production. She called to thank him for all the radio mentions and he couldn't believe his good fortune when he then asked her to appear in *Blonde* and she consented. Of course Madeleine Carroll, lovely and accomplished as she was, had decided it'd be to her career advantage to appear with Hope — a box office star she wasn't, probably because many American audiences thought her cold and remote. Hope, obviously, was being deputized to "warm her up" — in the picture, that is. Lanfield remembered Hope having trouble concentrating on the script when his head was so full of love fantasies about his co-star, fantasies never to be actualized, and for obvious reasons — obvious to everyone but Hope, that is. For Carroll was going hot and heavy for blonde, hunky, super-manly Sterling Hayden at the time (she was to do several pictures with Hayden) and Hope was just not in the Hayden league when it came to what the Paramount flackers, in ads, would call "Man-Flesh Megappeal."

Madeleine Carroll, determined to finish a picture that might possibly boost her filmic stock if some of Hope's box-office magnetism rubbed off on her, tried to handle his bumbling, schoolboyish advances as offhandedly and tactfully as possible. Hayden's attitude was more direct: he wanted to show up on the set and rearrange the famed ski-nose. Carroll lived in fear that if Hope knew about her and Hayden he'd toss her off the picture; so she employed her feminine wiles to keep Hope at bay while filming proceeded.

Soon the cats were out of the bags, when halfway through the shooting Carroll married Hayden in a private ceremony, the news of which was kept from the press. She knew she'd have to tell Hope, gambling that with so much of the picture in the can, it was too late for him to replace her. Hope put a brave face on the news, all smiles and quips in front of the happy bride and her groom, but privately he was angry. Lanfield consoled him by telling him the picture was going well and having such a "class act" as Carroll as co-star would enhance his "prestige stock" with the fans. That his personal stock was at an all-time low, after this rebuff, was something he just had to live with — especially when Sterling Hayden, an adventurous type who traveled the world in boats, was reputed to be extra-handy with his fists when any "vital interest" of his was threatened. Gale Sondergaard, who had a witchy tongue and had been waiting to get in her innings with Hope, didn't help matters when she remarked that "After all, young Mr. Hayden is a very handsome man."

Bing Crosby did the first of his fey, wry, sometimes-apt, sometimes-not cameos in Hope pictures in *My Favorite Blonde*, playing a brief walk-on as a truck driver. He was back full-force, however, in Hope's second 1942 film, *The Road to Morocco*, along with Lamour, Dona Drake, Monte Blue, Yvonne de Carlo, and Anthony Quinn as a sinister sheik. Quinn, though handsome and a devil with the women (he was to win over Katherine DeMille and become the great C.B.'s son-in-law), was often cast as a heavy in the early Road movies but was eventually to become a star in his own right. There was snickering around the set when director David Butler and crew heard Hope announcing loudly one day that "Anthony Quinn and I both suffer from gross miscasting when we were born for romantic leads." It's still moot whether Hope meant these words or was jesting.

The Road to Morocco shooting didn't find obese David Butler any the lighter, and he was the object of several unkind Hope gags, as usual. In fact, there were as many misadventures behind the cameras as before them. One time Bing and Bob were lying on what purported to be the North African shore when a camel started licking both of them and in a typical pseudo-homoerotic gag of the period, they each mistakenly assumed the other was kissing him. Something about the taste of Hope's skin must have alienated the animal, however, because right after the kissing-licking-whatever scene it flung a big glob of spittle in Hope's astonished and disgusted face. In another scene, the boys were to be chased down a narrow Moroccan street by a horse-riding tribe of Bedouins. Hope and Crosby could hear the horses but couldn't see how far off they were. Director Butler assured them he'd give the jump-out-of-the-way signal in plenty of time. But as they ran along the (sound-stage) street and the sound of horses' hooves got louder and louder, Bob and Bing wondered when on earth they were going to get the signal. Finally Hope panicked and jumped through the first available door. Crosby held on a while longer but finally crashed through a window just before the horses arrived and nearly trampled him to death. Both men were furious at Butler, who privately found their protestations and minor injuries amusing, and insisted, adding insult to injury, that they'd jumped too soon and ruined the shot.

Hope came up with a new nickname for Butler after this incident: The Murderer. Self-centered as he was, he seems never to have realized that the constant put-downs and fat jokes had brought David Butler to a saturation point. Crosby, equally a monster of self-involvement and ruthless self-projection, also seemed to have missed the point —that what goes around comes around. "There must be a mite of sadist in Butler," Bing loftily theorized later. The two stars were also irritated when Butler ordered that the one and only phone on the set be installed fully a block and a half away. Butler wasn't having them placing bets and making deals and buying real estate on his — and the studio's — time.

Morocco was only the third Road picture, but already the formula was wearing thin for some critics. Howard Barnes of The New York *Herald-Tribune* blasted the film as "a singularly tasteless and preposterous example of the witless-wisecrack-and-zany-situation school of moviemaking — it tosses away the talents of a couple of good performers instead of capitalizing on them." Bosley Crowther of *The New York Times*, however, took the opposite view. "The screen can hold no more diverting lure than Hope and Crosby, ambling, as they have done before, through an utterly slap-happy picture . . . a delightful 'escape.'"

Crosby and Hope also appeared in 1942's *Star Spangled Rhythm* as the most prominent of many Paramount guest stars in a surprisingly apt and fast-moving variety show. The slender plot had Eddie Bracken and Betty Hutton arranging a big show for the gobs while trying to get married. Well-directed by George Marshall, this wartime salute was handled with verve and many imaginative touches. Though Hope played emcee at the big show, he had comparatively little to do as compared to Hutton, who stole the picture with a cinematically snappy song-in-ajeep number and her hilarious attempts to scale the studio wall. Hope may not have particularly lusted for Hutton, but according to George Marshall, the womanly charms of Veronica "Peek-a-Boo Bang" Lake were very much borne in on him. Veronica put Ski-nose in his place in short order, though, according to Marshall. Dona Drake, Hope's "perennial," and Bing's son Gary also had small roles.

Eddie Bracken and Betty Hutton have at various times been quoted on Hope. Eddie once said that "The way to get along with Bob is to play stooge for him and never, ever hog his spotlight." Hutton is on record as feeling that he resented any attention given her. As she put it, "If he wasn't at the center, then he didn't wanna play."

It was now into 1943 and Hope began to protest he wasn't getting as much money as he was entitled to. Accordingly agent Doc Shurr talked Paramount into lending him to the Goldwyn Studios, where he figured Bob could be "gotten out ahead" with a snappy salary increase. Negotiations began with the colorful Sam Goldwyn, famous for two things: his tasteful, mature productions and his malapropisms. When Sam learned that Bob wanted $100,000 for one picture, he got up from his desk, walked over to the wall and began hitting his head slowly against it, with the Goldwynism gem: "He wants a hundred thousand, with me with not a thimble to pour in!" At the first confab, nothing was decided.

To ingratiate himself with the always-impressionable Goldwyn, Hope followed along on a Shurr suggestion and showed up at the premiere of a Goldwyn Gary Cooper film in Texas. Seizing every chance, he kept bringing up the Money Matter to Sam, but the producer always put him off. At the last show for the premiere, Hope did his bit from the stage and then introduced Goldwyn. Sam stepped right into a trap that Hope hadn't even thought to set up — until the minute he heard Goldwyn extolling his, Hope's, virtues to the audience. Seizing the moment, Hope chirped "But what about my salary?" Disoriented and taken off balance, Goldwyn tried to ignore the remark, but the audience — thinking it part of the act — was eating it up. Then Bob literally lay down on the stage with microphone in hand and insisted Goldwyn join him. Too stunned to do otherwise, Goldwyn did as he was told. Then Bob gave out with the 1940's equivalent of "Can We Talk?" — about money, natch. He and Goldwyn, to the astonishment of Doc Shurr, proceeded to work out the deal right there on their backs on the Dallas stage. Hope got his $100,000.

Goldwyn's first project for Hope was to have been a remake of

Eddie Cantor's *Whoopee*, but a battle with the aviation industry in which Goldwyn was engaged jettisoned that idea and gave Goldwyn a new one. About two years before the signing of Hope, Pan American Airlines, which had agreed to put their facilities at Hope's disposal, withdrew their support from his production of *Transatlantic Pilot* because it allegedly "emphasized the hazards of flying." Furious at their non-cooperation, Goldwyn then announced a substitute picture, *Thirteen Go Flying*, a Sidney Howard script about the crash of the airliner "Cavalier" in Bermuda. When Goldwyn finally calmed down and the war began overseas, he decided to commission a more "constructive" script about the airplane industry entitled *Sabotage*. This picture had been sitting on the shelf ever since, until — through this most convoluted of methods — Goldwyn hit upon the bright idea of turning the screenplay into a comedy with Bob Hope and Dorothy Lamour.

Sabotage, in any form, was never made. The picture Hope did finally shoot for Goldwyn, *They Got Me Covered*, started life as a serious thriller, *Washington Correspondent*, undoubtedly modeled on Hitchcock's *Foreign Correspondent*, and it shows. While it has a hilarious opening (Hope is fired from his job as a foreign correspondent when he alone missed the story of Germany invading Russia) and is interesting dramatically throughout, it's only sporadically amusing, lacking many of the Hope-style gags and situations that distinguished his later comedy-thrillers. In fact, told completely straight with different actors, *They Got Me Covered* would have been a creditable thriller. Although Hope is allowed some zaniness in key sequences — in one bit he pretends to be a mannequin when an enemy agent is throwing knives — his complement of gagwriters seem not to have figured much in these proceedings.

In typical Hope films it was accepted procedure for the other actors to play it more or less straight and let Hope get the laughs, but in *Covered* everyone but Hope is especially serious. Lamour, a pleasing if limited actress, must have been getting her usual private "mad-on" at Hope during this, because she seems somehow confused and preoccupied throughout the movie, as if she weren't sure how the hell she should play it; this was no farce like the Road pictures. On the contrary, *They Got Me Covered* betrays its serious origins in practically every scene. In spite of this, there are some genuinely amusing lines and situations. For instance, when Lamour catches sight of the overripe stripper Marion Martin she has a chance to put Hope in the shade by quipping, "There's enough peroxide there to disinfect the whole German embassy!"

Martin was a very top-heavy blonde whose twin talents were readily apparent to Hope and the other men on the set. But while Hope might have loved to play extra scenes with Martin in her dressing room, the woman who really got the lion's share of Hope's attention was the cool, statuesque brunette Lenore Aubert, playing a character called Olga. Their scenes in the picture — with Hope making suggestive remarks while acting schoolboy lovesick and Aubert maintaining her dignity and keeping him at bay — were not far off the mark from their offscreen confrontations.

Meanwhile Sam Goldwyn began to get worried that he'd make enemies of the FBI — let alone the aviation industry — if they took *Covered*'s script too literally. In it the FBI is shown up by Hope's bumbling, irresponsible nitwit who uncovers the spy ring in a beauty salon (albeit accidentally) long before the agents do. To hedge his bets, Goldwyn sent the screenplay to J. Edgar Hoover, a personal friend, who wired back: "The script is okay; anything can happen in a Bob Hope picture." Thus was a feud averted between one of America's first-rank film producers and the head of the Federal Bureau of Investigation. The gagman from Cleveland was flying high in big company as of 1943, that was for sure.

The same month *They Got Me Covered* was released, Hope's private and professional lives were coming together in an extremely unpleasant and downright messy fashion: his brothers Jim and Jack were facing each other in a courtroom.

In 1939 Jim Hope, at the time a real estate man in Hollywood, asked Bob if he'd hire Jim's common-law wife, Marie Mali, as a part-time secretary. She'd keep her full-time job with Texaco in the meantime. Marie was hired for $50 a month to assist Annabelle Pickett, Hope's full-time secretary, in answering fan mail and carrying out other related duties. She'd report for work in the evenings and stay two or three hours per weeknight.

At this time, Jim knew his brother Bob was making a lot of money, but he didn't know how much. Jack, who'd started handling Bob's business affairs, let it slip. Jim compounded the error by telling Marie how much his brother was worth. "And all he's giving me is a lousy fifty dollars a month!" she screamed. She insisted that Jim go to Bob and get her a raise. Bob announced to Jim that he couldn't promise Marie a raise but if things worked out she'd get a generous bonus at the end of the year. Needing money at the time, Jim asked his wealthy brother if he could at least lend him a thousand or so. Bob complied, grudgingly, but made it clear it was definitely just a loan.

Marie waited and waited for her bonus; when none was forthcoming, she began to get angrier and angrier. First she tried to sabotage Bob's relationship with Annabell Pickett — in the hope that she'd get her job — by sending Hope letters, lengthy and detailed ones, citing Pickett's alleged ineptitudes. At first Hope took some of the charges seriously, with a resultant office dissension and awkwardness, but later it dawned on him what Marie was up to. Although Jim told his brother he'd tried desperately to talk her out of it, Marie sued Bob Hope for two full years of back pay at $50 per week, retroactive. Furious at Marie and his brother, feeling that he was surrounded by leeching jackals, Hope accused them of being parasites and instituted a countersuit against Jim Hope for the amount of the loan.

The case reached the Superior Court in January 1943. Any anger or mixed emotions Jim might have felt over Marie suing his brother against his wishes (or so he claimed) had gone out the window with Bob's countersuit. Jim accompanied Marie to court, where the two of them glared at, but did not speak to, Jack Hope, who was there as Bob's representative but let the attorneys from Sturges and Russell argue the case. Marie's attorney proceeded to argue that people who did secretarial work for movie stars normally were paid between three and four times what Hope had paid Marie — and per week not per month. Hope's lawyers insisted to the court that Marie's claims that Bob had promised her a bonus were pure fiction.

Ultimately the case was thrown out of court when the jury was unable to agree on a verdict. Bob's relationship with his brother Jim was irreparably damaged. A few years later Bob would get even with Jim for having dared to show ingratitude, and worse, for having caused him public embarrassment, the case having been duly reported in the papers.

At this time, 1943, Hope had cordial, if distant, relationships with his other brothers, all of whom found varying degrees of success in one business or another. Ivor, the oldest, was running the Hope Metal Products Company back in Cleveland. (Bob had simply bought the company to insure his brother's employment, then set himself up as President and appointed Ivor Manager.) Fred has own meat provision business in Columbus, Ohio — reportedly Bob Hope had done the same for Fred as he had for Ivor. Sid also remained in Ohio and was a farmer there. George, the one who'd once entertained ambitions of following in Bob's show business footsteps, was by 1943 a sergeant in the Air Force at Santa Ana, where he wrote the script for the Army radio show, *Wings for the Army*. All in all, many in the know at the time felt Hope had behaved very generously toward his siblings.

But this generosity, as it turned out, had a price on it. Never really close to his brothers, and suspicious of their attitude toward him (weak and clinging and parasitical and bothersome as he found it) he'd grown tired long since of their jealousy and their demands, and one method of keeping them at arms length was to set up as many of them in business as their individual aptitudes and energies permitted. But he was always to resent ever having to do it in the first place.

Hope felt, with some justification, that he'd worked damned hard to get to his position in life at 40 — and with little or no support from his brothers — and refused to see their side of it (such as it was): that it wasn't easy being in the shadow of such a famous and wealthy person, that it was a strain to find oneself perpetually the comparatively "poor" relation of Bob Hope. Hope was never to let any of them forget what he'd done for them. Years later he'd grouse to reporters about how he had to support and sustain his brothers, getting nothing in return. When one friend who'd never had brothers or sisters once self-pityingly commented to Hope it'd been lonely being an "only child," Bob hooted nastily and informed the guy he didn't know how lucky he was! "The weak come to the strong and drain them!" he snapped.

His negative experiences with his family, of course, help to account for Hope's dual nature in manners monetary; why he can be so generous at one time and with one individual, and so incredibly miserly on another with someone else. Like many wealthy and famous people who've had to claw and scheme to the top, Hope saw everyone around him as a potential user and parasite out to take a bite out of him at the first opportunity (his instincts on the matter proving more correct than not in many instances). He could give thousands of dollars to what he considered a worthy charity or fund but was almost comically, not to say grotesquely, pinch penny in other ways. He never would tip cab drivers, for instance, citing it as a principle that he used cabs all the time and would have wound up depleted of a fortune had he tipped every cabbie over the course of time. Nor did he leave tips in restaurants, assuming, often self-importantly and blindly, that a man of his stature should not expect a check, let alone be forced to leave a tip. He's been known to say that people should feel absolutely honored to wait on him.

Hope was reunited with Eve Arden from the Ziegfeld Follies days when she appeared with him in *Let's Face It*, one of Hope's slighter

With Betty Hutton for 1943's *Let's Face It*

efforts released in 1943 by Paramount. Also on board were Betty Hutton, Zasu Pitts, and, yet again, Bob's perennial female favorite, Dona Drake. Danny Kaye had starred in the Broadway version. Kaye had run into Hope on the set of *They Got Me Covered* right after Kaye had seen his first screen test for Sam Goldwyn. Kaye told Hope he hated himself on the screen; this struck a reminiscent note in Hope obviously, recalling as he did how he'd felt in 1931, and Kaye was touched when Hope assured him he'd be just swell in movies, and moreover arranged for David Butler (he of the excess avoirdupois) to shoot yet another test that might highlight Kaye's distinctive attributes more fittingly. Kaye was to feel an entirely different reaction a short time later when he learned that Hope would be starring in the picture Danny had tested for.

In *Let's Face It,* Hope and two Army buddies (Dave Willock and Cully Richards) are hired by three women to make their husbands jealous. The trouble starts when the soldiers' actual girlfriends show up and want to know what their swains are doing with three strange women. The movie opened to mixed reactions in August 1943. The *Daily News'* Kate Cameron raved that it was "hilarious entertainment [that] produces laughter from beginning to end with scarcely a let up." *The New York Times*, on the other hand, claimed that *Let's Face It* was "a rather feeble and outdated contraption . . . if it weren't for Mr. Hope it would be a very sad affair indeed. No one can do more with poor material than Mr. Hope, but there are limits."

On the other hand, Hope's next picture, *The Princess and the Pirate* (1944), again for Sam Goldwyn, turned out to be one of his all-time best. Hope was always to find it strange working on Goldwyn's much smaller lot, but with *Princess* (as compared with *They Got Me Covered*) Goldwyn didn't stint on Grade A production values, classy, elaborate sets and even "gorgeous" Technicolor, all of which the film deserved, and exploited to the hilt.

The Princess and the Pirate had its origins in a bizarre, supposedly true (but more likely apocryphal) Hollywood story that had made the rounds for years. In the story two men get drunk together and pass out in a hotel room. During the night one commits suicide by jumping out the window. The other is accused of murdering him until the police discover the dead man wrote his last will and testament on his friend's chest in red pencil. In an improbable (and admittedly farfetched) quantum leap of a sort, from this tale came the farcical saga of a cowardly bogus pirate (Hope) who at one point in the film has a treasure map tattooed on his chest.

Hope plays an actor on a ship whose fellow passenger, a beautiful princess (Virginia Mayo), is running away from a marriage arranged by her father. When pirates attack the ship, Hope disguises himself as an old gypsy woman who catches the eye of the pirates' tattoo artist, Walter Brennan. (In a try at 1944-style pseudo-homoeroticism, Brennan has seen through Hope's disguise, but wants to save his life for ulterior purposes.) In the movie's most hilarious and memorable sequence, Mayo and Hope escape from the pirates only to wind up performing on stage at an island dive before a crew of terrifying cutthroats. As per the plot, if Hope doesn't succeed in entertaining these people, he'll literally die on stage. In this scene Hope has on grand display everything he's learned about the art of comedy and how to adapt it to his screen persona.

The picture also benefits from an excellent supporting cast that makes the most of the material. Victor McLaglen is a memorable gruff "Hook," leader of the pirate crew. Virginia Mayo, surprisingly, subdues the hard, trampy edge she exuded in other pictures and delivers her loveliest and warmest performance; although the "straight woman," she holds her own nicely with Hope throughout. The biggest surprise and delight among the supporting cast is Walter Brennan, nearly unrecognizable in his hysterical, lithe turn as the Popeye-like tattoo artist. Great gags in the picture have Hope forced to drink an absolutely humongous mug of beer in the aforementioned tavern, and his pantomime under the pillows when portly Walter Slezak, a sinister ruler of the "island paradise" sits on top of them with Hope hiding underneath. In an unexpected twist at the end Mayo is finally reunited with the man she truly loves — Bing Crosby.

Walter Brennan, a distant relative of mine whom I frequently saw when living in, and later visiting, Hollywood, always held Bob Hope's comic abilities in high esteem. "I'd go so far as to call him a genius," Walter told me back in 1964. "The timing, the rhythm, it all couldn't come just from his training, great as that was; it was native to him!" Walter added, "I always felt that Bob was put down unnecessarily as an inventive comic. I'd rather have seen him given his place as one of the top humorists of his generation. I know he did well, but he hasn't really gotten the respect he deserved." When I asked Walter if he agreed with those who thought Bob "ruthless," he shot back, "'Ruthless' is always a word they use against a man determined to make the most of his abilities. It's a hard world out there, and you have to run for it!"

Virginia Mayo has always looked back on *The Princess and the Pirate* as one of her more pleasant assignments; she looked most pleased when I once told her that, in it, she'd never looked more beautiful. "It was a fun assignment," she said, but shied away from anecdotes about the picture, Bob, or other members of the cast. Not so David Butler and Walter Slezak. David told me in 1960, "Bob was such a skilled comic that you didn't have to direct much — just put him in front of the camera and cut him loose!" Slezak said he had a deep respect for Bob's talent: "And he wasn't a scene stealer — not with me. He encouraged his co-players to do their best."

In late 1944 Bob decided to conquer yet another medium when he began a daily column, syndicated in newspapers around the country, called "It Says Here." The column consisted of a collection of gags put together by his staff of writers. Hope at one point complained that he might have to drop the column because it was a nuisance meeting a daily deadline, which made insiders — and his hard-working gagwriters, who really wrote the column — snicker among themselves.

Around this time Hope began his fourth Road movie with Bing, *The Road to Utopia*, released in early 1945. Once again the boys were vaudevillians and once again they ran into Dorothy Lamour, this time while traveling to Alaska. Once again (a tired device) a map, belonging to Dorothy, leading to a gold mine, figures in the action. Like most of the Road movies, *Utopia* is not that hilarious, but it does have its cute moments, adding up to a leisurely time-passer. The usual clever sight gags predominate.

Dorothy Lamour, discontented yet again with her secondary status, was assuaged with a nice number to sing in a saloon, but otherwise was fighting the boys for lines and screen time. They infuriated her in other ways too. One afternoon they went off to a charity function without telling Dorothy they wouldn't be back to continue shooting her number. She got all dolled up, came onto the set, waited and waited for them to return while director Hal Walker and the crew kept busy preparing other sequences. Finally Gary Cooper shuffled by the set and told her she was crazy to keep hanging around.

Cooper went on to suggest that Dorothy give the Hope-Crosby Combine a dose of their own medicine. With some initial misgivings — for all her anger, Dorothy knew how to gauge relative positions in the Paramount pecking order — she took Coop's advice and went home. Lamour to this day insists that though the boys kidded her about it from that day forward, they never again left her in the lurch. She tried to get even with them by pulling gags like blacking out her teeth so they'd crack up and interrupt a scene, but nothing, as she recalls it, that would get her into serious trouble. She was always making cracks, of course, but nothing that hit home — Bob's nose and Bing's toupee being, presumably, off limits. On a future Road picture, as will be duly noted, she almost did go too far.

Although David Butler was to be replaced by Hal Walker for the directorial chores (with Hal Walker getting sole credit) there were still the usual narrow escapes and accidents on the Utopia set. A supposedly "tame" bear that was to sniff around the two men as they lay in bed in a cabin became somewhat too feisty, and the boys ran for their lives — off the set and out the stage door, in fact. The next day this bear severely mauled its own trainer. When talking about the incident years later, Hope, in his usual approach to such matters, would make what happened to the trainer (who lost an arm) sound less important than what nearly happened to him. At another point Hope and Crosby were climbing an "ice" wall on a rope when the rope broke. Crosby tumbled onto the sound-stage floor. Hope maneuvered himself so he'd land on the comparatively soft Crosby instead of the floor. Crosby was not amused.

At first the ending of *Utopia* seemed as if it would break the rule of Hope never getting the girl, as Hope and Lamour go off together and get married. But when Crosby visits the duo years later he sees that their sons look just like him. Hope was worried that the censors would insist on an alternative ending — one planned was for Lamour to be split in half by a buzzsaw (offscreen) with half of her going off with Hope, half with Crosby — but to Hope's surprise, the censors, for once in their lives, reacted with humor and flexibility, telling them there was no problem, as the lookalike sons idea was "too absurd" for credibility anyway.

After the release of *Utopia* in January 1945, Paramount let it be known there'd be no more Road pictures, as it was too difficult arranging the schedules of the stars. According to Dorothy Lamour, fans sent in 75,000 letters protesting the decision. Paramount quickly announced preproduction on something called *The Road to Home*, which would have showcased Hope and Crosby as returning GI's, but it never materialized. Two years later Bob and Bing were to team, instead, in *Road to Rio*.

CHAPTER FIFTEEN

THE GREAT LOVER

In the latter half of the 1940's, after the war, Hope found himself slipping in the ratings. His radio show had always been bolstered by using eager GI's as the audience. As a May 1946 *Newsweek* article on Hope put it, "For years he had used the raucous and ready laughter of GI audiences as a sounding board for his jokes. Now he could rely on them no more." When Hope took his show to college campuses in order to regain the spontaneous feedback he felt he needed, he found that "jokes that tickled GI Joe laid eggs with Joe College."

He also had tax troubles. In March of 1945 he owed the Treasury Department $62,000 in income tax, but found he could only raise $12,000 in liquid assets. Reminding the Treasury of all he'd done to sell war bonds, he detailed the reasons for his predicament in a carefully worded letter. The Treasury granted him an extension if he promised to pay what he owed from what he made on his next movie.

His movies were still box office, and subsequently the picture business became even more important in his scheme of things. So did publishing. Hope not only set up a corporation for his movies but decided that the corporation would publish the latest in his ghostwritten volumes, *So This Is Peace*, and paid out $25,000 to a printer. The publishing firm of Simon & Schuster was paid another hefty amount to distribute the book. This time the profits would go into Hope's pocket, not to any charitable organization. Hope was determined to recapture any popularity — or money — he might have lost any way he knew how.

Hope had other troubles in 1946. Dolores decided to host a benefit for some Carmelite nuns and the lawn of the Hope estate was turned into a kind of country fairground. Dolores and cohorts spent a great deal of time in preparation for the day. It was decided to raffle off certain food items, such as hams and chocolate cakes, and several booths featuring games of chance were set up along the grounds. A wheel of fortune in which a prize might be won if a small fee were paid was a popular attraction. Everything was proceeding splendidly and Dolores was proud of her efforts.

Suddenly, several police cars from the North Hollywood precinct rode up the driveway and across the lawn, sirens blaring, scattering the startled guests in all directions. The cops disembarked and announced to one and all that a raid was in progress because of reported "gambling." Neighbors of the Hopes beat a hasty retreat while horrified Carmelite nuns ran screaming about the lawn in a panic. Dolores tried to explain to the officers what was happening, but to her dismay they insisted that she close up shop and order everyone — those who hadn't left already — to go home.

What made it particularly ironic was that the night before the "fair" Hope had hosted a benefit for the LAPD at the Shrine Auditorium. But he was less angry at the police — who were, he reasoned, just doing their job, if a little overzealously — than he was at whomever had made the anonymous complaint. There were any number of people who had a grudge against Hope by this time, but the one who'd really been hurt was Dolores, and he was furious at anyone who would take out their anger at him on his wife. While there were plenty of suspects, what was lacking was proof.

It was around this time that Hope toured the country in a "colossal" show featuring over forty radio, stage, and screen stars — and a full complement of beautiful chorus girls — all lorded over by the One and Only Ski-nose. Hope pulled out all the stops in publicizing the tour and for weeks in advance his publicity men did nothing else but make calls to columnists and others when not dreaming up new ways to hype the show. Hope was out to regain those of his audience who'd strayed by pushing himself down the throats of each and every American he could get within range.

Meanwhile his brother Jim had dumped ex-secretarial aide Marie Mali (he blamed her for his estrangement from Bob and for the complete cessation of cash gifts or loans that the estrangement engendered) and married a pretty young lady named Wyn Swanson, who had show business ambitions. The newlyweds decided to go out on the road with their own act and were booked into theatres in the boondocks by the Levey office, which figured that anyone with the last name of Hope would be bound to attract attention. They also figured that if they could somehow manage to get Jim and Wyn booked into a theatre when Bob and his massive road show were playing in the same town it would prove highly profitable.

This happened when both Bob and Jim were booked into theatres in Spokane, Washington — Bob at the huge Gonzaga Stadium, Jim and Wyn at the tiny Post Theater just around the corner. The marquee of the theatre read in big letters: BOB HOPE'S BROTHER, JIM. Apparently they reasoned that anyone who couldn't get tickets for, or couldn't afford, the big Gonzaga Stadium, could always walk a few yards and see Jim for less than half the price.

Bob was incredulous, then amused, then angry when he heard the news from a reporter who innocently asked what he thought of it. Bob knew Jim and Wyn would be no competition for him, but figured that his brother was once again trying to exploit him. (Whether Jim, on his end, actually realized that Bob would also be playing in Spokane is open to question.)

Unbeknownst to either Bob or Jim, a reporter in town got the bright idea of getting the two men together for a picture. First he called Jim and got his consent. Jim and Wyn, who didn't realize that the reporter hadn't spoken to Bob beforehand, assumed that the photo would mean a reconciliation. Then the reporter called Bob. The man's ear was nearly singed off by the language that come over the phone, as he was told in no uncertain terms that Bob hadn't the slightest intention of posing with his brother, sitting for a joint interview, or even seeing Jim Hope. Meanwhile, Jim and Wyn, believing that not only the reconciliation but an all-out endorsement of their act was in the offing, had excitedly started dressing.

Back at their hotel Jim and Wyn waited and waited for the reporter to call back until it finally occurred to them what must have happened. Bob had nixed the photo. A wave of rage and bitterness and even despair at being second best must have washed over Jim Hope as he realized there was to be no reconciliation, no blessing, no real publicity for his act.

After their show that evening, Wyn and Jim had supper at Bob's hotel and had to endure more humiliation. A whisper rushed through the dining room crowd about how Bob Hope and his company were in the lobby preparing to drive to the airport. Wyn and Jim went out into the lobby to see if they could talk to Bob, but he just brushed past them as if they were part of the crowd. As far as Bob Hope was concerned, his brother Jim might as well have been dead.

Reportedly Bob had sent his agent Doc Shurr to sneak into the Post and watch Jim and Wyn's act, and Shurr reported back that Jim was

175

an acceptable performer but simply didn't have the right material. Bob was not of a mind to lend Jim one of his many comedy writers, and was glad that the act was a bomb and his brother's stage career short-lived. Years later, when an LA *Times* reporter asked Bob if he'd ever helped his brother out during that period, Hope snapped, "Yes, I helped him out. I helped him out of show business." Bob had made up his mind that no other Hope boy would succeed in the entertainment business (his brother Jack as business manager didn't count) or become anywhere near as famous or successful as he was.

Hope's one 1946 release was *Monsieur Beaucaire*, a comic remake of the Rudolph Valentino 1924 silent, both based on a novel by Booth Tarkington. This was to be the first time that the team of Melvin Frank and Norman Panama actually got to work on a bona fide script (as opposed to just the story treatment) and they began their assignment with gusto. Two-thirds of the screenplay had been finished and handed into the studio when the team learned that Paramount had another writer also working on a *Beaucaire* scrip without their prior knowledge. Angered, they refused to submit the final pages until the studio let them out of their contracts.

Although George Marshall was the director, cartoonist-turned-screenwriter Frank Tashlin was brought in to liven up the climactic sword duel between Hope and sinister Joseph Schildkraut with a few hilarious sight gags. Tashlin later went on to write and direct some latter-day Hope features.

Monsieur Beaucaire is one of Bob's better films. He plays the bumbling, barely competent King's barber who winds up impersonating the handsome Duc de Chandre (Patric Knowles) who has quite a reputation with the ladies. Some of Hope's best scenes are with Cecil Kellaway as the fussy advisor to the King. Kellaway, a gifted and versatile character actor who had no trouble getting into the silly mood of the piece, gave — and got from — Hope everything that was required. Although Hope is targeted for death almost from the first, he manages to defeat Schildkraut in the duel and takes his girl, Joan Caulfield, to America where he sets up a barber shop — with a chastened Schildkraut as the shoeshine boy.

Both Schildkraut and Caulfield have been quoted on Hope at various times. Schildkraut, a famous character actor who'd seen better days in 18th Century France as the Duc d'Orleans in Norma Shearer's elaborate 1938 *Marie Antoinette*, was now reduced to a villainous comic spoof in *Beaucaire*, and let it be known he felt director George Marshall had "no feel" for the period and that Hope had grandstanded and mugged so grossly he'd thrown even the comic elements out of focus. "I'm really sorry I ever agreed to do that picture; I ended up looking like a buffoon. That kind of low comedy was never my métier anyway," Schildkraut snapped.

As for Caulfield, who tended to get lost in the proceedings, playing second fiddle as she did to Hope's clowning, she was guarded and faintly commendatory in what she said of the picture, declaring only that "any picture with Bob puts any leading lady's stock up" and that the picture had been "a lot of fun." No word was forthcoming from Patric Knowles, at the time regarded as one of the movies' all-time handsomest men. This confrere of Errol Flynn in the latter's more action-full Warner movies of the Thirties (Flynn, who swung both ways sexually was said to have been much in love with Knowles — they even looked alike) must have felt somewhat uncomfortable while doing *Beaucaire*, aware as he must have been that all his handsome predecessors in Hope movies had won Ski-nose's undying enmity and were pushed out of camera range at every opportunity. Helen Ferguson, the press agent who was rumored to have been Barbara Stanwyck's lover at one time (Helen had herself been a silent film actress) had one of the sharpest, gossipiest tongues in Hollywood, and once said maybe it was true Knowles and Flynn looked alike enough to be brothers but what Flynn felt for Knowles was hardly brotherly. In any event, handsome Patric emerged from *Beaucaire* essentially unscathed and his career went on apace.

Then it was back to Dorothy Lamour for Hope, with Dorothy sullen, defensive and wary as ever, playing the title role in a concoction entitled *My Favorite Brunette*, released in 1947. (Hope was by then a ripe 44.) Although made on the Paramount lot, it was Bob's first independent production under the arrangement he'd set in motion a while before, with stockholders in Hope Enterprises putting up $100,000 while banks added another million. Lamour was later to comment that Hope on this picture, in which he had a financial stake, didn't tend to goof off nearly as much as he had when Paramount was footing the bills. She decided it was her turn to indulge the luxury of assorted goofings-off. When Bob developed a habit of chewing gum to lubricate his vocal cords, Lamour took to aping him. During one love scene she blew a huge bubble just before they kissed; when the gum hit Hope's nose it spread all over both their faces.

Dorothy brought her new baby son Ridge to the set one day when

Hope's wife was visiting. Dolores took one look at the baby and noted he had a nose very much like Bob's. Counting off on her fingers, she quipped, "Hmmm, what was Bob doing at that time?" Dolores watched while Bob's on-set shenanigans drove Dorothy to distraction, commenting only, "Be glad you don't have to put up with him at home, too" — which Dorothy found small comfort.

Lon Chaney, Jr. was in the cast of *Brunette* as a lovable "heavy" whose dumbness is exploited by his nasty pals. He was essentially doing another turn on his memorable portrayal of the dimwit in the film version of *Of Mice and Men*. Chaney was to spend most of his career in the shadow of his famous father, who'd died in 1930 after a distinguished career playing grotesques. The adaptation of John Steinbeck's *Mice* was to be his rare "prestige" appearance. A sad and embittered man, Lon Jr. had found himself playing third and fourth fiddle in "A" productions while starring over at Universal in spinoffs of *Wolf Man* and *Frankenstein* fare. In *Brunette* he was seen, however, to good advantage, as his role was well-written and director Elliott Nugent threw some breaks his way. Bob reportedly felt sorry for Chaney, "probably," character actor John Hoyt commented, "because he saw elements of himself, as he might have been with less success."

Another actor on the downgrade was the famous Peter Lorre, who'd been a German film star and did memorable character portrayals at Warners and elsewhere in the early Forties. In *Brunette* he's a killer-for-hire who stabs assorted members of the cast when he's not throwing knives at Bob. Though Lorre's performance, basically a straight one, is effective, he felt much resentment at the downslide in his career as of 1947. Oddly, he was to say of Hope, "Had he lived in Germany in my era [the Twenties and early Thirties] he might have done very well in drama." What Hope thought of this has never been put on record.

My Favorite Brunette is a far more successful comedy-thriller than *They Got Me Covered*. Hope plays a baby photographer who winds up on death row (the film is in flashback, narrated from his jail cell) when he gets involved with the mysterious Lamour and is framed for murdering a government man. Like *Covered*, *Brunette* has an interesting plot and would have made a competent thriller, but the gag-and-comedy routines are inserted more smoothly into the mixture. The picture, exciting and humorous in equal measure, is one of Hope's better efforts.

Reginald Denny, a renowned character actor who'd played with the best since the Twenties, when he himself had been a silent star, held Hope's abilities in high esteem. Recalling his work with him in *Brunette*,

Denny said he felt Bob had latent dramatic ability he'd never exploited (oddly echoing Lorre's remark). "His timing was wonderful, he had wonderful control of his body and his face," Denny recalled.

During the Forties, Hope had become friends with one of his comedy writers, an alcoholic former newspaperman named Fred Williams. Hope was to carry on a kind of love/hate relationship with Williams for some years, finding him often exasperating. Hope always got furious with Williams' antics when the man was drunk, but found him a warm companion when sober, forgiving his alcoholic indiscretions when they were halfway amusing. Some friends of Hope thought Williams' hold on him came about because he reminded Hope of his father, a champion bottle-hoister. During wartime, when Williams was in the service, he'd call up his general, pretending to be Hope, and ask for an extended leave of absence for himself so he could "help Bob" with his show at the base. (He'd learned to imitate Hope's voice and pronunciation perfectly.) Most times Hope had never even agreed to do a show, but tolerantly adjusted his schedule to fulfill the promises his good buddy had made just to keep him out of trouble with the commandant.

What Williams, however, didn't have in common with Hope's dad, the bibulous Harry, was his tendency to show up with male pickups he'd met on his drinking excursions. Hope always dismissed these men as simple drinking buddies but others acquainted with Williams' didoes knew better.

Hope's continued palship with Williams caused a lot of raised eyebrows as time went on. Associates wondered why Hope let Williams take such terrible advantage of him. On one occasion Hope asked Williams to check out of New York's Waldorf-Astoria for him while he was busy elsewhere. Days later, Hope got a call from the hotel's manager — instead of checking out, Williams had moved into Hope's suite of rooms and was entertaining several male guests in rowdy drinking orgies. But no matter how outrageous Williams' stunts, no matter how they made Bob fume and fuss, Hope didn't break with him. Not at that time, anyway. "When Bob likes someone as a *person*, he mentally blocks out what he *doesn't* like," said Dorothy Lamour.

In 1947, the same year *My Favorite Brunette* was released, Hope took Fred with him and Dolores when they traveled to London to appear at the Odeon Theatre for the annual film command performance for King George VI and Queen Elizabeth. Hope demanded in advance that Fred keep on his best behavior, and above all, stay off the booze. For the entire ocean voyage, Fred complied. He remained sober as a judge through the first day in London. Then a mutual friend of Bob's and Fred's gave Williams a bottle of Scotch which Williams claimed he needed for a "sore throat." By the time the Hopes were set to leave for the Odeon Theatre that night, Williams was nowhere to be found.

It later turned out he was already at the Odeon, where he proceeded to fall flat on his face in front of the King and Queen. By the time Hope arrived, Williams was backstage in the green room making performers nervous. When Fred interrupted a rehearsal Hope was doing with Robert Montgomery, Hope insisted Fred go home. Fred refused; staring drunkenly at Hope, he said, "You're so beautiful in those tails." Finally Hope got Williams out of the theatre — he'd been humiliated enough for one night.

Hope eventually tired of Fred Williams and his shenanigans, and the two drifted apart. After that Williams' decline accelerated. By 1953, six years later, he was reduced to riding freight cars and cadging meals hobo-style. Trying to hop off one train, he fell under the wheels and was crushed to death (the second time in his life Hope lost a friend to a train). When the news got to Bob, friends recalled that he seemed more devastated than he had since his mother died. Williams' emotional hold on the usually cold and self-involved Bob Hope has never fully been deciphered, though speculations have continued for years. "Denial" may be a possibility.

My Favorite Brunette was still filming when Bob's brother Sid died of cancer at 41; he'd been two years Bob's junior. Both had known about Sid's illness for some time, so it didn't come as a shock. Whatever anger Bob might have felt toward Jim and other brothers, he could only pity Sid, who'd kept his family and himself sequestered on his farm; he'd leave a wife and five children behind. Hope went out to Ohio during Sid's final months for a bittersweet reunion. All the Hope brothers attended the funeral and Bob reportedly told Sid's wife, Dorothy, that she and the children would be provided for.

Later in 1947, Hope appeared yet again with Crosby in another all-star revue picture directed by their standby-perennial George Marshall and entitled *Variety Girl*. This picture celebrated the Hollywood "Variety Clubs" that assisted needy children. The plot had two young ladies, who'd been helped by the clubs in childhood, attempting to enter show biz. Hope and Crosby have some funny put-down routines. A young Deforest Kelley, who later went on to fame as

Bones in *Star Trek*, played a handsome talent scout. Director George Marshall put himself in front of the camera to do a turn and other back-stage types performed. William Demarest, who was in the film, later said, "Bob gave everything he had even to stints where he was a passing attraction; he never let down his professional guard for one minute!"

Where There's Life (1947) came next. In this Bob teamed with pret-ty blonde Signe Hasso and not-so-pretty William Bendix in a fairly good comedy about a would-be groom who's kidnapped on the night before his wedding. It seems certain factions in the Kingdom of Boravia are convinced he's the rightful ruler and want him to claim his throne. A lady general (Hasso) is employed to see he does. Hope's comedic gifts are in fine fettle in this, and the script, co-written by frequent Hope col-laborator Melville Shavelson, has some great one-liners. William Bendix, a great man for stealing scenes, later recalled that he had his work cut out for him getting the edge on Bob. "He's an old hand at grabbing all the attention," Bendix snorted. "I gave up after the first scene with him — and I'm not a guy who gives up easily!"

Paramount had as its prime Christmas release in 1947 *The Road to Rio*, one of the better entries in the series. For this one Bing and Bob had put together a special production company; they co-produced the picture with Paramount. Each man and the studio owned a third. Dorothy Lamour was never even considered or consulted. She was, however, insulted by all the financial maneuvering that left her out in the cold — and out of the money. Insult was added to injury, in her view, when the boys later deigned to give her a minuscule percentage of the picture and her eventual profit-sharing residual check came to a total of sixteen cents.

Dorothy was to have her revenge, even if inadvertently. The boys had invested $25,000 apiece in a new soft drink called Lime Cola, and used their two thirds ownership clout to convince Paramount to let them advertise the cola in *Road to Rio* via a big sign seen in one of the sequence backgrounds. Unfortunately, Lime Cola went out of business before the picture opened and both men lost their investment. It was too late to take the big sign out of the picture.

Bob and Bing and director Norman McLeod would play jokes on Paramount's top honchos by deliberately inserting obscene gags into each morning's rushes which they had no intention of using the in the finished picture. For Lamour, however, the "filthiest" Hope gags were the ones that cut her out of an appearance on Crosby's radio show dur-ing the filming. Both she and Hope were guest-starring but Hope ad-

Bob and perennial co-star Dorothy Lamour kissed and made up a lot during their careers, here in a publicity shot from 1947

With Signe Hasso in *Where There's Life*, 1947

libbed so much during the pretaping that, come airtime, the producers had no choice but to save time by cutting out Lamour's song number entirely. Nobody bothered to tell her either.

The night of the broadcast, Lamour held a dinner party and turned on her radio at the appointed hour so her guests could hear her song. By the time the Crosby show ended, she'd worked up a particularly foul disposition. So angry was she at the boys that they made a point of staying out of her way on the set unless juxtaposition was absolutely necessary.

In *Rio* Lamour plays a young heiress hypnotized by a sinister aunt who wants her to marry an associate of hers. Gale Sondergaard was again in a witchy role as the aunt and told friends she was fed up with those parts. As Norman McLeod recalled it, "Gale fancied herself attractive and beguiling, though romantic stuff had never been her forte — she was always some kind of freaky villainess. When some of the dialogue referred to her as unpleasant to the eye (which she wasn't) it made her hysterical, and she demanded script changes which unfortunately she didn't have the clout to get done. She felt these roles were beneath her — I guess she needed the money. But she was always professional."

The highlights of *Rio* are the hilarious high-wire act Bob participates in at the start, and his Carmen Miranda drag scene near the end. After a somewhat slack middle section, the finale — with Bing and Bob working overtime to short-circuit the hypnotized Dorothy's wedding — is amusing and suspenseful. The Andrews Sisters even contributed a catchy number, "You Don't Have to Know the Language."

Hope's next picture *The Paleface* (1948) was to turn out to be one of his most financially rewarding and critically acclaimed. Ginger Rogers had been first choice (and a bad one) for co-star but she wanted too much money, and was replaced by Jane Russell. An almost unrecognizable Robert Armstrong (from *King Kong*) put in an appearance, and Hope made sure, as usual, that Iris Adrian got a juicy supporting role. By 1948 Adrian's looks were "on the fade," as Armstrong phrased it, but she gave a decent account of herself as an aging, but still saucily sexy, dance-hall girl.

Jane Russell, who could be a feisty filly when she didn't like a picture or a leading man, and had no hesitation in telling off all comers, recalled that she "loved" working with Hope. As she put it later, appearing as his co-star was "a ball," adding, "He's even funnier offscreen than on, and everything's relaxed except his chocolate eyes, which never stop darting, never missing a thing." Hope, on his end, was to give Russell, whose generous figure caught his eye from the first time he saw her, the nickname of "Lumpy." Norman McLeod, on the team for yet another whirl, found himself playing reluctant and fuming stooge for Hope, who walked all over him as usual. When light changes or costume changes took too long, Hope would stomp off to the exit to play golf while McLeod would stamp his foot and stutter "S-s-stop, B-b-Bob!" in a whisper that could barely be heard. Hope would keep right on going. "Hope loved to tease McLeod and make fun of him," Robert Armstrong remembered. "I don't know why McLeod put up with it as much as he did; needed the job, I guess, and a Hope picture always helped a director in the industry. I, for one, wish Norman had hauled off and given Bob a nose-remodeling; the crap he put up with!"

The Paleface is a superior comedy about a dentist, "Painless" Potter (who's anything but) played by Hope, who becomes innocently embroiled in an attempt by Calamity Jane (Russell) to uncover a nest of white traitors who're selling guns to the Indians. As in the best Hope comedies, *Paleface* is not a total farce, being replete with a plot that contains some genuine suspense and holds the attention throughout.

Co-screenwriter Frank Tashlin worked up some great visual gags. An early scene in which Hope and Russell are married (to fool the traitors, who've been told to look out for a single agent) involves the camera's being fixed on everyone's hands during the ceremony. When the minister is through conducting the vows, he says: "And now — the kiss." This is followed by a kissing noise. "Not me, you fool!" shouts the minister.

In another scene Calamity Jane confronts Iris Adrian as the dance hall girl who makes a play for Hope. (The traitors figure that her jealous boyfriend will knock Hope off) and delivers a knockout punch to Adrian's jaw as they stand in the door of the saloon. The next shot shows Adrian picking herself up from the debris of a wall all the way across the street.

Hope's performance in the comedy scenes is good, but he's oddly listless and perfunctory in the one "serious" scene when he realizes Jane has played him for a fool; Jane thereupon confesses she's actually fallen for him. Hope's approach, whenever he was confronted with actual drama, was to underplay to such an extreme that he comes off like a drama student doing a "read-through." This approach continued to persist even when he played more serious roles in subsequent years. "He really had no confidence in himself as a dramatic actor," Frank Tashlin later said, "but the joke on Bob was he was a better all-around actor than he ever allowed himself to be. He was afraid of failure, I guess."

Like many of the cartoons that *The Paleface* resembles, the film employs the same pseudo-homoeroticism that frequently popped up in Hope movies (as it did in, of all things, Bugs Bunny cartoons). In these bits, an essentially asexual comic character (which Hope always was to play in certain respects in spite of his heterosexual appetites) becomes involved in what, under the circumstances, would be called "a compromising position." In *Paleface* an Indian gets a whiff of some of dentist Hope's laughing gas and invades the bedroom Hope and Russell are sharing. Mistaking him for Russell when his eyes are shut, Hope gives the Indian a kiss right on the lips. Unlike his kiss with the minister, this one is shown on camera. These kind of "gay" gags would be rife in *Son of Paleface* a few years later.

Although *The Paleface* is a period piece and not a picture that can be taken seriously, in retrospect its depiction of Indians is regressive, to say the least, as was true of all Hollywood pictures of the era. When a Native American gentleman sent Hope a letter about *The Paleface* in which he said, in part, "There's thousands of Indians who are a darned sight smarter and a darned sight more civilized than you. . . . to listen to you, one would think it is a disgrace to be an Indian." Hope's only reaction was amusement at what he felt was the fellow's thin skin. Superficial in some crucial ways, Hope never seemed to realize that the Indian man was reacting to hundreds of years of repression and the knowledge that Native American culture had not only been virtually wiped out by white settlers but that "original people" were in a constant battle for civil rights, even in the Forties. Hope tended to feel that every group was ripe for satire, but forgot that minorities who in the Forties were lacking equality with other American groups were certainly entitled to be more "sensitive." Scenes in which Hope shoots dozens of Indians (Calamity Jane is actually the markswoman) and dead Indian bodies begin literally to pile up on the ground, are in retrospect especially disturbing, and provide a dark undertone to the basic humor of the picture. Hope would continue making public and private jokes about Indians, Gays, Blacks, and Jews for the rest of his career, with the private ones much, much more vile than anything he said on camera or before a live audience.

The Paleface was Hope's biggest-grossing picture to date, garnering approximately $4.5 million at the box office. Part of the reason for its success was Hope's decision to take his radio crew on tour in order to play up the picture. Doris Day was his featured vocalist at the time, and she proved to be more of a pain than even Painless Potter could handle. She seemed to spend most of the tour in the bathroom, and would complain right before show time that she couldn't go on because her makeup wasn't right, or it was an unflattering dress she had on, or her tummy was upset. But Doris's chief complaint was that she wasn't making enough money. Hope was never to ask Doris to accompany him on his later U.S.O. tours, understandably, as conditions overseas would have proved too much for her — and him. She never made a picture with him either.

Hope was teamed with Lucille Ball for the first time in movies in a remake of *Sorrowful Jones* (1949), based on a Damon Runyon story. Hope had known Runyon back in the Thirties when they lived in the same hotel in New York. Runyon concentrated on writing stories that — at least in their screen adaptations — focused on cartoon versions of gangsters, gamblers, and other colorful New York lowlife "characters." In *Sorrowful Jones*, Hope plays a bookie who accepts an IOU for a bet from a desperate father. The father then leaves his little girl at the betting parlor while he goes to see if he can borrow the money from a big time operator (Bruce Cabot). When the father inadvertently discovers Cabot fixed some races, Cabot orders him killed and Hope is stuck with the youngster. Lucille Ball is a singer at Cabot's nightclub who helps Hope look after the child. The film was a remake of the 1934 *Little Miss Marker* in which child star Shirley Temple and Adolphe Menjou had made a big hit.

One flaw in their comedy drama is that none of the characters ever expresses any sympathy for the young father, who died simply because he was in the wrong place at the wrong time. The film seems to go too far in its avoidance of sentimentality. The casting of Hope undoubtedly makes the character of self-absorbed Jones more palatable, though whether such a character ever existed outside Damon Runyon's, and the screenwriters', imaginations is debatable. Although Hope does very nicely in an otherwise treacle-laced praying scene with the little girl. Throughout the picture he continues his patented emotionless underplaying. Fighting, as usual, any drift toward dramatic acting, Hope, when all else fails, falls back on the usual comedy shtick.

Rhonda Fleming was originally slated to play Lucille Ball's part of Gladys. (Fleming was to be Hope's leading lady in his next film.) Ball's previous film, *Her Husband's Affairs*, had been a ball-of-ice disaster, and *I Love Lucy* was still in the future; her agent found few offers coming in from producers who resisted her $75,000 fee per picture. Ball was no slouch when it came to asking favors of Hope, however; he'd hired Desi for his radio show at her request. She went to Bob and asked him if he could tell Paramount he wanted her to co-star with him in *Jones*. Not having a crystal ball on hand to tell her that a hit TV show and true super stardom were coming up in the relatively near future, Ball wasn't above begging. One story has it that she was even willing to go further to get the job. In any case, she got it.

Both Lucy and Bob were skilled comedians and not true dramatic actors (or didn't see themselves as such), and they worked extremely well together when the subject was comedy. But in the comparatively serious scenes in *Jones*, Ball subdued her natural spirited persona to drop to Hope's level of understated — sometimes somnambulistic (perhaps he'd returned to his childhood habit of sleepwalking?) — playing. The result is that the two of them seem to be just walking through half the picture. Director Sidney Lanfield was to recall that he had a time of it eliciting appropriately solid performances from either. Ball was also motivated by concern lest she overshadow her more popular (at that time) co-star; then, she reasoned, no more favors could be expected from him in the future.

Nevertheless, *Sorrowful Jones* is an acceptable trifle with its share of good moments along with more than a few missteps. To punch up the ending, the screenwriters had Hope bring a horse clear into a hospital bedroom to bring the child (winningly played by Mary Jane Saunders) out of the coma she'd fallen into after falling out a window. Though the horse-in-hospital scenes are elementarily amusing they're also utterly improbable, hence out of sync with the rest of the film.

Sometime before *Sorrowful Jones'* release in July 1949, Hope ran into a lovely 22-year-old starlet by the name of Barbara Payton in Texas, where Hope was playing in a golf tournament. According to Payton, she was introduced to Hope by a mutual friend, the millionaire Bob Neal, when Neal took her to a party Hope was throwing in his hotel suite. At the party Hope promptly pounced on Barbara, and Neal found himself out of the running. Payton spent the night in Hope's suite, and left for Houston, where she had an appointment, in the morning. That night Hope showed up at the Shamrock Hotel in Houston where she was staying, and the two had dinner. This time Hope woke up in Barbara's room.

From then on, Hope would arrange for Payton to be in whatever city he was bound for; this went on for several months. In New York for the premiere of *Sorrowful Jones*, Hope took his usual suite at the

Waldorf-Astoria — the same one where buddy Fred Williams had held his drinking parties — and put Barbara in an adjoining room with a connecting door. News of their involvement became widespread among insiders; all of Hope's entourage knew of it. Payton's studio, Universal-International, proceeded to warn her they'd drop her option if she continued the liaison. Payton, recklessly feeling that some way, some how, Bob would pull her irons out of the fire, kept up her involvement with him. Some time later, the studio canceled Payton's contract.

Whatever Payton had hoped to get out of Bob, she actually got very little. She complained to friends that instead of pearl necklaces or diamond earrings, Hope would give her jars of cheap jam. When Hope refused to star her in any of his pictures, or help her career in any concrete way (although he did introduce her to influential acquaintances in the hope one of them would take her off his hands) Payton got nasty, greedy, and indiscreet. She told everyone and anyone about her "fling" with Bob, accused him of being lousy in bed, and demanded money from him just to get rid of her but it was never more than a hundred bucks at a time. At this time Bob had passed his 45th birthday. ("Forty-five going on nineteen," Lucille Ball is reported to have said tartly — seems Bob wasn't delivering to Ball on promises he'd icily made to her, either.)

Hope had grown sick and tired of Payton and everything relating to her. Payton's threat to tell Dolores "all," however, would have gotten her nowhere as this sort of thing by 1949 was an old, old story to the patient, home-and-kiddies Mrs. Hope.

Hope proceeded to build a protective shell around himself, and assigned aides to deal with Barbara. Reportedly she was paid off with quite a large sum on condition she just shut up and disappear into a hole somewhere. She went through the money in months, and years later, still raging at Hope for not "doing more" for her, told the whole sordid story to *Confidential*.

Payton wasn't through yet, however, not in the early Fifties at any rate. She was to sink her hooks into such actors as Tom Neal (*Detour*) and the ex-Mr. Joan Crawford, Franchot Tone. When Payton took the measure of the admittedly younger and handsomer Neal and decided he'd never amount to much in the Picture-ville Pecking Order, she married the older, but more established Tone in the early Fifties. Tone, who'd reportedly beaten Joan Crawford while married to her, got paid back by fate when Neal beat him up so badly in 1951, in a confrontation in a Hollywood nightclub over Payton, that Tone had to resort to facial plastic surgery.

Snickers abounded in Hollywood when Hope's next picture was entitled *The Great Lover*. It was released, appropriately (or more likely, inappropriately) at Christmas time, 1949. In this Hope is a newspaperman chaperoning a troupe of scouts who've won a trip abroad. On the ship back to America, Hope encounters an impoverished duchess (Fleming) and the two run afoul of a sinister, homicidal cardsharp (Roland Young) who frames Hope for one of his murders. The only rationale for the title is a scene in which Young suggests Hope romance Fleming in order to snare her supposedly wealthy father, the Grand Duke (Roland Culver) into a card game.

Hope nearly drowned during one sequence in which director Alexander Hall wanted realism (meaning no stunt double) when he falls overboard and tries to climb back on the ship via the anchor, which keeps dropping Hope into the drink. Hope was attached to a special wire which would pull him up and down and into or out of a tank as warranted. The wire caught on part of the underwater rigging, and Hope was trapped beneath the water for several minutes until the assistant director, Henry Kaplan, dove into the water and got him untangled. Emergency lifesaving techniques were then employed to remove the water from Hope's lungs. He vowed never to do a stunt like that again.

The Great Lover is not top-drawer Hope by any means. Although there's quite an exciting final quarter, the picture is replete with too many long, long stretches without any laughs or even chuckles, and not a strong enough plot to compensate for it. One gets impatient for Hope — a grown man after all — to tell off the snotty head of the scout troop (and the boss's son) who insists (though he himself is only a kid) that Hope conform to the behavioral standards of the other scouts.

Unlike the polished-up and refined-up former "slut" Virginia Mayo in *The Princess and the Pirate*, Rhonda Fleming is much too coarse to be convincing as a European duchess; she seems in appearance and manner more like a standard Hollywood "B" girl. There are some funny bits — Bob hiding in a kennel with a hungry dog when he's on the run from the authorities; and a scene with him and Jack Benny (in a cameo) spoofing each other's toupees — but the result is disappointing.

Hope during shooting made no secret of the fact that he found Rhonda Fleming attractive, but as a movie duo they didn't click; she was to make only one more film with him, in the Fifties.

Now that Hope's movie stardom was assured, and his radio days almost over, he was to become ever more intrigued by — and move on to conquer all-out — a new medium: Television. As he was delightedly to discover, the Hope talents were perfectly suited to the "Boob" tube.

CHAPTER SIXTEEN

BOB AND THE PEACOCK

In the early days of Television, Hope had made a few tentative appearances, telling friends he was "feeling his oats." In fact, he said the same thing to me, when I did my first interview with Hope on the set of his 1950 movie *Fancy Pants*. He opened up to me pretty well on that occasion, as I was introduced to him by my old friend Billy Grady. Hope said at the time, "Television will expand — it is making large strides now, and it will improve more and more technologically. The regular people in it now will grasp its potential more firmly as time goes on."

In 1949 Hope had cut his TV teeth on the *Ed Sullivan Show*, for one, and shortly after he talked to me, he signed with NBC to do his own network special. That was in 1950. Hope was 47. The variety spectacular, for which Hope was paid $40,000, was sponsored by Frigidaire and broadcast on the evening of Easter Sunday, April 9th, from the New Amsterdam Theatre in New York. The guests included Beatrice Lillie, Dinah Shore, and Douglas Fairbanks, Jr.

Hope, with uncharacteristic modesty on the occasion of my first interview, had said moreover that it would be a matter of how television adapted to him and how he adapted to it, adding, "It's the second part I'm nervous about." Billy Grady, who sat in on the interview, immediately commented, "You'll ride high on it, Bob, as you have in every other medium," which made him beam.

It did take a while for Hope to adapt to the television medium — and vice versa — but one person who hated Hope's TV appearances from the first was Paramount's President, Barney Balaban. Balaban was convinced that Hope's box office would be badly affected if he could be seen for free on television, particularly if he — as Balaban expected — eventually did it on a weekly basis. This is exactly what happened after the first few specials. Hope's representatives and the Paramount bigwigs engaged in several heated phone conversations, with each side arguing what they felt was the realistic position. Hope's boys felt that television was the wave of the future; Paramount thought TV would destroy the movies. Balaban, like other movie producers of the era — the late Forties and early Fifties — declared to all who'd listen that it was bad enough that the studios had had to divest themselves of their exhibition outlets to satisfy Federal antitrust demands, but TV competition was providing Double Jeopardy (not the game show) in spades. It was true that movies by that time were not pulling in the crowds they had up to 1947.

Circa 1949, movie exhibitors, who were feeling the pinch especially, began sending Hope hate-filled letters (after seeing him on the Sullivan show) in which they chorused over and over their wariness of television and threatened to boycott his films from their theatres. The controversy began to die down only when it became apparent that Hope's shows could, in fact, be looked upon as hour-long commercials for his movies — anyway that was his shrewd selling point: a few back-slapping, quip-slinging luncheons, dinners, and parties with key exhibitors did the rest.

In 1950, for his third TV special, Hope decided to feature the entertainers who'd just gotten back from a tour of Korea with him. As in his first two shows, Hope was nervous, and this clearly shows up in kinescopes of the program. At one point, he gets caught behind the curtain after a skit and takes several moments to find his way out onto the stage — something one of his dorky characters would have done in his movies. But Hope also is likable and attractive, reaffirming his status as a truly irresistible comedian who'd honed to perfection his basic technique during vaudeville days, and expanded it on radio and in films.

The skits for this special were modestly entertaining, bolstered by fine support from Marilyn Maxwell (who once told me fervently, "Bob's the Best!") and others. While the bit with Judy Kelly, an athletic dancer and contortionist whose double-jointed movements bordered on the vulgar, was perhaps the low light of the show, the highlight was Hope's tap dance with the High Hat dancers, in which he proved he'd never forgotten the skills he'd shown to good advantage in vaudeville.

Hope's problems adjusting to television were, in fact, mostly caused by the many technicians and assistant directors, who'd be working overtime to demonstrate they were earning their pay by signaling to him, waving their arms, rolling their eyes, pointing to their wristwatches, and distracting him so much he could hardly concentrate on what he was doing. Finally he solved the problem in his usual forthright manner by insisting on no movement during the show. Once he made it clear that he, Bob Hope, was boss and that the crew would have to accommodate themselves to him rather then the other way around, things moved smoothly.

Hope was at first so aware of the visual element of television after his long haul of radio invisibility that he tried too hard to come up with gags that took advantage of the camera. But that meant an "overslide" into slapstick, which had never been his forte. He finally decided to settle back and do what he did best: the monologue, along with some light comic acting in the sketches. But the camera still presented a problem. The audience would see Hope holding his script as he'd done on radio, thereby depriving his monologue of a certain spontaneity. Because of this, the audience didn't laugh as hard. Hope was importuned to memorize his script before he went on the air, but this solution never did sit well with him.

Instead he preferred cue-cards, which were handy for him as he was far-sighted. Even when teleprompters replaced them in later years, he preferred the "idiot cards." This often caused unexpected problems, such as when guests who'd spent hours memorizing the script found out that Hope didn't have to, with a consequent verbalizing of their resentment. In another instance, a comedian hosting a London variety show with Hope as guest star deliberately read off all of Hope's cue-cards right after introducing him during a camera rehearsal, nearly inducing a Hope Heart Attack when he suggested he might do the same thing during the actual show. Another time an inexperienced cue-card man would simply throw each giant card behind his back, nearly decapitating members of the studio audience, until an assistant director came down and stopped him.

But the cue-cards were snaps to master compared to the TV censors. One early skit on his weekly show was a spoof of plugs and payolas, and actual products had to be mentioned on the air or the sketch just wouldn't work. Hope was annoyed by the "tight asses" at NBC who tried to remove the product-mentions and water down the script. Free mentions of products that were not sponsors were more upsetting to the NBC censors than sexual innuendo.

Another problem was the theft of material, which was particularly insidious because Hope's writers had offices right in the NBC headquarters. As Milton Berle remembers, "We could have had office space for our writers at NBC, but I didn't trust that set-up. Bob Hope once had his whole opening monologue, which he was going to do that night, delivered on a kiddie show the same afternoon by another guy whose writers had gotten it from an NBC secretary he was "friendly with."

Special effects brought their own headaches, literally, as Hope was to discover when a champagne bucket that was to be gently lowered onto the stage during a sketch slipped from prop man Al Borden's hands and clunked Hope right on the noggin. On another occasion, all the props were left behind when the crew went on location to shoot a special, initiating some quick creative thinking on the prop man's part.

One of Hope's chief TV rivals after Milton Berle was Jack Benny. Hope had known Benny well since their radio days. Like Bob and Bing, Hope and Benny had an odd love/hate relationship. Both got along together swimmingly while performing, but personally there was often a lot of friction. They were never more than "professional" friends. Given Hope's hyper-competitive nature, he was often jealous of Benny's equally high ratings and audience appeal. Privately Benny — although basically a nice man with a comparatively, and deceptively, gentle personality — could be bitchy when he felt like it, snapping at Bob and muttering under his breath when he felt his TV rival was getting too obnoxious or hogging too much of the action.

It was well-known among industry insiders that Benny was essentially homosexual, something that both amused and repelled Hope. When Crosby kiddingly made "gay" insinuations about Hope just to get his goat, Hope knew he couldn't really retaliate in kind, but with Benny it was another story. Benny told certain friends he felt Hope was the Fifties equivalent of a "closet case," which of course Benny himself was. The two never talked about it outright, but Benny would make occasional digs and Hope would pounce back mercilessly whenever he did.

Although Hope was hardly a paragon of masculinity with his manic mannerisms and "cowardly" posturing, Benny was undeniably quite effeminate — an effeminacy he deliberately underlined with theatrical flourishes and posturings, used in his comedy turns, and got away with because wife Mary Livingston was always on hand for "beard" duty (translate that "cover up"). Mary was always to be irritated with Hope's aspersions on her husband's manhood, and retaliated with imitations of Hope's cowardly, head-tossing shtick. Hope never let up on Benny's swishy walk and his tendency to hold his hand to his face like an elderly "auntie." Initially he did this only behind Benny's back at parties to amuse guests. Then he did it openly in front of Benny, and even in comedy sketches.

When they worked together Hope would throw in ad-libs (actually talked over with Hope's writing staff beforehand) of an obvious "gay" nature; one instance was an African explorer sketch they did when Hope guest-starred on the Benny program. The two men are carrying a tiger on a pole when one remarks that there aren't any tigers in Africa. Hope then swivels the tiger mock-up around to reveal that the other side of it is a leopard. "He must have gone to a veterinarian in Denmark," Hope says. "I wondered why he had his hand on his hip when I shot him." Benny fell out of character and bent over with laughter, then straightened up to slap Hope on the hand.

The irony is that during the entire interchange Hope is unconsciously standing with one knee bent and his hand delicately stretched out toward the tiger/leopard in what can only be described as a "light in the loafers" fashion.

Benny may have chuckled over all this in public, but he knew that Hope was viciously needling him and he didn't like it, particularly as he felt Hope was a complete hypocrite. He told friends, "Hope doesn't walk any differently than I do. He walks like a woman, too." In his later days when it was not so verboten to talk about such things, Benny would make the same comments on talk shows and do a mincing impersonation of the way Hope walked. He was not about to let Hope get away with it any longer.

In late 1953, Hope's Monday night show became the "first full hour commercial show on color television," and according to critic John Crosby was an "unqualified disaster." Part of the problem was that Arlene Dahl, who was co-starring in the movie *Here Come the Girls* with Hope at the time, had been contracted to appear on the show but did a last-minute walkout, greatly angering Hope. Dahl was also appearing with Jose Ferrer at the time in the City Center production of *Cyrano de Bergerac* and claimed that doing the Hope tour would "tax her voice." Actually, her lover, actor Fernando Lamas, had flown into town and captured all her attention. Janis Paige was quickly brought in as replacement, but didn't know her lines and didn't seem to have the vaguest idea of where she was or what she was doing. (Apparently Hope didn't allow anyone else but himself to use cue-cards, or else they're more difficult to master than one would imagine.)

To show off the new color process, the call went out for several "lovelies" — beautiful women, in showbiz parlance — to appear on the broadcast in the latest fashions. A crowd of about a hundred girls, each with an agent in tow, showed up to be personally auditioned by Bob and his associates. The choicest of these "lovelies" was then seen on the broadcast Monday night.

Critics had often accused Hope's program of being "tasteless," but the verdict on this show was simply that it was dull and unfunny. Allowances were made for it being a "dress rehearsal" (the same color show presented on Monday was performed all over again in black and white on Tuesday evening) but most reviewers, particularly Crosby, agreed that the color was the only noteworthy feature.

Of course John Crosby (no relation to Bing) and Hope had never been the best of friends. Three years before, when he was a radio critic, Crosby authored a piece in *Life* magazine that included the sentence: "Writers get $2000 a week in Hollywood for copying down Fred Allen's jokes and putting them on Bob Hope's program." Hope told *The New York Times* that Crosby's article "exposed him to the hatred and ridicule of the public and tended to discredit his standing in the entertainment business." A lawsuit was slapped on both *Life* and Crosby. Hope demanded one million in general damages, another million as exemplary damages, plus an extra $10,000 for his lawyer, Martin Gang.

Life publisher Andrew Heiskell called Crosby into his office and the two tried to come up with a way to placate Hope. Crosby was chewed out for "irresponsibility" in accusing Hope and his writers of plagiarism. Crosby argued that he'd been expressing a critical opinion primarily, which should have protected him from libel suits, and that the *Life* lawyers had seen nothing objectionable in the passage anyway. Heiskell did what he could to maintain "damage control," downplay all the media hoopla, and convince Hope that Crosby's statement had been inadvertent and would certainly have been excised from the article had it not been for someone's carelessness. Hope decided to drop the suit six months after he filed it. Through his attorney he issued the following statement: " . . . investigation and discussion have convinced me that *Life* was acting in good faith and without intention to harm me in publishing the article. Therefore, I have elected to drop the suit against *Life*. We have been good friends for a long time and I hope we will be good friends for a long time to come."

Insiders suspected that Hope's lawyer had advised him that since the article, entitled "Seven Deadly Sins of the Air, " was essentially a piece of criticism as opposed to an investigative report, they might have had trouble winning the suit in court. Hope had no intention of wasting his money if that were the case.

From then on, Crosby was always to be one of Hope's toughest critics. (One did have to admire his guts for continuing to take on the litigious Hope, although he knew his criticisms weren't essentially libelous.) He did grudgingly praise Hope on occasion, as in an April 1955 column in the *New York Herald-Tribune* that stated, "Bob Hope, who has not consistently or ever very intermittently entertained me for a good many years now, came up with the best show I've ever seen him [do] on Tuesday night. Unless my eyes were playing me tricks, there seemed to be a determined effort to remold the Hope personality into something a little less brash and a little more winning. This is a formidable task, Hope being the volcanic person that he is. . . ."

Crosby felt that in this instance Hope wasn't so determined to hog all the jokes in the sketches, but let his guest stars get some of the laughs, and it made for a show that was much more enjoyable. A highlight of the program was a filmed sketch — a parody of "This Is Your Life" with Lassie as the guest star — that employed about a dozen dogs dressed up in cute little outfits walking about on their hind legs. (Although Crosby suggested that it might have been funnier if they hadn't filmed it in bits and pieces first but just let the dogs go out on the stage to the expected calamitous results.)

Actually one of the strongest attacks on Hope — one of the most negative reviews he ever got throughout his career — came not from Crosby but from influential critic Jack Gould in *The New York Times* in 1953. Hope did a special show that was filmed on location during the sesquicentennial celebration of the state of Ohio. Gould's verdict: "A witless and tasteless charade, put on in the distinctive style of a road company Minsky, marked the return of Bob Hope to his video chores. . . . the program was the season's low."

Gould attacked Hope for resorting to his radio trick of avoiding "hard work" and resorting to sketches that were "rooted in suggestiveness and crudity." Gould bemoaned the fact that Hope embroiled the Governor of Ohio into his "excursion into commonness." "On the stage were numerous prominent personages who had passed their youth in Ohio and had returned especially for the occasion," wrote Gould. "It was in this framework that Mr. Hope scrawled his back-fence portraiture. Hope was back at his old stand, the glib connoisseur of the unpleasant and unnecessary way of life in show business."

Gould also objected strenuously to a sketch in which Hope, Phil Harris, and the Governor encountered two girls, one of whom, "a frightful hag," danced with Hope. "The dance was sheer vulgarity unrelieved by even a trace of comedy," screeched Gould. "One of Mr. Hope's lines was monstrous in its offensiveness. To add to the fiasco, Hope and Harris conducted an extended routine that substituted effeminancy for humor. This particular form of cathode nausea is an old story on TV, but by this time most comedians have wised up. Hope should too." Not since Hope had been condemned by a Catholic magazine in his radio days had he been subjected to such an outraged (and somewhat sanctimonious) critique.

On at least two occasions Hope tried to buy a TV station of his own, but it never worked out in his favor. In 1953 a company in which Hope held a substantial interest, Metropolitan TV, bought the Denver station KOA from NBC. Citing the strong relationship between Hope and the National Broadcasting Company (for one thing, NBC at that time owned half of Hope, Inc.) the FCC ruled that Metro's application for a TV station was not eligible "since it follows that NBC would then be acquiring a direct interest in the ownership, operation and control of a sixth TV station in contravention of the Commission's rules and regulations." The FCC further charged that through these convoluted financial arrangements NBC had "reserved to itself a position from which it has the ability to exert an effective influence on basic policy determinations which are, and should be, the prerogatives of the licensee of KOA only."

In July 1957, Hope was interested in buying a TV station in Rockford, Illinois, and formed the Continental Television Corp. with Ashley Robison, Albert Zugsmith, and Arthur B. Hogan "for the purpose of acquiring control of Greater Rockford Television Corp., which operated WREX, Rockford." Charged with "repudiating" the agreement to purchase the station, Robison and Zugsmith sued Hope and Continental for $1,185,000 in February of 1959, claiming that Hope's reneging had lost them commissions and profits. The suit was later resolved.

Another legal brouhaha erupted when Hope innocently appeared on Frank Sinatra's television show in October of 1957. Hope, whose own program was sponsored by Timex, had no idea that rival watchmaker Bulova was one of Frank's sponsors until a short while before airtime. He was assured that Bulova's ad wouldn't run until after the end credits. Somehow there was a mix up, and Bulova's commercial appeared before the end credits and hence was technically a part of the show.

For some time it was rumored that Timex wanted to get out of the deal with NBC and Hope, and sponsor only occasional specials instead of a weekly series, and they seized on Hope's appearance on the Sinatra show to charge him with violating his contract, which they promptly canceled. Five days before a major meeting between NBC and Timex to discuss this, Timex signed for half-sponsorship of a Bing Crosby special to be aired on CBS. NBC decided to threaten Timex with legal action. The following year Hope had new sponsors but he did six or so "specials" a year instead of a weekly series.

On occasion Hope would try something other than his usual mix of song numbers and comedy sketches. In 1958 he did a television adaptation of his Broadway triumph of 1933, *Roberta*, with Janis Paige, Howard Keel, and Anna Maria Alberghetti. He was to restage the whole thing again a decade later with John Davidson and Michele Lee in the cast. Occasionally he'd air specials that were centered on his film career, such as the one he did in the mid-Sixties that brought him together with nine of his leading ladies. (Arlene Dahl, who'd crapped out on that previous color telecast, wasn't even invited.)

A 1966 TV special, featuring nine former co-stars. Front row, left to right, Lucille Ball, Joan Fontaine, Hedy Lamarr, Signe Hasso. Back row, left to right, Joan Collins, Dorothy Lamour, Virginia Mayo, Vera Miles, and Janis Paige

Things occasionally got tense backstage, there being so many fragile female egos in the aging actress contingent. Dorothy Lamour and Joan Collins, who'd clashed during the making of *Road to Hong Kong*, didn't even speak to one another. Joan Fontaine, who'd hated the one film she did with Hope, *Casanova's Big Night*, simply wanted to get through her stint as quickly as possible. Virginia Mayo reportedly simply sequestered herself in her dressing room when her presence was not required. There were flare ups over dresses and who got to get her hair done first. "It was like a hotbed of hussies in heat," one insider quipped to friends. "The women appraised each other and wondered which of them was the bigger wreck, and some hadn't been on camera in years and everything had to be just so. Meanwhile Bob, who was older than all of them, could just go out and not worry about it. Women age, men grow dignified. It sucks, but that's the way it is. But Hope wore a lot of makeup too."

It was no secret that appearing on one of Hope's shows or specials could do wonders for an entertainer's career. Frank Sinatra always credited Hope with giving him his second chance in the early Fifties when he was having trouble finding work. "I couldn't get a job until Bob came along with his first television spectacular," Sinatra said. "He and his writers [constructed] the entire show around me. I didn't get a lot of money but . . . it was a tremendous psychological help to me." He conceded, "Bob wanted me for the show because he thought I was right for it — not because he felt sorry for me." Ironically, it was to be Hope's appearing on Frank's first show years later that got Hope into trouble with Timex.

Zsa-Zsa Gabor also credited Hope's show with saving her career. Gabor found her film work drying up in the Fifties, ostensibly because she'd blatantly cheated on husband George Sanders (no angel himself, who went her one better by cheating with both sexes). An actress of extremely limited ability, Gabor's film career might have dried up in any case. Hope, who felt the saucy Hungarian star had her uses, put her on one of his specials and kept her regularly employed elsewhere. Gabor once told a press conference at which I was present in 1957 that "Bob, he is big softie; Bob, he love me like his sister, like all the relatives he ever had. And I love Bob. He is sweetheart, darling!" Asked if there was a "romance," Gabor drew herself up and said, "Bob, he is married. I have my morals, darlings!"

That Gabor survived right into the 1990's to irritate and/or amuse millions with her idiotic statements, silly marriages, and inane cop-battering is due almost directly to Hope. It's certainly one thing he has to account to America for.

For a variety of reasons Hope has managed to outlast all the other TV comedians of the Fifties, including Milton Berle ("Mr. Television" himself, better known as Uncle Miltie), Sid Caesar, Red Skelton, and many others. Although nowadays he only does the occasional special, Hope still established — yes with the Big Nine-O at hand! — a distinctive presence on the tube that his camerados from the Golden Age of Television cannot match. He also set out early in the Fifties to avoid overexposure on the airwaves by switching from a regular series to the occasional "spectacular" — a pattern he was to ring varying changes on.

Hope has also employed several other tricks that ensure him high ratings.

As in the radio and early television days, he's happy to be associated with a sponsor and often includes the name of the outfit in the title of his show. In return, the sponsor does its bit, paying for advertisements in major magazines and for other publicity. Hope then books the trendiest guest stars he can find. It doesn't matter what he personally thinks of their talent, or lack of same, and he may not have even seen them perform; if they're hot, youthful, charismatic, and hot to trot — translated "available" — they go on his show. The better publicized the entertainer is, the greater chance of being cast in a Bob Hope special. Brooke Shields, whose acting career had been less than sterling but won her share of column inches in the media, wound up appearing on Hope's show more than once. Names who figured in the news at various times — Mark Spitz, Bobby Fischer — had a shot at the show more than once. Hope books the younger performers to attract a younger audience — he wants parents *and* their kids to watch him.

Once a show was on the schedule, Hope would personally make phone calls to TV columnists and reporters. As he put it, "I sit in my office out here in Burbank and shove those calls through. It's a wonderful idea. The columnists and writers ask me about my next show, and I tell them a few intimate things about it. Then they give the fact that I called them a lot of space." Hope was helped in his task by the NBC publicity department, which issued slick press kits about the shows, as well as public relations firms in New York and Hollywood.

In 1954 Hope discovered a new way to hold on to his popularity on television, which was really the old way he'd used to stay on top on radio during the war. He took camera crews with him when he toured the bases (the first show was from Thule, Greenland) and sold them to

NBC as specials. This ploy worked straight through the Korean War, the Vietnam conflict, and on up to the Persian Gulf engagement. For Hope, wars are good for business.

The author spent part of his Korean War hitch doing Army public relations. I used my Hollywood connections to interview Bob, who congratulated me on my "snappy uniform" and told me public relations were damned important and I should take a leaf out of his book in my future career and "always let them know you're alive and kicking." "That's what I do," he added. When I asked him what he thought of combat conditions in Korea, he replied, "It's the same sad old story. Men fight, suffer, die; if they're in shape to keep up with me, it's my job to make 'em smile and laugh. That makes me feel good."

CHAPTER SEVENTEEN

GLOBAL AFFAIRS

Just before Christmas in 1948 Hope got a call from the Secretary of the Air Force, Stuart Symington, who told him that President Truman wanted him to put together a show to entertain the troops stationed in Berlin during the airlift. The Red Army had completely surrounded the city, and food, fuel — and entertainers — had to be flown in for the starving and demoralized Berliners. Acceding readily to the request, Hope got together a showbiz troupe that consisted of Irving Berlin, Irene Ryan, and the singer Jane Harvey, among others. That was to be only the start of his post-World War II overseas adventures — and escapades.

First, Hope made arrangements for transport with MATS (Military Air Transport Service) which provided pilots, crews, and C-118 airplanes. Next, the members of the troupe updated their passports, if necessary, then got several shots — for typhus, typhoid, diphtheria, cholera, and tetanus — at the Army Medical Center. Then, when the itinerary had been reasonably settled, members of the troupe were given mimeographed timetables. Before each trip was over, there were plenty of penciled-in additions denoting the unscheduled stops the troupe might have to make.

In 1949, Bob Hope was 46, but for him there was no slowing down. He and his gang invaded Alaska; in 1950 they toured various Pacific spots including South Korea. In 1953, when I interviewed him, Hope brought his troupe yet again to Korea after special importuning by Special Services' Colonel Layden. Although there was a truce on at the time, the colonel felt the soldiers could use the distraction of top-grade entertainment. "It'll keep 'em out of trouble," he commented succinctly. Hope, as in 1950, found Korea bleak, with people literally living out of caves or in huts made from mud, and barely subsisting on what they could scrounge. "It's damned depressing," he told me, "but let's see what we can do to liven them up, some way, some how."

Children would run up to the army jeeps and walk off with everything they could get their hands on — tires, cans of gas, personal
belongings, you-name-it. They were dubbed the "Slickee Boys" of
Seoul. It was also in Seoul that Hope met Francis Cardinal Spellman of
New York, who was a great man for cracking down hypocritically on
sexy movies while earning himself the name of "Sadie" for his only thinly disguised and often overt approaches to young priests — and soldiers.
Sadie was in Korea to rub shoulders, or whatever, with "my boys," and
Hope like others found Spellman no Walt Whitman, as he preferred his
soldiers well rather than wounded. For appearance's sake, Spellman
would poke his nose in a hospital now and then, though the sight of
blood made him vomit. Hope's entourage on the surface treated
Spellman with all due respect while privately snickering at him. (A book
that later, in the 1980's, covered Spellman's gay affairs and assorted
didoes was suppressed by pressure from the Archdiocese of New York.)
Hope and Sadie found they shared a certain sense of humor, though
Hope, who never hesitated to visit the wounded in the hospitals, for
once found himself upstaged by Spellman's highly theatricalized and
well-attended "Masses" — which invariably featured the cutest young
servicemen as altar boys.

The 1954 tour to Greenland was the first of Hope's tours to be
televised. Hope brought along such heavy hitters as William Holden
(who'd just won a 1953 Oscar for his role in Stalag 17), his wife Brenda
Marshall, Jerry Colonna, Margaret Whiting, and others. Thule,
Greenland, was an early-warning radar station and SAC base in the
Arctic Circle where several thousand men were stationed. The cold
must have agreed with Hope because two years later he set off for
Fairbanks, Alaska, with Mickey Mantle and Ginger Rogers in tow.

In 1956, the pleasure of Hope's company was requested by Sir
Laurence (later Lord) Olivier in London for the "Night of 100 Stars"
charity benefit which Olivier was organizing at the Palladium. Hope
had met Olivier socially when the latter first came to Hollywood in the
late Thirties — the time of Olivier's Hollywood triumph as Heathcliff
in *Wuthering Heights*. Olivier enjoyed the company of comedians — his
own efforts in that métier always turned out rather grim — and he was
later to carry his affinity for funnymen further than that when he
became Danny Kaye's lover. Hope always made Olivier laugh, especially at the dignified way Hope carried himself socially in London as
against the borderline-vulgar routines he'd deliver on stage — so at
odds with his offstage conduct. Hope, according to one observer, had an

exaggerated idea that doing-as-the-Londoners-do gave him some "class" — especially when meeting royalty at a film benefit — quite a climb up for the Kid from Eltham who'd left England at an early age. Olivier found particularly amusing Hope's manner of coming out in front of the English audience with a slow, ambling gait more suited for the excess-avoirdupois Robert Morley, who once even laughed that Hope was stealing his act.

Hope came on late in the Palladium show, which began at midnight, and was still telling jokes at three in the morning. There were more acts to go, the crowd was getting restless, and Olivier was panicking. Finally, he thought of the perfect solution. He knew Hope had to board a plane very early that morning, so he walked out on stage and interrupted him, telling the audience about Hope's tight schedule and early morning call and begging them to let him leave. All the while Olivier was pushing Bob with tactful aplomb toward the wings. The trick worked and Hope was soon off and gone.

In 1957, Hope went off to Okinawa with Jayne Mansfield, Erin O'Brien, columnist Irv Kupcinet, and Mike Connolly of *The Hollywood Reporter* in tow. Mike Connolly, who was a not-too-closeted gay in Hollywood at a time when deep-in-the-closet was de rigueur, was a source of much inside gossip about homosexual manners and mores. A joke went around that Mike was out to rival "Sadie Spellman" in his attentions to the servicemen, and some of Hope's entourage picked up on it and, as Mike later reported, "made my life in Okinawa fuckin' miserable. Moreover, I didn't get to meet one damned serviceman alone — someone was always 'chaperoning' me!"

During a lunch break, when food boxes were handed out to the performers, Hope was struck by the sight of hundreds of children clinging to the fence surrounding the field where they entertained, all of them staring pathetically at the food. The 1958 tour, which went everywhere from the Azores to Iceland, employed younger performers than usual (inexplicably, Mike Connolly was not on hand that time around to pal with them) — among them folk singer Randy Sparks, dancer Elaine Dunn, and Molly Bee from the *Tennessee Ernie Ford Show* — none of them "names" by any stretch of the imagination. But things had changed, as even Hope noted; by the late Fifties the patriotic rah-rah-wave-the-flag-die-for-your-buddies-fight-and-die-through-thick-and-thin furor was but a dim memory. Déjà vu, translated in Americanese as "we've been that route, guys," was the "in" thing.

In late 1958, the by then 55-year-old Hope was in London where he attended a performance of the "Ukraine State Dance Ensemble" at Albert Hall. Reportedly he was so excited by the talents of these dancers he decided to do a show in the Soviet Union with Russian performers as guests. Hope with his usual shrewdness was betting that a trip to Russia would get a million dollars' worth of free publicity, and tapes brought back from the Soviet Union could be used to assemble what might turn out to be his highest-rated special ever. Hope also knew that the average American in 1958 had a strong curiosity about what their Cold War adversaries were really like.

When a trip to the Soviet Consulate in London didn't yield quick results (although Hope and Troupe were able to file for visas there), Hope pulled wires with a friend, John Hay (Jock) Whitney, who was then U.S. Ambassador to Great Britain. Whitney promised to take it up with the Russian Ambassador at a cocktail party that very night. Still, weeks went by and Hope never got his visa. Although he claimed at the time he was extremely disturbed by the delay, he was probably chuckling over how even the wait for visas was generating publicity of a sort. He had, of course, made sure his PR flacks were alerting the media to his impending trip — before it was even a certainty. At every appearance he made, reporters would ask Hope, "Have you got your visa yet?" He hadn't even left for Russia and already the columns were full of stories about the upcoming show and his trip preparations. Finally Hope was told he could pick up the visa at the Russian Embassy in Washington.

An amusing story, circulated reportedly by mischievous Mike Connolly, had it that when certain members of Hope's troupe went out in the dead of Moscow nights to find vodka and caviar, they wound up propositioning handsome Russian cops who — horrors! — turned out to be KGB agents. How these hapless ones got back to the U.S. in one piece remains one of the more recondite Cold War secrets. For the record, among the Hope entourage in Russia were such as press representatives Arthur Jacobs and Ursula Halloran; two of his writers, Bill Larkin and Mort Lachman; and lighting man Ken Talbot — heteros all, we hasten to add for the record.

The following year Hope went back to Alaska, this time with Steve McQueen and his then-wife Neile Adams, who fellow-travelers recall "fought a lot," and also in tow was busty Jayne Mansfield who later recounted that she'd bared her bosom while rubbing "soothing ice" on them and had almost been "raped by some Eskimos!" Jayne didn't specify the number. In 1960, Hope, by then 57, was trekking to Guantanamo Bay in Cuba with Zsa-Zsa Gabor, Andy Williams, Janis

Paige, Dolores Gray, and the future Gay-hater-supreme, Anita Bryant, who was to spend a lot of time with Hope in Vietnam a few years later.

Despite the basic gaiety of these mostly peacetime trips from the late Forties to the early Sixties, there were occasional sobering moments. When Bob barnstormed his way into North Korea, of all places, via wire-pulling, among the more unpleasant sights were the bodies, including those of children, that lined the roads, all stone-dead and covered with filthy straw, and then only barely. Then there was the bizarre, scary trip Bob and Dolores made through Berlin, armed, as she recalled, "only with a flashlight and a prayer," past tumbled walls and blocks of concrete under which were crushed dead bodies. In Weisbaden there was so much poverty that the hotel employees treasured the tissue paper wrapped around Dolores' clothing as if it were silk and, as she recalled, implored her not to throw it away but to give it to them. "It was an education, those trips," Dolores Gray later said, "a lesson in what real life was like over there, a lesson in man's inhumanity to man — and woman." What she witnessed in the bombed-out German capital was always to remain in Dolores's memory.

The weather the troupe encountered was often less than hospitable. The unbelievable frigidity of Thule in Greenland, where nights would last for months and the temps were North Pole-ish, involved such stratagems as never turning off engines because they'd just never turn on again, and life lived in quarters that amounted to insulated ice-boxes.

Winds in Thule would suddenly hurl along at forty miles an hour, then whip up to sixty, obliging people to lock arms with their companions just to keep from being blown away, finally whipping up to a hundred miles an hour or more. At such times it seemed impossible to stay outside for very long and still survive. "Bob was always on his best behavior with the opposite sex when he was in Greenland," Mike Connolly later quipped. "First because the natives wore so much clothing to ward off the cold that he would have had to dig and dig — like for gold; and second, because that damned frigid weather would freeze any guy's ass — and dick — off!" On Okinawa, later that year, some members of Bob's troupe were nearly lost when they were sucked into deep mud.

When a deluge broke out of the heavens on the *USS Forrestal* while it was moored in Naples, the men on board had to move all the equipment to the plane elevator so the show could continue below deck — prompting one Congressman in Washington to ask if Hope and Co.

were proving more nuisance than comfort in all these compulsive pere-grinations around the globe.

Sometimes there were mechanical difficulties. An elderly Madrileno, misunderstanding the directions he was given, drove off with the troupe's generator in Spain and was never seen again. In Guantanamo, a machine used in a sketch malfunctioned and the "clos-et space," as Andy Williams recalled it, that he and Bob occupied filled with so much smoke that oxygen tanks had to be employed to bring Hope back to consciousness. Jack Benny was to make malicious sport later of Hope's "globe-galumphings here and there, whenever the opportunity presented itself." According to Benny, Bob "was bored with Dolores at home and bored with the kids, and the only excitement he got was running all over Hell with his court retainers."

But Hope was to face, in that period, situations more concretely serious than bitchy allegations about the monkey business with distaffers. In Italy an army captain, bidding farewell to Hope and his gang at the airfield as they prepared to fly to Germany, noticed a smell of fumes around the plane. Recognizing the odor, he realized that the Hope party's planes had accidentally been filled with a fuel designed solely for jet fighters. Had the plane taken off, or so Hope's version of the story goes, it could have exploded.

Plane trips through the 38th parallel in Korea and along the "cor-ridor" to Frankfurt often brought the troupe close to enemy aircraft, including the Soviet MIGs. While flying in a B-47, Hope sat behind the pilot in the co-pilot's seat and was told he could get a better view by rais-ing his seat via a lever at his side, but he accidentally put his hand on the ejector knob. Had it worked (luckily it didn't) Ski-nose's parts would have been scattered from Tokyo to Guam, in Jack Benny's words "pol-luting the atmosphere beyond salvaging."

Hope, despite the ridicule by Benny and other comic rivals, loved to repeat stories along these lines, ad infinitum. But some of the narrow escapes he relates were never quite that narrow. The odor of that jet-fighter fuel was so distinctive that someone on the field would eventu-ally have noticed it before takeoff; moreover, there was no guarantee that the engine would even have worked with the wrong fuel. And enemy aircraft would only have been a problem if Hope's planes had flown into enemy airspace, which pilots were trained to forestall. And the famous ejector knob in the B-47 — famous because it figured repet-itively in Hope's tales of his overseas adventures — has always featured a special protective device that adequately prevents such accidents as

Hope claims almost happened to him.

Still the hectic — some said manic — pace of the tightly scheduled tours couldn't help but take their toll on a man now in his fifties. During the 1958 trip, when Hope was 55, he reached a point where he'd slept but seven hours out of the previous seventy-six. At the Moron Air Force base in Spain (pronounced "More-own," in case you're wondering), he developed the first symptoms of acute exhaustion — dizziness, nausea — and passed out as he was shaking hands with the commanding officer. Taken unconscious to the base hospital, Hope woke up during the examination, restless and all hot to trot again. The doctors prescribed sleeping pills to ensure he rested. In no time he was on his feet doing his show.

But a few days later, at a base in Germany, Hope suffered another episode, this time during a buffet supper at a general's house in Frankfurt. In front of the entire assemblage, Hope turned white, tumbled into a nearby chair, and had to be supported upstairs to the general's room, where he collapsed on the bed. Press flack Ursula Halloran did her best to keep the news of his illness quiet but too many people had witnessed the incident to insure adequate damage control. Stories hit the papers — wild exaggerations were noised abroad, including rumors of a heart attack — with Hope meanwhile refusing to go into a hospital for several days' rest and observation, as doctors urged. Soon Hope was back in harness, but his refusal to slow down, or modify or curtail tours, was to affect his career gradually, and in the late Fifties, to produce serious ramifications.

But these physical collapses in Spain, Germany, and elsewhere were not the worst of it for Bob Hope. Nor the frigid, stormy weather, overshot runways, badly placed ejector knobs or the seashells he collected in the South Pacific that sprouted hairy legs on his bed and gave columnist Hedda Hopper conniption fits. The worst came when Hope was in Moscow standing at a cocktail party given in his honor by U.S. Ambassador "Tommy" Thompson. The ambassador's wife came over to Hope and shook his hand as she gave him a big smile. "I do so enjoy your show, Mr. Benny," she told him. "Did you bring your violin?"

There were a number of other amusing incidents during the tours. The prop bottle that froze in Fairbanks didn't break away over Hope's head when Ginger Rogers hit him but instead made him see stars. The plane crew near Wake Island who "insisted" everyone who crossed the International date line for the first time had to jump blindfolded from the plane into the water fifty feet below but limited Hope to jumping off a suitcase in the luggage compartment. ("Whether in deference to his age or to his helplessness has never been determined," a wag on the tour later commented.) Then there was the time Bob was caught in a clinch with singer Jane Harvey and told everyone her nervousness made her break out in an itch that caused her to rub up against the first man who came along.

And when writer Chet Casteloff, who'd lost a lottery and therefore couldn't attend a luncheon with General MacArthur in Tokyo (only twenty from Hope's troupe were allowed in), turned up, after all, sitting right next to MacArthur while a befuddled fellow at the end of the table wondered what had happened to his seat.

Hedda Hopper, the acid-tongued columnist, commented to me in 1964 that she felt Hope was overdoing the round-the-world tours. "It's a compulsion with him," she said. "He doesn't know how to leave well enough alone. That was okay for wartime and special emergencies, I suppose, but did Bob ever stop to think that in his constant barnstorming to get attention for himself, he was wearing out his welcome with the officers who have to disrupt their schedules for his visits? Also," she added, "his acts had become stale and repetitious, and the servicemen were getting bored."

The much publicized trip to the Soviet Union had its own built-in frustrations for Hope and Troupe. The Russian cameramen insisted that the film Hope had brought from the States wouldn't fit properly into their cameras, so they had to use Russian film — which of course would have to be processed in Russian labs. This meant it was out of Hope's hands for days. Hope had brought along his own film precisely to avoid this "development." When most, but not all, of the film was returned to him, the Russians presented him with a stiff bill for the processing, and for the cameraman's services, and for film clips Hope planned to use for his show. Communists the Russians may have been, but as Hope later joked, they knew the value of a dollar better than any American. Hope later claimed he took the film but never paid for it, hence the title of his book about the Russia trip and other events in his life (also ghostwritten), *I Owe Russian $1200*.

As always, Hope brought along a bevy of beautiful women on each trip, ostensibly for the pleasure of the soldiers. On his Thule trip he tried to get the photogenic and cat-nippy-to-servicemen Marilyn Monroe to come along. But Monroe, neurotically messed up as usual, begged off due to "prior commitments" that could actually have been anything from an honest-to-goodness filming to a surfeit of sleeping pills to a "bad hair day." Searching around for someone similarly "stacked," Hope caught sight of a beauty pageant winner, Anita Ekberg, when he hosted a football banquet in L.A. at which she was a guest. He asked Ekberg to come along and she said yes. At the base, all the Swedish beauty had to do was walk on stage in a revealing gown and stand there as the boys and Bob "thrilled and throbbed" (in Anita's self-congratulatory words) at the sight of her pertly uplifted mammaries.

Back in the States, Hope prevailed on his buddy John Wayne to sign Ekberg to a long-term contract through his production company. Due to her double exposure, as it were, at Thule, Ekberg was to achieve a brief celebrity status, even appearing with Bob in two films, after which her popularity sagged.

The other Anita on some of the Hope tours (though she was to prove more active during the Vietnam years) was Anita Bryant. She joined up in the frank hope of raising her profile and she did achieve a sort of national prominence. Bryant never traveled without her husband of the time, Bob Green, who knew how wild show people could be and wanted to keep Anita safe from liquor, sex, and swear words. Although Bryant was not above wriggling around on stage and flirting "sluttish-ly" with the men, backstage, according to one troupe member, "she was as chaste and dull as a glop of wallpaper." She could not abide "bad" language, dirty jokes or the taking-in-vain of the Lord's name. One night during a bad storm, one of Bob's writers told her half-jokingly, half-reassuringly, that the weather was sure to clear up because Bob was having a talk with "The Man Upstairs." "How dare you say that!" Anita screamed at him. While some among the troupe liked Anita well enough and even admired her pluck, she was never to be considered a "party animal" and more than a few obscene jokes went around as to her sex life with hubby Bob Greene — if any. Years later, when there were no more annual tours to use for profile-raising-and-polishing, Bryant would make a desperate attempt to publicize herself and get her career back on the rails by starting a fundamentalist campaign against homosexuals. This effort, however, backfired on her badly.

One decided party animal was Jayne Mansfield, who accompanied Bob on several tours. Jayne's husband, muscle-boy Mickey Hargitay, would come along, too, and among the more bizarre sights for troupe members and servicemen to snicker at was muscle-bound Mickey painting Jayne's toenails. No slouch herself when it came to self-publicizing, Jayne on one occasion arranged for a lion cub to be waiting for her at the airport in Alaska. Posing with the cub, Mansfield snared the lioness's share of press and photographer attention. One time she ran around creating an uproar with all comers because a diamond earring had disappeared; she promptly enlisted the aid of several boob-smitten soldiers to locate it. The ice promptly melted as soldiers alternated between nosing in the snow and nosing upward into the anxious Jayne's bosom as she "hung solicitously" above them. Then it turned out she'd put two earrings on one ear — but the lucky servicemen caught between ice and boobs registered no complaints — which may have been the highly narcissistic and exhibitionistic Jayne's intention in the first place.

During the 1959 tour for U.S.O., Jayne deliberately came out on stage wearing a gown cut so low her nipples were showing. Hope was the last one to object to this turn of events, but the cameras were whirling for his TV special and he knew it wouldn't get past the NBC censors. Hope decided all he could do was stare fixedly at Jayne's breasts — which hardly took much effort — until she got the message and pulled the dress up "in embarrassment," which for once enlisted some genuine acting finesse from Ms. Mansfield.

Hedda Hopper was also along for the 1959 trip. She'd answer GI's questions about movie stars but, pushing 70, she was hardly "stare-bait." As she'd once been a young, and not unattractive actress in films, this singed her ego somewhat. Her famous obsession for wearing flamboyant hats was said to be her compensation for physical accoutrements that had, well, seen better days. Hope had brought her along strictly for the press coverage, as it was rumored he didn't particularly like Hedda. She didn't think much of him either.

Whether out of jealousy or propriety (doubtless a blend of both) Hedda took violent exception to Mansfield's nipple-revealing dress and a bitchy squabble ensued backstage; things really heated up when Mansfield, one of the few personalities who gave Hedda as good as she got, regardless of her awareness of the columnist's power, yowled that if she had it she showed it, unlike Hedda, who had "nothing to show."

Mansfield, of course, had her share of ambition, and she wanted to have it both ways. In 1961 she told me that Hope's tours "were a big publicity boost for me. They were exhausting but I enjoyed them. And all those wonderful guys out there expressing their loud appreciation for my, er, company made me feel just great!" When I asked her how Mickey Hargitay reacted to the waves of often lewdly proclaimed male admiration that came her way, she pursed her lips primly and declared, "He knows my body — I mean my personality as an actress — belongs to the public!" Though she may have wanted serious public attention as an actress and as a person, she would use her body to take her where she wanted to go. She thought Hope "vulgar and pushy" to place so much attention on her mammaries (pot calling the kettle black!); her flaunting of her nipple-revealing dress was her way of defying him along the lines of "If you're going to talk so much about my tits, Hope, here they are!"

During the tours, there were other minor squabbles among the ladies. Janis Paige was afraid she'd appear too boyish in her costumes next to curvaceous Dolores Gray (an expert at highlighting her womanly attributes) and caused a fuss backstage demanding she be allowed to showcase her femininity more "appealingly." Janis seems to have won that round, for one troupe member claimed she "out-titted Dolores for the rest of the tour." Zsa-Zsa Gabor, blatantly aggressive, as always, commandeered virtually everyone on one base and ordered them to get her what she needed to "look my very best, darlinks!" And meanwhile keeping all the other ladies fuming in the dressing rooms while she established an exclusive monopoly on the talents of the hairdresser. Bob's attitude toward Zsa-Zsa at this time seems to have been "She's a pain but she's a fun attraction for the men."

Long, long before her highly publicized fracas with a police officer some years ago, Zsa-Zsa was proving her lack of affinity with men in uniform (at least offstage) when she curtly informed one Air Force major that she positively refused to receive inoculations and that he could have her shots!

A supreme publicity hound, Gabor made a good professional partner for Hope. Despite his reservations about her, he understood and admired her craving for attention, which more than matched his own. Hope meanwhile was winning plenty of attention for his Christmas and other tours, and made a sack of dough selling them to the networks. Many other entertainers were to hit the road to military bases during this period, among them such hardworking personalities as Gil Lamb, Dave Ketchem, Sid Marion, Irish McCalla, Johnny Grant, and Roscoe Ates, but these relative unknowns were obviously not using it to further their careers or garner publicity.

Even before the Vietnam conflict caught fire in the mid-Sixties, Hope was being criticized in the media. In early 1959, The New York *Morning Telegraph* ran a brutally frank piece by Leo Mishkin that read: "There can be no question but that Bob Hope is a highly patriotic citizen, and that he has devoted many arduous hours, many long weeks, and a vast amount of energy and effort toward bringing joy and entertainment to the members of the armed forces stationed overseas. I just wish, however, that when Bob Hope appears on the TV screen in the corner of my living room, he wouldn't talk about it so much."

Mishkin went on to intimate, half seriously, that of course he knew that this might get him labeled a Communist, then continued: "There were moments the other night, when Hope televised the films of his recent Christmas trip abroad, that I got the distinctly uncomfortable impression that the journey was made not so much for the benefit of the servicemen in such faraway places as Iceland . . . but more for what Hope could get out of it himself. Over the period of the past ten years or so, he seems to have got quite a lot out of it. Perhaps even more than the soldiers and sailors he entertained."

Mishkin in his piece also complained that there were so many closeups of Hope and so few panoramic long shots of the servicemen (always shown laughing) or of the surrounding scenery that "Bob Hope on the flight deck of the *USS Forrestal* was just the same as Bob Hope on the platform of a ship berthed at the Brooklyn Navy Yard. . . . You know what I saw of Port Lyautey on this Bob Hope journey abroad? I saw Bob Hope playing golf, that's what I saw in Port Lyautey. For this he had to travel 10,000 miles?"

In the years to come, the criticism of Hope in the media and by word of mouth was to get more and more cynical. In the meantime there were more movies to make.

CHAPTER EIGHTEEN

OFF LIMITS

Domestically, the Fifties didn't begin auspiciously for Bob Hope. On January 9, 1950, he and his alcoholic buddy, writer Fred Williams, were driving from Palm Springs back to Hollywood through a downpour on Route 66 when the car skidded and smashed into a tree near the town of Riverside. Although it was Hope's car, it was never determined who actually had been at the wheel. Hope and Williams managed to get out of the wrecked vehicle, flagging a passing motorist who drove them into town. Williams had sustained a very minor injury to his leg, but Hope had to be taken from Riverside to Hollywood in an ambulance. His dislocated shoulder meant that Hope was unable to play the following week in Bing Crosby's golf tournament. It was said later that this was the incident that permanently soured Hope on Williams, who, as before noted, was to die three years later in another, much more grisly accident.

Three months later, Hope got into more trouble when he appeared at the Paramount Theatre in New York and made jokes about the Forrest Hotel on West 49th Street, claiming the accommodations were cramped and rat-infested. The Nesa Realty Corporation, which owned the hotel, was not amused, and filed a $100,000 libel and slander suit against both Hope and the Paramount Theatre in June. Nesa claimed that Hope's derogatory remarks about the hotel injured "its reputation, business, and credit." Attorneys for Hope and the Paramount argued that the comedian's remarks were "in jest and in the light of the circumstances surrounding their utterance could not have been understood by any reasonable person as having been uttered other than in jest." The matter was settled quietly out of court.

Hope's first film release in 1950 was a musical version of the 1935 Charles Laughton Paramount hit, *Ruggles of Red Gap*. It was retitled *Fancy Pants*. Hope's former co-actor Edward Everett Horton had even had a pre-Laughton crack at the role. This time Hope had no trouble convincing Paramount to go with Lucille Ball as his co-star; the studio was impressed by the grosses of their first teaming in *Sorrowful Jones*. Moreover, by this time Ball had racked up a solid radio hit with her *My Favorite Wife*. Lucy registered relief to all comers that this time around she didn't have to beg; Hope always kept his eye on the ratings — and on performers whose popularity would serve to boost his own.

My first interview with Bob Hope, as I noted above, was during the shooting of *Fancy Pants*. I also met Lucille Ball, on the set, for the first time (again courtesy of an introduction by my friend Billy Grady) and she couldn't have been nicer. I was 26 years old, and within months would be off to the service in the Korean War. One of my more pleasant memories as a private, corporal, and later sergeant in the U.S. Army during 1950-53 were the nice letters Lucy wrote me, always neatly typed as per her secretary and always full of kindness and cheer. While in the army, I mentioned her letters to Bob Hope when I encountered him on one of his tours, and he snapped, "Well she has good help and they keep up faithfully with admirers." I did make him laugh when I told him that Lucy didn't affect Joan Crawford's gushy "Baby Blues" (as Jerry Asher called her blue stationery) and was always simple and straightforward.

I never encountered, at least in that period, the hard-faced, hard-nosed, "tough to take" dame Lucille Ball was to represent to many who knew her privately. She was the soul of graciousness on the *Fancy Pants* set. Guarded in her statements on Hope, she remarked that "He always galvanized his fellow players and set them a high standard to follow." The words sounded, I recall, a little stilted and high-flown for a gal who (as I knew her) was always the soul of down-to-earth directness.

Lucy's mind wasn't always on her job during the shooting of *Fancy Pants*; she'd discovered she was pregnant by husband Desi Arnaz again and came across as both overjoyed and frightened that she might miscarry as she had before. (Some time after filming on *Fancy Pants* ended, Lucy did miscarry; she was in her late 30s at the time.) This mental combination of elation and fear made her edgy and occasionally difficult to work with. I noted while on the set that there was tension between her and Hope, only thinly layered by an overly polite mutual approach to each other. In retrospect, it seems to me that this edginess on Hope's part might have been a reflection of his concern over her pregnancy, with its morning sickness and other symptoms. I also recall that Lucy seemed pasty-faced and tired much of the time.

George Marshall was on hand to direct yet again, and when I

spoke to him he seemed full of enthusiasm about the project. When Hope's restless ways, perpetual phone conversations and preoccupation with golf rather than the task at hand made Marshall irritable, the director would take some of the pressure off himself by participating off-screen in certain sequences; in one where Hope is surrounded by hostile Indians throwing hatchets at him, George himself undertook to throw the prop hatchet as close to Hope's ski nose as he could, perhaps wishing it was a real one.

Marshall was concerned but not dismayed when Hope was thrown from a seven-foot-high mechanical horse (used in conjunction with back projection) and landed on his back on the cement floor. Marshall, it seems, didn't feel Hope enjoyed sufficient freedom of movement so he directed his assistants to remove the restraining straps from the horse, in effect contributing to the accident that ensued. The mechanical horse had bounced higher and higher as its speed increased, until Hope could no longer hold on. (These peculiar accidents began to become suspiciously typical on Hope pictures, as if some of his directors, frustrated because they couldn't really speak their minds on various matters and thus risk firing, had no other means of getting even with the cocky, often thoughtless comedian.) On this occasion Hope immediately bellowed he was sure he'd sustained a concussion and a possible broken back, but x-rays at Hollywood Presbyterian Hospital showed only soreness — to Hope's satisfaction and the relief of the studio.

In this new version of *Ruggles*, Hope is an actor impersonating a British butler (and, later, an Earl) who takes a position with a wealthy family in the American Wild West. Ball plays the daughter who becomes involved with him. The plot revolves around a ploy to turn the territory into a state, with Teddy Roosevelt himself putting in an appearance. Although the performances are good, *Fancy Pants* is quite disappointing considering the talents involved, with genuinely amusing sequences being vastly outnumbered by ones that are just silly. Eric Blore is again on hand for some gay camp, and Bruce Cabot, maturing but still handsome and masculine, gave Hope his usual uneasily competitive moments.

Hope's next film was *The Lemon Drop Kid*, released early in 1951, a remake of the 1934 Lee Tracy starrer. (Paramount seemed to be on a remake jag in this period, with Hope elected to reprise earlier Paramount players in their lead roles.) His attitude probably was that anything tried and true might as well get a reworking, but he missed sight of the fact that recycled material could also lose freshness. Certainly this had been true for *Fancy Pants*.

In *Lemon*, based originally on another Damon Runyon story, Hope is a smalltime operator who fleeces a gal out of the money she was supposed to place on a bet for her boyfriend, a hood named Moose Moran (played by a strangely subdued Fred Clark). Moran insists Hope come up with the $10,000 he would have won. "Have the money by Christmas," he threatens, "or Christmas morning you'll find your head in your stocking." Hope then commences his frantic efforts to raise the money, and finally hits upon a scheme to collect dough for a (very temporary) home for retired showbiz ladies; this "charity" loot he'll hand over to Moran as repayment. Trouble is: after Xmas, the "old dolls" will be out on the street again. Hope's exasperated girlfriend, played by Marilyn Maxwell, serves as his conscience, and all works out neatly in the end, as in all such pieces.

Maxwell is pleasing in this; she was always a "good interview" and very humorous into the bargain; she once said, "Bob and I played well together because we sort of understood each other. He knows how far he can go, and I always made sure he never got out of step." How Hope reacted to this attitude has been unrecorded. Hope at 48 was in fine fettle, his libido as active as ever. Director Sidney Lanfield and set workers noted that his kissing scenes with Maxwell, especially one late in the picture by a statue where Hope's character has hidden money, is especially sensual (Marilyn must have temporarily let Hope "off the leash" for that one) and in this picture Hope did seem generally more "sexy" than he had in many recent films. Once again Hope was here assigned the task of making an essentially selfish and sordid character more palatable for the audience.

A small role in the picture, as one of Hope's companions, was played by former vaudevillian Jay C. Flippen, who'd been big on the circuits when Hope was relatively unknown and struggling. There'd always been talk during Hope's early days that he'd borrowed a lot of Flippen's shtick — talk that Flippen himself might well have helped keep in circulation. Flippen's resentment was doubtless further fueled by having to play fifth fiddle to Hope in *Lemon Drop Kid*, where many of his lines were dropped from the script or left on the cutting room floor.

For instance, when Hope in the film enlists the aid of his associates to dress as Santa Clauses and collect money for him, each actor is given a little vignette on screen — except Flippen. By the time Hope was through with him, the hapless Flippen was left with precisely two lines of dialogue in the finished film. It had taken him years, but Hope had gotten even. It was typical of Hope to cast Flippen not as an act of charity but to remind him of how far he, Hope, had come in the industry and how low Flippen had sunk.

Hope wasn't satisfied with the first rough cut of the film, which was put together by Sidney Lanfield, already a veteran Hope director. After the first screening for the Paramount bigwigs in Hollywood, Hope went behind Lanfield's back and complained to studio president Barney Balaban about the movie. Hope couched his objections in terms that made it sound like he was chiefly concerned about the good of the picture, but the truth was he didn't like all the time that subordinate characters were getting. In his view, the picture had seemed to run away without him. Hope also felt that the song which the film introduces, "Silver Bells," hadn't been creatively staged. "Buttons and Bows" from *The Paleface* had become a big hit and had increased that movie's box office; he argued that "Silver Bells," if done correctly, could do the same for *The Lemon Drop Kid*.

When Lanfield heard about all these discussions behind his back, he was livid. Hope and Lanfield never worked together on a movie again. Frank Tashlin, who'd come up with so many great sight gags for previous Hope pictures, was brought in to script the new sequences Hope demanded (all featuring Hope, of course), but first Tashlin insisted he be allowed to direct these sequences as well. Hope quickly acquiesced, showing not the slightest guilt over having thrown Lanfield to the lions.

Tashlin's version of the "Silver Bells" number was an improvement over the original, which had been sung straightforwardly in the gambling casino/old ladies home by practically the entire cast, in the manner of a Hollywood choir. Tashlin took the song onto sets of New York City streets filled with falling snow, people with packages, Santa Clauses, children, and all the requisite hustle-and-bustle of Christmas. It's one of the best sequences in the picture.

There are other good moments in the film, such as when Hope, trying to get clothes off a dummy in a department store window, times his actions to the movements of a mechanical Santa next to the mannequin and strips the dummy naked without realizing a policeman is outside watching. Hope dresses in drag as an old woman at one point, and quips to the other ladies, "You still have your hour-glass figures but most of the sand has gone to the bottom." The sliding walls and hide-

"Gr-r-r-r-r!" With co-star Hedy Lamarr in *My Favorite Spy,* 1951

Jane Russell and *Son of Paleface,* 1952

away tables of the casino-turned-boarding-home are clever, but the old folks' home sequences border on the grotesque and are undeniably patronizing toward the elderly. In spite of its flaws, *Lemon Drop Kid* remains one of Hope's more engaging movies.

Lanfield, who in the early Fifties became one of the first film directors to move over into television (there were rumors that Hope had pressured to get him blackballed in films) wound up directing hundreds of TV shows. Later he said of Hope, "He was the worst egomaniac I ever worked with, was a back-knifing son-of-a-bitch, mean as sin. I feel sorry for all the directors who worked with him after me — he treated them like servants. His way was the only way; I tried to buck him, and he took it out on me."

After the release of *The Lemon Drop Kid* in March, 1951, Hope went to London for a two-week personal appearance engagement. He contacted the Reverend H. J. Butterworth, who was the founder and director of a London youth club that had lost its headquarters during the blitz, and told him he'd donate his salary to Butterworth's group so that they could rebuild. Hope's press flacks made sure stories of Hope's generosity appeared in all the papers back home as well as overseas.

My Favorite Spy, released in the Christmas season of 1951, was Hope's one and only teaming with the glamorous Hedy Lamarr, whose career was already on the downgrade. Worried and disappointed, and concerned for the future, Lamarr, though still beautiful at 36, was running scared, and she and Hope didn't hit if off all that well She later told an interviewer, "I didn't think we made that great a teaming. We didn't look right together." Friends of Lamarr feel that she took the part hoping (as other leading ladies before her had) that some of Hope's continuing box-office popularity would rub off on her. In *Spy*, Hope was cast as "Peanuts," a fifth-rate comic who bears a striking resemblance to an infamous spy. Peanuts is importuned to impersonate this spy, and encounters Lamarr as a foreign counterspy while on his mission. Iris Adrian popped up again in the supporting cast, which also included Francis L. Sullivan, Ralph Smiley, and Arnold Moss. *Spy* wasn't one of the happier moments in Hope's career; he squeezed what chuckles he could out of it, but aside from the chase scene at the finale, the laughs are pretty meager. Lamarr never found comedy her strong suit, and while she looks beautiful her performing lacks verve and animation.

Hope then reteamed with Jane Russell, who'd already shown she was more than a match for him, in *Son of Paleface* (1952). This was the first full feature Frank Tashlin was to direct with Hope (he also co-wrote the screenplay) and he proved as adept with the material (more his cup of tea than *The Lemon Drop Kid* had been) as Norman McLeod had been with the original *Paleface*. The title *Son of Paleface* has to be taken with a certain grain of salt, as in the previous picture Hope's nickname was actually "Painless" ("Son of Painless" just wouldn't have cut it) and only the Indians called him "Paleface," as they did every white man. Now in the sequel every character refers to Hope's famous "father" by the retroactively revised nickname of "Painless."

Russell liked working with Tashlin as much as she did Hope. She found the director "a big fuzzy bear of a man with a delicious sense of humor; underneath, however, Tashlin was a serious, moody guy."

The story has Paleface Potter's son leaving Harvard to go out West and claim his inheritance — at his fiancée's urging — after the death of his father. He learns to his dismay that all he's inherited is a lot of debts, and the townspeople threaten to string him up if he doesn't pay up. An old associate of his father's tells the younger Potter that Pop has hidden a treasure horde and he'll try to help him find it. Meanwhile a beautiful criminal named "Torchy" (Russell) is committing highway robberies all over the place, while Federal agent Roy Rogers tries to stop her.

There are more homoerotic gags in *Son of Paleface* than in any other Hope movie — so many, in fact, that there's every reason to believe it was deliberate on Tashlin's part. When Rogers grabs Hope angrily after Hope destroys the other's wagon, Hope pulls away and accuses Rogers of wanting to kiss him. Two cowboys on either side of Russell (she's also an entertainer and owner of the saloon) move in to kiss her, but when she steps forward they wind up kissing each other. When Rogers doesn't react to Russell's beauty, Hope asks him, "What's the matter — don't you like girls?" After Rogers replies, "I'll stick to horses," Bob once again backs away in a panic. Later on, as they stand at the bar, Hope leans over to give Russell a kiss, but Rogers switches places with her and Hope nearly plants a wet one on the handsome cowboy instead. Years later critic Andrew Sarris was to theorize that these were just "the teensiest suggestion of a wickedly gay routine," and that if Hope had been free to do as he wanted without regard to censors and standards, he'd have been even more "riotously and obscenely funny."

Son of Paleface also gets laughs from heterosexual situations, among them a now-classic sequence in which Russell and Hope finally get to embrace in a passionate smooch without Roy or any other cowboys in the way. First Russell lifts up one of her legs behind her. Then

223

Crosby, Lamour, and Hope, one more time, in *Road to Bali*, 1952

Bob does the same. As they continue to kiss, both of Bob's legs lift up in the air. These impossible gags, dreamed up by Tashlin, were products of his long apprenticeship in cartoons, where impossible gags were the stock in trade.

In another sequence, Bob is riding through the desert for days when vultures come down to roost on his wagon. When he passes through an icy oasis that's just a mirage, the vultures have turned into penguins. When Roy and Bob are tied together to a chair at one point, Roy struggles to get free, keeping Bob's head banging painfully against the back of the chair. "Don't stop," Hope tells him, "I'm beginning to like it." (More homoeroticism with a little S&M thrown in for good measure.) The climactic chase — Hope gets his wagon across an impossibly wide canyon by opening his umbrella — is genuinely suspenseful. The most memorable — and kinkiest — sequence has Hope and Roy's horse Trigger sharing a bed together and stealing the covers from each other. In the long run, however, *Son of Paleface* is perhaps more clever and inventive (and sexually creative) than out -and-out hilarious.

In July 1952, when *Son of Paleface* opened, Hope went to Chicago to be a television convention commentator. While there, he was sub-poenaed to appear before Special Commissioner William H. Murphy of the Superior Court. It seems the ex-wife of Hope's TV and radio producer, Albert "Cappy" Capstaff, was seeking increased child support payments. Hope testified that he'd paid Capstaff $23,800 in the previous ten months.

One of the lawyers asked Hope, "Does he also get an unlimited expense account?" "I wouldn't give anybody an unlimited expense account," Hope replied. As Hope left the witness stand he was given a check for $1.10 as a witness fee. "I've played a lot of benefits before," he said as he put the check away in his pocket, "but this is the first time I've ever been paid for it."

After *Son of Paleface*, it was back on the road again with Bing Crosby and Dorothy Lamour for *The Road to Bali* (1952). The director for this outing was Hal Walker. *Bali*'s script was a melange of all the other elements of previous Road pictures. Bob and Bing are again cheap vaudeville entertainers; again they run away when two girls want to marry them; again they run into Lamour on a South Sea island where she's seeking treasure, this time in the ocean. This was used as the framework for the usual quota of funny, and barely funny gags. *Bali* depended on guest star cameos more than the other Road films (except for the subsequent *Road to Hong Kong*): Jane Russell shows up amidst a bevy of lovelies in a magic basket, and Humphrey Bogart filmed a short bit spoofing his Oscar-winning role in *The African Queen* where he's seen walking (yes, walking) down a river with a boat in tow.

Jerry Lewis and Dean Martin, who were still partners at that time and a comedy team to reckon with, also had cameos in the film. At one point during the shooting, both Bob and Bing — preoccupied with the golf game they were hoping to play if they finished up in time — were blowing one line after another. Dorothy Lamour used to rib them as much as they ribbed her, but on this occasion she went a little too far. "Better warm up Martin and Lewis," she cracked. "They're not only funnier, but younger."

The director, the crew, and the other actors all cracked up. But there was not a smile to be seen on the faces of Hope or Crosby. Bob glared at Lamour for a few moments, then said, in utter seriousness, "You'd better be careful how you talk to us. You can always be replaced by an actress." Lamour, irritated but alerted, henceforth watched what she said around the touchy duo.

For a beach scene in the picture, tons of pure white sand had been brought to the set in trucks from Pebble Beach. Coincidentally, Hope was at the time installing a small golf course in his backyard and needed to fill four empty sand traps. After the sequence had been filmed, he ordered the prop man to have several truckloads of sand driven over to his house, but the prop man refused. "This belongs to Paramount," he said. When Hope reminded the rash fellow that he and Bing owned two-thirds of the movie — and thus two-thirds of the sand — he was forced to comply.

Hope's first release for 1953 was *Off Limits*, in which he teamed with Mickey Rooney. His lovely leading lady was again Marilyn Maxwell, with whom he always worked well. Hope played a manager, Rooney his new fighter, while Maxwell took the part of Rooney's aunt (that's right, aunt) who's opposed to the Mick's line of work. An added complication was that both the Hope and Rooney characters were in the army.

Rooney had had a longer association with movies than Hope, and was the more versatile and gifted performer of the two (critic James Agee, who was not easily pleased, thought Rooney a genuinely great actor) but at the time shooting commenced, Rooney's career was in a decided downswing. Part of the problem was his gambling, night clubbing, and other high jinks, which made Paramount nervous about hiring him. The producer, Harry Tugend, wanted him for the part, however, and put up a fight for him. Two old pros who understood each other, Rooney and Hope worked well together on camera but didn't become close offscreen. One day the crew was shooting a major sequence that took place in Madison Square Garden with several hundred extras, but Rooney failed to put in an appearance, having had a wild night on the town. Tugend found him passed out at his apartment, "hollered him awake," as he later put it, plied him with coffee and got him over on the set to keep the day from becoming a total loss. The Mick saved the situation, giving a terrific performance in the scene.

Jack Dempsey did a cameo in *Off Limits* and later probably regretted it because it got him involved with Hope and Rooney and other entertainers, including Milton Berle and Hank Williams, in the later promotion of a "magical" elixir called "Hadacol." The makers of this cure-all potion were putting together a road show to promote the miraculous properties of their product, and wanted all these names to appear in person as a massive publicity stunt.

Hope, for one, had his doubts about this undertaking, so he told his agent to get the money — $30,000 for two dates — beforehand or

With wife Dolores at an Adolph Zukor testimonial in 1953

he wouldn't show. In fact, Bob had his check in hand before he even stepped out on stage. Needless to add, the "Hadacol" elixir went nowhere with the public and none of the other entertainers ever received a cent for their appearances.

Hope was President of the American Guild of Variety Artists (AFL) in 1953 when he and the union were charged with unfair labor practices, accused by the Chicago Cafe Owners Association and the Entertainment Managers Association of the Midwest of "trying to force employees to pay $2.50 a week for each entertainer into a union welfare fund." The two organizations also slapped a $2 million-plus lawsuit on Hope and the union. The National Labor Relations Board dismissed the charges that July, saying the board had no jurisdiction in the case. According to the NLRB regional director, Ross M. Madden, "Commerce had not been affected by the union action."

Hope next appeared in Claude Binyon's *Here Come the Girls*, released in October 1953, with Tony Martin, Rosemary Clooney, Fred Clark, and redheaded Arlene Dahl, one of the mass-produced indistinguishable pretty ladies of the period. Although Arlene was said to have a weakness for comedians (one friend said of her, "Maybe she likes to laugh while she makes love") and had been rumored to have the hots for Red Skelton, Bob Hope reportedly left her cold. For one thing, Dahl was involved with hot-blooded Fernando Lamas at the time, and Hope knew he was no competition for Fernando and didn't even try to be. "Bob — yes, even Bob — knew his limitations and was satisfied to stay within them — sometimes," William Demarest, also in *Here Come the Girls*, said of him.

Here Come the Girls was an amusing enough little comedy musical, expertly directed by Binyon, with Hope as a chorus boy who turns into an overnight star but is unaware he's merely been drafted to serve as a decoy for a mad killer stalking Broadway. Saddled with highly unmemorable songs, the movie nevertheless has lots of funny lines and situations. Over the years it has been derided by some of those who appeared in it, but *Here Come the Girls*, seen today, is not nearly as bad as other films Hope was to make.

Hope's next, *Casanova's Big Night* (1954) got an even worse critical drubbing. In this Hope plays an apprentice tailor who's asked by a Duchess (Hope Emerson) to pose as Casanova (Vincent Price, in a cameo) so that he can test the fidelity of the Duchess's future daughter-in-law (Audrey Dalton). As he proceeds with this task Hope becomes entangled with the real Casanova's valet (Basil Rathbone) and grocer

(Joan Fontaine), who is owed money by The Great Lover.

In her memoirs, *No Bed of Roses*, Joan Fontaine dismissed the picture with nary a line, although *Casanova's Big Night*, expertly directed by Norman Z. McLeod, did have its moments. Even at a certified 50, Hope managed a youthful jauntiness and socked home his lines and jokes well.

I interviewed Basil Rathbone in Boston, where he was appearing in a summer stock production of *The Winslow Boy*, the summer after he'd appeared in the Hope film, and he was enthusiastic about Hope's comedy skills. Always a supporter of, and rooter for, other performers, Rathbone said Hope "had a natural gift, backed up by lots of hard work."

Critics blew hot and cold over the film, but it made a considerable profit. It was about this time, 1954, that Hope was starting to do regular TV specials, and when the Paramount execs saw the *Casanova* grosses they accepted the fact that his TV work would boost his pictures, publicity-wise.

According to *Cue*'s movie critic, *Casanova's Big Night* was "long on slapstick, short on wit, imagination, and invention. Hope is in his most familiar movie role: as the conceited, self-adoring oaf who fancies himself a great guy with the gals but is terrified of his own shadow. The jokes, skits, gags, and comic situations loosely scattered through the film follow this elementary pattern. Some are amusing, but many fall flat. Perhaps because we've seen these same gags too often in the past — and mostly in Hope pictures."

Around this time, a deranged Korean War veteran decided that several popular entertainers of the day were co-conspirators with the power to emit evil "brain waves," which they were using to force cars off the road and kill people. Among those he accused were Eve Arden, Audie Murphy, Bing Crosby — and Bob Hope. Most received death threats, and were subsequently approached by FBI agents. Fortified by their wealth and their private security measures, Hope and Crosby tended to regard the whole crazy business as something of a joke — and even as a publicity boost of a sort. Not so Eve Arden. She was appearing in *Auntie Mame* in San Francisco and the police had to post guards in the audience, and also back on the farm where her kids were. A few nights later, the man was caught and institutionalized.

Some months after the March opening of *Casanova's Big Night* in that same year, 1954, Hope was visiting London when he hopped over to Paris for a visit but forgot his passport. French authorities allowed him to go to a hotel, but warned him he'd be arrested if the passport wasn't forwarded pronto from London. It arrived shortly, after much intra-city fuss, and the incident, though trivial, was kept alive by the papers, providing an amused Hope with more free publicity.

Hope could use it, as he came out at the time with yet another ghostwritten autobiography, *Have Tux, Will Travel*. William Thornton Martin, who worked as Pete Martin, had just done Bing Crosby's life story, and Hope — never one to lag behind — had Martin do the same for him. Martin would do other books with Hope in the future — all tailored to produce for the panting Hope admirers cross-country the image Hope sought to impress upon them.

The year 1955 brought Hope *The Seven Little Foys*, which opened the week of his 52nd birthday in May. It was inspired by the life of vaudevillian Eddie Foy, a bona fide "character" who'd been notoriously difficult to work with. Whenever Foy engaged in a dispute with a theatre manager, he'd wait until ten minutes before show time to start picking up his belongings and heading for the exit. Naturally, on such short notice, his managers tended to accede to whatever demands were made.

Jack Rose had never produced a picture before, and Mel Shavelson had never directed, but the two offered their jointly written screenplay to Hope and the studio with the express stipulation they be hired for exactly that: to produce and direct. Hope, who liked ambition and feisty push in others so long as the ambitions didn't conflict with his own, backed the boys.

Paramount executives were willing to go along, but only if all three, Rose, Shavelson, and Hope, took a percentage in lieu of salaries. Hope had a certain instinctive feeling that the script would do him good — and his aggressive lawyers were always ready to check the books when needed — so he agreed. Rose and Shavelson, initially reluctant, had no choice but to take it rather than leave it.

In the subsequent movie, which contained some actual occurrences mixed in with fiction, Hope marries a pretty immigrant performer (Milly Vitale) and has the seven kids of the title by her, but when she dies suddenly (he's on the road most of the time), he's stuck between never seeing the kids or taking them out on the road — he elects for the latter.

Personifying showbiz nepotism at its worst, they prove to be a dismal act, but personally too adorable to get the boos they deserve. Trouble crops up when Eddie's late wife's well-meaning relative tries to get custody of the kids, but the children interrupt the subsequent courtroom battle to insist to the judge that they enjoy traveling with dad and aren't ill-treated or neglected. Moreover, the constant exposure to showbiz has improved their aptitudes miraculously. (Eddie Foy Jr. was decades later to be the best-known of *The Seven Little Foys*.)

In spite of the fictional trappings, much of the real Eddie Foy personality comes through. Foy was an egomaniac who badly neglected his wife and children in pursuit of his career (a clear Hope self-identification with the character, which is probably why he wanted to do the film) and his behavior was thoughtless at best and vile at worst — yet it comes across that his kids liked the ambiances he provided and actually wanted showbiz careers of their own.

While Hope had made such fictional crumb-bums as *Sorrowful Jones* and *The Lemon Drop Kid* palatable and even winning, he had his work cut out for him with the real-life Foy. The picture is too "cutesy" for sophisticated tastes, but deserves credit for not glossing over the truth about Foy. For instance, not once is Foy shown being affectionate toward his children. One is given cause to wonder if Hope, were he given a crystal ball enabling him to view a film on his own life, would have reacted with an equanimity equal to his "truthful" depiction of another monstrously self-absorbed funnyman father.

In any event, as more than one 1955 critic noted, it was a major irony that a man who so resembled Eddie Foy in his personal life — to say nothing of his career aims — was able to make the man seem at times even personable and sympathetic. This, however, was probably due more to Hope's "lovable" screen persona (lovable at least to the die-hard Hope fans, of whom there were many) than to any "great acting" on his part.

Although some critics fell into the trap of vastly over-praising Hope's performance — for instance, The New York *Daily News* critic gushed he was now on the level of Oscar winner Bing Crosby and could "hold his head up with Hollywood's dramatic thespians" — he in fact proved a distinctly limited actor in *Foys*. He didn't stop short of using — for mood enhancement — the death of his longtime buddy, Barney Dean, the vaudevillian turned gagwriter, to lend a certain dramatic sobriety to his climactic courtroom scene, which was shot the day after Barney's death (it was his best acting in the film). His essential thespian weakness really comes through, however, in the sequence where he comes home to learn his wife has died. He can only manage a kind of vague fatigue rather than the shock, desolation, and guilt the sequence calls for — cries out for.

The highlight of the film is when James Cagney reprises his 1942 role of George M. Cohan (in *Yankee Doodle Dandy*, for which he'd won an Oscar) and does a dancing duet with Hope on top of a table at an awards ceremony. Both show off their splendid soft-shoe routines to fine effect and great audience appreciation, onscreen and off. (At the time Cagney was 55.)

Hope's glowing notices in the film gave him a "temporary swelled head" as George Tobias, also in *Foys*, put it. Soon he was fancying himself a "serious" actor (Der Bingle's acclaimed performance the year before as an alcoholic performer making a comeback in *The Country Girl* continued to rankle) and he field-marshaled a search for scripts that would fittingly highlight his newfound (by himself) acting stature. Luckily his love of, and ongoing facility for, comedy and his basic common sense got the better of him — had they not, we might eventually have had to endure a Ski-nosed Hamlet.

Hope was to have, during 1955, a couple of bizarre accidents that for a change didn't occur on a movie set. He was on the patio at the Menger Hotel in San Antonio having breakfast with the staff of a local TV station when he started to clown around and leapt on the top of the table. Because of a thick tablecloth covering it, Hope didn't realize the top was made of glass. When he hit it with his full weight the glass shattered and he dropped through to the floor. His ankle was lacerated but not severely enough to interfere with his schedule.

He got even more press attention when he went to Iceland in December 1955 for the U.S.O. and put on an act with Joan Rhodes, a fashion model turned professional strongwoman who lost her balance while lifting Hope to her shoulders and proceeded to drop him head-first on the floor. An Air Force plane flew a shook-up Hope form Iceland to London where he was admitted to a hospital with two broken fingers, a sprained neck, a cut nose, and a very sore head. (Or so the original report had it. Later it developed that his fingers had been injured when Miss Rhodes fell on top of him, though x-rays showed they were sprained not broken.) Hope complained of headaches for days afterward, but the doctors soon released him with a clean bill of health.

Hope was also getting into more trouble with his jokes. England's Princess Margaret had recently broken her engagement to Group Captain Peter Townsend. (His divorce earlier had debarred him as a husband to a royal, and she was grief-stricken, claiming he was the only man she'd ever loved.) On his show that year, Hope quipped,

"Townsend should have known better than to try and play the Palace. I never could." He made a few more ill-chosen observations about the aborted wedding, only to learn later that the Canadian Broadcasting Station had been deluged by complaining calls afterward.

During the 1950's, Hope had won added fame as the clever and apt master of ceremonies at the Oscars; he was to continue this stint for many years, always to acclaim. To this day his successors as MC, including the clever and engaging Billy Crystal, are compared unfavorably with him. While from 1941 to 1953 — except for 1948 — Hope had ranked with the ten top moneymaking stars, he'd always lamented (via amusing banter) that no Oscar got within miles of him — at least an Oscar for acting. He was to win a number of "consolation" Oscars, for instance in 1940, 44, 52, 59, 65, etc., but they were for humanitarian work and general contributions to the film industry. He'd been particularly galled by a "consolation" 1944 Oscar, the year Bing Crosby won a real one for *Going My Way*.

Egoistic as always, Hope had belabored Academy Award audiences for years with his failure to win an acting Oscar, though he was shrewd enough to overlay his hurt with humorous kidding. The year that *Seven Little Foys* was released, 1955, saw Hope clowning around onstage and off at the Oscars in a skit about the "Best" of 1954, and he was photographed trying to "take away" Marlon Brando's Oscar for his performance in the 1954 release *On the Waterfront*.

"This is the only way I'll get one," he told reporters. He was to be proven spectacularly right. The next year he didn't even get nominated for what he and his flacks had spread the good word was his acting high point — *The Seven Little Foys* didn't get a little brother named Oscar.

CHAPTER NINETEEN

THE FACTS OF LIFE

Fresh from his "high-water" stint as an actor in *The Seven Little Foys*, Hope decided to appear next in a film that offered him a somewhat more complex screen characterization — at least by his lights. *That Certain Feeling*, released in June 1956, was based on a Broadway show by Jean Kerr and Eleanor Brooke entitled *King of Hearts*. In this Hope plays a queasy cartoonist who develops stomach trouble every time he gets emotionally upset. His ex-wife (Eva Marie-Saint) is working for a more successful cartoonist (George Sanders) who hires Hope as an assistant. Naturally Hope does everything he can to head off the budding romance between Sanders and his ex-wife, whom he still loves.

Despite the cartoon subject matter, the part was more of a character than the usual Hope caricature — at least it was originally — but Hope's associates Norman Panama and Melvin Frank (who also jointly produced and directed) saw to it that plenty of Hope-style gags were added to I.A.L. Diamond's and William Altman's script. The result, predictably, was closer to the typical lovable bumbler Hope had played so often rather than the character Kerr and Brooke had conceived. Al Capp, the "Li'l Abner" cartoonist who shared Hope's conservative political views, had a small part in the film, as did Jerry Mathers, TV's *Leave It to Beaver* star. Hope also gave his son Kelly, then a cute pug-nosed boy of 9, a small bit in the film.

George Sanders, who was by 1956 three years younger at 50 than Hope, though looked somewhat older to his annoyance, dismissed *That Certain Feeling* with his usual caustic put-down approach some years later. "In it Mr. Hope grandstanded and bitched-up a perfectly good play into a perfectly awful film. I did it purely for the money and during it was bored to extinction."

Eva Marie Saint, a lovely young star who was "hot" in 1956 after appearing with Brando in *On the Waterfront* and other well-received films, was the latest lady to be drafted by Hope to enhance his "ladykiller" prestige and guarantee his "class" status — predecessors to Saint having by now included Joan Fontaine, Hedy Lamarr, Madeleine Carroll, and still counting. The film didn't do much for her, and she knew it, for she was playing second fiddle (graciously and quietly) as Sanders was playing second fiddle (angrily and scornfully) to Hope's usual star shtick. "It was so good to work with him, he had a natural comedy sense," she told me at a 1956 party. (I was then film critic and reporter for *Motion Picture Daily* and *Motion Picture Herald*.) When I asked Saint if she'd appear with Hope again, she hesitated a few seconds too long, then replied, "If the vehicle were right." (She failed, ladylike creature that she was, to specify if the "vehicle" were meant to be right for him, or her.)

The needed, indeed expected, ego-salves for Hope in *That Certain Feeling* were forthcoming, to a point, via the critics. "Hope here gets another chance to prove that he can not only clown adeptly but project a warmly human personality from the screen," ran one verdict.

Hope's "certain feelings" nearly got him into hot — by which we mean boiling — water when Barbara Payton resurfaced in an unexpected way in the summer of 1956. That was the year, as before noted, that the ubiquitous and nettling Payton decided to sell her story about her relationship with Hope to *Confidential* magazine (a gossip-rag sensation of that era that put the revelations of today's tabloids to comparative shame, being biting, detailed, and shameless — *Confidential* finally outsmarted itself and a few years later was but a memory, but while it burned it gave a lethal light.)

The *Confidential* story hit the stands in July, 1956. At the time I had published a story in the fan magazine *Movie Life* called "Loves That Rocked Beverly Hills." It detailed the love lives of Eddie and Debbie, Grace Kelly, and others. (I was doing a lot of freelance work for the movie fan magazines in that period, in addition to my regular job at *Motion Picture Herald*.) In earlier years I'd interviewed Barbara Payton in connection with some film she was plugging, and always found her a sullen, moody type, a woman who held things in, and who could explode under the right conditions. Knowing this, I pressed Barbara's "bad buttons" by bringing up names of men she'd "had it in for." Then she'd blab away!

Certainly the story on Hope and Payton that I read in *Confidential* made my *Movie Life* piece on Hollywood Loves, trenchant and honest as it was, look like a recital of the didoes of Campfire Girls. It was obvious that the magazine's lawyers had gone over the whole story with

Payton — sentence by sentence — and decided to print it with every steamy situation-cum-insinuation intact and in bold black print.

Hope reportedly came nearer to a heart attack than he ever had, before or since, when Payton's tell-all hit the stands. His press people thereupon suggested to him this might be a propitious time to spend more time with wife and family. Soon the entire familial entourage was appearing at public functions and premieres, with nary a photo opportunity neglected. The usual weasel press agents were taken on the team to let the public "find out" only what the Hope camp wanted it to know. (Press agents from time immemorial have been hyper-adept at hornswoggling the public, concealing far more than they reveal, thus proving themselves eminently poor sources on stars for newspaper, magazine, and book biographers. They are, after all, stars' employees.)

In the shots taken of the Hopes at various events in 1956, Dolores looks matronly beyond her years (she was 53), 16-year-old Linda and 15-year-old Tony are attractive, winsome teenagers, 9-year-old Kelly and 8-year-old Nora are cute as buttons, and paterfamilias Hope, tenderly and protectively placing his hands across the shoulders of Mrs. and the Little Ones, is the very personification of the All-American Family Man: 1956 vintage. Few saw through the outrageous phoniness of this "Family Values" overkill.

Hope was enraged at Payton's actions and at *Confidential*, but of course a lawsuit, his lawyers insisted, was out of the question. It would only attract more attention to Payton's allegations and the article itself and — well, there were other reasons, as they warned him. Paramount executives were concerned chiefly with how the brouhaha would affect the box office of *That Certain Feeling*, released about the time the article appeared.

Hope's fundamental attitude toward the affair was, friends recall, mixed. It had showcased him, however vulgarly, as the Ladykiller Supreme he always longed to come across as; he knew his popularity as a star would suffer relatively little damage from a publication held in such low repute, and he realized that *Confidential* could have dredged up far more hurtful (to him anyway) truths and allegations (his friendship with Fred Williams, for instance, and his endlessly ongoing family quarrels). To say nothing of other involvements with the Fair Sex.

Dolores, her womanhood affronted, her maternal protectiveness of her brood of four ignited, viewed the whole matter differently. There's no doubt this woman, who knew her Bobby Boy better than any other human creature, had been on to his numerous entanglements

236

with other women, but to have it spread out all across the newsstands of America — even in a "rag" like *Confidential* — was quite another story. According to insiders, the decibel level of the fights in their California home had never before reached such shattering heights. Several associates are in agreement that if ever Dolores might have made up her mind to leave Bob, this would have been it.

Hope, fighting for his domestic life (and family-man public reputation) made haste to argue that Barbara Payton was a vindictive tramp who'd dreamed it all up; that her tale-bearing had no foundation in fact; that she was just another Hollywood nobody looking for publicity and was peeved he'd never cast her in one of his pictures or put her on his TV show. Dolores, no fool, wasn't buying any of his protestations, though she, who'd lived with him as his wife for twenty-two years and was on to every facet of him, was less angry at what he'd done with Payton than at the public humiliation she, and her kids, had to endure because of it.

Ruth Waterbury, Helen Ferguson, Hedda Hopper, Adela Rogers St. Johns, and other observers of the time were almost unanimous in their feeling that Dolores stayed with him not only because she continued to be susceptible to his charms and promises to behave, but that she enjoyed being Mrs. Bob Hope Forever as against the fate of divorcées she'd known, and that meant more to her than getting half his money in a settlement. Nor did she want the "four innocents" (a term she used to Hedda Hopper) subjected to a broken marriage. Also, and most importantly, Dolores still had affection for him. But that love was to be increasingly soured by disillusion, hurt, and bitterness as the years went on.

Reassured and strengthened in his position (relatively, anyway) Hope proceeded to turn his celebrated retaliatory vindictiveness on Barbara Payton. He worked overtime putting out the word she was a no-good slut who couldn't be trusted — and shouldn't be hired. Lots of starlets, he sneered to flunkies, associates, and anyone who'd listen, used their bodies to get ahead in their careers, but they never, ever went public with it. If they did, they weren't "good sports," they "didn't play by the long-established rules." Barbara had broken those primary rules; he'd see to it she became persona non grata.

After a promising start some years before (in 1950 she'd played Jimmy Cagney's girlfriend in a Warner opus called *Kiss Tomorrow Goodbye*) Barbara Payton in 1956 was pushing whatever levers would pay off. Her career had dried up; she needed money. (This didn't make her

Confidential charges any less true, as Hope's legal battery admitted.) Her marriage to Franchot Tone — a gentleman who was not himself averse to, or ever free of, recurrent scandal — had ended in divorce, and the money she got out of him didn't last long. She'd gone to England looking for work, then came back to Hollywood, where her last feature film, released in 1955, was to be *Murder Is My Beat*. After the *Confidential* affair, she subsided into alcoholism and prostitution, appeared in some smut films, and died in 1967 at 40.

Later in 1956, Hope was to jump — at least in his film work — from the smutty ridiculous to the classy sublime, so to speak. Certainly Katharine Hepburn was a class act. It has never been entirely clear why Kate the Great (who'd even made her then-fifteen-year status as married Spencer Tracy's mistress a dignified — for Hollywood — involvement that was protected from press scrutiny) wanted to join the list of other "respectables" whose mission as co-stars was to make Hope look more class-act than he was.

Paramount publicity man Charlie Earle, an old friend of mine, with whom I was doing interviews on such as Tony Perkins and Charlton Heston and Tom Tryon during that year 1956, confided to me at the time that the Payton mess didn't do Hope much good at Paramount, and though various reasons were given publicly, Hope did go over to MGM for the picture *The Iron Petticoat* with Hepburn, later returning to Paramount "when things had cooled down."

Earle told me in 1956, "Bob is well-liked at Paramount; his films did make money for them, but this Payton thing screams out for some cooling off. Working with Hepburn may give him some class, some respectability. God, I hope so!"

While Hepburn was certainly not in a position to condescend to Hope over his morals, or lack of them, and even had Spencer Tracy with her in London while she did the Hope film, observers never felt there was any particular warmth between them. Possibly she looked down on Hope because he didn't conduct his extramarital affairs with the discretion that was mandatory at the time. Ruth Waterbury told me that Hollywood "went easy" on the Kate-Spence relationship because Kate hadn't really broken up the Tracy marriage, which had disintegrated long since after Louise Tracy devoted her life and energies to hers and Spence's deaf son John — for whom she established a haven for the deaf called The John Tracy Clinic.

"No home-wrecker was Kate," Ruth added. "Spence drank a lot, and had a number of affairs, including a red-hot one with Loretta

Young. Kate was a latecomer to matters Tracy; if anything she was a blessing, for she stabilized him, helped him cut down on his drinking, and steer a steady course — steady for Spence that is."

Originally Hepburn was to have made *The Iron Petticoat* (released in December 1956) with Cary Grant, but when he proved unavailable, Hope stepped in. "One of the appeals of the picture was that he could get the hell out of the United States for a while," Charlie Earle told me. "English journalists could be vicious snipers at stars too, but they were three thousand miles away." He added, "And that's where Bob wanted to be — three thousand miles away!"

The Iron Petticoat was to be the first film Hope shot outside the States, and in the land of his birth. It was made at Pinewood Studios, and Hope — given to publicity as sedate as he could make it at the time — loftily informed the British journalists in attendance that he was impressed by the way the British crew lacked that manic American urgency about everything, and even stayed perfectly calm during such crises as a set catching fire. Naturally these prim, laundered observations didn't sit well with the Paramount flacks and set crews back home.

Petticoat was to be a sort of retread of Garbo's 1939 *Ninotchka*, with Kate as a Russian captain who lands her plane in Germany's American zone, and Hope as the American major delegated to teach her the ways of democracy. A love affair ensues and they get caught up in Cold War intrigue that almost finishes them both off.

In such films as *Bringing Up Baby* (1938) Hepburn had proved to everyone's complete satisfaction that she could be as adept in comedy as Hope would never be in drama. Unfortunately for her, Hope arrived in England with his overworked writers in tow and immediately set about making his part more of a typical Bob Hope characterization. First he called up Ben Hecht, who was polishing the script, and told him it needed work and he had suggestions. Sensing trouble, Hecht called Hepburn the minute he got off the phone with Hope and asked her to accompany him to the conference at Hope's hotel. To Hope it seemed as if he had barely gotten off the phone when Hecht and Hepburn were ushered into his suite. Hope at first pretended he had only "a few suggestions," nothing major, mind you, but the "suggestions" soon reared their ugly heads as a complete and drastic rewrite, replete with plenty of Hope gags.

Hepburn, intrigued with doing a variation on Garbo's portrait of a Soviet type, was committed to the picture, but Hecht was not. He walked out, leaving the field clear for Hope's writers. At this point,

Hepburn didn't care all that much. Tracy, back at her place, had given her what constructive advice he could; moreover, he demanded her off-set attention, and she was further preoccupied by an eye infection she'd picked up after a dunk in Venice's Grand Canal during the shooting of the previous year's hit *Summertime*.

But she was no fool, and she kept alert. Soon she and director Ralph Thomas (up to that point better known for his *Doctor* movies with Dirk Bogarde), did what they could to counteract the onslaught of Hope and his gagsters. Although some critics later were to opine that Hope and Hepburn performed together better than was to be expected, offscreen their relationship was distant (politely so) and wary. Such veteran character actors as James Robertson Justice and Nicholas Phipps — good English standbys — did their best to enliven the proceedings, which were received lukewarmly by most reviewers.

Determined to have his last word, Ben Hecht bought an ad in *Variety* (which has been widely published since) in the form of a letter addressed to "My dear partner Bob Hope." In the letter, Hecht told Hope he was having his, Hecht's, name removed from the film, and expressed his regret that Hepburn couldn't remove herself from the picture as well. He accused Hope of sabotaging and blasting out of the picture Hepburn's "magnificent comic performance," and strongly implied that Hope's ego had virtually destroyed the picture. In a subsequent issue of *Variety* Hope himself took out an ad that suggested Hecht's leaving the film had been the best thing that could have happened to it. Hope later claimed it was the studio, not he, that had made the cuts, and that his own suggestions weren't adhered to. (Nobody bought it.)

In 1992, when my researchist William Schoell wrote to Katharine Hepburn asking what she wanted written about her role in, and attitude toward, *The Iron Petticoat* and her feelings about Hope, her assistant, Sharon Powers, wrote back, in part, "Miss Hepburn said it's all too long ago — and water under the bridge." But in 1957, when I interviewed Hepburn on the set of *The Desk Set*, another of her co-starrers with Tracy, she'd said, "The less said about it the better. Just thinking about it gives me a headache. It was a mess!" And her thoughts on Hope? "No comment!" she snapped, but the glare in her eyes spoke volumes.

Typical of the critical opinions were those offered by Bosley Crowther of *The New York Times* and Alton Cook of The New York *World-Telegram*. From Crowther: "The hopeful offbeat teaming of Miss Hepburn and Mr. Hope as the ideological opposites who get together has resulted in something grotesque. Miss Hepburn's Russian affectations and accent are simply horrible, and Mr. Hope's wistful efforts with feeble gags to hold his franchise as a funny man are downright sad." From Cook: "The picture does not properly belong to Bob Hope, but that does not bother him in taking charge of most of the laughter. Miss Hepburn does a giddy caricature of her own behavior in romantic and dramatic roles."

Hope's next part was again based on a real person, as it had been in *Foys*, and was also more "serious" than usual. Jimmy Walker, the subject of *Beau James* (1957) and the Gene Fowler biography it was based on, was a colorful "playboy mayor" of New York City in the 1926-32 period. Walker was a married Catholic, but he flaunted his mistress, the actress Betty Compson (Vera Miles), thus putting his political fortunes on the line. Alexis Smith plays the hapless wife. Walker was credited with a number of civic improvements — subways, highways, the creation of the Department of Sanitation — but eventually was brought down in 1932 by the Seabury Investigation into suspect financial maneuverings during his administration.

The same duo responsible for *Foys*, Rose and Shavelson, brought *Beau James* to the screen (Rose and Shavelson co-wrote the screenplay, with Rose producing and Shavelson directing). This time they made a fairly successful effort to recreate the facts (including the downbeat ending detailing the mayor's fall from grace) and downplaying the usual Hope gags. Another unusual angle about the picture was that Hope played an actual adulterer for the one and only time on screen rather than a married man innocently embroiled with a hot patootie. Both Smith and Miles were cast against type for interesting results.

As in the case of Eddie Foy, Hope fails to completely submerge himself in the persona of his subject. Still, he and the film got more than respectful notices. The New York *Daily News* critic wrote: "The production is characterized by fine craftsmanship and solid appeal, largely of a humorous vein. Most of the scandal and pathos is circumvented or so padded with dramatic license that nobody feels like singing sad songs for New York's 100th mayor — and undoubtedly this is the way that Walker himself would have liked it."

Hope mulled over a few possibilities for a follow-up to *Beau James*, including playing P.T. Barnum in another biopic, essaying a professor of criminology in *Experiment in Crime*, based on a Philip Wylie story, or starring in an original western, *Westward Ho*, by Bert Lawrence. Any of these would probably have made more worthwhile projects than the picture he did do, *Paris Holiday* (1957). Co-starring the

French comedian Fernandel, it's one of Hope's all-time worst.

Bob Hope was no longer making movies at Paramount. His new contract with United Artists was for two pictures a year, and under its terms he'd have to split the costs of each film with the studio. The plus aspect was he'd have more control than before. He figured a teaming with Fernandel, very popular in his native France, would make a lot of money for him, and for added insurance he added two "very luscious dishes," Martha Hyer and Anita Ekberg (whom he had previously "discovered") to the mix.

Although it turned out that the two never hit it off — and with the language barrier hardly understood each other much of the time — Hope found he could identify with Fernandel's struggles upward from second-rate clubs in Marseille to the better-class places in Paris, and finally to the stage and movies. But Hope also felt he'd worked just as hard to get where he was, and wasn't about to give any quarter where Fernandel was concerned. Hope, vain and egoistic as always, never really thought of Fernandel as being in his league; he saw himself as the much bigger star, someone the French comic would have to pay court to.

Bad feelings had erupted between the two about a year earlier when Hope asked Fernandel to appear on a TV show he was taping in London. At first, Fernandel asked for $40,000 to appear — an outrageous sum for a TV stint in those days — but when he and Hope met face to face he had his interpreter tell Hope he'd do it for free as long as Hope covered transportation and expenses for the French comic and his family. Hope, in his usual penny-pinching style, readily agreed to this apparent bargain — but regretted his action when he saw the astronomical charges Fernandel and his entourage accumulated during their London stay. "Parasites!" Hope hollered when he saw the bill.

Hope, however, was high on doing a picture in Paris, and he felt that he and Fernandel would work well together. He hired Gerd (*A Kiss Before Dying*) Oswald to direct; Hope himself would produce. Using his own story, he had Edmund Beloin and Dean Riesner work up a script according to his specifications, making sure there were plenty of love scenes between him and the luscious leading ladies.

When Fernandel saw a copy of the script, he hit the ceiling. Even someone who couldn't read English could tell that Hope had the lion's share of the lines and action; Fernandel's part amounted to no more than one supporting characterization among many. Fernandel issued a press statement that Hope had misled and betrayed him, that you couldn't trust Americans, and that he had no intention of appearing in this awful film with Mr. Hope. The teaming of these two international stars had, it seemed, hit a snag.

Hope, however, had no intention of canceling the production; it was already getting reams of publicity, for Fernandel's outraged remarks at his press conference were picked up by the American papers. To cancel the film now would be criminal — everyone was talking about him and the Frenchman. Hope didn't want to replace Fernandel, but knew he had to get him back in the game — without paying through the ski nose.

Representatives arranged a talk in Paris between the two comedians at Hope's suite. Fernandel walked in with great pomp accompanied by a half dozen of his associates. Hope had more than that in *his* retinue. When Fernandel saw Hope he ran over and embraced him as if nothing had ever happened. (Fernandel wanted badly to appear in a major American movie, giving the lie to many of his angry public pronouncements.) The Frenchman then proceeded to go through the script page by page, pantomiming his disappointment at his lack of lines. Many, many hours later he'd made it clear to Hope he'd do the picture only if his part were expanded. He'd not report for work until the script was completed to his satisfaction. Ten days and $200,000 later (that's what the delays cost the production) Hope and Fernandel finally agreed on the shooting script and other concessions, chiefly financial, that Fernandel insisted upon, and the filming began.

Now that Hope himself was producer, he discovered all the little problems studio people had taken care of before were now his to deal with, and in all their maddening detail and endless ramifications. One sequence had to be re-shot because the negative turned out to have been scratched at the English laboratory. Shooting was delayed for several days at an unheated chalet when there was an unlikely snowstorm in the middle of May. There was no power to light up certain scenes on cloudy days, and since gas was rationed, there wasn't nearly enough for the generators.

Hope was especially perturbed to learn that the box-like lunches served to casts and crews on location for American films wouldn't do at all for the French crews, who demanded huge meals and wine. Hope was even more infuriated when he and Fernandel went to a premiere of Otto Preminger's *Saint Joan* to plug their own picture and the French comic got many more laughs than he did when they came out on stage together, Bob speaking French, Fernandel English. The French audience thought Fernandel's mispronunciations of English words were hilarious, but were afraid Hope would be insulted if they laughed at his mispronunciations of French. Hope didn't understand this until it was explained to him much later, and even then he seethed.

Paris Holiday is a comedy in name only. Hope and Fernandel, essentially playing themselves, get embroiled in a misadventure with a gang of counterfeiters and a pretty spy (Ekberg), and the gags are incredibly old. Even the climax, with Hope dangling from a helicopter (though it does feature some great shots of the French countryside) has no real laughs. *Paris Holiday* could almost function as a catalogue of the missteps of Hope's bad movies (and there were worse to come). Also, at age 55, Hope was beginning to look a little peaked to play a romantic lead (even in comic terms) and lovely Martha Hyer makes a highly implausible love interest for him. To see ski-nosed Hope teamed with busty beauties in farces like *The Paleface* is one thing, but movies like *Paris Holiday* ask us to believe that young, attractive women like Hyer would go into fits of jealousy upon catching Hope in compromising situations (Dolores maybe; Hyer no). But no one on hand was summoning the guts to tell self-absorbed, self-aggrandizing Hope that his "loverboy" pose was getting a little long in the tooth (especially as all were in his pay).

The critics were for the most part unamused by the goings-on in *Paris Holiday*. Hope's treatment of Fernandel was also roundly criticized. Wrote Bosley Crowther in *The New York Times*, "Here [Hope] has that most distinguished of French comedians, Fernandel, as his co-star, and how does he use him? As a second-rate tag-along foil!"

During the filming of *Paris Holiday*, Dean Martin (who was making *The Young Lions* in Paris at the time) called up Hope and took him to dinner at La Cremailliere, where Hope's attentions became engaged with an attractive Marilyn Monroe lookalike who passed by their table and gave Bob lascivious winks. A few days later, Fernandel threw a party for the cast at another restaurant and Hope saw the same young lady walking over to the table, where he was sitting with Anita Ekberg. As Ekberg sat there highly amused, Hope kissed this new addition's hand, complimented her figure and fussed over her like a schoolboy suffering his first crush.

Taking pity on Hope, and before things went too far, Ekberg leaned over and whispered to him, "That isn't a woman. It's a man."

The would-be Monroe was actually a famous French female impersonator and nightclub star named La Cochinelle. Once Hope had bounced back from his embarrassment and disgust, he still had to admit that La Cochinelle was a fascinating creature. He invited him/her out to the set to see him and Fernandel working. Hope's encounter with this drag queen, replete with a surfeit of unsavory implications, wound up being reported in yet another racy rag, *Whispers*, in October of 1957. Hope later wrote about the encounter himself in one of his books so as to make light of it, his initial attraction to the impersonator having made him extremely uncomfortable.

The year 1958 did not usher in the best of news for Hope. It was hassles-with-relatives time again. He got a call from his brother Ivor, who informed him that the business he'd entrusted him with, Hope Metal Products of Cleveland, was about to go under. Ivor had tried everything to forestall the inevitable, but the company was ridden with over two hundred creditors, and its assets of approximately $90,000 were far outweighed by liabilities of almost a quarter million. Hope had put $100,000 into the firm in 1955, but this time refused to throw good money after bad. The company filed an involuntary bankruptcy action, and its assets were auctioned off in September 1958. Hope had lost his investment, but worse, it severed a bond with his oldest brother.

Hope was finishing up work on his next picture, a return to *Paleface* territory entitled *Alias Jesse James*, while this was happening. His other brother Jack served as producer on this 1959 film while Hope executive-produced. In this one, Hope is an insurance salesman who's sent out west to cancel "poor risk" Jesse James's life insurance policy. He finds himself attracted to the beneficiary of the policy, James's girlfriend (Rhonda Fleming), which gives the outlaw two reasons to hate Hope's guts. Jim Davis and Gloria Talbott were also on hand in smaller roles. As in *Paris Holiday*, Hope didn't hire any of his usual screenwriters, but this time the results were somewhat more felicitous. He also had old hand Norman McLeod at the directorial helm to hedge his bets.

There were some Frank Tashlin-inspired cartoon-type gags in this picture also, such as a scene in which Hope takes a shot of Arizona red eye. For this the special effects crew attached tubes to Hope that ran up his back and into his hat, and at the proper moment would release air that made the hat puff out comically with its brim folding up, as well as shoot streams of incense (resembling steam) out Hope's ears. For other scenes, such as when Hope was chasing a runaway buckboard, such standard devices as back projection screens and treadmills would be employed. Hope was running on a treadmill for one scene — the final one to be shot — when he suddenly passed out and had to be taken to the emergency room of the nearest hospital. He recovered after a period of rest, but this incident was to inaugurate a train of physical problems.

Alias Jesse James had its admirers, but the *New York Herald-Tribune* critic expressed the majority opinion when he wrote that the picture "suffers from a sameness of material, and a lack of spontaneity."

One of the cast members, Jim Davis, who was later to win a career in television after a highly abortive 1948 start in Bette Davis's *Winter Meeting*, later told me in an interview that he felt Hope was doing too much physically for his age, and should slow down: "He's a perfectionist, and carried too far, that always leads to trouble."

Hope was on a U.S.O. tour that Christmas of 1958 when a clot developed in a vein in the cornea of his left eye, brought on by stress and too much work. Returning from the tour, he did as doctors ordered and relaxed for a while, but finding domesticity (as usual) a bore, he was soon back on his regular schedule and suffered a relapse from the eye condition. This forced him, in February 1959, to cancel a benefit appearance in Miami, which added to his stress. In March of 1959, he was in New York at the Institute of Ophthalmology of the Columbia-Presbyterian Medical Center, getting cortisone treatments to thin the blood, and, hopefully, dissolve the clot, which had already reduced the vision in his left eye by 50 percent. At this point doctors warned that if he didn't slow down and make serious adjustments to his lifestyle, he stood to lose 100 percent of his vision in that eye.

When news of this hit the papers, Hope began to receive rather grotesque letters and telegrams from veterans and others who offered to give him one of their own eyes if, God forbid, his eye should go blind — this because of all Hope had done for them and the American people. One impassioned offer from an Edward O'Daniel in Grant Park, Illinois, ended with a postscript that asked Hope for an autographed picture. "How much will it cost?" O'Daniel asked.

If anyone at that time needed any proof of how poorly Hope was feeling, and how badly he was bothered by the lingering blood clot and symptoms of fatigue — which included dizzy spells and frequent collapses — they needed to look no further than Hope's announcement he was withdrawing as host of the Emmy Awards in April 1959. Hope, all agreed, *had* to be sick to miss that big an audience.

There was no doubt that his condition severely depressed him. Always he'd hated being inactive. The ruthless little boy in him, who kept repeating to himself "a man who *won't* be beat *can't* be beat" hated the infirmity and the fear, at age 56, that he might have to give up entertaining and get relegated to has-been status. He was also put off when sudden movements made his eye flare up, and then there was the threatening possibility he might have to give up golf because of it. Golf and Show Business — they were his two loves, and for a while he feared they might be behind him. He let Dolores fuss over him and nurse him, but he was a difficult man to live with at such close quarters, as she knew only too well. For her part, Dolores was glad to have him home with her again for a spell, in this case a long spell, but was sorry, mostly for his sake, about the reason for it. Hope's doctors, for their part, continued to monitor him closely and gave him heavy doses of drugs for his condition.

"One good thing about this situation is I'm seeing more of my family," Hope told an interviewer. "The first few days I suffered from the jitters sitting around doing nothing. Fortunately, I've always been able to turn myself off and go to sleep anywhere, anytime. The drugs have helped keep me calm too."

But Hope in 1959 desperately missed being in front of an audience. He added to the interviewer, "I took on all these projects back in 1952, and that's when the dizziness started. It was all because I'm a big ham. An audience is like dope. Once you're used to it — the applause and excitement — you have to have it again."

The rather pitiable talks with reporters, including me, continued, with Bob throwing out intimations of an enforced retirement, or at least a slowing down of his activities. "I'm not ready to give up," he told me later in 1959, "Damn, if I go they'll be carrying me out! Once a trouper, always a trouper!" But retirement — and even a slowdown — turned out not to be in the cards. Those who knew him were not surprised.

His first post-illness film project was yet another picture with Lucille Ball, *The Facts of Life* — his only film release for 1960. Ruth Hussey, Louis Nye, Louise Beavers, and Mike Mazurski were on hand for able support.

It began as a serious script by Hope's former comedy writing team, Mel Frank and Norman Panama. Earlier they'd attempted an American variation on Noel Coward's *Brief Encounter*, to star Olivia deHavilland and William Holden. Unlike Coward's story, the wind-up was to be amusing rather than depressing — which to many lovers of the original seemed a highly illogical idea. But when *Peyton Place* and *Strangers When We Meet* and other jocularly termed "adultery" films became the rage in the later Fifties, Frank and Panama decided their story needed a whole new slant. So they rewrote the script with Hope in mind. As they designed it, the picture would begin "straight," but with lines and situations appropriate for Old Ski-nose. Lucille Ball was brought in as leading lady.

Hope had of course worked with Ball in the past and had guest-starred on her *I Love Lucy* show. Now *I Love Lucy* was off the air and Desi and Lucy were divorced. Lucy's contract with Desilu was so written that had she attempted another TV series at the time she'd have wound up working for her ex-husband. Her film career had waned, and to her *The Facts of Life* came as manna from heaven, even if, in hers and others' opinions, the script was a little moldy around the edges. (It had been rejected time and again by other studios and performers.)

Hope had bitter set battles with Melvin Frank, who directed the film his partner Panama produced. Frank wanted Hope to play a bona fide character, not just give them the usual Hope persona. Frank wanted-ed the two married people embarking on their first affair (which doesn't get consummated) to register unease and trepidation. Instead Hope wanted to put in the same overactive libido shtick he'd displayed in his Road movies — an approach completely wrong for the insecure husband he was playing.

Frank was to find himself forced to film two versions of several sequences, one in which Hope displayed the "innocence" and uncertainty the director felt the film required, and another in which Hope could go straight for the easy gag, characterization be damned.

At later screenings, Hope's variations would always get the bigger laughs, to be sure, but Frank was adamant about going with the alternate sequences in the finished picture. Hope would storm off the set shouting that Frank was afraid someone might suspect he was making a comedy. Still, some of what Frank advised must have sunk in because Hope often let the director do what he wanted. Ironically, many critics complained that the film was too dull and staid and didn't give the Hope-Ball combine enough opportunities to do what they did best: be funny. The same people who'd praised Hope's acting in more serious ventures such as *The Seven Little Foys* were now, it seemed, opposed to his attempting anything different.

According to Lucille Ball, in an interview a year later in 1961, "Bob just didn't believe in his abilities as a dramatic actor. That was unfortunate because in my humble opinion he could have been a really fine one if he'd believed in himself. But he played it safe and stuck to comedy. He should have branched out, given himself a chance."

Filming on *The Facts of Life* had to be shut down for a month while Ball recovered from injuries she received falling out of a rowboat in an artificial lake at the studio. Though the water was only three-feet deep, as she fell, her head smashed against the boat and she was knocked unconscious. When she was pulled out of the water, there was a deep wound in her leg, and her face was black and blue. Even when she returned to the set weeks later, she had to wear heavy makeup to disguise the bruises.

In addition to her painful physical injuries, Lucy had to face the unpleasant "fact of life" that she was, at nearly 50, in the "aging actress" category circa 1960 and that moreover she was hardly cut out to play the "cinema grotesques" essayed by women of her era such as Bette Davis and Joan Crawford. (She was, however, to work opposite Hope in a film one more time, two years later.) Still unwilling to work for Desi, she eventually moved toward Broadway, appearing in *Wildcat*.

The Facts of Life was one of four films Hope always was to feel he deserved an Oscar nomination for (and this despite the comic-versus-serious problems that had sent director Frank up the wall). His other Oscar might-have-beens, in his opinion, were *The Seven Little Foys*, *Monsieur Beaucaire*, and *Beau James*. With all his special and honorary Oscars over the years, including a Jean Hersholt Humanitarian Award, he's always been bitter there was never a separate Oscar category for outstanding performance in a comedy. Not one of his performances was ever considered. "You know," he told one interviewer, "you really have to go on a campaign for that."

But Lucille Ball, and others, had put the finger on Bob Hope's Oscar troubles: he never summoned the will to give an all-out straight dramatic performance; he was too fearful audiences wouldn't accept him in that incarnation. Would he have proven his dramatic mettle had he tried? Neither he nor we shall ever know.

The Sixties would bring more movies for Hope, and keep him very busy indeed in one of the hottest spots he'd ever visited, onscreen or off. Vietnam. He'd also become something he'd rarely been in the past — controversial.

CHAPTER TWENTY

THE "SPONSOR" OF VIETNAM

Bob Hope planned to include Vietnam in his 1962 Christmas tour of bases from Japan to the Philippines — until the Defense Department told him it was too dangerous and canceled his shows. His primary reason for wanting to do Nam was to beat the competition. Other TV entertainers, such as Perry Como and Ed Sullivan, had started doing shows from bases (like Cuba's Guantanamo Bay) themselves, after taking note of Bob's high ratings. Hope felt — even in that early 1962 phase before hell really broke loose in Vietnam — that if he were the first to televise from Nam it'd be quite a coup. A more than appropriate place for one.

Two years later, Hope finally got an okay from the Defense Department to do Vietnam. The tour started out in Korea, and there were stops at bases in Guam and elsewhere along the way. Among the entertainers Hope took with him were Janis Paige, Anna Maria Alberghetti, Jill St. John, and the ubiquitous Anita Bryant. In the following year, 1965, he brought along singer Jack Jones, Kaye Stevens, Joey Heatherton, Miss World Diana Lynn Batts — and, again, Anita Bryant. Hope wasn't the only one organizing tours in Nam; others included Raymond Burr, Martha Raye, Kathy Nolan, and country-western singer Roy Acuff.

It was during the 1966 tour that Hope became friends with General William Westmoreland. General Emmett O'Donnell, president of the U.S.O. at the time, recalled that "Bob and Westy would sit up talking a lot on that trip. They'd talk about the war, what was happening at home, what it all meant. And that reinforced what Bob was seeing in the hospitals. He was terribly torn up by those wards, trying to be amusing and funny with a guy whose guts are coming out. He'd put on a bold front, but when he got into the back room with his drink — vodka and orange juice — he'd ask why we subject our boys to this, to get killed and maimed for what — to fight but not to win."

Like many Americans at that time, Hope felt the United States should have officially declared war and been done with it. "If the White House had just let all the B-52's in Thailand, all the B-52's in Guam, and all the Air Force go in," he said, "they'd have won the war in ten days and saved three million lives." (American lives, that is.) The trouble was that Hope continued making statements like that long after the rest of the country was sick of the conflict and favored de-escalation if not complete withdrawal.

By 1967 anti-war sentiments were being expressed — among the young and the liberal — throughout America. Hope had trouble getting some entertainers, who were against the war, to go with him on his U.S.O. tours. To his credit, he refused to name them. "They're in the minority. We're not at war and they're entitled to their opinion." He was also shrewd enough to know he might need some of those entertainers — big names especially — for his TV specials once the conflict was over, and there was really no profit in starting feuds with any of them.

Although many major names were skittish about joining Bob, he did get well-known second stringers such as Phil Crosby, Barbara McNair, Raquel Welch, and even the columnist Earl Wilson, to go with him in 1967. The following year, he had to content himself with Ann-Margret and former football player Rosey Grier, among a string of those unknown and likely to remain so.

The Anti-War Movement reached its peak in 1969, with demonstrations on virtually every college campus, and raging debates between Americans as to the worthiness of continuing our involvement in Vietnam. Still focusing on his beloved soldiers — and the high ratings his Vietnam specials got — Hope continued his treks into the combat zone into the early Seventies, along with such entertainers and celebrities as Connie Stevens, Romy Schneider, columnist Irv Kupcinet, Neil Armstrong, Ursula Andress, Jim Nabors, Redd Foxx — and even wife Dolores. Whatever their individual feelings about the Vietnam conflict, the performers — many of whom would never have gotten on television otherwise — knew they'd show up prominently in a major Bob Hope NBC special just a short while after they returned to the States.

These tours only did a couple of shows in Nam; the rest of the stops were in non-combat areas like Alaska, Korea, and Thailand. Hope did his Vietnam shows in the field, but afterward would fly to Bangkok to stay in comfortable quarters in the Erawan Hotel. The "difficult conditions" and "cramped quarters" Hope would mention as being staples of the tour referred more to the backstage dressing rooms at the bases than to the actual places the cast and crew stayed.

Not that there never was any danger. The Defense Department tried its best to reduce it by giving Hope and Company strict warnings about their behavior while in Nam. They had to walk down the center of streets, away from the sidewalks and the buildings in case of bombs. They were allowed only to walk in pairs or at most in groups of three, because larger groups would make good targets for terrorist attacks. They were told to protect themselves from deadly flying glass in the event of a mortar attack.

Hope got a lot of publicity over a near-miss in 1965, although it didn't come to light until two years later, when the U.S. 25th Infantry Division captured a secret Viet Cong document in which VC leadership rebuked some Saigon terrorists for a bomb that went off ten minutes too early and exploded before Hope and his troupe arrived at their hotel. Whether Hope was the actual target is debatable, as the explosion didn't destroy the Caravell or Majestic Hotels where he and his entourage were staying, but the Brinks across the street.

The VC had loaded up a truck with TNT and dynamite and parked it in front of the Brinks. Dozens of people were either killed out-right or severely injured, but Hope's gagwriters even found this a fit subject for quips in one of Hope's ghostwritten volumes years later: "There were fire trucks, people shouting, and a big hole in front of the Brinks Hotel, which had been bachelor officers' quarters housing some 125 people. Now every room had a southern exposure. The walls had been blown out. So had some of the bachelors." (The taste displayed here is extremely questionable.)

Yet Hope was undeniably disturbed by many of the things he saw in Nam. One of the Brinks explosion victims, a young kid, lifting his bloodstained head to say Merry Christmas to him as doctors picked glass shards out of his body. An incoherent soldier in the hospital who was too wracked with pain and emotional distress to react to him when Hope brought him a message from his buddies. The boy, who'd stepped on a land mine, watched his comrades get blown to bits, and now had no legs. And a burn ward full of boys with ravaged bodies and disfigured faces that required of their visitors and consolers more intestinal forti-tude than most had handy.

These were places the TV cameras did not go. Hope always said his chief reason for taping these U.S.O. shows was to enable the parents and sweethearts at home to actually see their soldier boys on their TV sets, but Hope's cameras never showed the reality of war, only has-been entertainers and would-be starlets and make-believe "over-sexed" showgirls who waved to, hugged, and kissed the soldiers with one eye always on the close-up camera.

America of the late Sixties was by now thoroughly sick of the war. Hope continued to emphasize escalating the conflict when by then most people at home were fed up with bloodshed and body counts and wanted it *ended*. The soldiers who bore the real brunt of the war were the most exasperated of all. As the early Seventies came in, and Nixon had still not managed to bring an honorable end to what Lyndon Johnson had begun, and whether he intended to or not, Hope had come to represent the Ultimate Hawk of the Seventies, to become the very personification of the conflict in the eyes of many Americans and even quite a few GI's.

Part of the trouble was that Hope was busy palling around with the men who'd been forced to continue the war. Hope had known Richard Nixon and indeed been good friends with him since he'd run for Governor of California in 1962. Hope would arrange for Nixon to play golf with any of the big Hollywood stars Nixon wanted to meet and know better, such as Jimmy Stewart or Fred MacMurray. Hope had met Spiro Agnew in June 1968, when Agnew was governor of Maryland at an awards banquet where they sat together, in no time becoming fast friends. Since they enjoyed the same kind of humor, Hope made Agnew a member of his "gag-telling circuit" — those friends he called early in the morning to try out new jokes on. Many of these gags were "dirty" or anti-gay, and in extremely poor taste — along the lines of, What were Robert Kennedy's last words when he lay bleeding on the hotel kitchen floor in Los Angeles in June 1968? Later on, Hope was to feed Agnew, who later resigned under a cloud of scandal as Nixon's first Vice-President, some special material when the Veep's staffers suggested that Agnew needed a more self-deprecatingly-agreeable image.

Though all fair Americans knew Lyndon Johnson's administration had bogged the United States down in Vietnam and that Richard Nixon had inherited the undeclared war in 1969 and was trying to end it rationally and honorably, the pace of the administration's policies left many impatient and often exasperated. Given Hope's friendship with the top panjandrum in Washington, it was small wonder, and perhaps inevitable, that he became — perhaps unintentionally, given the position's unpopularity — a "spokesman" for the war. His constant remarks about wanting to bomb the hell out of everything when the American

death toll was mounting and more and more dismembered and disfigured boys were brought home, aroused considerable misunderstanding,
and despite Hope's protestations that acceleration and heavy bombing
and other extreme measures would greatly shorten the war and save
lives. .

The Leftists and Anti-War protesters found it in their interests to
charge Hope and others like him with "warmongering" and "insensitiv-
ity." Even to many soldiers in Vietnam he'd become a symbol of
America's involvement and what seemed an irrational need to escalate a
conflict nobody seemed to be winning. Hope also, on his end, couldn't
seem to accept the reality that the so-called "peaceniks" were made up
as much of sensible and outraged ordinary Americans as of "oddballs"
and "lefties" and "draft dodgers."

As of 1971, Hope, regardless, had become something of an
American icon, in the same class with Mom and apple pie, and the vast
majority of servicemen, at least in the beginning, cheered his arrival at
their bases and appreciated his and his troupe members being "there for
them." Over the decades since World War II, soldiers saw the Hope
Troupes as being "a little piece of the United States, of back home,"
come to the war zone, and this was the case, for a while, in Vietnam.
The more gung-ho servicemen, the "straight arrows" and small-town
mid-Americans saw Hope as representative of the patriotic core of
America that was rooting for the right cause, the furthering of the
American dream abroad, the defeat of encroaching Communism as per-
sonified by Soviet Russia and its allies in Asia. Hope's appeal had always
been primarily to the more simple and innocent servicemen; no one
ever accused his comedy of being subtle or intellectual.

But Vietnam was a vastly different conflict from World War II,
when a vast patriotic surge and an urge to win against the Nazi and
Japanese scourges had united all Americans. Now America was bogged
down in an unwinnable war because policy at the top wouldn't fight to
end it on American terms. Frustration and disillusion were the notes
increasingly struck. And the soldiers, culled mostly from the disenfran-
chised and the disenchanted — working class boys and blacks who had
no college deferments or the "inside pull" that would exempt them from
service — were a different breed of soldier than any Hope had known.

And so all the contributing factors came together to produce in
many of the fighting GI's a brutal kind of cynicism and resentment.
Vietnam had become a vast battleground filled with men who found
release, and insulation, in marijuana and stronger drugs. The drugs and

the sense of futility led to a breaking down of barriers. Homosexual activity became more common among the servicemen (a form of comfort and closeness in their womanless environment). Men were even killing their own officers. The political changes taking place at home also inevitably affected the servicemen. Moreover, the sex-starved servicemen, trapped in unspeakable conditions, could no longer react with "innocent" glee to coy, teasy ladies in the Hope troupe — action was their sexual criterion by then, with whatever partner came to hand. The breakdown had become frighteningly real — even, finally, to Hope.

Hope made an effort — a real effort — to change with the times. He knew these boys of early Seventies Vietnam were no longer his contemporaries. To many he was an "old fart," a joke, someone their fathers used to laugh at — so he attempted to win them over with "new-fangled" jokes about marijuana along with the old standbys about broads and bosoms — juiced up for contemporary tastes . Or so he believed.

The soldiers, like most Americans, came of course from a star-struck society that treated its movie stars the same way the English treated their royalty (at least as they did back then). Even in the eroded atmosphere of the Seventies, to some of these kids from hick towns and depressing urban projects, kids who'd never dined in a fine restaurant or even seen a Broadway show, Bob Hope *was* royalty. And seeing his show at the least was surcease from monotony, tension, and fear. Hope had also become the kind of classic comic at whom you laughed naturally, even before he opened his mouth. One was expected to laugh; one was *supposed* to laugh. Egged on by frantic officers who wanted to make a "good impression" on the visitors, they did what they were told. What Hope was saying didn't matter. The service audiences — many of them — responded like Pavlov's dogs.

Many of the soldiers cared not at all about Hope but did care about the women he brought with him. Soldiers in World War II, a more innocent, sexually-repressed, boyishly masturbatory group, had always reacted enthusiastically to the women of the troupe, true, but now something new had been added. The Vietnam servicemen exhibited a sensuality and vulgarity when the women appeared that was sinister, even frightening. It was as if the servicemen of World War II would have been satisfied with a little kiss or hug, but the Nam-era soldiers — fed up, angry, resentful, in stark touch with their male sexuality in a way World War II boys hadn't been, would settle for nothing less than a full-bodied experience. When Raquel Welch got back from her 1967 tour of Vietnam, she told a *Time* reporter that Hope shouldn't bother taking entertainers to Nam, but hookers. (Hope never hired hookers, but he did sign up Dean Martin's Golddiggers, a sexy group indeed.) Hope was furious at Raquel's observation. In response, he fell back on an old line from World War II: "We take pretty girls to remind the guys what they're fighting for." Unfortunately, by 1967 — and even more starkly so by 1972 — it had a quaint, old-fashioned sound.

Hope also failed to comprehend what that trite business of "what men were fighting for" implied. Was he saying that wars were fought just so men would be left in peace to pursue and make love with women? Was this to be, à la the Second World War, a fight for good old heterosexuality, against "pervert" Nazis, and "mass-rapist" Japs? Also, it seems never to have occurred to Hope — certainly never to his "second," Anita Bryant — that many of the men fighting and dying in Vietnam might be bisexual or homosexual. Values, in all areas, were different. Hope, try as he might to overcome it, was badly out of step.

Although attendance at the Bob Hope shows in the Vietnam of the early Seventies was generally voluntary, there were times when GI's from some battalions were told bluntly they either went to the show or would be confined to quarters. "Many times an entire battalion would be ordered to attend, " said Russell Bice, the national director of U.S.O. shows. This didn't sit well with some of the soldiers, who saw Hope as a reflection of two administrations that had put them in a hellhole that they — and eventually much of their country — didn't want them in.

Ron Kovic, the former Marine sergeant and paraplegic whose story was told in the book and the film *Born on the Fourth of July*, was extremely disillusioned by Bob Hope. Kovic was in Chu Lai in December of 1965 when he went to see Hope's show. "When they filmed us, they tried to make us feel we might be seen by our families back home — Hope exploited every soldier who ever fought in that war. And I don't think he sacrificed anything in going there. He realized it was a great tool for his advancement as a personality. Our response to him came out of fear and loneliness — convicts in a prison would have done the same. And I saw how he used women to get a rise out of us — it seemed like he was always leaving with the women and we were always staying with the war. The *Apocalypse Now* scenes with the Playboy bunnies typified what it was really like in those troop shows — the terrible frustration and anguish."

Kovic was on his second tour of duty when Hope came again. "I remember not wanting to go to the show, and the men who did go came back very cynical. People didn't laugh at his jokes; the war wasn't funny anymore, and a hundred Bob Hopes wouldn't have made any difference. Back in Vietnam, Hope symbolized an American myth that had been shattered by our war experience — and that's why the troops began booing him. That's how he really made us feel."

Kovic was typical of those more literate and intelligent soldiers capable of seeing through Hope's self-sacrificing, patriotic veneer to the bedrock of his self-centeredness. The less educated or more naive soldiers couldn't perceive that they were being used — that they were, in fact, taking part in their own exploitation.

On both the overseas and domestic fronts, things might have proceeded more smoothly had Hope stuck to telling jokes and entertaining the troops and kept his mouth shut when it came to matters of policy. Bill Faith, who was Hope's full-time publicity director for several years, said, "Until [Vietnam], people saw [Hope] as a kind of elder statesman without a portfolio, someone hopping around the world being a good ambassador. Then, instead of insisting he was a comedian, taking potshots were he thought they belonged, he became fairly partisan. Suddenly, he was an ambassador for a single cause. That's where I think it weakened him. I think the cause that Hope espoused became so controversial and was perceived by so many people as immoral."

Certainly Hope's U.S.O. tours accomplished things of a positive nature — one soldier was called up on stage and shown pictures of his children, whom he'd never seen. Some of the performers made calls to parents of GI's when they got back home — and many of the soldiers gave the shows unqualified raves. But negative incidents, moments when GI's would be vocal in their displeasure, while in the minority, did occur, something Hope — aided by friends high up in the military — always did his best to cover up, minimize, or outright deny.

Around 1970, a U.S.O. employee gave an interview to an Ohio paper in which he intimated that Hope was less than acceptable to the soldiers in Vietnam. The story went out over the wire services. When Hope saw it he was livid. The first thing he did was get in touch with his pal Jim Rhodes, the Governor of Ohio, asking him to help prevent further interviews. Next he contacted friends at the Pentagon, who contacted the offending party at the U.S.O. and demanded a retraction. The employee immediately sent Hope a wire of apology. Hope bandied it about with a self-satisfied smirk for weeks.

In 1970 he was doing a monologue at Lai Khe before the First Infantry Division, when his remark, "I saw the President and he has a plan to end this war" was met with a chorus of boos. Startled, he continued his monologue but was met with virtual silence from the entire audience. He was probably correct in his assertion that the original boos weren't so much directed at him as indicative of the cynicism these tired, impatient GI's had toward any talk of "an end to this war." Hope went astray, however, in imagining that he himself hadn't been the object of the soldiers' scorn or contempt. By this time, Hope's stance on the war and his feelings about escalating it were well known even to the GI's, as was his close friendship with Nixon and other Washington higher-ups. In that respect, those men were indeed booing Bob Hope.

In any event, the incident badly bothered him. He made excuses for the men, coming up with new reasons for their behavior every time he was asked about the incident or "wrote" about it in one of his books. The men were shell-shocked, they'd experienced heavy casualties the day before, he'd say. (But wasn't that usually the case when he visited bases in combat areas?) The men knew they'd be picked up by television cameras and wanted to express their feelings to Nixon and the country. But those men also knew Hope's broadcasts were heavily edited, and they'd be cut out — as they were.

Hope was angered by the way the increasingly liberal press seized on the incident at Lai Khe and seemingly blew it out of proportion. But Hope has always been strangely silent about an incident at Long Binh a year later that in no way could be considered ambiguous. There were pickets already waiting for him outside when he arrived. Anti-war, anti-Hope placards were held up by many of the men in the audience, and the officers were roundly booed as they were introduced. "After about fifteen minutes of Hope's show, he was being drowned out by the boos," war correspondent Richard Boyle said. "When the TV camera panned the crowd, the GI's were standing up and giving it the finger and making power salutes. Then the troops started throwing things and tried to rush the stage . . . it was getting very menacing — pretty close to a riot."

Military Police had to come out to guard the stage, and Hope, "who was visibly shaken, had to shop the show." Clearly many of the soldiers felt Hope = the administration = the war. When asked about the incident by one journalist, Hope flatly denied it ever took place. "I've *never* been booed," he protested, even though he himself had freely admitted that was just what had occurred, for whatever reasons, at Lai Khe the previous year.

Hope's utter failure to realize how identified he'd become with the "war machine" that wouldn't give up on Vietnam was credited to his closeness to the politicians and generals who were gung-ho for continuing the fight. Hope never saw any other side of it but theirs. Even after the vast majority of Americans — including many of those who'd formerly felt as Hope did that acceleration was the solution — favored a complete withdrawal. He may have entertained the common foot soldiers, but he didn't get down with him and "rap," rarely broke bread with them as he did with the higher-ranking officers, thus giving himself a chance to hear their individual viewpoints. Even when he spoke with injured or dying soldiers in the hospitals, they were too preoccupied with their suffering to really talk. Hope was now not only out of touch with the GI's he professed to care about, but with the average American back home, who didn't tell jokes late at night with Spiro Agnew or play golf early in the morning with Richard Nixon.

Back in the United States, even some of Hope's friends and professional associates were becoming impatient with his attitude. Several of his writers of the more liberal persuasion resented having to write jokes for Spiro Agnew, as well as gags that reflected their boss's right-wing bias. Hope almost had a falling-out with Missouri Senator Stuart Symington, the former Secretary of the Air Force, who'd asked him to entertain GI's during the Berlin airlift way back in 1948, and who for years had been one of his closest friends in Washington. As year after year saw the United States bogged down more and more in the Vietnam mess, Symington finally said, "I used to think a lot like [Bob] does when I was only on the Armed Services Committee listening to generals. Then Bill Fulbright asked me to come on the Foreign Relations Committee, too, and I've been getting both sides. I'm afraid Bob still hears only one side."

Hope's reply to this was, "Stuart Symington used to be the biggest hawk ever known. Then he got all mixed up with Fulbright and they became picky, picky, picky." At that late date, 1970, Hope still preferred to think of Vietnam protesters as a limited assortment of Communist agitators or out-and-out wackos. Some of his supporters even trotted out the famous statement made by Josef Stalin in the Forties — that the way to lick the United States was to drain its military resources via a series of small wars fought with minor Soviet allies, and that this proved true over the years with the battle with North Korea (1950 – 53) and then with North Vietnam,. But this only incited Hope to insist again that a knockout escalation — hadn't Truman done it with Japan in 1945? — would make an end of the war.

Hope had planned to reunite with Lucille Ball for a new movie (never made) in which he played a character much like himself, entertaining the troops in Vietnam, and Lucy was to have been a nurse who helps Hope get some children out of the country by way of the Mekong River. Mel Shavelson's secretary was typing up the script for this when she heard American troops had been ordered into neutral Cambodia. Disgusted and angered, she asked her boss, "How can Bob Hope even *think* of making a comedy out of the Vietnam War?" Adding, "I'm not typing another word of this!" Shavelson called Hope and was surprised that he readily agreed it might be a good idea to put the picture on the shelf; always the good businessman, Hope was smart enough to reason that if his movies released during the Vietnam conflict, all of which had been completely apolitical, hadn't done well at the box office, a film that might be construed by many as politically slanted would certainly be a hot potato. And a cold turkey. Paying customers could be scared off by the inevitable picket lines. He looked, instead, for a less volatile film project.

There were other ripples of dissatisfaction with Hope. In March 1971 The New York City Council of Churches decided to give him its annual Family Man Award when objections arose over the only other candidate, New York Governor Nelson Rockefeller. The entire sixty-man board endorsed the choice of Hope. When a Brooklyn Lutheran pastor named Reverend Richard Neuhaus found out about the decision, he marched into the council's next meeting with twenty young liberal ministers in tow and asked the council's executive director, Dr. Dan Potter, why Hope had been chosen. He was told Hope's credentials were "unimpeachable," and, more importantly, Hope's presence would guarantee a large turnout at the $150-a-plate dinner that coming fall.

Neuhaus and his associates charged that these reasons for giving Hope the award were "ludicrous" and demanded it be given instead, posthumously, to Whitney M. Young, Jr., the black civil rights activist. The Neuhaus statement read in part, "There is nothing in Mr. Hope's record [regarding] public commitment to the three pressing issues that confront the council — poverty, racial injustice, and peace. On the contrary, Mr. Hope has uncritically supported the military establishment." In a recount, the Board voted 34 to 22 to rescind the Hope designation and give Young the posthumous award.

After news of this hit the papers, the council was overwhelmed by a cascade of abusive and vulgar phone calls, with a spokesman declaring himself shocked by the "ugly obscenity" of some of the calls. When asked to comment, Hope said it was more appropriate that the award (which had previously been won by three Presidents of the United

States) go to Young rather than to him. This elicited public comment by columnists such as Harriet Van Horne, who, while admitting she "abhorred his politics," nevertheless felt the comedian was being punished for having the wrong friends.

The degree to which Hope had become identified in the public mind with the Vietnam conflict was finally driven home to him when a teenager approached him as he was leaving a Van Nuys ice cream parlor and asked, "Hey, aren't you the guy who sponsored the Vietnam War?"

Hope came in for even more criticism than in the past on the issue of televising all his tours. When one interviewer, citing the extensive media coverage and commercialization of his tours, suggested that his TV specials came across as virtual advertisements for the war, Hope responded it was at the Pentagon's urging that he took cameras with him into the combat zones.

One thing that should be made clear is that Hope himself didn't pay for these tours. The Department of Defense (which of course gets its funding from taxpayers) provided all the transportation. Hope's televised sponsor paid the filming expenses, and NBC also paid Hope a salary of $150,000 for each TV special. The whole package was then sold to NBC for a generous amount. The performers were given a small living allowance from the U.S.O. and again paid scale by NBC if they appeared on the telecast. According to Russell Bice, the U.S.O. didn't receive one single penny from the highly rated and lucrative broadcasts; the money all went to NBC and Hope. Although Hope representatives claim that Hope enterprises lost millions on the tours, insiders say this was highly unlikely.

There were indications that Hope's primary objective in going to Vietnam wasn't so much to entertain troops but to put together his profitable TV specials. Everything possible was done by the military to accommodate Hope's TV crews. One time they were filming the show on board the *Ticonderoga* aircraft carrier, whose planes were actively engaged in war missions, when Hope was told by his lighting men that the constant motion of the ship would necessitate the use of cross lighting unflattering to the women in the show. It was intimated that it'd be so much easier if only the sun would hit the ship at just the right angle. Word went out that the men on the bridge were instructed to turn the ship around and lower the speed to five knots so that the sun would be in just the right spot. Here is an example of how the services did all they could to please Hope, knowing that his specials were an extremely effective form of propaganda.

Each special was put together from approximately 180,000 feet of film (no videotape back then). A project that would normally take months had to be condensed to a couple of weeks so that the special could be aired for, say, a projected Christmas showing. The best reaction shots of the servicemen — usually laughing hysterically at Bob's jokes or expressing an appropriately stereotypical masculine reaction to the female entertainers — had to be carefully chosen from hours of film. The only time NBC ever raised any objections to the content of the specials was when its executives found out Hope planned to include some "pot" jokes; NBC insisted these be cut, but when Hope told these same jokes on the *Tonight Show* to Johnny Carson, NBC said it was okay because the *Tonight Show* was a news program. Which was news to practically everyone.

Hope himself had admitted to trying marijuana back in his vaudeville years, but later informed one paper that he hadn't sampled it until around 1975. To more conservative publications he'd say he knew pot wasn't good for people, but to more liberal ones, like *Rolling Stone*, he'd say, "It's just like liquor; it all depends on the dosage and frequency, you know."

In 1971, Hope made an effort to entertain in Hanoi by flying to Vientiane, Laos, to meet with the North Vietnamese consul, Nguyen Van Thanh, from whom he hoped to get a visa. The meeting between Hope and Thanh instead turned into a negotiation for freeing the prisoners. Thanh posed with Hope for pictures, but as to freeing the prisoners, he'd say only that it was up to Nixon and his acceptance of the seven-point peace plan. When Hanoi eventually turned down Hope's visa application, he blamed it on the press leaking details on the "negotiations" despite Hope's press people's attempts to keep a lid on it.

In 1975, Hope tried yet again to get a visa to Hanoi, and let it be known he had a plan to bargain for the POWs in exchange for ten million dollars. When Hanoi again refused to let him in, Hope abandoned his efforts, citing as the reason a newly unveiled American peace proposal. Hope also had probably come to feel that the Pentagon itself might turn against him if his efforts to do a televised show from Hanoi — POWs on TV! — and consequently net the ratings of the century, interfered with the government's agenda.

Apparently Hope had gotten all he could out of Vietnam. It was time for other, newer professional debacles.

CHAPTER TWENTY-ONE

THE PITS

During the Sixties and Seventies, Hope continued in other activities besides "sponsoring" the Vietnam War, including the making of films. Although still under contract to United Artists, he frequently did pictures for other studios. His 1961 release, *Bachelor in Paradise*, for MGM, carried on the tradition of suggestive titles (*The Great Lover*, *Casanova's Big Night*) that coyly perpetuated Hope's persona as an unlikely (and by 1961, at 58, rapidly aging) "lover boy."

Bachelor in Paradise was directed by Jack Arnold (*Creature From the Black Lagoon*), who was apparently unable to repeat the success he'd had with Peter Sellers two years earlier in *The Mouse That Roared*. In *Bachelor*, Hope plays a well-known author who moves into a community incognito to do a book on life in the suburbs, in the process getting himself involved with several housewives and their jealous husbands. Lana Turner was the latest feminine star to hoist up Bob's onscreen loverboy shtick, in this playing a woman who works for the development Hope has chosen to live in, and with whom he carries on a romance.

While Turner at a ripe 41 was no longer in the first blush of loveliness on display in such as *Love Finds Andy Hardy* (1938) or in the full bloom of womanly lushness featured in the 1947 *Green Dolphin Street*, she was still far too glamorous and beautiful — she'd romanced onscreen Gable, Taylor, Stewart, and other male powerhouses — to make a likely love interest for Bob Hope.

As if Lana weren't enough, MGM also threw at Hope some younger cuties to cavort with, including perky Paula Prentiss and the always sensual Janis Paige. By this time Agnes Moorehead and Reta Shaw, also in the supporting cast along with John McGiver and Jim Hutton, were much too old for romantic leads opposite Bob, though they'd have been more appropriate choices, given his age at the time. Given the plot's and premise's comic possibilities, the picture doesn't

Bachelor in Paradise, 1961, with Lana Turner

exploit them to any particular advantage, and some critics even came right out with it and declared Bob Hope too superannuated for such hijinks.

Hope's one 1962 film project was a new team-up with Bing Crosby for what was to be their final Road picture, this time called *The Road to Hong Kong*. Both boys — Hope at 59 and Crosby at 58 — looked too tired and old for such boyish excursions by now, and some critics felt the net effect was pathetic. The film was made in England, and Hope and his family, and Crosby and his family (the unfortunate, neglected and grossly mistreated sons of his first marriage excepted) all cohabitated in a 56-room, stately manor house between Ascot and Windsor, but close enough to London and whatever passed in Britain for the golf courses that represented a big chunk of their environment, as always.

In fact, Overgrown Boys Bob and Bing spent so much time on the golf courses that the director of *Hong Kong*, Norman Panama, was forced to drive out personally and drive them back after applying what pressure he could. At this point in their lives there's little doubt that the two nearing-60-ers enjoyed the relaxation of golf far more than they did the "work" of moviemaking — in Bob's case it was to show increasingly in the films after *Hong Kong*.

Louella Parsons, the 77-year-old gossip columnist who'd retire within three years, and whose "bladder control" problem in the age before adult diapers was never worse (she left little puddles behind wherever she sat) was the first to mention in her column that Dorothy Lamour, it appeared, would not be participating in the new Road movie. Lamour, to her chagrin, got word that Gina Lollobrigida or Sophia Loren might be the new "girl." Lamour's son, William Howard, Jr., who worked for Hope's agent Doc Shurr, was the first to tip her off. As it turned out, she was to be in it, but when Shurr dropped by her house with the script she was horrified. She'd been a co-star with "the boys" in six previous Road pictures, but this time she was to be barely on hand in a cameo. She'd simply be singing a new Sammy Kahn song in the background, not part of the action at all, while Bob and Bing ran around maniacally in the foreground. Her total number of lines in the script: four.

Lamour was livid. As she put it, "My number was not at the beginning of the picture. Not at the end of the picture. It was just stuck in somewhere in the middle. And while I would be singing, the script called for Crosby and Hope, in Chinese clothes and Chinese makeup, to be involved in a chase with the police! Over all this, I would be singing my one number!"

Lamour sent the script back with a flat refusal. She'd participate only if her role was expanded, she told Shurr and Panama. Producer Melvin Frank tried to tell Dorothy it was too late to make any changes in the script, even though both knew that, as in the old Road movies, the gagwriters would be coming up with new lines almost to the second they began shooting a scene.

Then Lamour read that Joan Collins had been signed for a major role in the movie — the middle-aged men who were making *Road to Hong Kong* had opined from on high that Lamour at 47, a decade younger than the Bing-Bobsters, was "too old" for the part! She figured that was that, but negotiations continued. She was later to learn that her name was tied up in the distribution deal and it might cause complications if she wasn't in the film, which is why she eventually got her way and her part was accordingly juiced up — somewhat.

When Lamour went to London to appear in the film, a major "bitch fight" broke out between her and saucy Joan Collins. First, Collins told the papers that Lamour was looking for trouble because she, Collins, had the bigger part. Lamour shot back that if she was going to start a feud with someone, it'd be the star of the picture, not some nobody. Collins then really unsheathed her claws and declared that of course it was too bad that the men could still play their roles and Dorothy was given a hassle — Collins characterized it as "a blow against feminism" but added cattily (her job, after all, was at stake) that Bob and Bing still looked remarkably fit for their ages but poor Dorothy had let her looks go. With each sally reported eagerly by the notoriously vicious British press, both ladies would fume behind closed hotel-room doors and let off pressure by throwing bottles and screaming.

Joan Collins, 28 at the time, was appearing in *Road to Hong Kong* not only for the exposure but to get away from Warren Beatty, as her affair with him was winding down to its conclusion and he was being difficult. Beatty, inclined to meddling, looked at the script and pronounced it "crap!" But Collins enjoyed working with Hope; like many people, especially women, she found him utterly charming and down-to-earth, and she was particularly impressed by the aggressive confidence he exuded. Crosby, on the other hand, she found disgusting. He had a habit of constantly spitting into the sawdust on the floor, which didn't sit well with the men who had to sweep it up. Joan hated kissing him, not only because his breath was fetid but because his manner was always preoccupied if not downright unpleasant. The voluptuous Joan, who had a high (and admittedly justified) opinion of her womanly charms, naturally had no use for a man who, as she described it, "looked through" her. But Hope knew how to play to her ego and could probably have seduced her had he been a younger man at the time.

One of the highlights of the picture is a sequence in which Peter Sellers plays a zany Indian doctor who attempts to cure Hope of his amnesia. These two giants of comedy, whose styles are so very different, nonetheless work together marvelously (with good support from Bing) in a scene in which both men do what they're best at: Sellers employs a full repertoire of dialects and movements and twitches while Hope reacts in his inimitable fashion.

At one point Sellers plays a pipe and causes a snake to appear out of a basket. He explains to the frightened boys that if a snake ever bites them all they have to do is "cut the wound and suck out the poison." When Hope asks what to do if the bite's in a place he can't reach with his mouth, Sellers replies, "That's when you find out who your friends are."

In his vaudeville days (off the stage, not on) Hope had heard the joke in its original form: "What do you do if a snake bites you on your cock?" He was afraid that even this extremely bowdlerized version wouldn't make it past the censors, but luckily it did, and got one of the biggest laughs in the picture.

Although generally dismissed (particularly by Lamour) as the worst of the Road movies, *Hong Kong* in retrospect is actually one of the better ones. The plot has Bob and Bing getting involved in a sinister organization, run by Robert Morley, that sends the boys off in a space-ship as part of an inexplicable plot to take over the world. Bob and Bing (although Crosby doesn't look particularly healthy) are both in top form and some of the gags are the most memorable in the series.

As Bob is being tied into a "fly it yourself" contraption at the beginning of the picture, he complains about the quality of medical help Bing always gets him when he inevitably breaks his bones during a stunt, and is particularly livid over the last doctor. "How was I to know he was an elephant doctor?" Bing rejoinders. Bob replies that the size of his thermometer should have been a clue. "When he was shaking it I was still on it!" Hope says. And Hope's estimation of Morley, "I think he rolls his own," was certainly ahead of its time.

Bob and Bing have a very inventively staged song number early in the movie, and in Lamour's number — which was clearly expanded beyond a mere background bit — Bob and Dorothy get quite a few laughs as some fish he'd earlier hidden in his clothing keep popping out to give Dorothy conniptions. (Lamour's part is still tiny, however.) A scene in a spaceship when the equipment malfunctions and the boys are force-fed at a rapid rate approaches genuine hilarity. The entire pro-duction is good-humored and has some amusing cameos by Frank Sinatra, Dean Martin, and especially David Niven.

The film got only lukewarm notices but it made a lot of money. It was in box office terms the fifth most successful picture of 1962. "I never did see the accounting books," Lamour claims. She was still bit-ter over being cut out years ago when Hope and Crosby got together to secure ownership of two-thirds of all their Road pictures. "Those guys have so much money," she told columnist Cindy Adams, "and I helped make it for them. Well, I'm better off if I save my breath to cool my cof-fee."

Over the years Lamour had compiled quite a few reasons to be more than annoyed at her co-stars' behavior. She didn't get a single phone call from either while negotiating her deal for *Hong Kong*. When she opened a new act at New York's Latin Quarter a short while before leaving for England to make the picture, neither of the men sent good-luck telegrams or even bothered to answer her letters. Bob had her on one of his specials to promote the picture, but Bing told her there was no time to include her in his promotional show and used life-sized cutouts of her instead!

Years later, when Lamour and Bing were both signed to appear on the *Hollywood Palace* TV show on the same night, Hope refused to do a walk-on. "He won't do anything for nothing." Lamour said at the time. When Hope did a TV special featuring many of his leading ladies, Dorothy later said, "I did all the publicity work on the show, meeting with the press and so forth, and I made [all those] pictures with him, so how come I didn't get a bigger part in the program?"

As with Hope and Crosby, Hope and Lamour have often been characterized as "good friends," when the relationship they really have is a professional one, of shared experiences — 50 percent fun, 50 percent exasperation — and not true friendship. Some of those shared memories were captured on the set — all too briefly — on *Road to Hong Kong*, but such memories hardly began to offset the understandable bitterness and resentment of decades.

Hope had next planned to do *The Road to India* with Crosby, using Indian financing and Indian stars and appointing himself associate producer, but the project never got off the planning board. It would be almost thirteen years before there'd be discussions for another Road film.

Hope's son Anthony (Tony) graduated from Georgetown University in June 1962, and while not the official commencement speaker, Bob was asked to say a few words at the ceremony. President Kennedy heard about Bob's jokes — mostly about the recession — and through Pierre Salinger relayed to him that he'd like to hear them personally. This began a friendship between Hope and the star-fucking JFK. "Every time I'd go to Washington," Hope said, "Pierre would call me and say, 'Come on over.'" Hope and JFK would not only trade jokes — as Hope was later to do with Spiro Agnew — but there were reports that Hope introduced Kennedy (and other presidents) to more than a few Hollywood glamour girls.

Also in 1962 Hope set up a trust for the Bob Hope House, Inc., a charity in Cincinnati, Ohio, which Hope has operated, mostly in absen-

With Lucille Ball in 1963's *Critic's Choice*

tia, like a latter-day Father Flanagan. The Bob Hope House is a home for underprivileged and delinquent boys, who are usually sent there direct from the Ohio court system. Hope used to do a show for the House once a year (he now raises money via an annual "golf outing") and tells the boys that he himself didn't start out with much but that it's still possible to make something of oneself, etc. The irony implicit in this Bob Hope "Boys Town" setup — the house's motto is "If you treat a human being like a human being, he will act like a human being," a spinoff on Father Flanagan's "There are no bad boys" — is that it espouses the most bleeding-heart-liberal sentiments while bearing the name of an arch nonsentimentalist and pragmatist who was to be dubbed Mr. Superconservative in his later years.

On August 6th of that same year, Bob lost one of his closest relatives when his brother Jack died in Boston of chronic hepatitis. Certainly the two had had their differences but Bob had often come to rely on Jack's judgment and to think of him as a genuine friend. His anguish was compounded when less than two weeks later, Jack's son, William John Hope, a machinist at Douglas Aircraft Corporation, was diagnosed as having a serious case of leukemia. He was only 41 at the time and had a wife and two daughters.

After all this, Bob was in no mood to put up with what he termed his "renegade" brother Jim when he got back in Bob's hair later that year. Having flopped in show biz — with help (or, rather, no help) from his brother — Jim had turned to writing. He'd written a book about the Hope family (with plenty of pages devoted to Bob) entitled *Mother Had Hopes* and proceeded to sell it to a Boston publishing firm called Bruce Humphries Publishers. Jim and his wife Wyn had told absolutely no one about the book and wanted it to be a big "surprise" for Bob, containing as it did things about his famous brother only Jim knew about.

Unfortunately, the publisher — with one eye on sales potential — insisted that Jim get his brother to write an introduction. Jim wanted no part of that idea; it was his book and his alone. Besides, he knew Bob would certainly not consent to write a foreword. Reportedly, the editor at Humphries undertook to contact Bob, telling him about the book and asking if he'd help his brother out and submit an introduction. Bob's reaction was predictable. He threatened to sue the firm if they proceeded with the book; Humphries, a small house whose owners knew where their bread was buttered, decided to cancel the publication, citing Jim's refusal to ask his brother to do the introduction as the cause. When Jim later died, in 1975, an utterly bitter and disgusted man, Bob insisted Wyn surrender the manuscript to him, which she did.

Lucille Ball was still otherwise unemployed and nearly unemployable when Hope again rescued her by making her his co-star in his next film, *Critic's Choice* (1963). Warner Bros. put it on the shelf for a year because of disastrous previews, then released it to coincide with Lucy's return to television in *The Lucy Show*. It didn't help much, as the picture didn't fare well with critics and public.

The movie was based on a Broadway show by Ira (*Rosemary's Baby*) Levin. In the film Hope plays a newspaper drama critic who insists (against all reason and probability) on reviewing his own wife's lousy play. The picture never quite recovers from this basic contrivance; in real life a critic would rightfully claim conflict of interest and someone else would get the assignment. Even if one accepts the admittedly amusing premise, it's all Hope and Ball, as his would-be-playwright wife, and a fine supporting cast (including Rip Torn, Jessie Royce Landis, Marie Windsor, Jim Backus, and Jerome Cowan) can do to keep the movie afloat. Scenes were obviously thrown in just so Hope and Ball could mug shamelessly, but there are some genuinely funny moments — particularly when Bob gets drunk with Marilyn Maxwell (pleasing as always) and goes to the theatre to see the play in a near stupor.

Originally it was planned to film Hope's next picture, *Call Me Bwana*, in Kenya, but the political situation there necessitated a switch to the sound stages of Pinewood Studios in England, which actually proved more appropriate for such a lightweight exercise. Hope had signed up for the film primarily for the opportunity to visit Africa, as well as a chance to work with Anita Ekberg again. It may have been "Goodbye Kenya" but at least Ekberg was still on board. Edie Adams was also signed, as well as the British character actor Lionel Jeffries. Hope's golfing buddy, Arnold Palmer, also got into the action.

In this, Hope as a phony explorer whose books are actually based on the adventures of his uncle, is asked by the government to search for a space capsule that's landed in Africa (a premise taken from more than one Fifties science fiction film) and takes a pretty secret agent (Adams) along with him. Ekberg plays (yet again) an enemy spy. The director, Gordon Douglas (best known for the giant ant thriller *Them*), got his start directing Hal Roach shorts, but by 1963 betrayed no particular comedic bent.

With *Call Me Bwana*, Hope's films became "deals" instead of movies. The "deal" setup ran like this: Somebody needed a picture. In this case, Harry Saltzman, later co-producer of the James Bond movies. Hope also needed a picture. A deal was cooked up over cocktails. Even less attention was paid to the script, concocted by a pair billed as Nate Monaster and Johanna Harwood. Hope was satisfied so long as he could get to the golf course every day and there were one or two attractive ladies in the film. Hope was probably less surprised than anyone when the reviews of this uninspired effort were lukewarm.

Hope almost got his eye poked out by a bad-tempered ostrich in one scene, but the bird didn't peck enough sense into him to prevent the comedian from going into *A Global Affair*, released in January 1964. An MGM release produced by Hall Bartlett with Jack Arnold again on hand as director, *Affair* was yet another "deal." Hope was chiefly interested in the picture because it would again capitalize on his "lover boy" image (at 60 yet!) by teaming him with a bevy of international beauties. Hope plays a United Nations official who finds an unclaimed baby in the UN building. Soon afterward a variety of foreign lovelies approach Hope to try to convince him that their country should adopt the child.

Call Me Bwana, 1963, with Anita Ekberg

Lilo Pulver, Yvonne DeCarlo, Robert Sterling, Jacques Bergerac, and John McGiver were among those trapped in this unmemorable mess, which wound up, sentimentally and unbelievably, with Hope adopting the baby himself. The critical reaction on this was predictably zilch.

In March of 1965, the 61-year-old Hope was the guest of honor at the U.S.O.'s Silver Anniversary Celebration, at which he accepted an award from President Lyndon Johnson, who was in rare form, and getting as many laughs from the star-studded crowd as Hope. One of the more glamorous attendants was a certain board member of the U.S.O. (and of Pepsi-Cola) named Joan Crawford. After the banquet, Hope continued the festivities in his suite upstairs at his hotel, but Crawford was nowhere to be seen. She'd already retired to her own suite and was nursing a bottle of vodka and calling her friends — including me — to tell them how the evening had gone.

In between phone calls, while Crawford was refreshing her drink, an associate of Hope's got through and told her Hope wanted her to join the party. "I can't come. I'm naked," she told him. The man misunderstood her and thought she was saying "I'll make it." Joan made a few more phone calls, then shimmied into her dress but didn't bother putting on her underwear. She showed up at Hope's suite, snookered, vodka flask in tow, and went over to Hope and Stuart Symington. "I haven't got anything on under this gown," she said, "and I don't give a fuck."

Later Joan called me again and told me exactly how she felt about Hope. "He's the worst self-promoter and self-aggrandizer I've ever known," she growled between swallows. "He thinks everyone should jump at his command. I'm a bigger star than that fucker will ever be. He's just a cheap vaudeville comic, loves only himself, and he can go straight to hell." After that, mumbling, "I'm tired love, gonna go beddy-bye," Joan got off the phone. Some days later I reminded her of what she'd said about Hope that night. "That's the best damned capsule commentary on him ever given!" she chortled.

Hope's next film, released shortly after his 62nd birthday in 1965, was entitled *I'll Take Sweden*. It was another "deal" under United Artists auspices and was produced by Edward Small and directed by Freddie De Cordova. In this hastily concocted mess Hope did his best to tap into "youthful" concerns that were already dated by the time the film came out. To attract a younger audience, Hope cast Frankie Avalon, the teen idol famous during this period for his Beach Party movies. The thin plot, badly scripted, has Hope a widower who objects to Frankie's dating his daughter, Tuesday Weld, but becomes even more concerned — after a move to Sweden to get Weld away from Avalon — when the girl is romanced by a sophisticated playboy, played by Jeremy Slate. Dina Merrill was on hand to play Hope's romantic interest.

I was on the *I'll Take Sweden* set several times during the shooting during one of my annual lengthy sojourns in Hollywood in that era. Dina Merrill, whom I interviewed later at her press agent's, Helen Ferguson's, home, was gracious about Hope, saying she admired his durability and energy. "He'll go on forever and ever," she laughed, proving more of a prophet than she knew. Frankie Avalon spoke respectfully of Hope, saying, "He's got wonderful humor, and I'm picking up a lot of tips from him on how to put over scenes. With young people, he's a good listener too." Tuesday Weld also thought Hope "a legend, an inspiration," citing his patience with her during their scenes together and his advice on her career. But Hope himself was the *piece de resistance* interview subject. Sitting with him on the set, and later in his dressing room, I was told, "I try to keep up with what's going on. Young people are very stimulating to work with. Frankie, Tuesday, the rest, they're today, and that's where I wanna be — in today." Asked if he'd continue to make movies, Bob said, "As long as I can make it to a set, as long as the deals keep coming. Retirement is for the birds. I need to keep busy."

As it turned out, *I'll Take Sweden* didn't prove to be worth the efforts of all concerned, and the critics dismissed it with terms like "witless" and "trivial."

During the next year, not yet under fire for his Vietnam activities, Bob was getting his share of criticism from another quarter. Civil Rights activists felt he ought to get involved in their struggle. During this period, he was telling borderline racist jokes in private. One that got around Hollywood, being repeated often enough in the Polo Lounge of the Beverly Hills Hotel, was, "LBJ wants the pope to make Martin Luther King a cardinal so he won't have to kiss anything but his ring." At home, Hope's favorite entertainment routines for guests were lapses into offensive "colored" dialects, along with the continuing "faggot" routines. Two years later, after the 1968 Oscar ceremonies were delayed for two days because of Martin Luther King's assassination, MC Hope stunned a number of people by not only remaining loudly silent on the murder but for making gross jokes about the postponement.

His choice of pictures remained as bad as his choice of jokes. In 1966 he made what is arguably his worst picture (a possible tie with *8 on the Lam*). This was called *Boy, Did I Get a Wrong Number*. It inaugurated a three-picture association with Phyllis Diller in the late Sixties.

In a September 14, 1992 letter from her Los Angeles home to our researcher Bill Schoell, Phyllis Diller wrote: "I met Bob Hope in 1961 when I was bombing in a horrible club. The Lotus Club in Washington, D.C. An agency had sent me to a place where I should never have attempted to play. A line of girls were to mingle after the show — oh, whoopee! My material was very cerebral, quite highbrow for this terribly low-brow audience, so of course I bombed every night. But Bob was already a fan from my *Tonight Show* appearances and he grabbed me as I was trying to sneak out and told me I was great. This was the beginning of a beautiful friendship and much collaboration. I have made more guest appearances on his TV specials than any other female."

In her letter, Diller added, "I believe that the political climate affected the reviews of our movies." Phyllis also felt that when it came to casting romantic co-stars in that period, "Bob should have had more realistic love interests, girls not so young. I felt Marjorie Lord in *Boy, Did I Get a Wrong Number* was the most realistic and worked well."

Phyllis revealed that she even got to crash Bob's golfing activities. As she put it, "I've had many happy hours caddying for Bob. He loves to see an old bag carrying an old bag."

Hope, for his part, was to remember that the Washington, D.C. club in which he discovered Phyllis was so poorly frequented that "only the cocktail waitresses formed the audience."

Although Diller with her wild hairdos and pseudo-shrewish manner may have seemed an unlikely match for Hope professionally, she wasn't an unattractive woman in private life and Hope liked her immediately. She was also closer in age to him than many of his nubile and almost-nubile co-stars of the period. A warm friendship ensued that some labeled a romance but it's more likely that common interests and spiritual affinity were the ingredients. Phyllis was one of many that Hope helped, often without any publicity fanfare.

Producer Curtis Roberts, who knew Hope through the years, told us, "He did a lot of favors and kindnesses nobody ever knew about. He was like Frank Sinatra in that respect. And he gave a lot of his time gratis to charity and other events of the kind. Measured in money, time is valuable, especially to an entertainer, and he gave lots of it. His reputation for stinginess and wariness in matter of finance sprang, understandably, from the fact that a lot of people over the years tried to take a bite out of him, his relatives, old friends from the past, hangers-on. He got tired of being a patsy. He got to feel that too much kindness to such people only weakened them rather than encouraged their self-reliance. And he didn't like being played for a sucker. And can you blame him?"

There was the usual insider gossip about the casting of buxom Elke Sommer in *Boy, Did I Get a Wrong Number* as the temperamental movie star ("The Divine Didi!") with whom the Hope character becomes involved. "Hope — he is divine, divine — I love to be around him. He brings everyone fully alive," Sommer told me in 1966. It was as if the older Hope got, the more obvious and talentless the sex symbols were in his pictures. At least his early co-stars, beautiful as they were, were also reasonably talented actresses, but anyone who sat through five minutes of *Number* could see Sommer wasn't in the league of, for instance, Madeleine Carroll. But dumb beauties were Hope's casting cup of tea in the mid-Sixties. Even in the comedienne department, and with the notable exceptions of Diller, Lucille Ball, and Martha Raye, Hope rarely sought out skilled performers who might outshine him. In *Number* he had it his way, more or less.

The picture has Hope as a happily married man (Marjorie Lord, as Diller noted, was appropriate age-wise as his wife) with two kids. When he calls his wife at the beauty parlor, a line gets crossed, and Hope winds up speaking to an actress (Sommer) who has run away from her latest picture because she's tired of taking bubble baths. Afraid she'll be recognized if she orders from room service, she begs Hope to bring her something to eat, and after some trepidatious cogitation, he does. This sets off an involvement with the lady that gets Hope in dutch with his wife, Didi's boyfriend, and even the police, who accuse him of the sex bomb's murder when they mistakenly think she drowned.

The critics were merciless. Even in retrospective reviews since, such as William Schoell, who wrote, "The situations in *Boy, Did I Get a Wrong Number* must have seemed perfectly amusing on paper, but as enacted on the screen in this lethargic production they only merit a few chuckles. Diller adds some fun to the proceedings, but her big gags, such as riding a motorcycle through a trench and making all the workmen pop out like jumping beans, really don't work at all, and the situations and assorted mishaps that might have been hilarious had they happened to Diller are mistakenly turned over to Sommer. Marjorie Lord's horrible teased hairdo (the latest 1966 style!) resembles a mushroom cloud and is unintentionally funnier than Diller's finger-in-a-socket coiffeur. This movie is really awful!"

In an attempt to recapture his now sadly sagging film popularity circa the mid-Sixties, Hope had drafted as director the same George Marshall who'd worked long before on more successful Hope features like *Monsieur Beaucaire* and *Ghostbreakers*. Marshall helmed both *Number* and Hope's next film in 1967, *Eight on the Lam* (sometimes rendered *8 on the Lam*) but Charlie Chaplin himself, in his prime, could have done next to nothing with these screenplays. In *Lam*, Hope is a bank teller who finds $10,000 and spends it. When $50,000 turns up missing at the bank, Hope is afraid he'll be accused of embezzling, and with his seven kids takes off until he can prove his innocence. Diller is again cast as the family housekeeper (in the film Hope is a widower) and Jonathan Winters as her boyfriend, the detective pursuing Hope.

Any picture that offers a teaming of two top comedians like Hope and Winters, and their fans looked forward eagerly to the occasion, should have been hilarious fun, but such was not the case in the pitiful *Lam*.. Winters was reined in by a bad script *and* Bob Hope, neither giving him enough decent material, or time, to pitch successfully his special shtick. Jill St. John and Shirley Eaton were the saucy wenches on hand this time.

Bombing out with George Marshall twice in a row, Hope turned in desperation to writer/director Frank Tashlin for help. Tashlin had always been reliable in the past when it came to producing great gags, and he'd helmed some of Hope's funnier movies, such as *Son of Paleface*. The movie Tashlin wrote for Hope, however, *The Private Navy of Sgt. O'Farrell*, which Tashlin also directed, wasn't in Tashlin's, or Hope's, usual league. The critical reaction to *O'Farrell* was scathing, which may have had as much to do with the political climate of 1968 (liberal critics of that year didn't much care for Hope's stance on Vietnam) as it did with the fact that the script seemed a throwback to the Forties, the time period in which the film takes place in fact, and indeed may have been an old script polished off, inappropriately, for Hope's use in the Sixties.

In the film Hope actually plays an army NCO, and the "private navy" refers to the crew he puts together to sail for some beer being delivered in a ship torpedoed by the Japanese. Some of this beer has already floated to the island Hope's based on, and has instigated several drinking parties, but the supply is running low. In addition to beer, the men are looking forward to the arrival of nurses, but in a funny scene that's very well edited and directed, the only ones to get out of the plane are several male nurses, and Phyllis Diller. Never a topflight actress, though a wonderful comedienne, Phyllis is okay in a role that in the Forties would have gone to Martha Raye. Indeed Diller seems to

With Jeffrey Hunter in *The Private Navy of Sgt. O'Farrell,* 1968

imitate Raye at times. She's given a few good lines, as when she tells how her parents used to make booze in the bathtub and would let her bathe in it, too. "To this day," Diller says, "whenever I see a martini I start to take my clothes off."

At 65 years of age, Hope exhibits quite a bit of energy in the picture (although his patented virile "gr-gr-growls" over women seem dubbed) and he even manages some juicy kissing scenes with no less than Gina Lollobrigida. Of course, had Tashlin *not* had such scenes in his screenplay Hope would no doubt have insisted he insert them. In a funny parody of *From Here to Eternity*, Gina and Bob roll around the beach as bigger and bigger waves break over them. "When Burt Lancaster does it it's very sexy," Hope says in the film. "I do it and I almost drown!"

The picture seems, in retrospect, to be an honest, if not entirely successful, attempt to recapture some of the good-natured wackiness of the Road films and Hope's better wartime comedies, but it was released in the wrong decade. Tashlin did turn in a briskly directed swan song for what was to be his last film. There were the usual funny sight gags and the obligatory pseudo-homoeroticism. When Hope and the commander, handsome Jeffrey Hunter, start hugging each other at the moment of victory, Hope pulls away and says, "We don't have to hug each other. We got the real thing [girls] on board!" But by this time wild horses wouldn't have dragged in audiences who'd been burned by *Number* and *Lam*.

Jeffrey Hunter, who was to die tragically a year later at 43 after brain surgery following an accidental fall, was a good friend of mine, and some months after he completed the film I talked to him in Hollywood about *Private Navy*. "It was really a swell picture, I thought," he said. "And Bob gave it everything he had. I really thought it was going to go over big, and I was very disappointed when it failed. Bob kept us all going with his wonderful gags and it was a good-time set all the way."

Hope may have had a failing film career in the late Sixties, but he kept busy on the domestic front by marrying off both his daughters in 1969 alone. That year Linda married a producer-director named Nathaniel Greenblatt Lande. That was on January 12th in North Hollywood, and on August 19th, Nora followed suit by marrying Samuel Boyd McCullagh, Jr., the assistant director of admissions at the University of San Francisco.

While both women were married at the same church, the Roman

Catholic St. Charles of Borromeo, they had different ideas for their weddings. Linda's was described by *The New York Times* as "strictly Cecil B. DeMille, with a cast of 1000 guests," among them Spiro Agnew and Governor Ronald Reagan, as well as Bing Crosby, Dorothy Lamour, and other Hollywood luminaries. The reception was spread out all across the grounds of the Hope estate, upon which big tents had been erected in case of rain. In contrast, Nora, who was described as "publicity shy," had "only" 400 people, and her reception fit neatly into the garden around the Hope pool.

On the sadder side, in June of that same year two of Hope's brothers, Ivor and George, died within a week of each other.

By 1970, at 67, Hope was onstage at the Royal Albert Hall in London doing a monologue at the Miss World contest while the judges picked the semifinalists. Although feminists had been threatening for days to disrupt the proceedings, as they felt such contests were demeaning to women, Hope was unaware that many had already infiltrated the audience. He was halfway through his routine about women's libbers and peaceniks when the demonstrators made their move and the hall erupted with the sound of whistles and firecrackers. As Hope stood there wondering if he should continue, the activists ran down the aisles assaulting the members of the audience and those on stage with bags of flour, bombs of blue paint, and decaying tomatoes. It was a scene far funnier than any that had appeared in Hope's recent movies.

But it wasn't funny to Hope, who was splattered by one ink bomb and began to panic. He flashed back inwardly to the bombs he'd heard go off in World War II, Korea, and Vietnam. He was still out there "taking chances" in Vietnam in that very year. Thoughts of the IRA and anti-war protesters who might not stop at violence to make their point rushed through his head as well. He quickly made his way off the stage and didn't return until things had quieted down and the demonstrators had left the hall. He was later criticized for leaving the stage.

After the event, Hope spoke out angrily against the feminists, but was probably more irritated that they'd chosen his monologue to disrupt than that they'd demonstrated. He trotted out the usual tiresome remarks about how women's libbers were always ugly, and what was wrong with beauty if a pretty woman could win a contest and get to travel, see herself on TV, and make some money? Never a great brain on such matters, Hope hadn't stopped to ponder that perhaps these women were demonstrating precisely because their alleged lack of good looks rendered them dismissible not only in the eyes of judge and con-

The Dynamic Duo receiving a "Show Business Hall of Fame" award from
columnist Earl Wilson in 1968

Daughter Nora's Hollywood wedding to Sam McCullagh, Jr., 1969

Head to head with Jackie Gleason in 1971's *How to Commit Marriage*

test organizers, but of the movie producers and directors, and men like Hope himself, who were perhaps too willing to exploit that female beauty for their own gain.

Hope was not to star in a feature film from 1969 to 1972. Meanwhile, anxious for and badly in need of a successful movie project, he swallowed his pride and agreed to *co-star* with Jackie Gleason in *How to Commit Marriage* (1969), released one year to the month after *The Private Navy of Sgt. O'Farrell*. Hope went into the project fully aware that, unlike Jonathan Winters and "that Frenchman" Fernandel, Gleason was every bit a match for him in ego and will as well as in talent. Neither man was the first choice for his role. Cary Grant had turned down the part Hope was to play, and Hope had tried to get Peter Ustinov for the part Gleason later played. Ustinov was a fine, sometimes funny actor but was not quite in Hope's comic league.

United Artists was so disappointed with the grosses of Hope's last three films that Hope had to make *Marriage* in partnership with NBC and talk Cinerama into releasing it. The story had to do with Hope's daughter, Joanna Cameron, deciding to live with her fiancée, Tim Matheson, instead of marrying, when she finds out that her parents are on the verge of a divorce, with ensuing plot complications of a somewhat predictable nature. Jackie Gleason, who got equal billing with Hope although his was really only a supporting part, played the fiancé's father.

The role of the wife was to have gone to Lana Turner, Bob's *Bachelor In Paradise* co-star, and then to Ava Gardner, before it was offered to Jane Wyman, who hadn't made a film in years, and never made another after *Marriage*. "The studios are afraid to hire the old stars because they're afraid we might bomb," she said at this time. "Then they bring in people who bomb anyway because they've had no experience."

Marriage bombed in spite of such experienced players as Wyman, Hope, and Gleason on the screen and veteran director Norman Panama at the helm. While the movie pretended to be Sixties "hip" in its attitudes toward sex and marriage, it was essentially middle-class in its ambiance and sentiments, and, moreover, badly dated. Hope playing golf with a chimpanzee named Mildred was the highlight of the picture, which gives a good indication of what the rest was like.

Hope was oddly prescient in a book about his movies when he wrote, "Finally a few words about two of my latest pictures (you'll note that actors never refer to 'my last picture' — it's liable to be)." He was

With The Three Degrees singing group, 1970

prescient because the films in question, *Marriage*, and his next, *Cancel My Reservation* (1972) were indeed Bob Hope's last film appearances.

As was the case with *They Got Me Covered* years before, *Cancel*, based on a Louis L'Amour novel, betrays its origins as a "serious" picture in virtually every scene. Hope plays a host of a daytime TV show who's feuding with his new co-host, his wife, Eva Marie Saint. He leaves New York in a snit and goes off for a rest at his Arizona ranch, where he finds the body of a dead Indian girl. Hope is accused of the crime. When his wife comes out to reconcile, there are more murders and attempts on their lives. Eventually the killer is unmasked.

Hope had at one point planned to produce the script, then titled *Broken Gun*, with someone else in the lead, but when the deal fell through, NBC suggested he do it himself. Hope, who served as executive producer, contacted two scriptwriters he'd worked with before, Arthur Marx and Robert Fisher, and got them to convert the script into a comedy. Unfortunately, the comic elements were inserted haphazardly, lending the movie an uneven quality and an odd, hybrid nature. Some scenes, such as the one in which a car in a garage is slowly low-

284

ered onto the unconscious bodies of Hope and Saint and nearly crush-
es them, are simply played straight, with some minor suspense but
absolutely no laughs. One waits for the hilarity to break in but it's never
forthcoming, and Hope gives the impression he's just standing in for a
more serious actor.

Dream sequences, such as one in which Bob imagines himself surrounded by a lynch mob consisting of the likes of Bing Crosby, Johnny
Carson, John Wayne, and Flip Wilson (calling cameo central) seem
dragged in from another picture. A good movie obviously got lost
somewhere in the mess, but Paul Bogart, essentially a sitcom director,
fails to find it, and doesn't include, in his inexperience, sufficient closeups to get the audience more engaged in the action.

The movie employed a supporting cast of fading actors such as
Ralph Bellamy and Forrest Tucker, playing the heinous villains, and
Chief Dan George, the Seventies' answer to the departed Maria
Ouspenskaya. Plus there were the requisite "sweet young things," most
notably Anne Archer, who went on to relatively greater fame years later
as the wife in *Fatal Attraction*. Here she plays "Crazy" Hollister, a nubile
neighbor of Hope's who also gets embroiled in the proceedings. Then
as now, Archer was a very talented and extremely sensual performer, and
undoubtedly the 69-year-old Hope's favorite scene in the movie was
when Archer gives him mouth-to-mouth resuscitation — a dirty old
man dream in glorious Technicolor.

Eva Marie Saint is also good as the wife. Ironically, some of her
speeches make her sound like Bob's real-life wife Dolores, in the early
days, particularly one in which she explains to "Crazy" why she went to
work with her husband: "He'd just visit me from time to time. Even the
visits didn't pay off. We still don't have any children."

While the critical notices and low box-office returns would have
been enough in 1972 to make this Hope's last movie regardless, there
was another reason for Hope to call it quits. He didn't like the way he
looked on screen. He was, after all, some months short of 70 when
Cancel was released in October 1972. In it, he completely lacks the energy of his younger or even middle-aged days. His old shtick lacks spontaneity and most of the time doesn't work at all. Even his much vaunt-
ed timing is off, as well as his delivery.

Moreover, in this his last film Hope gives far too much emphasis
to lines that would be funnier had he thrown them away, and vice versa,
and his straight lines are delivered with such blatant lack of enthusiasm
that it's obvious Hope would rather have been playing golf or doing

anything, anywhere but making this picture. He seems like a tired old man doing a bad impression of Bob Hope. In some spots, it's a truly pathetic exhibition.

William Wolf in *Cue* magazine wrote that it's "about as funny and exciting as a forgotten punch line. Hope started off with a very funny career, if you dug his brand of comedy, but in the string of awful films he has appeared in these latter years, the notion has persisted that he must walk through them spewing one-liners. . . . This one [has] all the excitement of a funeral."

Hope was momentarily elated when *Cancel* became the first, and of course last, of his films to open at New York City's Radio City Music Hall, but he needn't have been. On the last night the picture played there, the run shortened even more abruptly by a musicians' strike necessitating the closing of the hall, only 300 of the 6200 seats were filled. To all intents and purposes it was now Hope's movie career that had been canceled. Hope would make one last attempt to appear in yet another motion picture with Bing Crosby before the Seventies came to an end, but perhaps it was fortunate that Crosby died offscreen, in 1977, before he and Bob died on it.

CHAPTER TWENTY-TWO

STAVING OFF THE REAPER

Although they were "professional" friends rather than close personal ones, Hope was still affected by the deaths of Jack Benny in 1974 and Bing Crosby in 1977. If for no other reason, they reminded him of his own mortality. He had known good times with both men, as well as fine professional associations in film, radio, and television. Like him they had remembered the early years — vaudeville, touring, the hectic, exciting "radio days" and the bold new experiment that television had represented in the late Forties and early Sixties. He'd shared a lot with both of them.

George Burns had originally planned to do the eulogy at Jack Benny's funeral but he became so overwhelmed by his emotions that Bob had to take over at the last minute. One of the highlights of the Hope tribute to Benny was, "He only gave us eighty years and it wasn't enough."

In 1975, Bob had first gotten the idea to film an original script by Ben Starr entitled *The Road to Tomorrow*. In this Bob and Bing and Dorothy Lamour, essentially playing themselves, would have reunited and cast off into misadventure. (In retrospect, they might have made a pathetic threesome visually. Bob's, Bing's, and Dottie's ages circa 1975 being, respectively, 72, 71, and 61.) By 1977, the plans had been firmed up somewhat, and Sir Lew Grade, the British producer, expressed an interest in what was by then entitled *The Road to the Fountain of Youth*. Unfortunately, filming had to be postponed when Bing Crosby "celebrated" a bit too much backstage at a gala tribute to his fifty years in showbiz in Pasadena, and managed to fall 25 feet into the orchestra pit. His injuries kept him hospitalized for several months, but the real finish came when Bing insisted on playing golf in Madrid and underwent a fatal heart seizure.

Hope was planning to do a hospital benefit in New Jersey and was staying in New York at the Waldorf-Astoria when he heard the news of

Bing's death from a friend, Bill Fugazy. "I had a very funny reaction to that," Hope was to say later. "My head just got so tight that it felt a little dangerous to me. So I laid down and rested, because the whole thing was such a shock. I didn't cry at all. I don't cry easily. I just felt that tightness." Bing had been 73. As one friend put it, "At least he went out doing what he best enjoyed — playing golf."

In 1976, Hope's daughter Linda's marriage of six years came to an end, and Hope offered her a job to take her mind off things. She would run Hope Enterprises as well as develop and produce TV series for the company. She'd already chalked up experience in film production, but tongues wagged in the industry over what seemed like blatant nepotism, and there was comment on Bob's paying his daughter only $600 a week for all her tasks when the industry standard would have been twenty times higher — and that to produce just one series. Linda claimed at the time that her father had been generous to her in other ways and had helped her get through her divorce, so she didn't mind. There were also rumors that Hope was "looking over her shoulder" all the time anyway, and was really in charge, with Linda taking care of details. Linda managed to develop one show, the short-lived *Joe and Valerie*, but didn't share in the profits or get any royalties. "You see, I'm a salaried employee," she explained.

Linda was to keep her hand, off and on, in Hope Enterprises right up to the present, working under various titles and assuming a myriad of responsibilities. Over the years she did her best to influence her father to accept his age and adapt to the times, usually without success. For instance, she thought it'd be good and fitting for Bob to play aging men who try desperately, if not pathetically, to attract younger women, whether it be with money or power or contacts or whatever. But Bob insisted on hanging on to variations of the Lothario persona that he considered, against all evidence, his strong suit and which he worked hard to keep alive. Linda was quoted as saying, "I would like to see him expose the softer, gentler side of himself." At that point, though, it would have been news to a lot of people that he had such a side. She added, "I'd like to see him take risks. His image is very much that of the ladykiller — your basic Loni Andersons and Brooke Shieldses and all these young girls kissing him. That's not something that really happens to people who are 83, 84. It could certainly have humor, but you'd have to be able to see the underbelly, see the pain, for it to really work." Linda was speaking of her father circa 1987.

Hope and some of his associates, however, felt it was still too early

Grand Marshal and Queen (Stephanie Hix) of the 1974 Orange Bowl

Celebrating fifty-three years of marriage, Dolores and Bob, 1987

for Hope to "play a George Burns role," that he may have been in his 80s but looked 60. Linda was unable to convince anyone that even at 60 it would be a little grotesque for Hope to be coming on to the likes of Brooke Shields. Whenever Hope was offered a script that dealt realistically with his age and situation, he'd reject it. At one point in 1981, when Hope was 78, Linda finally threw up her hands and quit over "creative differences," accepting that, at the time she was merely a supernumerary at Hope Enterprises. There were, however, to be professional reconciliations and re-alliances in subsequent years for Linda and her father. Part of the problem was Hope's difficulty in taking seriously any woman in an executive capacity, one of his "out of date" foibles Linda found trying, as did others of "distaff" staff.

At the time of the temporary 1981 parting, Linda said of her father that he "didn't really want to change. His feeling is that he's had a very successful career, and I certainly can't argue with that. I'm grateful for the opportunity he gave me, but there does come a time when you have to make a break and try your own wings." (Right up to 1998 Linda is her parents' chief aide.) Now, at 95, he may feel a greater need of her input, "knowing especially that it's based on loyalty and love and a lot of seasoning on Linda's part over the past twenty-two years of her many assignments," as an associate puts it in.

Though the film career by the late Seventies had conclusively dried up, as even Hope realized, he tried to stay active in other areas. He appeared at Harvard University in the fall of 1979 and, oddly enough, discovered he appealed more to this post-Vietnam college crowd than he had to the students of earlier eras. The students did like him, and it wasn't just an obeisance to advanced age. His gags were more contemporary, more racy, focusing on drugs, though characterized by one critic as "sexist or anti-gay." The only really awkward moment came when Hope introduced The Village People, who were trendy at that time, and was told by the assemblage that "Disco sucks!"

Also in 1979, on May 7th, a tribute to Hope was held at Avery Fisher Hall at Lincoln Center. Joanne Koch, the executive director of the Film Society of Lincoln Center, got the idea for the tribute when she saw Woody Allen enthusiastically discussing Bob on Dick Cavett's talk show. Allen, in fact, selected the clips that illustrated the high points of Hope's career, and wrote the narration with Cavett, but didn't attend the event himself, leaving Cavett to do the podium honors.

Cavett got disastrous notices from the critics, who disapproved of the way he slammed Jerry Lewis during his opening monologue. "If he could be so beastly to Lewis in public, what did he really think of Hope in private?" asked Andrew Sarris. After slamming Lewis, according to Sarris, Cavett had turned around and done "a knowing aside for currently chic Jane Fonda," whom Hope had roundly despised since her "Hanoi Jane" adventurings during the Vietnam War. The selection of clips, moreover, was criticized, and everyone felt the shy Woody Allen should at least have put in an appearance when he himself had, if indirectly, generated the idea for the tribute.

Hope's monologue at the tribute won higher marks, and he was to impress most of the audience with his energy, timing, topicality, and ribaldry. Once he was offstage, however, it was a different story. Whereas previous recipients of Lincoln Center tributes, such as pixieish George Cukor and Joanne Woodward and Paul Newman, had mingled graciously, and even enthusiastically, with the guests, Hope set up a barricade of security guards who kept him sequestered from press and public alike as he made his way to his table at the reception. Only a chosen few were allowed to approach him.

The acerbic *Village Voice* columnist Arthur Bell was in the audience that night and wrote that Hope's jokes had always left him with a bad taste. Bell added, "His humor, which I'm sure he'd construe as harmless, ridicules the underdog, thereby making the 'regular guy' feel superior. A lot of harmless adds up to harmful. In *Fancy Pants* the American Indian is depicted as a wooden clod who says 'How.' What Hope does with women would make both Jane Fonda and Sigourney Weaver cry 'Why!' And when he came out in person for ten minutes of standup he told an anecdote about Bing Crosby. The two men would go away on golf weekends and share the same room. Hope couldn't sleep because of Crosby's snoring. Each morning, Crosby woke up refreshed, always beating a tired Hope at golf. Bob finally solved the problem by kissing Bing on the mouth just before beddy-bye. Crosby would spend the rest of the night watching him. Hilarious? I cringed."

In the early Eighties, Hope suffered a recurrence of eye problems, this time in the right eye. It became inflamed and sore and so affected his vision that while rehearsing a TV special in late 1982 he was forced to use cue cards that were twice the normal size. Finally the eye hemorrhaged and Hope was rushed to New York for a consultation. The left eye had already had four laser operations, but doctors would leave that as a last resort for the right one. "This is caused by stupidity," Hope said at the time. "It's caused by going too fast. Most of the time I think I'm about 40 and I just fly, fly, fly." He was a few months short of 80 at the time.

The doctors succeeded in controlling the hemorrhaging but again told Hope he'd have to slow down or risk serious complications. Although he hated to do it, Hope canceled plans to go to Lebanon in December to entertain the troops. Ten months later, in 1983, he was back in New York. In London the eye had been troubling him yet again. He went to see his ophthalmologist, Dr. Robert Ellsworth, who was associated with the New York Hospital-Cornell Medical Center, for a check-up. Afterwards he went with his friend, the limo king Bill Fugazy, across the street to Gleason's tavern for some "anesthesia" and to watch the America's Cup race.

Part of the secret of Hope's longevity was that he tried to care for his health as best he could. He walked about a mile a day, including brisk constitutionals in the early hours of the morning. He also ate lean, healthy food, and didn't smoke. He was unable to drink due to a bladder irritation. "If I drank," he said, "I'd piss all over the place." He took care of what had turned out to be a nagging back pain by hanging from gymnastic rings attached to a support beam on the balcony outside his bedroom. With 90 on hand in 1993, he was sticking to these habits, or at least intelligent modifications of them (now largely abandoned). In 1983, after his eye was checked out, he felt so good about everything that he had his name added to the list of potential space-shuttle passengers. His essential good health during this period kept him out of the papers, except for a 1991 incident, a minor one. At 88 he tripped at a benefit in Florida and required several stitches above the nose. That same year Dolores fell at home and broke her arm (she was 87) while Hope was taping a TV special in Nashville.

Though in 1983 Hope's doctors would have much preferred that he slow down after the second right-eye emergency in September, he was on the road again the following month, to visit the troops in Beirut. His actions struck many as foolhardy, almost desperate, for an 80-year-old, and Dolores was worried and furious. Hope had brought several entertainers with him including Ann Jillian, Brooke Shields, and Cathy Lee Crosby, but the ladies were told to remain behind with the Sixth Fleet in Haifa Bay while Hope "insisted" he be taken from the USS Guam via Marine helicopter to visit the barracks where 241 men had been killed by a terrorist blast.

This was Hope's first trip to servicemen overseas since the end of the Vietnam War. He knew that he owed his career in large part to his visits entertaining troops, so he had no intention of missing them after he'd traveled so far already — accompanied by the usual photographers. Newspapers made much of the fact that artillery fighting between the Lebanese Army and the rebel forces could be heard in the background as Hope was ushered around the base, given an Arab headdress to clown around in, and did a five-minute monologue in front of a closed-circuit television camera which all the men were directed to watch. Hope stayed at the base for 75 minutes and then was helicoptered back to the *Guam*. Only thirty minutes later, the base was peppered with fifty rounds of machine-gun and small-arms fire.

Part of Hope's circa-1983 obsessive need to enter these danger spots and entertain "his boys" was to prove he could still cut the mustard, that at 80 he was as brave and energetic as ever. Benny and Crosby and others had succumbed but he was going to fight the grim (or grin?) reaper with every weapon he had. He was still taking his role as a patriotic symbol very seriously. He knew that, as he got older, new and younger comedians were coming in to take his place, establishing themselves in movies and on TV, and it wouldn't be too long before he could no longer compete. But there was one thing they couldn't take away from him, his "war record," his boys, his soldiers. As long as he could broadcast from besieged army bases and show America a carefully monitored slice of what was happening in foreign hot spots, he felt there'd always be a place for him.

Meanwhile Dolores, only a year his junior, and whose children were grown and absorbed in their own lives, sat at home and thought of ways to fill up her time. In the mid Eighties, President Ronald Reagan made her a trustee of The Kennedy Center in Washington, but this didn't really keep her busy. There were big parties, such as the gala bash she threw for up to 600 people to coincide with the Bob Hope Desert Classic Golf Tournament in Palm Springs in January 1984, and little social gatherings with other wives and friends. In 1985 she got together with another golf widow, Betty Ford, and the two bandied about the idea of writing a guide for women whose husbands were always on the golf course or on the road. They planned to call it "Guess Who We Saw at the Airport?" But it was Bob who got the book off the ground — this time it was another ghost-written effort, *Confessions of a Hooker*, about his love affair with golf.

Always he kept up the assorted benefits, but one he did in New York in early 1984 caused quite a commotion behind the scenes. Hope had been approached by representatives of the Fire Museum and a committee of volunteers who wished to raise money for it. They were plan-

293

ning a benefit at Radio City Music Hall in May and told Hope they desperately needed him as a draw so that as many tickets as possible could be sold. Hope was forced to cancel another date, but agreed to do the benefit as scheduled. The event actually ballooned into becoming a major 80th birthday celebration, and raised about $400,000 for the museum. But when all costs were subtracted, the amount was reduced to between $75,000 and $100,000.

It was the understanding of the Fire Museum and the volunteer committee that Hope would be donating his usual $50,000 fee to the cause. Fire commissioner Joseph Spinnato and Dennis Smith, the President of the Fire Museum, sent Hope a letter indicating they expected him to keep his promise to either contribute his fee or donate money to the museum. Hope denied ever making such a promise. "I do all kinds of benefits," he said, "but when I was approached to do this show for the Fire Museum it was for a fee, and everybody I came in contact with knew that. If they'd lost money, then they could have had a gripe. They should be jumping up and down. They grossed $400,000. That's not bad, is it? They hired me to draw a crowd and I did."

Hope insisted only he could have made the decision to return the $50,000, "and I knew nothing about it." He'd done more than his share of "straight" (no fee) benefits and although publicly he'd only admit he was upset over the criticism he was receiving over the money, privately he was fuming over what he claimed was the way they'd "tricked him" out of the $50,000. But there was no way he could hold onto it without looking like a heel.

In 1985, Fred Hope died, leaving Bob the last surviving brother of the original seven. "Now I really feel old," Hope, then 82, told a friend. But he also liked to remind people that his grandfather, James Hope, had died in England in 1943 at an almost-centenarian 99. "Maybe I'll top that," he joked.

There has always been speculation as to exactly how much money Bob Hope has, but the roots of his fortune can be traced to 1938, when he bought a plot adjacent to the Lakeside Country Club, not far from his house, for $18,000. He turned it into a profitable golf driving range, then twenty-five years later sold it to the Music Corporation of America (MCA) for a cool million. Jim Saphier, who'd died in 1974, had been Hope's business agent and sometime partner in various ventures starting in 1936, and he'd been credited with advising Hope wisely in money matters.

The profits Hope made from an oil deal he'd gotten into in 1949 with Bing Crosby and a Texas golf partner and from which, reportedly, Hope made anywhere from $1.5 to over $3 million when his share was later sold to a major oil company, went into more real estate investments. In 1970, Hope let it be known that, at least in his estimation, his estate was worth $40 million. "Thirty-five million of it in property." At that time Hope owned more land than anyone in the San Fernando Valley, and since today real estate in Southern California is worth over ten times what it was in the Seventies, it's a safe bet that those who rank Hope's fortune in the $400 million range aren't far off the mark, no matter how much Hope may deny it.

To get around the high income taxes that were gobbling up most of his earnings, Hope formed several companies, including The Hope Corporation, to handle his book projects; Hope Records, to make recordings of his broadcasts; and Hope Enterprises, Inc., which handled his independent feature films and personal appearances. As of 1950, Hope Enterprises was doing nearly a million dollars in business annually, with the IRS supposedly gouging 92 cents from each dollar. Nowadays it's estimated that Hope must gross about $3 to $4 million per year to net the approximately $2 million he needs to meet all expenses and salaries of employees and continue his charitable donations.

In addition to the real estate — which reportedly includes properties in Phoenix, Arizona, Puerto Rico, Malibu, Thousand Oaks, Palm Springs, and North Hollywood, in addition to San Fernando Valley acquisitions — at one time or another Hope held shares in the Cleveland Indians, the Los Angeles Rams, an organization that distributes TV sets, and Big Crosby's old racetrack at Del Mar, among other venues.

Occasionally Hope's holdings will cause controversy, such as when in 1991 he decided to sell hundreds of acres of the Jordan Ranch in the Santa Monica Mountains, to the Potomac Investment Association of Gaithersburg, Md., a development company that planned to build a golf course. Maria VanderKolk, the Ventura County supervisor, was one of the environmentalists outraged by Hope's decision, which would have stymied their plans to do as much as they could to preserve the vanishing open land. "The man is 87 years old," VanderKolk said at the time. "What does he need another $25 million for?"

The environmentalists proceeded to offer Hope an alternative: if he donated the land to the government it could be turned into a state park named after him. This attempt to appeal to Hope's vanity only backfired, however. Furious at the way these "activists" were interfering with his plans, Hope let it be known that if the deal to sell the land didn't go through, he'd sell off other portions of his property to corporations looking for garbage dump sites. When crossed crucially, as in this instance, it was apparent that Hope could be extremely vicious.

An alternative solution proposed that Hope swap land with the National Park Service, though it'd be less profitable for him in the long run. He'd sell the government various parcels of land for about $70 million (less than they were worth). The park service would then give the development company fifty-nine acres of Federal land in Cheesebro Canyon. Not everyone agreed with this solution, fearing it would set a precedent and the Santa Monica Mountains would become like the Brazilian rain forest.

Julie Zeidner, however, a spokeswoman for the Santa Monica Mountains Conservancy, felt it was the best alternative. "Profit is clearly the bottom line for Mr. Hope," she said.

In the early Eighties, *Forbes* magazine was claiming that Hope's fortune amounted to nearly $200 million, a low estimate according to some observers. Hope got in touch with a staff writer named Richard Behar and asked him to prove it. "If my estate is worth over $50 million," Hope told the writer, "I'll kiss your ass." Setting to work, Behar was soon able to confirm that Hope was worth at least $115 million and told people he was almost positive Hope still had additional holdings that he, Behar, had yet to uncover. When *Time* magazine estimated Hope's fortune at half a billion as far back as the Sixties (!), Hope quipped, "If I had that kind of money I wouldn't bother to go to Vietnam, I'd just buy it."

Whatever the ultimately discovered facts of the matter, it's undoubtedly true that Hope is one of the wealthiest, if not the wealthiest, men in show business.

Although Hope has never run for office like some of his Hollywood peers, his son Tony decided that was just what he'd do in 1986. By that time, the once-handsome Tony was a portly 45-year-old man with a wife and two children. He'd graduated from Harvard Law School in 1965, served in the Air Force briefly, then went to work at the TV division of 20th Century-Fox as director of business affairs. As did his sister Linda, he flirted with television production, and was an associate producer of *Judd for the Defense*. He was a $150,000-a-year partner at the national accountancy firm of Touche Ross and Co. when he decided to quit and run for a $75,000 job in Congress, hoping to gain the seat once occupied by Republican Bobbi Fiedler. Tony's politics were as conservative as his father's.

First Tony, who lived with his family in Spring Valley, bought another house in Northridge — prompting his opponent, Elton Gallegly, the mayor of Simi Valley, to charge that he'd moved to the 21st District, much of which his father owned, just to run for office. When Bob found out what his son planned to do, he rejoindered, "How much is it gonna cost me?" Hope's campaign contribution was legally limited to just $1000. In spite of that, Tony thought it was practically a cinch that he'd win. It was his father's district, after all.

Tony has always given his mother all of the credit for "keeping the Hope kids out of jail and off the psychiatrist's couch. She 'brung' us up right," he said. "She taught us a sense of values. She made sure that none of us had a lot of free time, and she pointed to our dad as an example. [She] always said, 'Your life is going to be as interesting as you make it. Keep active. Keep trying. And don't be afraid of change.'"

Tony in 1986, however, had underestimated the odds in the gamble he'd taken. In the primary he got only 35 percent of the votes cast, losing to Gallegly. His father had promised to campaign for him, but citing his busy schedule he wound up doing comparatively little. Just as Bob didn't like the idea of his brothers, or even his wife, stepping into the spotlight he considered his and his alone, he undoubtedly breathed a sigh of relief when son Tony didn't make it into public office. To date, Tony has made no further attempts in politics. The two other children elected for quieter lives. Son Kelly became a schoolteacher, daughter Nora a housewife.

In 1987, Hope was off again on yet another overseas jaunt, an exhausting journey to the Persian Gulf, the Philippines, the Azores, and elsewhere. It was televised in early January, 1988. "Hope is bound to go through the ratings roof with this one," wrote Kay Gardella in the *Daily News*. "Who doesn't want to see how our boys are doing over there?" The special was called "Around the World in Eight Days," and featured such entertainers as Connie Stevens, Barbara Eden, and Lee Greenwood, not exactly heavy-hitters by late-Eighties standards.

Hope would continue his overseas tours in the following years, and his specials. In mid 1990, for instance, it was "Bob Hope's U.S.O. Road to the Berlin Wall and Moscow," with Rosemary Clooney, Dolores Hope (getting into the limelight, to her kids' and others' delight), Brooke Shields, and La Toya Jackson. (In an earlier, 1989 Easter special from Nassau, one of La Toya's numbers had to be cut because even Bob felt she was too sexy — too many bumps and grinds — for an Easter show.) The show in Moscow got damned by one critic as "a tedious and badly produced special [with] Hope's trademark blend of mean-spirited jabs and self-deprecating jokes."

At the time, Bob had expressed much enthusiasm for glasnost. "I'll never again entertain troops in wartime," he said. "I credit Reagan and Gorbachev for it. And you know when it got me? When Gorbachev came to this country and I saw him [on TV] getting out of the car and shaking hands of people in the street. I said, 'What the hell is going on?' I knew then everything was changing."

But of course there were more wars, and more trips overseas. On August 2, 1990, Iraq invaded Kuwait and American troops were sent overseas. This trip, in December 1990, gave the 87-year-old Hope possibly more headaches than all of the others combined. The Defense Department was carefully monitoring news reports because of the special skittishness of the Muslim religious leaders in Saudi Arabia. For instance, reporters couldn't observe any non-Islamic religious service attended by U.S. troops for fear that the Iraqi government would use this to further complaints that Islamic holy places were being defiled by non-Muslim soldiers.

But there was an outcry from the media when a security lid was clamped over the Bob Hope tour. Although Hope's show would be filmed for his obligatory special, reporters wouldn't be allowed to cover the troupe shows in progress. One USA Today reporter howled, "Suddenly Bob Hope's humor is classified?" Adding, "Something has gotten a little bit out of whack here. If it's okay to show on television next month, it should be okay to publish tomorrow." There were also comments that Steve Martin had gone to see the troops and reporters had been allowed to go along with him so why the blackout on Hope?

The Defense Department explained that it had restricted the media coverage for reasons of security, and because "it is felt that media coverage of [Hope's] shows and visits, however well-intentioned, have a very great likelihood of being exploited by the Iraqis for propaganda purposes." Hope told everyone that it certainly wasn't his idea. "Did I ever say keep the press away?" he asked at a news conference. "I live for the press!"

There were other problems. Since Saudi women had to be veiled in public, Ann Jillian, Marie Osmond, and the Pointer Sisters had to be left out of the show in Saudi Arabia. Hope's jokes had to be monitored by the Pentagon. Those that dealt with the style of dress of Saudi women were considered too inflammatory. Dolores, however, was allowed to sing "White Christmas" to the troops on Christmas Eve. By this time Mrs. Bob Hope had had enough of being left house-sitting as usual and had persuaded Bob to let her accompany him on his trips whenever feasible.

Hope's TV special made from the Gulf War program aired just in time to help publicize his new 1990 book, *Don't Shoot, It's Only Me*, which was co-written with longtime associate Melvin Shavelson. *The New York Times* described it as "definitely more Hope than glory," adding, "Some of the stories included are in their anecdotage. . . . a tiresome rat a tat tat as told to a tape recorder quality [that] comes off rather like an attenuated, pretentious, heavy on the patriotism Bob Hope special." To *Variety*, the book was burdened by "a chronic insistence on lashing every anecdote with a barbed tongue and strangling each recollection with one-liners." The book also contains inaccuracies and inconsistencies which create odd passages, such as the one in which Hope confuses the release date of *The Facts of Life* (1960) with the release of *Brief Encounter* (1946), the original film which inspired it; he talks about the country's attitude toward adultery when he was making *Facts of Life* "back in 1946." (!)

When Hope wasn't busy entertaining the troops, his TV specials went to exotic locations or celebrated special anniversaries or holidays, such as an X-mas special filmed in Bermuda in 1990 or a birthday special put together in Paris. And since movies were out of the question, Hope did the unexpected and went back to the stage in 1989, for one night only.

The occasion was a re-teaming of Hope and George Burns for a highly publicized comedy show at Madison Square Garden. There were, of course, a lot of pretty girls on stage for the "boys" to bounce jokes off, and Dionne Warwick was brought out now and then to sing. At the time Hope was 86 and Burns 93. Hope was more nervous than he thought he'd be. He wasn't facing a group of entertainment-starved, captive, grateful GI's here. This was a hard-boiled New York audience, and they had paid a pretty penny for their seats. The audience, it turned out, seemed to enjoy it. Politeness? Deference to the performers' respective ages? But critical reaction was divided. Wrote the *Newsday* critic: "By-the-numbers comedy, some of it funny, some of it borderline blue (that was how you could tell it was different from television), some offensive, none of it memorable." The *Daily News* critic wrote, "George and Bob gave a show to remember," while *Variety* called it a "fun-filled

"Acapulco Spring Fling of Comedy and Music" TV special, on location in
Mexico, 1990

evening that failed to fill a lot of seats." In truth, the evening wasn't a record-breaker for the Garden in terms of attendance.

That same year Hope was saddened by the death of another professional friend, Lucille Ball. Hope had first realized that Lucy might be slipping when she guested on his 85th birthday special the previous year and had trouble doing a dance number. Then the following February, Bob and Lucy introduced a big production number at the Oscars, receiving a standing ovation, and Hope noticed that Lucy seemed a little "wobbly." Approximately two months later she was dead from a full cardiac arrest at age 77.

To Hope it seemed increasingly as if all the friends who remembered the "good old days" with him were slowly slipping away. That was probably why he was enthused about the show with Burns some months later. By this time all of Hope's brothers were gone. Cancer had claimed Sidney, Jack, and George. Jim had died of emphysema and Fred's heart had given out. Bob's children circa 1990 all had lives of their own. He began to turn to Dolores increasingly for support — Dolores and his audiences.

Although approaching 90, Hope wasn't to be spared in the early Nineties from being the subject of gossip, making headlines in the tabloids, attracting the attention of neurotic oddballs, or making unintentional waves among minorities. He was even to be the inspiration for a filmic roman à clef.

Jan King, who'd been Hope's secretary for several years, asked him for a small pension when she retired, and was refused. She'd been planning to write a book praising her former boss and all his kindly deeds and charitable works. Instead, she decided to write a hard-hitting exposé-type book from her trailer in Palm Springs. This was in contrast, certainly, to the laudatory ass-kissing biographies some of Hope's former publicists and employees had ventured upon over the years.

Circa 1991, as in the old *Confidential* days of 1956, stories of Hope's slave-driver tactics with employees and wild affairs with wanton women began steaming up the pages of the supermarket tabloids. Insiders felt Hope might not have been as bothered by all this as the public imagined. He knew that tabloids were given to inflating, and had a low credibility level, and if people believed the stories, so what? Also, if they made him look like a stud-womanizer, wasn't that the image he'd been carefully cultivating with all his might and main for the previous seventy years?

Another, weirder woman had already turned up. She was one Sally

Fox from New Orleans, and she appeared to be out to "get" Hope. Following in the footsteps of that deranged veteran of the Fifties who claimed Hope and his friends were using brain waves to force cars off the freeways, Fox started complaining to the media and the FBI back in the Eighties that Hope was an insane person who had the ability to interfere with the thinking processes of ordinary people. She claimed that the FBI got nearly a thousand calls a day from assorted individuals who were also upset about the dangerous thought waves Hope was allegedly projecting into their consciousnesses. Fox's theory was that Hope could take over people's minds by literally projecting himself into their brains.

By 1989, Fox was writing to President Bush and members of Congress asking them to "stop this heinous and vile mental abuse by Bob Hope." According to the FBI, Hope's mental abilities or what-have-you didn't "reveal a violation of federal law."

The whole idiotic business came up again in the summer of 1990 when another woman in New York wrote to Fox to tell her that she, too, was a victim of Hope's "horrible" thought projections. Wrote the New York *Post*, "Of course it's absurd to think that a man who for half a century has permeated TV, radio, movies, and advertising could 'interfere' with the thinking of Americans. Of course it's daft to imagine that, after playing golf with a half-dozen presidents, he might not be a citizen above suspicion." Among the theories concerning Fox and her lady friend: that they might have had sons who died in Vietnam.

A Bette Midler film of 1992, *For the Boys*, seemed to have odd parallels with the career of Bob Hope. In the film James Caan plays a comic who neglects his wife and children in pursuit of his career, chases women, and entertains the troops overseas from World War II up until Vietnam — always with cameras at the ready. Midler plays a singer who does a TV show with him until Caan's firing of a blacklisted writer causes an estrangement. A brief reconciliation is shattered when Midler accompanies Caan to Nam and sees her officer son shot and killed before her eyes; he then dies in her arms.

The film veers off in its own fictional directions, but it's hard to believe that the Caan character wasn't based, in part anyway, on Hope, and that the filmmakers weren't dealing, among other things, with Hope's "pro-war" stance. In the picture, the main difference between Hope and Caan is that Caan — a more handsome and typical leading-man type — registers none of Hope's charm, wackiness, or basic amiability. It's one reason why more critics probably didn't make a connection between the two. The film did poorly at the box office. There were rumors that Hope had pulled strings behind the scenes, but such theorizing smacks of the paranoid. The film was heavily advertised and marketed and Hope couldn't have kept audiences out of the theatres had they wanted to go. In the meantime, *For the Boys* remains the closest thing to a screen biopic of Hope that Hollywood has yet offered. Hope remained silent on the matter, but Martha Raye was to claim that Bette Midler had taken her life story and appropriated it for her own uses. Actually the Midler character resembles Raye only vaguely. Interestingly, at a Friar's Club event celebrating Raye's 76th birthday, Bob Hope was scheduled to re-present Raye with the Oscar she received for "outstanding service in entertaining servicemen during three wars." This was in August 1992, when Raye was getting someone from the Writers Guild of America to show up at a deposition with Raye's original film treatment — the one which the besieged producer swears wasn't the source of the *For the Boys* screenplay. But in honoring Raye at the Friars, Hope, many felt, was making his own tacit statement.

For decades, Hope had been having a field day with the gays, making mean-spirited jokes about them of all types and descriptions, but the gay community started fighting back in the early Nineties after Hope appeared on the *Tonight Show* with Johnny Carson and passed remarks they found unconscionable. It was far from the first time Hope's homophobia had drawn sharp criticism. His gay routines had had a long, long history. Like many vaudeville comics, Hope used to clown around in pseudo-homoerotic sketches that garnered laughs precisely because in that era the idea of two men being attracted to one another or "married" or "keeping house" was considered outré and weirdly hilarious. If the jokes weren't homophobic per se, it was because the gay community hadn't yet become a recognizable minority.

Although showbiz people were thoroughly aware of the presence of homosexuals, many in their own field, and to some extent had always practiced a sophisticated tolerance, they also knew that to the ordinary member of the audience gays might just as well be Martians. Hope came from the generation in which only the most obvious, stereotypical gays let it be known, however inadvertently, that they preferred their own sex. In the Twenties and Thirties, there was a tremendous hypocrisy going on, for, as in the Nineties, only under more open conditions, perfectly masculine, "straight-acting" guys were carrying on homosexual liaisons, whether purely physical and transitory or on an emotional level.

With wife Dolores and friend in 1991

But in that benighted area, the idea of one of these more obvious types, these silly, limp-wristed pansies, however nice they might be, fighting for their country or having normal, everyday feelings was completely alien to the public consciousness. Like many other comics of that early period, Hope loved to get easy laughs by imitating the effeminate gestures and lisping speech of "screaming queens" — the only gays he ever encountered that he knew were gay. Some felt Hope was too naively un-perceptive in this regard to be believed, however. Meanwhile, gay men who could pass for straight rarely came out of the closet except to other men like themselves.

With Gay Liberation on the ascendancy after the Stonewall Riots of 1969, Hope began to replace the old pseudo-gay routines with out-and-out jokes about homosexuals and their "silly movement." Sometimes these jokes would be reasonably funny and inoffensive, such as one in which he quipped that gay lib and the mafia were joining forces: "Now with the kiss of death you get dining and dancing." Told by an openly gay comedian, some of these gay gags wouldn't have been considered homophobic; told by the conservative, old-fashioned Bob

Hope, they told a different story.

In July 1986 Hope was doing a $1000-a-plate charity benefit on the *Princess* yacht when he told guests from the podium that the Statue of Liberty had AIDS. "Nobody knows if she got it from the mouth of the Hudson or the Staten Island ferry [pronounced "fairy"]." Again, a joke that might have gone over if told by a self-deprecating AIDS activist to gay friends, seemed completely vile and insensitive when mouthed by Hope. When he was severely criticized for the joke, he claimed he only told it so he could comment on how "awful" it was later, at the same time admitting that he found it funny.

What made it all the worse was that Hope followed up this gag by getting up and doing the can-can with two men, General William Westmoreland and former New York Governor Hugh Carey.

When some people objected to Hope taking beautiful women on his overseas tours during the Vietnam era because their presence would only lower the morale of the men who could look but not touch, Hope was furious. He responded, "I'm glad we have the kind of guys over there who do get excited when they see a pretty girl. It's comforting to know that when the Cong wave a white flag our boys don't wave back. Thank God the only fliers [read "queens"] we've got over there are in the planes."

One gay veteran was especially condemnatory of Hope's attitude, saying, "I resent the notion Hope seems to be propagating that if a man is homosexual he's some kind of sissy or coward or weakling who's incapable of doing anything that requires force or roughness. Most gay men, and there were far more of them in the Armed Forces than you might think, aren't swishy or hysterical. Like many gay veterans, some of whom gave their lives for the United States, I served my country honorably and faithfully, and I didn't see Bob Hope beside me on the battlefield. I really liked Bob Hope and his shows, and I certainly didn't expect him to trot out a troupe of half-naked guys just to please me, but when he stood in front of the troops and did his limp-wrist jokes and talked about purses and all that, it made me feel really angry and heart-sick inside. Talk about low morale. I was doing my job as well as anybody else, wasn't I?"

In fairness to Hope, he had nothing to do with the Anita Bryant anti-gay campaign of the Seventies, which he disagreed with, and he's claimed that he really has nothing against homosexuals. According to Hope, "I've worked with so many gays over my years on Broadway, knew so many of them, liked so many of them." But because he knew his middle-American, middle-class, anti-intellectual, and anti-gay audiences didn't like them, he continued (cravenly, many feel) to do the anti-gay material. Finally some gay activists had had enough when he passed the homophobic remarks on the Carson show. Formerly, Hope had cavalierly dismissed the activist complaints. "They're threatening to get together and hit me with their purses," he cracked. But this time around, he was to get whacked with much worse than purses.

Rumors flew that certain gay insiders of a more militant stripe had gotten to Hope and told him flatly that if he didn't cut the homophobic routines, certain stories about him from his past would be trotted out for all the world to hear. What would most of his GI's think, they declared, if stories about gay Fred Williams' all-night, all-male drinking orgies at Hope's Waldorf suite (admittedly not attended by Hope) were to get out? It would be easy as pie, they said, to accuse Hope of being a "Don Juan Homosexual," covering up his essentially homo-or-bisexual nature with phony heterosexual exploits, using women as "beards," as so many ostensibly "straight" men did.

With anti-gay violence rising, even the less-hostile gay leaders flatly told Hope that his anti-gay jokes had become a menace. Put under this extreme, and ominous, pressure, Hope finally consented to do a public service spot denouncing anti-homosexual prejudice and violence. The spot he taped was shown all too infrequently on late-night television in major markets.

When a Native American in 1948 had tried to tell him how much his "Injun" jokes in *Paleface* had hurt him, and when feminists over the years tried to tell him how much they were offended by some of his routines, Hope only laughed in their faces. Now, with the gays, he'd responded affirmatively. Was this a sign of a new maturity in the comedian, an acceptance of the fact that times were changing and he'd better change with them? Or were there deeper, darker motives behind his actions? Or had the implications that many Hope friends in Hollywood who hypocritically "came on straight" to the world might find themselves "outed" played a role in his turnabout? And then there was his own vulnerability.

Although many gay activists charged Hope with being a "closet queen" — as so many of his Hollywood friends were, the long-standing joke in Hollywood being that closet gays were the worst homophobes and the more powerful among them in the movie hierarchy were blocking positive gay movies and images — what was probably more accurate was that Hope had always been one of those men who covered up inse-

Thanks-for-the-Memory Lane ca. 1991

Ho ho ho Hope making like Santa on a 1992 Special

curities of various kinds, including doubts about their own "manliness" — as opposed to their sexuality — with a homophobic attitude that seems to say, "I may not be much of a man — too short, too fat, too old, not virile enough — but at least I'm not a fag." While there were stories, put out by the pro-Hope hangers-on, that it was Dolores, not Bob, who was unable to produce natural children, the Gays had not allowed Hope to forget that his four children had all been *adopted*, that he'd never, so far as anyone knew, produced a natural child of his own.

As of 1993, having hit the big N — his Ninetieth birthday — Bob Hope was ridden with insecurities of all kinds. He hadn't made a movie in twenty years, so had faded from the "current movie star" firmament. His by-then-infrequent TV "specials" took dips in the ratings when they weren't filmed at military bases, and even then heavy promotion was required and they had to be shown at just the right day and hour. Johnny Carson having left *The Tonight Show* circa 1993, there was for a time serious talk of his replacing Hope as the man who did all the specials and as King of NBC — Carson being, at the time, twenty years younger and all that. Carson had already been told he could do pretty much what he wanted when it came to special projects. NBC executives had taken cold, objective note of Hope's diminishing audience by 1993, to say nothing of his obviously fading energy and Carson's comparatively youthful and still-extant celebrity status.

The many professional friends Hope had made over the years were dead and dying, as were those on the personal level. And then there was the situation on the Home Front. . . .

A source in close contact with Bob and Dolores Hope circa 1993 — indeed, for some years before — a source that wishes to remain anonymous but whose credentials are impeccable — gives us a picture of the Bob Hopes' domestic scene as of that time.

His hearing was failing badly, yet he still refused a hearing aid. His midsection was sagging; even corsets, however carefully designed, didn't do much for *that*. The usual exercises of the past were behind him, though he'd swing a golf stick at times, more to reassure himself than for any other reason.

The Toluca Lake house had the atmosphere of siege. There were the security men who stood constant guard, the two locked doors that protected his sleeping quarters from the outside world, the phone in his bedroom he kept constantly employed with numerous snappish business complaints, usually over money. On that subject you could hear his failing, but still shrill, voice through a whole wing of the house. The staff of eight servants had a frequent turnover rate, for Bob and Dolores Hope, then 90 and 89 respectively, had developed a baleful reputation as difficult employers.

By 1993 a cold, irritable distance had developed between husband and wife. Yes, when they appeared in public they seemed devoted and mutually attentive. But behind the locked doors in Toluca Lake they were short and tense with each other.

The long succession of infidelities Bob had been guilty of — stretching now over decades — had finally broken down Dolores's essentially benign attitude toward him. She'd operated for years on the philosophy that had gotten him off the hook — that men were like that, curious, roving, obsessive to a degree women could never match. She'd closed her eyes to much of it; but inwardly the anger seethed. Finally, circa 1993, it was there on the surface, reflected fiercely and hauntingly in her eyes whenever they lit on him.

Her corrections and criticisms of him multiplied; he avoided her by retreating to his own quarters. According to this source, Hope's happiest, most relaxed hours came when Dolores was absent. Then he could wander anywhere in the house, have in what few old cronies were left, relax and laugh and kid around, free from the bitterness and disapproval Dolores showed, the distaste for him, amounting to a steady contempt.

On his part, consistently self-absorbed and insensitive into his 90s, Hope felt no twinges of conscience, no retrospective spells of remorse, only an impatient annoyance that Dolores held against him the obsessive through-the-years womanizing, the frequent absences of the earlier years, the indifference toward their kids, whose visits he barely tolerated.

And then there was the lady friend he sneaked out to visit, this Cavalier of 90, although a security man acompanied him to her place (she lived nearby). According to the insistently anonymous insider, Hope didn't turn to her for sexual release or even for romance — these were past needs by then. But what she did give him was concern, emotional reassurance, friendship, even a form of tenderness. These were what he needed from a woman now. These the ever-carping Dolores never gave him.

As of 1993, when Linda and the other kids visited, they felt like strangers in the house. Linda, often hired and fired by her father, found him distant, filled with criticism of anything and everything concerning her. She left after these little visits with a sigh of relief. She'd come to realize that despite her best efforts, there was no pleasing her father — or her mother either. Both wanted to be left alone. Nor was their attitude any different toward the other three kids. Both Bob and Dolores felt an essential coldness to these children who were not their biological own, who had not, in their view, turned out satisfactorily — granted that several of them had tried their honest best to please — and pleased not. The personal lifestyles of several of them, which would have had Hope fuming and yelling in past years, now elicited only his cold indifference.

The insider recalls that circa-1993 Dolores had religious shrines all over the house — candles lit to the Blessed Virgin, whose statue was prominently and strategically placed. "Dolores was a devout Catholic, sure — still is — but in the wrong way," the insider recalls. "She was great with the literal parts but she'd missed the spirit of it. She was mean with the servants, never satisfied; the 1993 turnover was so horrendous that some leading employment agencies had given up on them entirely. And she didn't show true charity where it counted." One older woman employee collapsed with what seemed a serious physical attack just as Dolores was leaving for mass one day. "Mrs. Hope just shrugged, ordered the casualty taken care of, and jumped into her car," the insider recalls.

On their 60th wedding anniversary (1933-1993) Hope had ordered flowers to be placed in Dolores's room. When she saw them, she swept by with total disregard. An aide remembers Hope asking just how many years he and Dolores had been married. He'd forgotten. Even though it was the Milestone Sixtieth. When he was told he commented, "Oh, was it that long?"

Hope on that Sixtieth Anniversay was overheard telling a friend on the phone, "What the hell does she have to kick about?" He'd never divorced her, had he? For six decades she'd been The Lady of the Manor. "What more could a woman want?" Waspish, demanding, carping, and mean, with the servants as with her husband, that is how her servants and aides saw the then-89-year-old Dolores Hope. A tragic departure from her younger, sunnier self.

An aide has described the dinners at home. The couple would sit there in uneasy silence. Hope couldn't wait to get away from her and back to his part of the house. Then there was their eternal stinginess in small things. When they went out together to events, the hosting operation paid for every last thing: the limousine, the flowers, the accessories, escorts, anything.

Nothing changed that much over the next five years. As of 1998 Bob had grown ever weaker, his personality fainter, his troublesome eyes worse, his hearing lamentable. When he attempted routines in public, his failing eyes darted sideways to catch the words written in giant letters on the cue cards. There was an increasing air of pathos, even of desperation, about Hope at 93, 94, and finally, 95 on May 29, 1998, this man who'd rather die than do without an audience.

The year 1998 finds the 95-year-old a shadow of what he once was, yet he works up sufficient energy to appear in person to accept such recent kudos as an Honorary Veteran from President Bill Clinton and an Honorary Knighthood from Queen Elizabeth.

In 1994 he'd won an Emmy for his NBC Special, *Bob Hope, the First Ninety Years*. (In 1996 he did what he said was his final Christmas special for NBC.) In the years that followed, honors had seemed to come from Left and Right. Two he especially cherished came in 1997. The U.S. Navy named a newly commissioned transport ship after him. The Air Force then did likewise with a new aircraft.

That same year saw Hope receiving the Ronald Reagan Freedom Award for what Nancy Reagan cited as his "tireless efforts on the front lines of liberty." She called him "America's most honored citizen and our favorite clown."

Dolores's attitude toward these constant honors seems, in public, to have been graciously forebearing; in private she indicated they were monotonous. Restlessly, indeed competitively, she decided that — yes, even at age 93 — it was *her* turn to get into the spotlight. She put out, in 1997, a new CD called "That's Love." Earlier, she'd done a CD called "Now and Then." Another CD has celebrated "the spirit of World War II." Then, also in 1997, she went on as a guest with Rosemary Clooney during the latter's two-week gig at New York City's Rainbow and Stars. The critics and other commentators were tactful and upbeat; yes, her once-dulcet tones had faded, even cracked, but she made up for it (they said) with personality and interpretive skill. Bob Hope's attitudes toward his wife's spotlight-competition, while publicly mellow and acceptive, are privately (an inside source notes) patronizing, comtemptuous, dismissive — and mightily irritated.

At 1998 events, he seems truly a ghost of what he once was. The 95-year-old eyes, almost sightless, are red-rimmed and swollen, the movements ever more feeble and uncertain. Aides and security men carefully help him from cars and guide him across sidewalks, negotiating — often avoiding — such hazards as stairways and platforms and multi-levels.

Bob Hope has always kept in mind that his paternal grandfather almost, at 99, hit the century mark, and this has helped reinforce his desire to reach age 100. Asked by a friend in early 1998 if that were indeed his ambition, he smiled wistfully and replied he wouldn't mind making the 200 mark if he could have back his full sight and hearing and a reasonable modicum of his former energy. What saddens him most, he's said, is that if he goes on *too* long the public memory of him in his vigorous and charismatic prime will fade — all they'll remember is that frail old nonagenarian-aiming-at-centenarian.

When another friend repeated to him Bette Davis's famous apothegm, "Old Age Ain't for Sissies," he chuckled breifly, then retorted, "Old Age ain't for pessimists and worrywarts either!"

Obviously, some Bob Hope Obsessives cross-country have lately been overdoing the Bob Hope Death Watch. On June 5, 1998, his "death" was incorrectly announced due to a glitch on the Internet, which prematurely released an obituary of him they, like other news organizations, had been holding — a standard media practice for famous people over a certain age. Compounding the problem, a Republican Congressman from Arizona, Bob Stump, was on the house floor at 3 p.m. that afternoon when Majority Leader Dick Armey (R. Texas) gave him the Hope obituary which had been prepared by the Associated Press. After a consultation, Stump proceeded to make a death announcement on the House floor; it was carried live by C-Span. "It is with great sadness that I announce that Bob Hope has died," he told his fellow Congressmembers.

Meanwhile, other news organizations, out to verify the report, got to Hope's daughter Linda, who refuted the news all-out, adding that at the moment Congress started "mourning," Hope was eating breakfast at his Toluca Lake Home. According to Linda, Hope had a good laugh about it, saying "I'm still here," and later graciously accepted the apologies of Congressman Stump, an old friend, and the AP.

Eldest daughter Linda will be on hand, her friends feel, to the real end, serving as executive producer of her father's company, engineering Dolores as well as herself through public appearances, lessening the burdens every way she can. Loyal and understanding, if admittedly saddened and disillusioned, Linda has consistently praised her father's talent, felt that he'd never achieved his total artistic potential. She's been backed up by a critic who wrote that her father "never got the parts he deserved," adding, "People in Hollywood lacked the imagination to see that he could have been an earlier version of Jack Lemmon."

Son Tony later settled in Washington, D.C. as a practicing attorney, and seems, at least to date, to have largely abandoned his political ambitions while making occasional half-hearted forays. Little is heard from the Hopes' other two children, Nora and Kelly, who prefer to live their lives out privately, for the most part. Linda's position as her parents' mainstay, as of 1998, seems to be permanent and secure. "It ought to be," a friend of Linda's has said. "She's faithful and steadfast, someone they can rely on — *now, at last.*"

It's true that through the years, and indeed right up to his mid-90s, Bob Hope continued to cling persistently, even pathetically, to the same old routines, or variations thereon; to the same old comic persona, with all its self-limitations; voicing the same old prejudices he felt would sell with a majority of his audiences; belaboring his "beloved boys" in the services overseas with stances that finally were to turn some of them away from him; never, as his daughter Linda noted, ever really changing or growing into anything stronger creatively, more meaningful and universal — as would have been appropriate for a man of his years and talent.

Yet Hope can probably look back on his 95 years of living and working with few regrets, really. Though neglecting his artistic potential, indeed thwarting it at times in favor of his popular persona, he nonetheless parlayed his chutzpah and strong, driving ego and genuine gifts (however, at times, misused and underexploited) into an unstoppable force that made him one of the world's most popular, most instantly recognizable entertainers.

Bob Hope may have few really close friends, probably never did, and five years shy of a hundred, having outlived so many who traveled with him along life's road, he must feel, in the depths of his spirit, a chilling loneliness. It's strongly to be doubted that he faces a relatively imminent Eternity with positive or hopeful, let alone spiritual or sentimental, feelings.

Were he a man of more self-flagellating or self-condemning spirit, which he is not, he'd be suffering conscience pangs over his flagrant infidelities with countless women, famous, also-ran, and obscure, and the consequent neglect of his eventually wounded and embittered wife, and those four children, over the years. Were he a more sensitive and self-analytical and empathetic human being than he was or is, he'd come to terms with the fact that he never truly cued-in to them as persons, as a man more in touch with his feelings would have. At times he endangered his health, played havoc with his emotional well-being, destroyed his peace of mind, womanized more sophomorically than compulsively, took occasional, sometimes catastrophic, wrong-life-turns that hurt others as well as himself.

But granted all of the above, Bob Hope has always, all the way up the years from those drab, negative, dark beginnings in Cleveland, nurtured a dread of the dull, pedestrian, dehumanizing workaday world where the bulk of human beings, in Thoreau's famous words, lead "lives of quiet desperation." Highs, excitements, piercing joys, and enthrallments born of living fully; a manic, all-encompassing need to remain in the warming, galvanizing super-beams of the Spotlight, and at what he conceived to be the Dead Center of Life and Living — these have driven this consummately self-involved man right up to the end. Can there, then, be any argument that Bob Hope has fulfilled the destiny he earmarked for himself in the long ago, that indeed he *has* done always what he *wanted* and *needed* to do? No, none.

But what if Bob Hope were asked on what note he wanted to end that long life? Would his deep subconscious finally come to his rescue and point out to him the logical one, the right one: sailing out to sea on one of the ships now named for him, clowning and entertaining "his boys" on deck, with the waning sun of a Pacific day warming him, and the cool, sharp wind egging him on to do his best, his very best, for those young servicemen who, alone in all the world, over all the years, he truly, deeply loved in his Heart of Hearts? Just possibly.

At Eventide, the philosopher once truly noted, All That Will Count Is Love.

A Selective Bob Hope Bibliography

Adams, Cindy. "Thanks for the Memories." *Ladies Home Journal*, December, 1987.

Arden, Eve. *The Three Phases of Eve*. New York: St. Martin's, 1985.

Barthel, Joan. "Bob Hope." *Life*, January 1971.

Berle, Milton. *B.S. I Love You*. New York: McGraw Hill, 1988.

Berle, Milton, with Haskel Frankel. *Milton Berle: An Autobiography*. New York: Delacorte Press, 1974.

Cahill, Tim. "Bob Hope." *Rolling Stone*, March, 1980.

Carter, E. Graydon. "America's Greatest Hope." *Family Weekly*, May 26, 1985.

Chierichetti, David. *Hollywood Director*. New York: Curtis Books, 1973.

Collins, Joan. *Past Imperfect: An Autobiography*. New York: Simon and Schuster, 1978, 1984.

Crosby, Bing, as told to Pete Martin. Call Me Lucky. New York: Simon and Schuster, 1953.

Edwards, Anne. A Remarkable Woman. New York: William Morrow, 1985.

Faith, William. *Bob. Hope: A Life in Comedy*. New York: G.P. Putnam's, 1982.

Harris, Warren G. *Lucy and Desi*. New York: Simon and Schuster, 1991.

Hope, Bob. *I Never Left Home*. New York: Simon and Schuster, 1944.

— . *I Owe Russia $1200*. New York: Doubleday, 1963.

Hope, Bob, as told to Eleanor Harris. "My Favorite Mother-in-Law." *McCall's*, October 1955.

Hope, Bob, as told to Pete Martin. *Have Tux, Will Travel*. New York: Simon and Schuster, 1954.

Hope, Bob, as told to Pete Martin. *The Last Christmas Show*. New York: Doubleday, 1974.

Hope, Bob, with Melville Shavelson. *Don't Shoot, It's Only Me*. New York: G.P. Putnam's Sons, 1990.

Hope, Bob and Bob Thomas. *The Road to Hollywood*. New York: Doubleday, 1977.

Hope, Dolores. "My Life is Full of Hope." *Woman's Home Companion*, November, 1953.

Lamour, Dorothy, as told to Dick McInnes. *My Side of the Road*. New Jersey: Prentice Hall, 1980.

Lukas, J. Anthony. "This is Bob (Politician-Patriot-Publicist) Hope." *The New York Times Magazine*, October 4, 1970.

Morella, Joe and Edward Z. Epstein and Eleanor Clark. *The Amazing Careers of Bob Hope*. New York: Arlington House, 1973.

Nattin, Pete. "I Call on Bob Hope." *Saturday Evening Post,* April 26, 1958.

Quirk, Lawrence J. *Jane Wyman: The Actress and the Woman*. New York: Dembner Books, 1986.

Rochlin, Mangy. "Funny Man." *Los Angeles Times Magazine*, February 1, 1987.

Russell, Jane. *Jane Russell: An Autobiography*. New York: Franklin Watts, 1985.

Streete, Hobton. "Have Tux, Will Travel and That's What Bob Hope Did With That Blonde." *Confidential,* July 1956.

Thompson, Charles. *Bob Hope: Portrait of a Superstar.* New York: St. Martin' s, 1980.

A Bob Hope Film Listing

The year noted is the film's formal release date.
* denotes important films,

*1. *The Big Broadcast of 1938*, 1938
 2. *College Swing* , 1938
 3. *Give Me a Sailor.* 1938
 4. *Thanks for the Memory.* 1938
 5. *Never Say Die*, 1939
 6. *Some Like It Hot,* 1939,
*7. *The Cat and the Canary.* 1939,
*8. *Road to Singapore.* 1940,
 9. *Ghost Breakers.* 1940,
 10. *Road to Zanzibar.* 1941,
 11. *Caught in the Draft*, 1941,
 12. *Nothing But the Truth*, 1941,
 13. *Louisiana Purchase*, 1941,
 14. *My Favorite Blonde*, 1942,
 15. *Road to Morocco*, 1942,
 16. *Star Spangled Rhythm.* 1942,
 17. *They Got Me Covered*, 1943,
 18. *Let's Face It.* 1943.
*19. *The Princess and the Pirate*, 1944.
 20. *Road to Utopia*, 1945,
 21. *Monsieur Beaucaire*, 1946,
*22. *My Favorite Brunette*, 1947.
 23. *Variety Girl*, 1947,
 24. *Where There's Life*, 1947,
 25. *The Road to Rio*, 1947,
*26. *The Paleface*, 1948,
 27. *Sorrowful Jones*, 1949,
 28. *The Great Lover*, 1949,
 29. *Fancy Pants*, 1950.
 30. *The Lemon Drop Kid*, 1951,
 31. *My Favorite Spy*, 1951,
*32. *Son of Paleface*, 1952.
 33. *Road to Bali*, 1952,
 34. *Off Limits.* 1953,

35. *Here Come the Girls.* 1953,
36. *Casanova's Big Night,* 1954,
*37. *The Seven Little Foys.* 1955,
38. *That Certain Feeling.* 1956.
39. *The Iron Petticoat,* 1956,
*40. *Beau James,* 1957,
41. *Paris Holiday,* 1958,
42. *Alias Jesse James,* 1959.
43. *The Facts of Life,* 1960,
44. *Bachelor in Paradise,* 1961,
45. *Road to Hong Kong,* 1962.
46. *Critic's Choice,* 1963,
47. *Call Me Bwana,* 1963,
48. *A Global Affair.* 1964.
49. *I'll Take Sweden.* 1965.
50. *Boy, Did I Get a Wrong Number.* 1966.
51. *Eight on the Lam.* 1967.
52. *The Private Navy of Sgt. O'Farrell.* 1968.
53. *How to Commit Marriage.* 1969.
54. *Cancel My Reservation.* 1972.

Bob Hope also made the following shorts:

+ denotes comedy shorts

+ 1. *Going Spanish*. 1934.
+ 2. *Paree, Paree*. 1934.
+ 3. *The Old Grey Mayor*. 1935.
+ 4. *Watch the Birdie*. 1935.
+ 5. *Double Exposure*. 1935.
+ 6. *Calling All Tars*. 1936.
+ 7. *Shop Talk*. 1936.
  8. *Don't Hook Now*. 1938. (Golf)
  9. *Welcome to Britain*. 1943. (Instruction for servicemen)
10. *All-Star Bond Rally*. 1945. (War bonds)
11. *Hollywood Victory Caravan*. 1945. (War bonds)
12. *The Heart of Show Business*. 1957. (Variety Clubs)
13. *Showdown at Ulcer Gulch*. 1958. (*Saturday Evening Post.* promo.)
14. *Hollywood Star-Spangled Revue*. 1966. (Treasury Bonds)

Notable Bob Hope guest appearances/cameos:

1. *The Greatest Show on Earth*. 1952. (Hope appears briefly as a member of the circus audience.)
2. *Scared Stiff*. 1953. (Remake of *Ghost Breakers* with Martin and Lewis.)
3. *The Five Pennies*. 1959. (Hope plays himself in a cameo.)
4. *The Oscar*. 1966. (Hope plays himself as emcee at the Oscars in one scene.)

INDEX

Adams, Cindy, 90

Adams, Neile, 206

Adrian, Iris, 132

Agnew, Spiro, 253

Alias Jesse James, 245, 246

Alice Adams, 109

All Quiet on The Western Front, 55-56

Allen, Fred, 101

Allen, Gracie, 100, 120

Allman, Elvia, 99

Anderson, Eddie "Rochester," 120

Antics, 56-57, 59, 60

Arbuckle, Fatty, 24

Archainbaud, George, 121

Arden, Eve, 75, 167, 229

Arnaz, Desi, 313

Asher, Jerry, 134

Astaire, Fred, 68

Ayres, Lew, 55

Bachelor in Paradise, 263

Ball, Lucille, 101, 186, 187, 216, 248-249, 259, 270, 301

Ballyhoo, 65, 67

Bandbox (Columbus, Ohio), 24

Barnes, Howard, 162

Barthelmess, Richard, 17

Beal, John, 123

Beatty, Warren, 216

Beau James, 91, 241

Bennett, Joan, 143

Benny, Jack, 50, 63, 64, 97, 99, 101, 107, 113, 119, 194-195, 208, 287

Bergen, Edgar, 94

Berle, Milton, 63-64, 70, 193

Berner, Charlie, 111

Big Broadcast of 1938, 94, 107, 112, 113

Blore, Eric, 118, 119, 132, 133, 174

Boasberg, Al, 50, 56, 63

Bob Hope House, 268-269

Bowes, Major Edward J., 92

Boy,.Did I Get a Wrong Number, 275

Bracken, Eddie, 162-163

Brennan, Walter, 170

Brice, Fannie, 74-75

Bromo-Seltzer Hour, 93

Bryant, Anita, 211, 250

Burman, Bob, 44

Burns and Allen, 50, 116, 128, 299

Butler, David, 156, 161, 168, 170

Byrne, George, 27-31, 34, 36-39, 46, 112

Byrne, Mary, 40

Cagney, James, 302-303

Caesar, Sid, 64

Call Me Bwana, 271

Calm, Alan, 34

Cameron, Kate, 169

Campbell, Louise, 91

Cancel My Reservation, 284

Capone, Al, 55, 72

Carlson, Richard, 124

Carroll, Madeleine, 159, 160, 161

Carmichael, Hoagy, 121

Casanova's Big Night, 200, 228

Cat and the Canary, The, 122-124

Caulfield, Joan, 176-177

Cavett, Dick, 290-291

Chandler Motor Company, 23

Chaney, Lon, 178

Chaplin, Charles, 17

Chicago, 1, 42, 43-44, 46

Cleveland, Ohio, 1, 7, 8-9, 11, 13, 15, 16-17, 21, 24-25, 40, 59, 60

Coburn, Charles, 130-131

Colbert, Claudette, 109

College Swing, 116-119

Collins, Joan, 200, 265, 269

Colonna, Jerry, 99, 119, 144

Confessions of a Hooker, 283

Confidential, 235, 236

Connolly, Mike, 205

Coogan, Jackie, 116

Cook, Alton, 240

Cooley, Charlie, 43-44

Cooper, Gary, 171

Crosby, Bing, 1, 67, 101, 103, 110, 124, 127-131, 133-139, 161-162, 170, 172, 225, 264, 286, 288

Crosby, Dixie, 138

Crosby, Gary, 133, 135, 163

Crosby, John, 196-197

Crosby, Lindsay, 134-136

Crouse, Russell, 75

Crowther, Bosley, 156, 162, 240, 244

Critics Choice, 269

Cue, 229, 286

Cukor, George, 36, 37, 39, 112, 119, 146

Dahl, Arlene, 195

Davis, Bette, 313

Davis, Jim, 246

Day, Doris, 98, 186

Dean, Barney, 44

Dean, Jimmy, 43

DeFina, Theresa, 82, 89

Dennis, Richard, 122

Denny, Reginald, 178-179

Desilu, 102

Detroit, 30

Devine, Andy, 121,122

Diller, Phyllis, 275-277

Dillingham, Charles, 34

Don't Shout, It's Only Me, 153

Dooley, Ray, 34

Douglas, Jack, 96

Dowling, Eddie, 34

Drake, Donna, 159, 163, 168

Dunne, Irene, 68

Durante, Jimmy, 76-79, 111

Durbin, Lloyd "Lefty," 23-27, 46, 53

Earle, Charlie, 238

Ed Sullivan Show, 191

Edward VII (King), 7

Educational Films (Shorts), 104

Eight on the Lam, 277

Eisenhower, Dwight, 150

Ekberg, Anita, 211

Eltham, England, 4-5

Facts of Life, The, 2, 47

Fairbanks, Douglas, 17, 58

Fairmount Boys, 113

Fancy Pants, 191, 215

Fernandel, 242, 243, 244-245

Ferguson, Helen, 136, 274

Fields, W.C., 115

Fix, Paul, 126

Flagstad, Kirsten, 115

Fleming, Rhonda, 189

Flippen, Jay C., 46, 218-219

Flying Down To Rio, 118

Flynn, Errol, 177

Fonda, Jane, 291

Fontaine, Joan, 210, 228

For The Boys, 302

Forbes Magazine, 296

Fowler, Gene, 122

Foy, Eddie, 230

Frazier, Brenda, 99

Gable, Clark, 62, 147

Gabor, Zsa-Zsa, 200, 201, 206, 213

Garbo, Greta, 70

Gardner, Hy, 86

Garland, Judy, 98

Gaxton, William, 75

Ghost Breakers, The, 124

Gilbert, John, 48, 70

Gilbert, Leatrice Joy, 48

Gill, Frank, 91

Gleason, Jackie, 283

Global Affair, A, 221

Godfrey, Arthur, 102

Going My Way, 135

Going Spanish, 104, 112

Goddard, Paulette, 123-126, 156

Goodrich, Frances, 120

Goldwyn Samuel, 163, 165, 169

Goodwin, Bill, 100

Gould, Jack, 197

Grable, Betty, 116, 118, 120

Grady, Billy, 65-67, 70, 111, 116, 146, 191

Gray, Dolores, 213

Great Lover, The, 189

Greenstreet, Sidney, 68-69

Hackett, Albert, 120

Haines, William, 39, 112, 120

Hall, Alexander, 189

Hanley, Jimmy, 34

Harbach, Otto, 69

Harlow, Jean, 19

Have Tux, Will Travel, 230

Hayden, Sterling, 160-161

Hayes, Helen, 57

Hepburn, Katharine, 238-240

Here Come The Girls, 228

Hillie, Verna, 91

Hollywood Reporter, 205

Hollywood Royalty, 146

Hoover, Herbert, 56

Hope, Avis Townes (Mother), 3-5, 7-8, 11, 18, 53, 55, 71-72, 80

Hope, Dolores (Reade) (Wife), 80-86, 89-91, 109-110, 142, 173-174, 236-237, 247, 293, 310-12

Hope, Emily (Sister), 14

Hope, Fred (Uncle) 19, 21, 166

Hope, Frederick Charles (Brother), 4, 72

Hope, George, 9, 30, 40, 53-56, 59, 67, 166, 280

Hope, Ivor (Brother), 4, 5, 59, 245, 280

Hope, James Francis (Brother), 4, 29, 165-166, 174-176, 270

Hope, Kelly, 87-88, 297

Hope, Linda (Daughter), 86, 88, 90, 279, 288-290, 310, 313-314

Hope, Nora, 297

Hope, Tony (Son), 87-88, 90, 279, 288-290, 310, 313-314

Hope, William John "Jack," 4, 14, 116, 165, 196, 269

Hope, William Henry "Harry" (Father) 3-5, 7-8, 11-12, 18, 71, 72

Hopper, Hedda, 132, 209, 210, 212-213

Horton, Edward Everett, 118, 134

Hudson, Rock, 43

Hunter, Jeffrey, 279

Hutton, Betty, 162-163

Hyde, Johnny, 37, 47, 49

I Love Lucy, 102

I'll Take Sweden, 273, 274

I Never Left Home, 151, 155

I Owe Russia $1200, 210

Iron Petticoat, The, 238-239

It Says Here, 170

James, Harry, 116

Jennings, Whitey, 14-17, 23

Johnson, Mrs. Lyndon, 253

Jolson, Al, 34

Josefsberg, Milt, 96

Joy, Leatrice, 48

Kaye, Danny, 168, 204

Keeler, Ruby, 34

Keith, B.F. Keith Circuit, 47-48, 55, 63, 67

Kendall, Norman, 24

Kennedy, John F., 268

Kern, Jerome, 68-69

Knowles, Patric, 76, 177

Kovic, Ron 256-257

Kupcinet, Irv, 205

Lamarr, Hedy, 222

Lamour, Dorothy, 112-113, 128, 131,164, 171, 177-178, 181, 185, 225, 265-266, 268

Lanfield, Sidney, 159, 219, 222

Langford, Frances, 101, 104

Lastfogel, Abe, 32, 145

Leisen, Mitchell, 111-112, 115, 135

Lemon Drop Kid, The, 217

Let's Face It, 169

Lewis, Milt, 36-37

Liggett & Myers, 102

Lincoln, Pamela and Damien, 90, 91

Lloyd, A1, 37

Lillie, Beatrice, 61

Lindsay, Howard, 75

Livingston, Mary, 94

Loesser, Frank, 121

Lorre, Peter, 178

Loves That Rocked Beverly Hills, 235

Loy, Myrna, 74

Luciano, Lucky, 72

MacLean, Barbara Barondess, 146-147

MacMurray, Fred, 68-69, 109, 253

Mahoney, Wilkie, 96, 122

Manhattan Melodrama, 205

Mansfield, Jane, 205-206, 211-212

Marsh, Joan, 132

Marshall, George, 126

Martin, Dean, 256

Martin, Pete, 230

Marx Brothers, 109

Maxwell, Marilyn, 192, 218, 226

Mayo, Virginia, 169-170

McCall's Magazine, 89

McFarland, Packy, 15

McGovern, Jack, 72

McMahon, Horace, 91

McQueen, Steve, 206

Menuhin, Yehudi, 100

Merkel, Una, 19, 122, 131

Merrill, Dina, 274

Merman, Ethel, 75, 76-79

Middlesex, England, 314

Midler, Bette, 302

Mishkin, Leo, 213-214

Moncrief, Monty, 137

Monroe, Marilyn, 37, 103, 210-211

Monsieur Beaucaire, 176

Morris and Fell (Agents) 147-148

Motion Picture Herald and *Daily*, 235

Movie Life, 235

Mowbray, Alan, 121-122

Murdock, Toots, 54, 56

Murphy, George, 68-69, 80-81

My Favorite Blonde, 159

My Favorite Brunette, 177

My Favorite Spy, 122

Neal, Tom, 101, 188

New York City, 31, 36,47-48, 55, 61, 68-69, 72-73, 75, 92

New York Daily .News, 120, 169, 231, 299

New York Morning Telegraph, 213

New York Mirror, 69

New York Times, 90, 124, 156, 197, 240, 244, 280

New York World-Telegram, 240

Newsweek, 173

Nixon, Richard, M. 253

Nothing But the Truth, 156

Nugent, Elliott, 121, 157

Nugent, Frank, 124

Oberon, Merle, 143

O'Donnell, Bob, 47

O'Donnell, General Emmett, 250

Old Grey Mayor, The (Short), 105

Olivier, Laurence, 70, 204, 205

Olsen & Johnson, 56

Oriole Terrace, Detroit, 30

O'Rourke, Billy, 35, 36

Oscars, 233

Palace Theatre, New York, 50, 60, 62

Paige, Janis, 194-195, 206, 250

Paleface, The, 132

Panama, Norman, 96

Pangborn. Franklin, 118,-120

Paris Holiday, 24l-244

Parsons, Louella, 265

Payne, John, 118-119

Payton, Barbara, 187-188, 235-238

Patton, General George S., 5, 150

Pepsodent Show, 98, 100

Photoplay Magazine, 118

Porter, Cole, 75

Powell, Dick, 94

Princess and the Pirate, The, 169

Prinz, Leroy, 131

Private Navy of Sgt. O'Farrell, 277-278

Queen Christina, 70

Quinn, Anthony, 126, 130, 161

Rainer, Louise, 74

Raymond, Gene, 118

Raye, Martha, 113, 115-116, 120-121, 250, 305

Reagan, Ronald, 80

Reid, Jim, 135, 138

Reid, Wallace, 7

Rhodes, James, (Governor), 257

Rhodes, Joan, 232

Richman, Harry, 73

Road to Bali, 225

"Road to Greenwich Village", 134

Road to Hong Kong, 200, 264

Road to Morocco, 161

Road to Singapore, 128

Road to Zanzibar, 131, 156

Roberta (Film), 109

Roberta (Broadway Version), 68, 69, 71, 81, 199

Roberts, Curtis, 275-276

Rockefeller, John D. Sr., 111

Rogers, Ginger, 68, 70

Romano, Tony, 144

Romanoff, Mike 73, 74

Rooney, Mickey, 226

Root, Johnny, 22, 23

Rosequist, Mildred, 19-23, 25, 29-30, 35, 37, 52, 53, 55, 59

Ross, Shirley, 113, 115-116, 122

Russell, Jane, 183, 184, 185, 222, 223

Saint, Eva Marie, 23, 285

Sanders, George, 234

Saphier, James, 103, 294

Say When, 72-74, 84

Schoell, William, 240, 276

Schwartz, A1, 96

Sellers, Peter, 26, 267

Seven Little Foys, The, 230

Shavelson, Mel, 96

Shearer, Norma, 62

Showboat, 68

Shurr, Louis, "Doc", 70, 71, 93, 104-106, 116, 163, 175, 265

Sitting Pretty, 70

Sidewalks of New York, 34

Sin of Madelon Claudet, 57

Skirball, Jack, 105

Snow, Ted, 30

So This Is Peace, 155, 173

Some Like It Hot, 121

Sommer, Elke, 276

Sondergaard, Gale, 161

Son of Paleface, 222-224

Sorrowful Jones, 184, 186

Speck, Gregory, 146

Specimen Days, (Walt Whitman), 145

Spellman, Francis Cardinal, 204

Stander, Lionel, 105

Star Spangled Rhythm, 162

Stitt, Fred, 30

St. John, Jill, 250, 275

Stevens, Connie, 297

Steward, Blanche, 99

Stewart, Jimmy, 65, 253

Stewart, Lee, 49, 55

Sullivan, Norman, 96

Sutton, Grady, 134

Sykes, Barbara, 34-36, 39-40

Tamara, 144

Thanks for the Memory, 113, 120

That Certain Feeling, 234

They Got Me Covered, 155, 164

Tone, Franchot, 101, 188-189

Troxell, Louise, 45-46, 50-52, 55-57, 65-67, 71, 83

Up Pops the Devil, 120

Ups-A-Daisy, 65

USO Tours, 143, 144-146, 151

Valentino, Rudolph, 58, 176

Vallee, Rudy, 92

Van Leer, Arnold, 61

Variety Girl, 180

Village Voice, 291

Walrath, Florence, 86, 87

Walsh, "Happy", 16

Walsh, Raoul, 120

Westmoreland, General William,. 250

Weston-SuperMare, England, 5

Where There's Life, 181

Whiting, Jack, 120

Whitman, Walt, 145, 204

Wilder, Patricia (Honey Chile), 93, 120

William Morris Agency, 32, 37, 44, 48

Williams, Andy, 206

Williams, Fred, 179, 180, 215, 306

Winchell, Walter, 65, 105

Winters, Jonathan, 277

Wolf, William, 286

Woodbury Soap Show, 94

Woolley, Monty, 121

Wright, Cobina Jr., 99

Wyman, Jane, 283

Your Hollywood Parade, 94

Young, Whitney M. Jr., 260

Ziegfeld Follies, 34, 74-75

JAMES STEWART

BEHIND THE SCENES OF A WONDERFUL LIFE
by Lawrence J. Quirk

This startling, intimate biography of James Stewart frankly and freshly reveals with new facts and over 200 interviews a fully dimensional insight into this revered figure and consummate American icon. This book eminently bears out the philosopher George Santayana's observation that if we knew all about a person, all the factors and conditionings that went into his or her makeup, we would love that person more, not less, for with total knowledge would come total understanding, compassion, and in Jimmy Stewart's case, profound respect.

Here is the Jimmy Stewart who put his action where his mouth was, becoming a real-life World War II hero and later Brigadier General. Here is to be found not only the Legendary Shy Knight who loved, on screen and off, spritely elusive witch Margaret Sullavan and sassy lady Ginger Rogers but courted heart-hungry widow Norma Shearer, pulled a comic gaffe with the Great Garbo herself, matched wits with feisty Kate Hepburn (in his Oscar-winning Philadelphia Story stint) and humorously fended off a Jimmy-Happy Marlene Dietrich.

Lawrence Quirk's book is a nuanced and subtle human account that will open our hearts even further to the incomparable Jimmy Stewart.

CLOTH • ISBN: 1-55783-329-X